AF478152

SPANISH FICTION IN THE DIGITAL AGE

Spanish Fiction in the Digital Age

Generation X Remixed

Christine Henseler

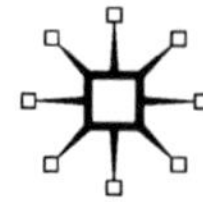

SPANISH FICTION IN THE DIGITAL AGE
Copyright © Christine Henseler, 2011.

First published in 2011 by
PALGRAVE MACMILLAN®
in the United States—a division of St. Martin's Press LLC,
175 Fifth Avenue, New York, NY 10010.

Where this book is distributed in the UK, Europe and the rest of the world,
this is by Palgrave Macmillan, a division of Macmillan Publishers Limited,
registered in England, company number 785998, of Houndmills,
Basingstoke, Hampshire RG21 6XS.

Palgrave Macmillan is the global academic imprint of the above companies
and has companies and representatives throughout the world.

Palgrave® and Macmillan® are registered trademarks in the United States,
the United Kingdom, Europe and other countries.

Permission to use the following photographs is gratefully acknowledged:
Photograph of Agustín Fernández Mallo courtesy of Agustín Fernández
Mallo and Aina Lorente.
Photograph of Gabi Martínez © Carles Mercader.
Photograph of Gabriela Bustelo © Gabriela Grech Gomendio/IPA Press.
Photograph of Ray Loriga courtesy of Ray Loriga.
Photograph of José Ángel Mañas © Thomas Canet
<www.thomascanet.com>.

ISBN: 978–0–230–10291–0

Library of Congress Cataloging-in-Publication Data

Henseler, Christine, 1969–
    Spanish fiction in the digital age : generation X remixed / Christine
  Henseler.
      p. cm.
    ISBN 978–0–230–10291–0 (hardback)
     1. Spanish fiction—21st century—History and criticism. 2. Popular
  culture—Spain. I. Title.

PQ6144.H46 2011
863'.709—dc22   2011005466

A catalogue record of the book is available from the British Library.

Design by Newgen Imaging Systems (P) Ltd., Chennai, India.

First edition: October 2011

10 9 8 7 6 5 4 3 2 1

Transferred to Digital Printing in 2012

For *Leah*
my sweet little punk

Contents

Acknowledgments

At the end of the novel *Nocilla Dream*, Agustín Fernández Mallo constructs a map of his book using four axis points: the rational, emotional, analog, and digital. I would like to begin this book by acknowledging the four wonderful women who fit into a similar set of directionals and whose influence on my life and work have contributed significantly to mapping my career. Jan Gorovitz has spoken to my heart for over a decade now, and it is thanks to her incredible love, patience, generosity of heart, laid-back personality, and eternal sense of humor that I have had the time, space, emotional stamina, and stability to write this book. Thank you for always making me laugh when times got tough and for reminding me of always having fun. My colleague and best friend, Valerie Barr, is located on the opposite side of my map's axis point, for as a computer scientist and a deeply intellectual and strategic thinker she has mentored me in the arts of the (computer) sciences and has helped me discover new critical and creative spaces along the way. I thank you for your support, kindness, friendship, drive, and eternal quest for knowledge. Your photographic memory and strategic, savvy mind continue to impress me every day. For a better understanding of my own generational consciousness as an "X-er," it takes a pre-Baby Boomer on one end and a post-Millennial on the other to gauge my location in the present. I am eternally thankful to my mother, Trin-Madlen, and to my daughter, Leah Madlen, both of whose unconditional love, trust, spirit and love of life and laughter continue to infuse my every word. Baby girl, you are the reason why these quests for knowledge and innovation must continue to reach for new ideas and change the future. Thank you all for being my central axis, for balancing me in the most supportive and loving of ways, every day.

The map of this book connects dozens of individuals whose contributions have allowed the links in this project to come to life. Several friends and colleagues edited my work extensively, gave me suggestions for improvement, and challenged me along the way. My special gratitude goes to Jing Wang, whose wisdom leads me every day; to Elizabeth Garrels, whose attention to detail I am in awe of; to Edward Turk, whose organizational advice I will always follow; and to Ian Condry, whose kindness drives me forward. My beloved mentors and friends, Robert Spires and Debra Castillo, and my close friends, Ofelia Ferrán, Gema Pérez-Sánchez, and Jessica Folkart, also read the entirety of my book and provided valuable editorial feedback. Thank you for always being there for me, for your support, advice, and encouragement. I couldn't have done any of this without you. Juan Manuel Espinosa copyedited this book with the utmost of intelligence and insight, and I can't thank you enough for your dedication and professionalism. A guiding light since graduate school is Roberta Johnson. Thank you for always believing in me, Roberta, for always being there for me. And, John, John Kronik, I miss you very much. You will always be in my heart and in my work, looking over my shoulder, making sure I do not make too many editorial mistakes. I hope this book would have made you proud.

The interactive and participatory quality of this book has been an incredibly enriching process; it has reminded me of the need to reach out, to remain open to criticism and ideas, and to learn from the rich trove of intellectual and creative minds that surround me. I would like to begin by thanking all of the authors who contributed to this book. A special thanks goes out to Agustín Fernández Mallo and his partner Aina Lorente for designing the cover of this book. Thank you for being such a down-to-earth *Mensch*, Agustín, always willing to share ideas, material, and your unique vision on art and life that truly turns the world upside down. It has been an honor to work with all of the authors whose work I analyze in this book—José Ángel Mañas, Ray Loriga, Gabriela Bustelo, Gabi Martínez, and Agustín Fernández Mallo. They all shared enthusiasm, ideas, books, articles, references, and granted copyright permissions. I would like to give special thanks to Gabriela, Gabi, and Agustín who provided extensive comments to their respective chapters, enriching them tremendously. The "Hybrid Storyspaces" conference I coordinated with Debra Castillo in April of 2010, and the conference "Nueva Narrativa Española" that took place in Lausanne, Switzerland, in April of 2011, gave me the distinct privilege of getting to know several members of the *Mutantes*. Thank you, Jorge Carrión, Germán Sierra, Vicente Luis Mora, Doménico Chiappe, Juan Francisco Ferré, Eloy Fernández Porta, Manuel Rivas, and Robert Juan-Cantavella for sharing with me your novels, essays, and ideas. Thank you for your friendship, kindness, and generosity, and a special thanks also goes out to Edmundo Paz Soldán who has been, for over a decade now, like a brother to me. I greatly appreciate and respect you.

The scholars and authors whose comments are placed in the side boxes of this book are my heroes. Despite often short deadlines, they were immediately willing and happy to read my work and add their insight and expertise. It is thanks to them that this book can lay claim to a dynamic collaborative quality that allows ideas and material to spill out of these pages and into future conversations. And so it is with utmost of respect that my gratitude goes out to Gema Pérez-Sánchez, Michael Ugarte, Edmundo Paz Soldán, Paul Julian Smith, Cintia Santana, Samuel Amago, Carmen de Urioste, Santiago Fouz-Hernández, Randolph Pope, Yaw Agawu-Kakraba, Eva Navarro Martínez, Alfredo J. Sosa-Velasco, Paul Begin, Kathryn Everly, Nina Molinaro, Debra Castillo, Vicent Moreno, Jorge Pérez, Vicente Luis Mora, Juan Francisco Ferré, Gabriela Bustelo, Care Santos, Gabi Martínez,

Germán Sierra, Jorge Carrión, Eloy Fernández Porta, Agustín Fernández Mallo, Andrew Brown, Javier García Rodríguez, Juan Manuel Espinosa, Carlos Manuel Gámez Pérez, Jara Calles, and Laura Borrás. In addition, I would like to thank my friend of many years, Care Santos, for her continued friendship and support.

The faculty, staff, and administration at Union College have supported me in many influential ways. My special thanks goes out to Gail Golderman, the super-librarian who could make the most difficult-to-find material appear on my screen in an instant, and the staff at the Schaffer library who never ceases to provide me with dozens of books and articles from around the world. I appreciate your support. Mary Parlett-Sweeney, my lovely friend and academic head of ITS at Union, and Kevin Barhydt, my incredibly supportive colleague, did not only answer any and all of my questions about computer technology, but they helped me learn and provided constant support in my quest to navigate computer games, adventure into Second Life, remix videos, visually enhance my conference presentations, teach with Wikis, use Google maps to develop digital storytelling projects, and so on. Thank you! And special thanks goes out to you, Kevin, and your student Omar, for helping create a fabulous DVD presentation of my chapter on MTV. I love your enthusiasm and constant willingness to help and work on new projects. In addition, I would like to thank my summer research student, Felisa Williams, for the initial insights and references on video clips and computer games. You definitely made me look cool!

I would like to thank the administration at Union College and the Program for Cultural Cooperation between Spain's Ministry of Culture and United States Universities for grants that allowed me to conduct research in Spain. In addition Union College provided me with the funds to publish the extra side boxes in this book and to hire an indexer and copy editor. This was invaluable help and I can't thank you enough for your kind support. I also want to thank Bill Regier from the University of Illinois Press whose belief in my work and fabulous writing tips I still follow, and Anne Cruz, who directs the *Hispanisms Series* and first believed in this project. With the greatest of respect for your work, I thank you for believing in mine. I also want to thank Niko Pfund from Oxford University Press for his valuable negotiation advice. Many thanks! Lastly, I want to thank the editorial staff at Palgrave Macmillan for publishing this book and for being flexible and willing to experiment with a different book format. Your flexibility has allowed my creativity to take flight into new directions.

The love and support, belief and guidance, enthusiasm and input of all of the above individuals (and so many more) map the many coordinates of this book. As a project made up of so many voices, on so many levels, I dedicate this book to all of you.

Introduction

Generation X:
Identity, Technology, and Storytelling

The form of the traditional novel is a metaphor
for a society that no longer exists.

—Ronald Sukenick

When a new cast of Spanish authors appeared on the market in the early 1990s, young readers flocked to bookstores. Ray Loriga, the *rock and roll novelist*. Benjamín Prado, the *grunge author*. José Ángel Mañas, the *punk writer*. Lucía Etxebarria, the *Spice Girl*. Their works spoke to their fans, but their unconventional writing styles, steeped in colloquial speech and popular media culture, were not well received by Spanish critics. Rock and roll? Grunge? Punk? How could the subcultural dynamics of these musical forms be reconciled with the aesthetic expectations and values of the literary canon?

At a loss for the right interpretive words, some critics readily rejected these writers as trendy, unrefined, and selling out to commercial culture.[1] Other critics tuned into their texts by making reference to earlier literary periods. They looked to such neorealist forerunners as Camilo José Cela's *La colmena* (1951) and Rafael Sánchez Ferlosio's *El Jarama* (1955) to absolve these authors' perspectives on everyday life. They associated the young writers' physical and metaphysical escapades with American Beat writers William S. Burroughs and Jack Kerouac. They praised their colloquial writing styles as Spanish versions of the American dirty realists Raymond Carver or Charles Bukowski. And although all of these literary references were justified, it became readily apparent that they told only part of the story.[2]

The novels of Generation X writers displayed characteristics that pointed to larger social and cultural transformations. These authors grew up on music, film, television, and advertising. They were the children of MTV and reality television, of the Video Home System (VHS), the TV remote control, and the cell phone. They developed a sophisticated language and perspective from which to evaluate and consume media technologies. They created

HAVE YOU SEEN THIS?

GENERATION J.A.S.P.

(Joven Aunque Sobradamente Preparado)

Spain's Generation X has often been called the *JASP* Generation based on a Renault Clio car commercial produced by the ad agency Tiempo BBDO in 1996.

The ad beautifully displays the generation gap and perspective of the Baby Boomers concerning the GenX individual, one that undermines their hard work ethic, intelligence, and level of innovation.

You can see the ad at:
www.lifeisalemon.net/2008/02/la
-evolucion-espanola-de-la-generacion-x/

—Christine Henseler

COCA COLA AND GENX

This Coca Cola commercial, called "Treintaytantos," clearly targets Spain's Generation X.

www.youtube.com/watch?v=RObZkBdLLlY

—Christine Henseler

characters who defined themselves through brand names like BMW, Swatch, or Sony; who got drunk on Japanese anime while listening to the Red Hot Chili Peppers; and who metaphysically moved in time and space to Road Runner cartoons. Popular culture and media technologies served to highlight emotional states, moments in time and movements in space; they projected actions or ingested personalities; they defined worth and desire, rebellion and conformity. They intimated an ever more multimedia and fluid reality that demanded a larger set of cultural literacies. But, how did critics of Spanish literature integrate this broader set of cultural signifiers into their interpretive toolkits?

Broad critical strokes concerning Spanish Generation X fiction's role in a changing society have remained relatively static and monodisciplinary. At the two extremes, scholars have either taken linear, cause-and-effect perspectives on the relationship between social reality and GenX narrative or theoretical, abstract approaches that sidelined material reality. Carmen de Urioste, in *Novela y sociedad en la España contemporánea (1994–2009)*, courses along Spain's changing social and cultural landscape through contemporary fiction. She centers on the work of GenX and non-GenX novelists such as Lucía Etxebarria, Benjamín Prado, Care Santos, Ray Loriga, and Almudena Grandes to regard Spain's real relations to sexuality, family and politics, desire and violence, the city, and memory, respectively. She and Cristina Moreiras Menor, in *Cultura herida: literatura y cine en la España democrática*, appropriate the theoretical studies of Jean Baudrillard, Fredric Jameson, and Guy Debord, among others, to understand the role of consumer society at the end of the twentieth century. While both of these studies acknowledge the role of media technologies in a globalizing world and present some fascinating interpretations, they move between the extremes of social and cultural reality, hyperreality, spectacularity, and violence to justify a more negative, destructive, and disillusioned Generation X worldview.

In line with these studies, other scholars have literally broken down the word and read characters' appropriation of the commercial image as consuming, negative, and emptying sites of meaning-making. For critics such as Carter Smith, Jason Klodt, and Gonzalo Navajas visual media

> *RAY LORIGA ON WRITING*
>
> "He utilizado el ordenador como una Polaroid y he querido que el olor y las vibraciones de las ciudades empaparan el texto" (1).
>
> —Mercedes Monmany,
> *"Rock and roll en la plaza Roja"*

have corrosive, ephemeral, and minimalizing effects; media instantly replace identities, erase *real* subjectivities, turn characters into actors of themselves, and present little ethical substance and appeal to the young.[3] When characters' worlds are taken over by the simulacrum, it either leaves in its wake a fascination with the obscene, the extreme, and the violent, or nothing at all. These critics believe that the creative potential of Generation X texts is more traumatic than transformative, and popular culture and technology leave little upon which the word can grow and evolve.

When scholars shifted their focus and viewed popular culture and media technologies as intellectual live wires instead of abstract theoretical constructs, the results added energy to the discussion.[4] In her book, *La novela de la Generación X* (2008), critic Eva Navarro Martínez examined the role of film, television, video, and music on GenX novels' themes, structures, and styles. She believes that these authors liberate the novel from fixed styles and parameters, proposing a democratization of the writing process and the introduction of new cultural references (276). Her meticulous work presages the effects of audio and visual cultures on the construction of contemporary subjects and realities. Navarro Martínez's scholarship attests to the integration of structural and thematic levels of text and popular media culture through critical models that are more integrative and participatory than oppositional and minimizing. In his essay "Other Lives: Rock, Memory and Oblivion in Post-Franco Fiction," Dutch scholar Maarten Steenmeijer compares non-GenX writer Antonio Muñoz Molina's *El jinete polaco* (1991) to Ray Loriga's novel *Héroes* (1993). He discovers that Muñoz Molina uses rock as a soundtrack that accompanies and reconstructs the protagonist's memories of a past made present. In *Héroes*, rock functions like an emphatic presence and a metaphysics of metamorphosis; it is the fuel of a higher existence that transcends time and space. Rock does not suggest a separate metaphysical state, but rather an embodied presence, a *Dasein*.[5] His essay differenciates rock in GenX texts as articulated and valenced on a variety of levels simultaneously: the thematic, stylistic, and existential.

Hispanist Jorge Pérez takes Steenmeijer's argument a bit further by stating that in Spain, film, music, and comics merge into new aesthetic codes that are transnational; they embody a global network of cultural references; and they are fully assimilated into storytelling mechanisms ("Reckless" 153). Pérez examines the transatlantic and multidisciplinary dimensions of several

GenX "rock and road novels," including those by Ray Loriga, José Machado, and Eugenia Rico. His goal is to capture the accelerating pace of cultural transformations occurring along what he calls "Superhighway Spain" (153–54). By analyzing rock music as a crucial and interactive component of Generation X texts, he invokes new layers of meaning that accentuate rock's function in narrative as one with "porous generic margins, as cultural hybrids that juxtapose words, images, and sounds" (155). His insights recognize the function of music and media as more integral, assimilated, and mutating of the novelistic enterprise.

The goal of this book is to unravel some of the theoretical abstractions that have driven scholarship on Spanish Generation X narrative. I perceive that previous perspectives have been tainted by the absence of a comprehensive, historical, and cross-cultural examination of the evolution of the "Generation X" moniker. By examining the term's roots and outgrowths, this study has several goals. First, it advances that although "Generation X" is considered a youth cultural phenomenon of the 1990s, it should not be viewed as a static literary or social category. Second, by understanding the essence of Generation X as a category that has evolved over time, this project identifies its main axis as found in the acceleration of media technologies, as converging in the f(r)ictions between subcultural and commercial capital, and as expressed in the spaces that open the "X's" blank to innovative and expanded aesthetic paradigms. Third, this project proposes the need to examine Spanish Generation X literature through more material-based research connected to the fields of media and digital studies. How do media inform GenX narrative structures and styles? What multi- and metamedia paradigms take shape when we examine the synergy between prose and technology? And what relationships emerge between the so-called "X'ers" and the *Mutantes* writers of the twenty-first century through this lens? Fourth, this project advocates for more gender-inclusive studies, more interdisciplinary perspectives, and a more global approach to Generation X in both the twentieth and twenty-first centuries. And, finally, this book's structure encourages more open, less hierarchical, more collaborative, interdisciplinary, and multi-platform critical practices.

> *What does this have to do with the new twenty-first-century Spain? I'm referring to the changing demographics especially in terms of race and immigration. Check out a very controversial writer in this generation from Equatorial Guinea: Guillermina Mekuy. Her first book was written when she was in her twenties.* El llanto de la perra *was met with scorn by the Guinean exiles and "serious" writers. I also have had some critical things to say in my* Africans in Europe *book. I'd love to see how you handle this novel, which is, among other things, another version of Almudena Grandes'* Las edades de Lulú (1989) *by an African woman in Spain. Also check out the pop or world music stars, "Las hijas del sol," also of this generation. So my question is, what does postcolonialism have to do with all this?*
>
> —*Michael Ugarte, in response*

Generation X Criticism in Spain

When critics talk about "Generation X" in Spain they must necessarily walk through a door marked "history." On the Iberian Peninsula, generational categories have structured literary classifications for over a century. Theorized by Spanish philosopher José Ortega y Gasset in *En torno a Galileo: esquema de las crisis* (1930), labels such as "Generation of '98" or "Generation of '27" delineated some of the greatest canonical works in literary history. The categories were known as much for the authors these classifications conjoined as the ones they left out. "Generation X," as Hispanist Nina Molinaro affirms, was no exception, and critics either "conflated the Spanish Generación X novelists with the entire generation, thereby effectively eliding the vast differences between the two, or they identified the subgroup as most worthy of attention" ("Facing" 303). When the limelight was placed on a more narrow definition of the Generation X group, the results were usually negative and damaging, with critics pointing to the publishing industries' role in the hyping of their images rather than in the literary quality of their texts.

> "Hoy, en países con sentido crítico actualizado y con algún debate no necesariamente vasco, resulta más notorio que la novela es un quehacer desfallecido. Nuestros mejores novelistas —dos o tres— lo saben y lo proclaman cuando se les atiende. Casi todo lo interesante que puede ofrecer hoy una novela pertenece a otro género: al ensayo, a la autobiografía, al diario, al cine, a la antropología, a la filosofía. Cuando se argumenta aún que en la novela 'cabe todo' es que, efectivamente la novela se encuentra vacía. ¿Contar una historia? Todavía hay diversos novelistas que alardean de que su máxima pasión, su vocación sagrada, lo que de verdad les mueve es contar historias. Que se hagan guionistas. Si conserva algún sentido ejercer la episodiología es, sin duda, el estilo; si tiene algún sentido escribir es producir algo que sólo se pueda decir por la escritura. Las historias las cuenta mucho mejor el cine, el vídeo, la televisión, los cómics, incluso."
>
> —Vicente Verdú,
> *"¿Vivir o leer novelas?"*

Discussions on the underlying logic and continued relevance of generational categories continue to this day, but I think it is fair to say that in the case of Generation X, Spanish critics held on to their modus operandi for reasons that were motivated by ideology rather than analytical perspicacity. The label unsettled critics' traditional, nationalist, and purely word-oriented critical perspectives; its "X" factor simultaneously allowed them to acknowledge and discredit the moniker's North American and popular cultural alliances, shunning the elusive "X" from their well-known repertoires. The illusory and intangible dynamic of the "X" marker released critics, or so they thought, from rigorous and justified scholarship, leading to reactions that stereotyped, homogenized, and discredited Generation X literature on a large scale.

The delimiting practice of Spain's generational model, together with the highly negative and unjustified reactions of the Spanish literary establishment toward Generation X texts, has led some US scholars, such as Cristina Moreiras Menor and Robert Spires, to call for a less polarizing and more plural approach to the new narrative of the 1990s.[6] They suggest that generational models be dismantled altogether for a better understanding of larger historical transformations, and that more connections be made between the novelists who belong to the GenX group (like José Ángel Mañas) and those who do not (like Javier Cercas, author of *Soldados de Salamina* [2001]). Nina Molinaro also calls for a more inclusive approach, recognizing the workings of larger historical and aesthetic movements and the need for a more multi-cultural and less homogenizing perspective on issues pertaining to gender, sexuality, race, ethnicity, immigration, or disability.[7]

In this project, I argue for a more fluid approach of inclusion, difference, and multiplicity that does not deny or erase specificity and narrowness of understanding. Without invalidating or negating the existence of a diverse spectrum of contemporary writers, I believe a better-defined conceptualization and evaluation of Generation X is sorely needed. Scholars notably include such writers as Belén Gopegui and Juan Manuel de Prada into a group whose literary roots, stylistic outcomes, and philosophical goals are radically different. In addition, scholars have used the GenX term interchangeably with *neorealismo* or *realismo sucio* [dirty realism] without entertaining their inherent differences; they limit the Generation X repertoire to literary models that have lost part of their foundational history in the process of translation, as is well analyzed by Cintia Santana.[8] They make direct connections between social realities and narrative outputs, discounting the complex web of glocal cultural influences that determine the Generation X worldview (especially in regards to race, class and gender). In addition, a partial understanding of the GenX designation has led scholars to relegate GenX'ers engagement with violence to the extreme by decontextualizing and displacing their narratives. Most importantly, scholars tend to push the role and meaning of popular culture and media technologies to the sidelines or demonize their effects, when they must be viewed as central metaphysical and structural determinants. For example, scholar María T. Pao appropriates the influential work of James Annesley on blank fiction to understand the role of commodity culture in José Ángel Mañas's *Historias del Kronen*. Her generally fascinating analysis concludes with the claim that the novel "contains an implicit warning against the objectifying ethos and consumerist tendencies embodied in its protagonist and stimulated by North American cultural products" (258). By not leading her assertions with a deeper understanding of "Generation X" and its relation to blank fiction, the subversive and integrative roles of commercial culture are lost, leaving behind empty takes on morality.[9]

A few critics in the field of Hispanism—Paul Begin, Eva Navarro Martínez, and Adelaida Martín Caro among them—have based their discussions on more comprehensive studies of the GenX label.[10] Their scholarship has contributed to the rich fabric of Generation X narrative by examining its relationship to punk, to audiovisual culture, and to the figures and movements related to popular culture, pop art, and the cultural underground and counterculture in the United States. Their approaches attend to the term's roots as well as its global and transatlantic outgrowths, especially as it relates to Latin American McOndo writers Alberto Fuguet and Edmundo Paz Soldán.[11] Their work foresees the need to move in multiple directions in order to conceive of this group of writers in more encompassing ways.

In this book I claim "Generation X" as an age cohort *and* a worldview, a group with a particular experience and conscience, as a term pertaining to a specific demographic and a label that metamorphoses through space and time. I am interested in how a multiplicity of voices and perspectives feature a distinctive, generational worldview that is not universally shared by the entire demographic. In regard to its application as a literary demographic, Spanish "Generation X" includes a particular base group, or first wave of writers publishing in the early to mid-1990s, including the well-known names of José Ángel Mañas, Ray Loriga, Benjamín Prado, Lucía Etxebarria, and Gabriela Bustelo. These authors fit perfectly into the GenX demographic: they were born between 1962 and 1977, and they began to publish in the early 1990s. Their lives were defined by socially improved conditions, by high levels of education and a variety of professions. These writers were and are active in the music industry, visual arts, and television as actors and film and television directors. They consume movies, television, computer games, and music from around the world. They are multilingual and have lived and traveled abroad, often for long periods. They are the first generation to grow up fully immersed in technology. Their worldview was shaped by MTV when its repertoire consisted of 100 percent music video clips and when advertising became a source of entertainment rather than an interruption of it. Their lives were first determined by technologies that asked them to get up and change a channel, record a video, listen to a tape, or pick up the phone. Today, the first group of Spanish GenX writers' comfort with technology displays itself readily in their webpages, their blogs, and their use of electronic mail.

THE FIRST WAVE OF SPANISH GENX WRITERS

José Angel Mañas, Ray Loriga, Lucía Etxebarria, Gabriela Bustelo, Benjamín Prado, Roger Wolfe, Pedro Maestre, Daniel Múgica, Ismael Grasa, Josán Hatero, José Machado, Francisco Casavella, Juan Madrid, and Caimán Montalbán.

THE SECOND WAVE OF SPANISH GENX WRITERS

Agustín Fernández Mallo, Germán Sierra, Jorge Carrión, Juan Francisco Ferré, Mercedes Cebrián, Manuel Vilas, Eloy Fernández Porta, Isaac Rosa, Javier Fernández, Vicente Luis Mora, Robert Juan-Casavella, Carmen Velasco, Jordi Costa, Javier Calvo, Imma Turbau, Alberto Olmos, and Doménico Chiappe.

—Christine Henseler

I extend the "Generation X" label to a second wave of writers who have been dubbed the "Nocilla Generation," based on novelist Agustín Fernández Mallo's trilogy *Nocilla Dream* (2006), *Nocilla Experience* (2007), and *Nocilla Lab* (2009); the "After-Pops," in line with Eloy Fernández Porta's much-acclaimed critical work in *After-Pop: la literatura de la implosión mediática* (2007); and, the term I prefer, the "*Mutantes*," as best expressed in the short story volume *Mutantes: Narrativa española de última generación* (2007), coedited by Juan Francisco Ferré and Julio Ortega.[12] Although also born in the 1960s and 1970s and belonging to the "Generation X" demographic, their work suggests a maturation of the GenX perspective, a positive change in worldview, and a do-it-yourself philosophy that wholeheartedly embraces social and digital media on a narrative and a critical level.[13]

The *Mutantes* clearly view themselves as global citizens; they are multilingual and they live, travel, and work abroad. Case in point is Jorge Carrión's description of himself on the inside flap of his novel *La Brújula* (2006) as "profesor en Guatemala, Chicago y Barcelona; y escritor en los cinco continentes" [professor in Guatemala, Chicago and Barcelona; and writer in the five continents]. Although they are highly educated and knowledgable in the history of Spanish and world literatures, film, popular culture, philosophy, science, mathematics, and media technologies may also be found at the thematic and stylistic center of their narratives and their personal and professional lives. Most of them have their own webpages and blogs, and they understand the benefits of living and working in a networked society. Most importantly, their work disrupts conceptions of culture, space, time, and reality, presenting more fluid mutations in genres and character identities. Their implicit and explicit attention to new models of authorship and readership force the literary establishment to imagine new ways of portraying the narrative landscape in Spain in the twenty-first century.

The *Mutantes* do not view themselves as Generation X'ers, or even within a clearly defined generational framework, but rather, as Jorge Carrión well articulates, as a "web of friendships," or in Germán Sierra's words, as "un 'embrión de red literaria' " [an embryonic literary web] (Azancot "Generación Nocilla"). They do not place fixed boundaries around their literary identities, but view themselves through more fluid metaphors that retain a certain level of liquidity. Despite this liquidity, Ismael Grasa (b. 1968) observes a clear connection between these writers and his own identity as a Generation X author of the 1990s, especially as it relates to the assimilation of language. Grasa contends that today's authors have sipped from,

> esas historias hiperrealistas y desestructuradas que hablaban de amor, sexo y marcas de champú [que] son los que hoy se han enmarcado en la llamada Generación Nocilla, capitaneados por Agustín Fernández Mallo y Ricardo Menéndez Salmón. Entre ellos se encuentra también Juan Manuel Gil (1979), quien reconoce la influencia de Ray Loriga.

> [those hyperrealist and unstructured stories that talked about love, sex and shampoo brands which are what today have been included in the so-called

Nocilla Generation, headed by Agustín Fernández Mallo and Ricardo Menéndez Salmón. Among them is also Juan Manuel Gil (1979), who recognizes the influence of Ray Loriga.] (Corroto)[14]

Grasa identifies stylistic and thematic relationships between the two groups of authors, suggesting that, "Los X de ayer son todavía los treintañeros de hoy" [The Xer's of yesterday are still the thirty-somethings of today]" (Corroto). And as I demonstrate in this book, the second GenX wave may very well be viewed within the changing configuration, but coherent base, of the Generation X designation.

Generation X: A Demographic Overview

In chapter 1, I examine at length the birth and evolution of the Generation X designation and its sociological and cultural outgrowths. Here, I provide a brief demographic overview of Generation X'ers in the United States and Spain by centering on their historical, political, and social experiences. This analysis provides an empirical basis from which Spanish GenX narrative can be questioned and reenvisioned and its aesthetic practices reevaluated. I do not present this material as self-defining of individual GenX experiences, but as determining each person to different degrees. By presenting a demographic overview on one hand and a cultural one on the other, my goal is to sidestep the problematic engagement with stereotypes most often hyped by the media in the 1990s and associated with negative, disadvantaged, and countercultural images of youth.

Generation X'ers were born between 1961 and 1981 (some sources reduce their dates of birth to between 1964 and 1981). They were the smallest cohort of individuals to be born in the United States and Spain, consisting of roughly 25 percent of the population in each country (vs. 30 percent for Baby Boomers and

---

HISTORY OF THE PILL

According to a Public Broadcasting Service (PBS) website on the history of the pill, in 1960, the G. D. Searle Drug Company of Skokie, Illinois, tried to license the first commercially produced birth control pill, Enovid 10. The company received Food and Drug Administration (FDA) approval on May 11, 1960. In 1962, 1.2 million American women were on the pill. By 1964 one-quarter of all American couples were using birth control, and the government sought support for birth control for the poor. By 1967, 12.5 million women worldwide were on the pill. By the early 1980s, 10.7 million American women were on the pill.

www.pbs.org/wgbh/amex/pill/timeline/timeline2.html

The nine-year difference between the two countries' (the United States' and Spain's) legalization of the contraceptive pill perhaps contributed to the first inklings of a GenX narrative to appear in North America in the mid-1980s, and their work to impress upon the full-blown version of a GenX aesthetics in the early 1990s in Spain and elsewhere.

—Christine Henseler

Millennials).[15] Their inception was most closely linked to the legalization of the birth control pill in the United States in the early 1960s and in Spain in 1973. Generation X'ers were tagged the "in-between generation" because they were born between the Baby Boomers and the Millennials.[16] They were deemed the "after" generation because they matured after grand social movements—the women's movement, the civil rights movement, antiwar demonstrations—had already taken place. They were the "lost" generation because they were, metaphorically speaking, lost in the present, arriving too late for the sweeping social movements of the recent past and too early for the Internet revolution that was to connect Generation Y babies from their cribs.[17]

In both the United States and Spain, Generation X'ers experienced a series of political and economic developments that marked their worldviews. In the United States, X'ers lived through Watergate, the Iran-Contra affair, the explosion of the *Challenger* Space Shuttle, and the Whitewater debacle. In Spain the population felt the growing pains of an emerging democracy and witnessed the corruption scandals of the Felipe González administration. Both populations experienced a global recession in the early 1980s, a stock market crash in 1987, and another recession in the early 1990s. They both felt the effects of a past marked by excess: the Reagan era in the United States and the radical growth and increase in living standards in Spain, kicked off by the exuberant *Movida* years (1975–86). As witnesses to the exploitation and failed political policies—real-world problems and situations that became increasingly macroscopic—neither country's GenX citizens felt compelled to act politically. They recognized the outlines of very real problems ahead—fiscal, social, and environmental—but in the nations' political systems they perceived no leadership on issues that concerned them. They encountered instead self-serving politicians who indentured themselves to the highest bidders, leaving the marginalized, the unemployed, and the sick to fend for themselves.[18]

> ### LA GENERACIÓN "X" ESPAÑOLA — ¿QUIÉNES SOMOS?
>
> "Somos la última generación que hemos aprendido a jugar en la calle a las chapas, la peonza, las canicas, la comba, la goma o el rescate y, a la vez, somos la primera que hemos jugado a videojuegos, hemos ido a parques de atracciones o visto dibujos animados en color.
>
> Se nos ha etiquetado de generación X y tuvimos que tragarnos bodrios como *Historias del Kronen* o *Reality Bites*, *Melrose Place* o *Sensación de vivir* (te gustaron en su momento, vuélvelas a ver, verás que chasco).
>
> Aprendimos a programar el video antes que nadie, jugamos con el Spectrum, odiamos a Bill Gates, vimos a Perico Delgado anunciar los primeros móviles y creímos que Internet sería un mundo libre."
>
> —Selecciones de un bloguero español
> http://86400.es/2005/12/
> 07/la-generacion-x/

In Spain, Generation X'ers grew up during and matured after the so-called *desarrollismo* period of 1960 to 1975, which effectively moved Spain into a modern society before the death of Franco.[19] The social changes during this period were indeed striking, and they included a shift from a predominantly rural to an urban society, a per capita increase of nearly two and a half times, a lowering in the birth rate (from 5.0 children per family to 2.5 by 1975); a rise in the number of people calling themselves atheists (from 3 percent to 26 percent), an increase in those with an "indifferent" religious allegiance (especially those born after 1960), fewer working-class individuals and a greater equality in income thanks in part to a better education system and a decrease in illiteracy, and finally, a series of advances in technology and communication.[20] The ownership of televisions went from 1 percent to 90 percent of households between 1960 and 1975, of refrigerators from 4 percent to 87 percent, of cars from 4 percent to 49 percent, of telephones from 12 percent to 44 percent, and of record players from 3 percent to 39 percent. Indicators show that by the beginning of the political transition, Spain had already transformed itself into a modern consumer society (Zaldívar).

Several Hispanists have pointed to the paradox of a dynamic and growing society and the social difficulties that stifled youth's optimism in the early 1990s because of high levels of unemployment, lack of affordable housing, the AIDS epidemic, drug addiction, and political corruption scandals. The leadership of Felipe González, Prime Minister of the Spanish Socialist Worker's Party (PSOE) from 1982 to 1996, implemented a vigorous program of economic reforms that included privatization of public companies, liberalization and deregulation, and restructuring of whole industries such as steel and mining. Under his tenure he extended the network of highways and airports, and the creation of a new infrastructure, including the high-speed train; free universal health care and reform of the pension system to needy people; universal public schooling; and the construction of new universities. González also played an important role in securing Spain's entry into the European Union and in Spain being a founding member of the Euro. On the economic front, Spain's entrance into the European Union in January 1986 demanded an opening of its economic borders, an increase in foreign investments, and a move toward industrial modernization.

González's work paved the way for a long period of declining interest rates, low budgetary deficits, and a stronger economic growth above the European average. These changes led to a sense of enrichment through consumption, which in turn was spurred by a positive stock market and the increasing value of real estate.[21] With this, Spain increased its gross domestic product, reduced its public debt, reduced inflation beneath 3 percent, and became the third-largest economy in Europe and the seventh largest in the world by the end of the 1990s (Zaldívar).

The early 1990s, the years most commonly associated with the Generation X boom in fiction and film, embodied Spain's high and immediate low. The year 1992 marked the 500-year anniversary of the Columbus voyage, the year in which Madrid was hailed as "The European City of Culture," and the year when the World Expo took place in Seville. It was also the year when the government-funded project Arte Contemporáneo (ARCO) hosted multiple artistic events in Spain and throughout Europe. In fact, the 1990s are hailed by many as a golden age in the arts in Spain. But in 1992, Spain's previously spectacular growth began to show signs of slowing down. In 1992, Spain was most touched by the late-1980s recession, which lasted well into 1995–96, when unemployment hit a high of 17 percent, and when the public began to lack confidence in its governmental administration (Zaldívar).

The result of Spain's rapid growth and subsequent sobering entrance into the world economy presented a series of conflicting emotions in the population. Data show that in 1992 Spaniards were highly satisfied with the collective situation of the country. Spaniards questioned between 1985 and 1990 expressed the highest level of satisfaction of all European countries, after Germany, with 61 percent expressing very high hopes for the future (Zaldívar 42). But Spain also had one of the highest number of people dissatisfied on a personal level. In other words, they were generally optimistic about the country, yet their hopes did not always coincide with the reality of their personal lives (Zaldívar 42), a condition well expressed in the article "La generación de los mil Euros." Spaniards appeared to be preoccupied with unemployment to the same level as the Germans, English, French, and Italians, but they did not appear to be as worried about immigration (contrary to France and Germany) or issues concerning political deterritorization (contrary to Italy and France). They were much less disquieted by the economic situation but more involved in issues pertaining to drugs and crime (Zaldívar 42). What made the case of Spain unique was that in the last thirty years, Spaniards did not only have to contend with a diversification and internationalization of the market and globalization of the media and cultural diversity, but also an increased recognition of Spain's political democratization, regional diversity, and search for autonomy (Graham and Labanyi 312). Change was converging on a variety of levels simultaneously, often creating situations that were inherently contradictory.

Generation X and New Media Technologies

An understanding of Spanish GenX demographics would not be complete without a discussion of the rise and role of media technologies in young people's lives. As Spain was contending with a complex web of developments in the post-Franco era, developed nations all around the world were moving from an industrial age to an information age. In other words, the technological revolution presented an additional layer of challenges to a society in which only 0.39 percent of households in 1980 owned video recorders and rarely any individuals had personal computers.

DID YOU KNOW?

While Generation X'ers have become part of the group of global consumers of media technologies, it is important to note that they were also a significant part of its producers and innovators. As one Spanish GenX'er explains in regard to his role in world developments:

"Los 'X' hemos estado trabajando todo este tiempo en hacer avanzar técnica y tecnológicamente, pero también 'ideosincráticamente' un mundo que depende cada día más de soluciones inteligentes y no de la fuerza bruta o el consumo ilimitado de los recursos naturales".

—Raúl Ernesto Colón Rodríguez
www.kaosenlared.net/noticia/
la-generacion-x-en-el-poder

In 1985, the Spanish government took on a bold and broad initiative to promote scientific and technological growth and modernization. With the "Plan Nacional de Investigación Científica y Desarrollo Tecnológico," the government succeeded in attracting large electronic companies from the United States, Japan, and Europe and advancing scientifically through financial and technological exchange programs with European nations. Their goal was to develop two main infrastructural changes centered on the period between 1986 and 1995: the creation of new telecommunications industries and an increase in educational and human resources in the sciences and engineering, with special focus on information technologies (Zaldívar and Castells 188). The results were spectacular in both cases. They lead to a duplication in scientific output from 1982 to 1990 and a 33 percent hike in doctoral theses. As of 1992, thanks to governmental foresight and modernization efforts by individual companies, Spain became the seventh-largest market in the world for electronics and ranked eleventh in the world in regard to its capacity to install products related to telecommunications (Zaldívar and Castells 192).

> **NEW TECHNOLOGIES IN SPAIN, 2009**
>
> "Spain represents more than 2.1 percent of the world's total [gross domestic product] GDP and has enjoyed a remarkable fourteen-year streak of economic growth above the 3 percent mark. Spain is fast becoming a leader in innovation and generating advanced solutions in the industries of aerospace, renewable energies, water treatment, rail, biotechnology, industrial machinery and civil engineering."
>
> *Technology Review*
>
> www.technologyreview.com/microsites/spain/

But how did this explosion in the economic and education sectors translate into consumption on a daily basis? The assimilation process regarding the integration of new media technologies in the home space can be summarized—as does Zaldívar—as "reasonably optimistic." In 1984, 61 percent of Spaniards considered the general process of modernization to be a positive one, while only 21 percent entertained a negative opinion. The positive attitudes were mostly found among urban youth of higher social standing and high levels of education (Zaldívar and Castells 184). That said, Spanish television became the technological emblem of a new window to the world and an expression of political dissidence against the last stronghold of the Franco regime. Although not broadcasting until 1959, and despite tight political control, the television found its way into 70 percent of homes by 1974 (de Riquer 265). By 1986, Spain's audience was the highest in Europe after Great Britain (Zaldívar 58–59). By 1992, 98 percent of Spanish households (compared to 99 percent in the United States) owned a television set and 90.7 percent of Spaniards watched television; 86 percent of the population owned a color receiver, 76 percent a radio, and 42 percent a VCR. In the 1990s the television screen became one of the most socially accepted and integrated media outlets in Spain, to the point of popularizing the phrase "La familia que ve la televisión unida permanece unida" [The Spanish family that watches television together stays together] (Zaldívar and Castells 200).

Cyberspace and its various online technological outgrowths such as the Internet, virtual reality, the blogosphere, multiplayer computer games, human-computer interfaces, and so on, appeared in Spain a few years behind the United States. Internet penetration in Spain was only 2.7 percent in 1997, and was mainly limited to individuals in universities and research centers. In the first half of 2003, Internet use rose to 25.2 percent ("Spain") and to 56.5 percent in 2007 ("News"). By 2007, frequent users, those who had access to the Internet on a daily basis or at least once a week, represented 85.3 percent of the Spanish population. Projected Internet use for 2012 is 62.8 percent ("News").

Spain, despite its challenges, setbacks, and rapid comebacks, made significant strides on institutional, economic, scientific, technological, and educational levels. Helen Graham and Antonio Sánchez said it beautifully when they portrayed the speed of Spain's developments as providing "the rest of Europe with a kind of technicolour close-up of a worldwide cultural and economic process" (408). Apart from speed, these critics point to one of the most important characteristics of this process of change: hybridity. The term as it relates to Spain's developments in the post-Franco period was based on the convergence of time frames and spaces. Spain's identity was determined by the collision between old, archaic morals and models and a youth culture heavily steeped in commercial culture, new technologies, and secular values; it was also shaped by an internal process of reform that intersected with larger European and North American pressures and visions. This was a society of contradictions, of prejudices, and of increasing openness whose schizophrenia was well exemplified in the juxtaposition of cosmopolitanism and traditional Spanish values in films such as *Women on the Verge of a Nervous Breakdown* (1988)

Hybridity is a very troublesome concept to apply. If applied without rigor, it takes us back to the idea of original, pure entities—cultures, social formations and identities as sealed containers—that then are mixed up. This would mean that GenX'ers are just a contaminated by-product of otherwise pure stereotypes. I don't think this is the hybridity you're talking about. I think hybridity here may be understood not as a concept but as an action, a transitive action. Like a verb, it is an action that has a direct object it affects—those containers that are thought to be pure. It goes from one place to another. It transforms something into something else. It has always done so, it always will. If we zoom in on the process of hybridity we realize that there are no pure containers, only petrified ideas of what a social formation or culture or identity should be. That is why existential descriptors like cynicism, nihilism, disempowerment—which are states of affairs in particular moments in time—cannot quite be subsumed into the process that is hybridity. In this book, hybridity is a tool to dissolve stereotypes.

—Juan Manuel Espinosa, in response

by Spanish director Pedro Almodóvar, and in the convergence of genres and styles from the underground music, fashion, and film scene during the *Movida Madrileña* (Graham and Sánchez 410). Since the beginning of the 1970s, if not earlier, hybridity was at the center of Spain's social and cultural identity, and it continues to be so to this day.

Global Flows and Hybrid Spaces

Generation X's characterization as an "in-between" generation and their growing-up experience in a country innovated by the artistic and social effects of hybrid relations function as an important base upon which further convergences—in this case, that of regional and global flows—can convene. Generation X matured in the 1980s and 1990s, a time in which old and new regimes and systems collided and collapsed—for example, the Berlin Wall and communism.[22] During this period, societies left behind old metaphors and developed new visions and practices that responded to the challenges of what Spanish sociologist Manuel Castells called "Information Capitalism".

On a macro level, these changes centered around the accelerating role of information technologies as the material basis of societies, an economic global interconnectedness that introduced new forms of relationships between economies, states, societies, the collapse of communism, and a restructuring of capitalism with major consequences worldwide (Castells 1–2). This was a media-driven world, always in a state of process and change, in which global capitalist ventures and individual consumptive practices were increasingly coexisting with new technologies.

> *TELEVISION AROUND THE WORLD*
>
> Empirical data on the existence and use of television shows that the existence of televisions in individual households has increased significantly all around the world since the 1970s. To put things into perspective: between 1975 and 1996, the number of sets jumped from 9,000 to 90,000 in the West African nation of Burkina Faso, from 1.2 million to 394 million in China, and from 121 million to 217 million in the United States (Miles 2003, 299).

This complex web of interconnections is, in the case of Generation X, intimately intertwined with youth's engagement in the globalization process. My goal here is not to delve into an extensive study on globalization or the subcultural dynamics of youth culture, but to consider a few of the results described in the United Nations–sponsored World Youth Report of 2003 titled "Young People in a Globalizing World." This well-researched document talks about the deep-seated and divisionary effects of the process of globalization on young people's identity construction. The report makes use of the definition set forth by Anthony Giddens, who speaks of globalization as "the intensification of worldwide social relations which link distant localities in such a way that local happenings are shaped by events occurring miles away and vice versa" ("Young" 292). The authors believe that the increasing economic and cultural interdependence of societies on a world scale, in so many areas and on so many levels, makes it necessary for us to talk about "globalizations" in the plural ("Young" 292). These multileveled shifts, which are "sharply differentiated as well as differentiating" ("Young" 292), affect and are affected by changing cultural perceptions.

The report clarifies that, contrary to the impression of globalization as a means of uniformity and North American submission—a criticism often directed toward GenX texts— globalization both universalizes and individualizes culture. Some have argued that young people are more familiar with US popular and commercial culture, Hollywood movies and television, than the culture(s) of their own country. There is no doubt that this is in part true; American mass media does account for 75 percent of broadcast and cable television worldwide, and American books make up 35 percent of the world market. But it also warrants restating that people's everyday experiences are anything but uniform. Youth partake in a global consumer culture, but they also interact with and produce their own culture based on local and personal experiences ("Young" 299–300). In effect, what the report highlights through a series of case studies from the Republic of Korea, China, Sudan, and the United States is that "young people use global culture and consumption as a means of narrating their own life stories" (300), they use it as a sort of canvas upon which they paint what P. K. Klitgaard calls their own "style landscapes" (qtd. in "Young" 300), or their own "textscapes," as is widely used in the literary context.

I agree with the authors of the report that it is inappropriate to make assumptions about the impact of globalization when local identities are also constituted through face-to-face relationships that occur in social contexts in which there is often little territorial movement: "Local meanings are constructed according to environmental and personal circumstances—and within the framework of wider political, economic, and social disparities— that inevitably play a role in determining the context within which those meanings can operate" ("Young" 301).[23] The result is a multifarious "third space" within which youth simultaneously accept and reject their home and the foreign cultures; this provides a hybrid cultural space of production that young people use "creatively insofar as it allows them to create meaning in a de-territorialized world" ("Young" 301). I find this idea of a "third space" particulary valuable since it does not deny the integrity or purity of a singular local or global expression, but rather presents an alternative realm of construction, separate yet integral of both.[24]

There is a belief that inherently underlines studies on Generation X, which is that globalization is unstoppable and that it "is a process young people react to rather than actively negotiate" ("Young" 293). Because of this vision, social scientists and literary critics have exaggerated and reinforced the stereotype of young people's marginalization and pathology ("Young" 294), and they have focused on the subcultural and reactive nature of their more visible expressions. Dick Hebdige's seminal book *Subculture: The Meaning of Style* (1979) and the subcultural theory of the 1970s British Centre for Contemporary Cultural Studies (CCCS) are often used as benchmarks for an understanding of these marginal and countercultural dynamics (Muggleton and Weinzierl 4). While the visions of both Hebdige and Muggleton and Weinzierl perceive counterhegemonic radical change in largely symbolic gestures, the 1990s, the period of the GenX boom, demands a more pragmatic and nuanced approach that David Muggleton and Rupert Weinzierl define as "post-subcultural" (and that Toshiya Ueno identifies as "Urban Tribal Studies" within their volume). Their edited book presents a post-CCCS approach that retheorizes and reconceptualizes "youth (sub)cultural phenomena on the shifting social terrain of the new millennium, where global mainstreams and local substreams rearticulate and restructure in complex and uneven ways to produce new, hybrid, cultural constellations" (3). Muggleton and Weinzierl argue that this restructuring has a direct impact on youth cultural studies and justifies why terms like *subculture, clubculture* (Susan Thornton), *tribe* or *neotribe* (Michel Maffesoli and Andy Bennett), and *lifestyles* (Steven Miles) better capture the fluidity and hybridity of youth cultural experiences in the 1990s and beyond.

In this book I engage with this social fluidity and individuality by highlighting the hybrid complexity and dynamics at play in new media technologies. From music video clips to computer games, these electronic spaces applied to print culture point to youth's agency instead of pathology, erasure, or lack of power. The audiovisual design and structure afforded by each medium empowers Generation X authors to reimagine characters through changing notions of space, time, and reality without denying their regional roots. They also license writers to problematize notions of authorship, of reading, of editing, and of constructing identity within a world of global flows.

> *When you revitalize the X Generation by getting rid of the platitudes of pathology, erasure and lack of power—this three-pronged continuation of the leitmotif of cynicism and skepticism in the young—you place your bet on hybridity, a hybridity that is highly-dependent on technology. You go from an existential point of view—the way youth understands the world—to a pragmatic point of view—the way youth deals with the world. This begs the question: Does this pragmatic point of view help us answer the existential question?*
>
> *—Juan Manuel Espinosa, in response*

Generation X Goes Global

Studies on Generation X literature have motioned toward the existence of GenX texts from other countries, but no scholar has looked more deeply into the web of interconnections that this global phenomenon portrays of Generation X. While an examination of international economic, technological, and social landscapes goes beyond the scope of this book, it warrants pointing out how some GenX texts intersect with the work of Spanish writers to identify characteristics that converge on a global scale.

The confluence of political and commercial content varies in GenX texts depending on an author's country of origin and their personal experiences. Speaking in broad strokes, in the late 1980s and early 1990s, authors such as Alberto Fuguet (Chile), Edmundo Paz Soldán (Bolivia), Jáchym Topol (Czech Republic), and Viktor Pelevin (Russia) all contended with the collapse of communist or dictatorial regimes and the surge of commercial capital-ism into everyday life. To differ-ent degrees, these sociopolitical collisions became part of their generational identities and nar-rative strategies. Viktor Pelevin, in his novel *Homo Zapiens* (orig. *Generation P*, 1999), fed into the post-Soviet metaphor of a Russian "Pepski Generation." His char-acter used sarcastic, cynical, and humorous language; advertising images and jingles; and mythi-cal figures and stories to create a prose of contrasting proportions that engaged with the commu-nist/Russian contention with commercial capitalism.

> **EXCERPT FROM *HOMO ZAPIENS* BY VIKTOR PELEVIN**
>
> "Once upon a time in Russia there really was a carefree, youthful generation that smiled in joy at the summer, the sea and the sun, and chose Pepsi.
>
> It's hard at this stage to figure out exactly how this situation came about. More likely it involved more than just the remarkable taste of the drink in question. More than just the caffeine that keeps young kids demanding another dose, steering them securely out of childhood into the clear waters of the channel of cocaine" (1).

Similarly, Jáchym Topol's novel *City Sister Silver* (1994) captured the opening of Central and Eastern Europe in the 1990s.[25] He portrays myths, nightmares, and stories through rapid shifts in syntax, style, spell-ing, dialogue, tone, and meaning, conjoining colloquial language and traditional literary forms. As translator Alex Zucker notes in the preface to the novel, Topol changes language in response to the new political landscape. He uses atypical terminology, a variety of Czech idioms, dia-lects, and slang, plus assorted words and phrases from other languages, to identify the fast-changing reality around him (viii). Chilean Alberto Fuguet, a writer who spent many years in the United States, appropriated the designation "McOndo" to replace Gabriel García Márquez's use of the town name "Macondo" in *One Hundred Years of Solitude* (1967). He sub-stituted several globalizing brands—McDonalds, Macintosh computers, and condos—for a familiar, already globalized notion of Latin American magic realism.

In societies where commercial capitalism had been part of the sociopo-litical landscape for a longer period, the collision of worlds and languages is less obvious and conflicted. Their language seems to have ingested com-mercial culture, leading to more flat linguistic patterns and a more self-centered search for meaning. *Faserland* (1995) or *Crazy* (1993) by Germans Christian Kracht and Benjamin Lebert, *101 Reykjavík* (2002) by Icelandic author Hallgrímur Helgason, *Praise* (1992) and *1988* (1995) by Australian Andrew McGahan, or *Trainspotting* (1996) by Irvine Welsh display many similarities to Spanish GenX texts. They include varying degrees of sarcasm and humor, lack of critical distance and political engagement, violence, and explicit sexuality. All present narratives that emulate linguistic patterns derived from everyday life—colloquialisms; neologisms; and references to film, music, and popular audiovisual culture. They also connect to technology on a thematic and/or stylistic level, using fragmenting techniques defined as televisual zappings, MTV aesthetics, and DJ remixings.

Spanish GenX novels display significant similarities with the novels of their contemporaries from around the world. Contrary to the working-class individuals and slang found in *Trainspotting* or *City Sister Silver*, Spanish characters are mostly middle- to upper-class individuals and their vernacular language has been cleansed into a commercially viable form of yuppie countercultural slang. Spain's texts are saturated equally with images from television, music, advertising, and audiovisual culture, and they are marked by short sentence structures and linguistic transpositions of the English language. Characters' physical or mental escapes and marginal positions are, in the case of Spain, often less politically direct in the questioning of societal norms and values than in Douglas Coupland's *Generation X* or Viktor Pelevin's *Homo Zapiens*. Their narrative style is generally as flat as the work of the German authors, despite their indulgence in more lyrical and emotional landscapes. Sarcasm and cynicism are found less frequently, except in the work of Spain's female novelists. Women writers decry societal norms through alternative

---

McONDO

"Now, thanks to Fuguet and his peers, there is a new voice south of the Río Grande. It is savvy, street-smart, sometimes wiseass and un-ashamedly over the top. Fuguet calls this the voice of McOndo—a blend of McDonald's, Macintosh computers and condos. The label is a spoof, of course, not only on García Márquez's fictitious village but also on all the poseurs who have turned these latitudes into a pastel tequila ad. ¡Hola! Fuguet is saying. Latin America is no paradise.

The new genre was born in 1996 with a collection of short stories by eighteen authors, all under thirty-five, called 'McOndo.' The book was launched, somewhat ironically, at a party at a McDonald's in Santiago, where Fuguet and coeditor Sergio Gómez signed copies to the sound of Friolators. The tales are irreverent, often aggressive, scatological riffs on contemporary urban life, told to a backbeat of sex, drugs and pop music. The mood swings from hallucinatory to suicidal, with a heavy emphasis on the blasé."

—Mac Margolis

It is important to note something that is usually rarely mentioned: McOndo may have seen itself as a Latin American anthology, but it also included three Spanish writers: Ray Loriga, Martín Casariego, and José Ángel Mañas.

—*Edmundo Paz Soldán, in response*

For some critics, to focus on media meant to be apolitical, sold out to American pop culture; that clearly was not the case.

—*Edmundo Paz Soldán, in response*

> *In Mexico the Crack writers—chief among them Jorge Volpi—published their manifesto in 1996, the same year McOndo was released.*
>
> *—Edmundo Paz Soldán, in response*

models of identity formation steeped in commercial culture and cyberculture, but they also engage with the effects of depression and drug use, as in Elizabeth Wurzel's *Prozac Nation* (1994). In general, first-person interior monologues dominate, short sentences and fragmented forms simulate MTV editing techniques, and popular media culture composes individuals' identities, their *being*.

These novels from the early to mid-1990s display the making of a larger phenomenon, one that defines a series of mutual characteristics and cultural idiosyncrasies. These global expressions go beyond the novels mentioned previously to display a movement that mutates the GenX label according to the convergence of cultural signifiers at play in each individual country and in a variety of genres. The result is a series of generational labels/labs with distinct manifestations: in Germany, "Generation X" metamorphoses into "Generation Golf" or "Popliteratur"; in France, the "*Whatever* Generation" comes to light with the work of Michel Houellebecq and Amélie Nothomb; in Russia, the "Pepski Generation" pushes vodka aside for a soda drink; in Iran, the "Burnt Generation" erupts and disrupts tradition; in South Africa, the so-called Y-Culture and *Kwaito* music—a blend of beat-heavy house music and African rhythms—embody a more musical Generation X; in China, there emerge the male "Hooligan Writers" and the female "Beauty Writers"; and in Japan, the consumptive habits of the *shinjinrui* present compelling interconnections with the US and Spanish phenomenon.[26]

> ## *GENERATION GOLF: EINE INSPEKTION* (2001) by Florian Illies
>
> The book *Generation Golf: Eine Inspektion*, sold six million copies in Germany. The book was a major success due to the fact that it described in a realistic manner the lives of youth born in the 1980s post–Cold War period.
>
> The term "Generation Golf" served as a German equivalent to America's "Generation X" and was based on the advertising campaign for the Volkswagen of the same name and the advertisement, which read "The search for a destination is over" (Hachtmann 12).
>
> According to Illies, the characteristics of the "Golf Generation" revolve around oneself, one's career, and a fascination with brand names. This generation was also the first to be hooked on soap operas such as *Melrose Place* and *90210*, resembling artificial drama that could always either be erased or eventually turn out alright (Hachtmann 12–13).
>
> —Christine Henseler

In sum, to talk about Spanish Generation X narrative, one must understand how it relates to and positions itself within a much broader global dynamic and alongside a variety of different genres.

A Network of Narratives

In the first pages of this introduction, I asked how Hispanists were integrating a broader set of cultural signifiers into their interpretive toolkits. While popular culture and media technologies present a particular set of challenges, placed within complex global and local cross-currents, reading practices have become ever more demanding. In 1999, in "Posmodernismo: ¿Cómo leer una novela de hoy?" ["Postmodernism: How to Read a Novel Today?"], Hispanist Gonzalo Navajas certified that the text, the novel, could no longer be read in cultural isolation or through a historically deterministic lens. Reading needed to occur, rather, within a web of multiple and interconnected signifiers. Navajas called for a more transtemporal and multidirectional reading practice that he referred to as "anti-reading" or "no reading." This process was less linear and successive in focus, more fragmented and dynamic in its approach to temporality, active instead of passive in its appreciation of the literary process, and embracing of a plurality and diversity that could be contradictory and oppositional (149–52). He called this approach "correlational," suggesting that fiction be read next to visual art, music, and other aesthetic practices.[27]

Navajas identified the need for a new approach to literary criticism that was put into practice by a group of individuals in Spain a few years after the publication of his essay. In 2006 and 2007, several new projects pointed to a perceptual change on a creative and critical level. In 2007, Eloy Fernández Porta published his influential book *Afterpop: La literatura de la implosión mediática*; cultural critic Vicente Luis Mora opened new analytical spaces in his much-acclaimed blog "Diario de lecturas" and books such as *La luz nueva: Singularidades en la narrativa española actual* (2007) and *Pangea: Internet, blogs y comunicación en un mundo nuevo* (2006). In addition, the short story collection coedited by Juan Francisco Ferré and Julio Ortega, *Mutantes: Narrativa española de última generación* (2007), was significant in identifying a change in the cultural tide.

These works, among others, now allow critics to take a first, second, and third look at Generation X narrative through a reading practice that I prefer to understand through the metaphor of the Semantic Web, also known as "Web 3.0." The fast transformational potential that has moved the Internet from a Web 1.0 to a Web 3.0 application, and will undoubtedly move beyond this point, allows us to identify the Internet's technological power in the art and practice of meaning-making. How can we learn from the process by which a computer makes meaning of an

---

WHAT IS "WEB 2.0" AND "WEB 3.0"?

For introductory videos, take a look at these:

WEB 2.0
www.youtube.com/watch?v=nsa5ZTRJQ5w

WEB 3.0
www.youtube.com/watch?v=OGg8A2zfWKg

—Christine Henseler

almost infinite number of topics and requests? Instead of the static and separate webages that marked a Web 1.0 application, the Semantic Web advances a way of creating meaningful connections between disparate elements drawn from film, video, photography, comics, music, art, and so on. Close readings of texts not withstanding, the Semantic Web can suggest that literary critics engage in a more interactive, communicative, open, collaborative, and participatory relationship. The Semantic Web provides a common framework that allows information to be shared and reused across disciplines and community boundaries. The writing and the study of narrative in Spain, then, must take place within this increasing web of organic and virally moving connections, the convergence of media technologies, and the hybridization of media and social cultural forms on a variety of platforms around the world. As the powerful video clip on the acceleration of technology indicates, "Shift Happens." But what are the innovative potentials and outgrowths of print culture within these shifts? And what changes need to occur within the field of literary criticism to accommodate these happenings?

> ### SHIFT HAPPENS
>
> To get a sense of the impact of the acceleration of media technologies on everyday life, take a look at this video clip:
> "Information Age…The Future of Technology":
> www.youtube.com/watch?v=OSjRpgT_hXM
>
> —Christine Henseler

To rival the Semantic Web in print format, *Spanish Fiction in the Digital Age: Generation X Remixed* includes side boxes to emulate a more participatory and networked approach to the subject. These boxes incorporate material that engages with the main narrative, information meant to advance a dynamic and fluid conversation in print in both English and Spanish (without translations, to boost the hybrid quality of the experience). In some cases I speak directly to you, the readers, asking if you have seen a particular clip or advertisement, or adding critical remarks to my own interpretations. Increasingly, the chapters involve the "responses"—comments, ideas, and material—of over thirty scholars and authors from the field of Hispanism. All of these contributors have read parts if not all of this book, and all of them have engaged in scholarship and creative work concerning

> *I like the reformatting of the traditional look of the written page of an academic book to incorporate side boxes such as those that one finds when navigating the Internet, thus inviting the reader to break with linear reading and unidimensional thinking, to embrace the type of reading typical of Internet hyperlinks, or what is called here the reading practice of the "Semantic Web." The change in page layout illustrates the present book's arguments that the Spanish Generation X cannot be understood without a serious look at how they fit in the network of global influences and youth culture, and how its members have been affected by and take narrative modes from new digital and web-based media experiences.*
>
> *—Gema Pérez-Sánchez, in response*

Hispanic narrative in the late twentieth and twenty-first century. Their voices join to provide a networked reading experience that unsettles the word from its unmoving location in the book. Their involvement helps disrupt hierarchies, cross and converge disciplines, and develop a more inclusive, participatory, mobile, and expanded modus operandi in the field of literary criticsm.[28]

Overview of the Book's Nodes

In this book, I examine the hybrid aesthetic effects of media technologies as they are impressed on the printed page. I call for a more fluid and interdisciplinary application to Generation X literature that invites the convergence of a series of nodes, or connection points, in a network of narratives. This network embraces both diachronic and synchronic movements across time and space in order to arrive at a better understanding of the cultural production of Generation X in Spain. The first node engages with the social and cultural development of the "Generation X" designation in the United States, Britain, and Spain. I trace its main characteristics and examine the role of commercial culture and media technologies in prose. What commonalities thread throughout the evolution and expression of a Generation X worldview? And how does Spanish Generation X literature fit into this general picture? My ambition is to show that although the generation's "X" space has been most often viewed as ephemeral and empty, negative and nihilistic, its blankness also identifies a positive space of alternative meaning-making and innovation. I advance this less discussed positive space as it relates to the construction of the GenX individual and his or her relation to new media technologies.

I tend to side with the Hispanists you mention who don't see anything lasting in the cultural production of these GenX'ers. Your quotation of Gonzalo Navajas comes to mind. Also, I wondered about the fleeting nature of this phenomenon, as soon as they turn of age and start having children their entire movement is relegated to something that "wasn't" like futurisim or "new criticism" which by now is anything but new. And it's not as though these writers (I have Lucía Etxebarria in mind) are contributing pioneering ideas and devices and perceptions as did the vanguardists of the 1920s, it seems to me they are almost exclusively a market phenomenon, commercial in their own way. Remember the "Movida"? The only lasting figure has been Almodóvar.

BUT: You are making me take another view of this. Your review of the entire movement, the way you put it in historical perspective, your articulation of the importance of this phenomenon in global terms, all this is very convincing.

—Michael Ugarte, in response

Generation X has been viewed as a youth cultural phenomenon that came to life and ended in the 1990s. For this reason, many Hispanists have studied GenX narrative as a *trend* whose influence has run its course, a *trend* tied to superficial and flat narrative styles whose stereotypes continue to be reiterated ad nauseum. In this book I question the static use of the moniker and call for a dynamic reconfiguration of Generation X whose main axis shifts over time and space. A closer examination of the evolution of the "Generation X" label since its inception in the US Baby Boomer years allows us to separate the term's stereotyped imaginings from its central axis points. Through a comparative approach to the term's birth and evolution in the United States we can gain a better understanding of its roots and outgrowths, and entertain new critical approaches to the topic.

To support my claim of an advancing and reshaping Generation X worldview, I move chronologically, from novels of the 1990s to 2010, and I engage with each individual text's relation to technology and what I call the reconfiguration of reality, or "reality projects." My selection includes three of the most visible and well-known texts by familiar GenX writers José Ángel Mañas, Ray Loriga, and Gabriela Bustelo; an intermediate figure, Gabi Martínez; and the most well-known author of the second wave, Agustín Fernández Mallo. The novels I examine in this book present the clearest examples of the movement toward a symbiosis of technological and linguistic models and the presentation of new cultural paradigms. The texts do not deny the existence of other styles and visions within and without the same group or similar narrative outgrowths in the work of authors not immediately or only labeled "Generation X" writers, such as the work of Care Santos, Juan Bonilla, or Mercedes Cebrián.

> *From an intellectual-history point of view, you seem to be positioned in a very interesting nowhere land. On the one hand, you are trying to leave behind the concepts of nihilism, cynicism that come from the loss of certainty that fell upon philosophy at the beginning of the twentieth century, an uncertainty that developed, in Continental Europe into Existentialism; you are trying to separate yourself from that continental tradition of philosophical discourse and ideas incarnated in Martin Heidegger, Albert Camus, Jean-Paul Sartre. In order to do so, you are grasping for the cultural sprouts of the analytical tradition. This tradition also suffered the loss of certainty in the way we handle the world, but it decided to focus its energies in the search for the absolute and permanent foundation of Math and Logic. Bertrand Russell wanted to find the foundations of mathematics, but soon Kurt Gödel showed the dead-end of such a project with his Incompleteness Theorems. All that effort was not lost, however, since from it came the work of Alan Turing on algorithms and computation, which produced simple formal models for complex abstract systems. This was not only the rise of computers, Information Theory and the World Wide Web, but in a more cultural frame of mind, it has allowed us to imagine the world as a web, as an interconnected entanglement of meanings.*
>
> *You seem to be standing on a place where the image of History as a line that has brought us nowhere is being replaced with the image of a web of communication that has to be curated in order to produce new subjectivities. This path, this process, is the hybridity you are describing in this book.*
>
> *—Juan Manuel Espinosa, in response*

The next node of this book regards the theoretical lens—media studies and digital theory—through which I interpret the novels. I take a theoretical and an empirical approach to popular media technologies, and I examine MTV, reality TV, single-player computer games, and the rhizomatic and participatory qualities of the Internet in isolation and in relation to their effects on narrative structures. My goal is to gain a better understanding of the connections between design, structure, and identity as cultural markers of a changing perception of the world. My interpretations benefit from the critical insights of scholars such as Carol Vernallis on MTV; Mark Andrejevic on reality TV; Espen Aarseth on video games; Katherine Hayles on data structures, and, Lev Manovich on hypermedia, hybrid media, and remix culture, among many others.

My theoretical approach flatly ignores studies on high postmodern theory because I believe the results of the most pertinent works (Baudrillard, Jameson, and Derrida, among others), while fascinating and enlightening in their own right, have been overused and remain too abstract in their formulations to be useful for this project. I agree with Henry Jenkins's viewpoint that media studies, and digital theory in particular, offer explanations and interpretations that allow for a better understanding of the impact of technological change on social, cultural, economic, political, and personal lives ("The Work of Theory"). My book makes clear that for a study on Generation X, a more empirical understanding of the interrelationship between technologies and cultural products is essential, and as such, digital theory offers "a point of intersection between the languages and practices of science and engineering on the one hand and the arts and humanities on the other" ("The Work of Theory"). My ultimate aim in this book is to challenge both realms—literature and media studies—by using each to inform, question, and intersect with the other, allowing for a deeper understanding of global narrative practices in media studies and a more observational and experiential approach to media studies in literary criticism.[29]

> *Derrida, Jameson, Baudrillard, and so on are not pertinent despite their brilliance and importance in the history of thought. It's much better to look at this cultural phenomenon through the lens of media studies. Look at what I say in the last chapter of my* Africans in Europe. *I very briefly ask questions about how the Internet might be an antidote to the lack of recognition of African writers in Spain.*
>
> *However, keep the following in mind: while you seek to eschew the "big" critics of the latter part of the twentieth century, you use them unwittingly, especially Jameson: "History is what hurts."*
>
> *—Michael Ugarte, in response*

Studies on Generation X cannot be complete without considering social theories of modern identities that center on mobility across wide-ranging landscapes or cultural maps, as indicated earlier. In the chapters at large, I adopt a postsubcultural stance in which more fluid and integrative frameworks replace dichotomies and hierarchies, most specifically as they relate to the role of commercial culture and media technologies on youth. The works of David Muggleton and Rupert Weinzierl, Sarah Thornton, Tracey

Skelton and Gill Valentine, Andy Bennett, Steve Redhead, and Steven Miles forward nuanced studies that respond to shifts in cultural experiences and expressions of youth at the end of the millennium. While deep theoretical analysis of their research cannot be the focus of this book, their insights underline the theoretical framework of this project. In particular, the work of sociologist Michel Maffesoli in *The Times of the Tribes* and the investigation of Italian philosopher Rosi Braidotti on the female nomadic subject reside in the subtexts of this project. Their models value in-between locations or interlocutions, which are positions that Generation X'ers—the *in-between* generation—naturally interiorize. Their theories allow me to emphasize GenX'ers' changing social relationships—they look at the world differently and they move differently within this world—and their use of expressive models that are more multiple and hybrid, integrative, and even contradictory.

A clarification is needed to understand the gender equilibrium of the GenX repertoire. The Generation X worldview is most commonly represented through the work of male artists. Despite the brand-making influence of Douglas Coupland, Richard Linklater, and Kurt Cobain, the label in the early 1990s also came to define a female style of looking at the world, which critic Andrea L. Harris called "Generation XX." On the Spanish literary front, among a host of male writers, Lucía Etxebarria and Gabriela Bustelo are the only two women who can be fully considered GenX

> *For any literary critic, in the beginning, there is a historiographical impulse: to find a place for a young generation of writers. But the Generation X writers that you talk about in this book have certain traits that make this impulse a difficult one to carry through. First, they go beyond nation-based, print-based notions of literature. And second, they do so by taking up new tools and new objects that populate the reality in which they live, using them to create their works.*
>
> *The tools of Gen X writers are not simple tools, like a hammer, or a pen, or a typewriter. Yes, the tools make it easier to do certain things: talk, write, listen, multiply, have a conversation. But the problem with the new tools, like photography and cinema, is that they are tools that represent reality. And when they do so, they change the way people relate to reality. So they represent, but also change ways of being in reality. And since reality is changed because perceptions of it change, subjects are ultimately also transformed by the process they themselves started. This makes it very difficult to tell a story about them, because they are continually changing the way they produce the interpretations of their own reality. Someone who tries to historicize this moving conundrum has a lot on their plate.*
>
> *To historicise this group, I think you have come up with a nice alternative: zoom in on certain tools, or certain goggles through which Gen X sees the world, and show how these tools and goggles change that world and them in the process. As presented in this book, these tools and glasses are the punk goggles, the music video tools of scripting and editing and creating soundscapes and soundtracks, the Avant-pop goggle, reality tv, the videogame goggle, and the goggles that map and mash with Google.*
>
> *—Juan Manuel Espinosa, in response*

writers in the 1990s. It is not my intention to explore why only these two women have entered the GenX ranks in Spain.[30] My goal, rather, is to engage with the effects of new media technologies on Spanish narrative independent of gender issues. That said, it is important to underline that women GenX'ers did not disappear in the early 1990s.[31] Yet, all too often, Hispanists have not questioned the purely male perspectives presented through the GenX worldview, nor have they identified the idiosyncrasies of a female vision. How does a female GenX worldview compare to that of her male colleagues? On what levels do they coincide? What has been left out? How can a more inclusive understanding of the GenX term allow scholars of Spanish literature to better identify the paradigms used to construct female subjectivity in the digital age? Do media contribute to a particular vision/version of the female subject in Spain? Do novels of the second wave of GenX writers, the *Mutantes*, include female writers whose ideas coalesce and contribute to this vision? Although the scope of these questions resides outside this book, I do entertain them in subsequent projects and encourage more critical work on the subject.

To ground Spanish GenX literature, its free form and floating "X" must be imbued with a multiplicity of voices without undermining its negationist, escapist, and innovative powers. This is a methodological operation in which the meaning and evolution of the GenX term itself intersects with a series of interconnected narratives and images, theories and practices. This web of links goes beyond the United States, Britain, and Spain—the main geographical frame of this project—to point to the existence of GenX expressions found in other countries as well. To engage with this multi-dimensional network of narratives, this book challenges us to become, in the words of Néstor García Canclini, "nomadic critics" and read through, within, and beyond cultural cross-currents to make new and unexpected connections.

Chapter 1

Tales of Generation X

Generation X wasn't discovered in 1991 any more than the New World was noticed in 1492 (Gordinier 21).

Scholarship on Spanish Generation X literature has been hampered by the absence of in-depth studies on the development of the "Generation X" label. Apart from Paul Begin's excellent analysis on the evolution of Generation X and its relation to punk, Hispanists have viewed Generation X as a phenomenon that lived and died in the 1990s.[1] In the introduction, I gave a short overview of the GenX demographic and located its dynamic within a world of global flows and technological advancements. My aim in this chapter is to examine in depth the sociological and artistic development of Generation X as a label whose roots reach as far back as the post–World War II era and whose outgrowths continue to this day. I have divided the chapter into four subgroups. In part I, I examine the designation's evolution from the 1950s until the 1970s, paying special attention to the term's appropriation in British punk, punk's relation to commercial culture, and the meaning of the blank attributed to its "X" marker. In part II, I relate GenX's "prehistory" of sorts, to its first manifestation in fiction in the 1980s. I present some of the parallel dynamics found in the US Brat-Pack writers and in Spanish GenX novelists seven years later. What did the emergence of these young and hip writers say about the need for new models of storytelling? In part III, I indulge in an analysis of the main GenX "boom" years, the 1990s. I discuss how the work of Douglas Coupland and Richard Linklater moves beyond stereotypes to uncover aesthetic innovation and mode of thought. To shift into new critical paradigms, in part IV, I engage with the work of James Annesley on blank fiction. Through the lens of "blank fiction," I propose more comprehensive and empirical readings to understand the evolution and value of Generation X texts. I end this chapter by untangling and placing into perspective some of the tales that have constricted continued scholarship on Spanish Generation X narrative. My hope is to put some of these perspectives to rest and allow other, more fruitful approaches to emerge.

Noticing Generation X, 1950–70

One of the few most comprehensive essays to document the historical development of the GenX label has been written by John Ulrich in his introduction to the book *GenXegesis: Essays on Alternative Youth (Sub)culture.* In this piece, Ulrich delves into the term's roots, back in the Baby Boomer period of the 1950s. He found that photojournalist Robert Capa, best known today for his images on the Spanish Civil War and World War II, proposed a project that documented the lives of twenty-four young people from fourteen different countries. These individuals were twenty years of age in 1950 and had a reasonable expectation of celebrating the year 2000. Capa found that the overarching theme of their lives was an uncertainty about the future and a reaction against the possibility of going to war (Ulrich 5).[2] Their post-warfare view of politics and adult life was filled with disillusionment and detachment, they distanced themselves from world affairs, and they located their personal lives along the family/work axis. This group was generally seen as cautious and conservative, and their worldviews were varied enough for the results of Capa's photomontage to be inconclusive. Capa called this unknown generation, *Generation X*, a placeholder for a generational vision that was yet to be determined (Ulrich 5–8). Unbeknownst to himself, Capa laid the groundwork for the future of a label meant to create history.

> *DID YOU KNOW?*
>
> "Generation X" was the name of a television film produced in 1996 based on the comic of the same name. It was also a possible pilot for a syndicated TV show. It was based on a group of young mutant-humans with a genetic variation that gave them superpowers.
>
> You can see a clip of the film version at: www.youtube.com/watch?v=yLc-F-HiFlw
>
> —Christine Henseler

The second development of the Generation X label occurred almost a decade later, in 1964, when Charles Hamblett and Jane Deverson published a book titled *Generation X.* In pink print, the front cover of the Gold Medal Books edition asked: "What's Behind the Rebellious Anger of Britain's Untamed Youth?" "Here—in their own words—is how they really feel about Drugs, Drink, God, Sex, Class, Color and Kicks." The young people to whom they referred were teenagers in the sixties and the results of their hates, hopes, and fears were to become the cornerstones of future Generation X'ers.[3] The interviews unveiled a series of commonalities that included a high level of tolerance for personal differences, the taking of drugs, a rejection of parental authority and mainstream society, a perspective on life as boring, a vision of the future as bleak and uncertain, and a daily environment filled with music and violence (Ulrich 11). Perhaps one of their most impactful findings was that they concluded that this group's problems were more acute, more universal, and more rapidly absorbed than that of any other generation before them precisely because of developments in mass communication.

To put these developments into perspective, it warrants reminding ourselves that in the 1960s, people witnessed the first televised war, the Vietnam War; they benefited from the digital production of newspapers and magazines in 1967; in 1968 the Philips C-Cassette was introduced for the recording of music; and in 1969 human beings first landed on the moon, an event broadcast to 600 million people around the globe. The increasing reach and individual use of technologies, especially television and radio, and the role of advertising within these media, allowed for the spread of mass-disseminated information and self-identification. As such, the "X" that was embodied by Hamblett and Deverson's particular group of lower-class and subcultural youth was not simply an unknown blank as it had been for Capa's; it was a space of unrest and resistance that had begun to recognize the artificial influence of commercial culture and technology on the construction of grand social narratives.

Youth culture's rebellion and search for meaning in a world whose signifiers were being absorbed and represented at greater speeds best expressed itself in the punk culture of the 1970s (a culture based on noise and speed). Punk's do-it-yourself philosophy presented an alternative space for identity construction separate from mainstream, an "X" space of resistance that defined a new Zeitgeist. This period was marked by the shocking words and actions of bands like the Voidoids, The Clash, Elvis Costello, the Buzzcocks, and the Sex Pistols, whose line, "No Future," quickly turned into a GenX anthem. When Britain's punk rock star Billy Idol found Hamblett and Deverson's book on his mother's shelf, it inspired the singer to call his own band "Generation X" in 1976 and unknowingly become a cornerstone to the evolution of the term as it grew into its demographic.[4] With the song "Your Generation" and the words "I say your generation don't mean a thing to me," Idol gave "Generation X" lyrics and melody.

> ### RUIDO LITERARIO
>
> "Para mí una 'nobela' aglutina todos esos elementos heteroglósicos que la literatura novelesca de hoy excluye o entrecomilla. Todo ese 'ruido' —y por 'ruido' entiendo desde interferencias ortográficas hasta incorrecciones coloquiales y cualquier tipo de jerga o lenguaje obviado normalmente por la literatura— al que el auténtico novelista tiene que recurrir si quiere revitalizar e inyectarle sangre nueva a un género capacitado como ningún otro para darle forma artística al lenguaje vivo".
>
> José Ángel Mañas—Author's Note to *Sonko95*

Most critics point to punk's negative, defiant, destructive, and anarchic stances to better understand GenX'ers' anti-authoritative, marginal, and nihilistic patterns. Yet for the results of this project, I would like to focus on punk's engagement with commercial culture as a blank site of meaning-making. Jude Davies, in "The Future of 'No Future': Punk Rock and Postmodern Theory," has indicated that punk lyrics "problematized the politics and transcendence brought about by commodity culture and mid-70s disillusionment with the post-war consensus" (4). These sentiments were considered in songs like "Complete Control" by The Clash (1978), which invoked the essential GenX concept of artistic freedom and resistance to the selling-out process. At the same time, the Clash's music displayed a horrified fascination with North American culture, which presented listeners with "a far more thoroughgoing ironization of conventional modes of subjectivity than is present in many of the critical discourses on postmodernity," observes Davies (8). For example, in their song "Lost in the Supermarket," the Clash juxtaposes the ugly realities of social marginalization with commercial culture's false promise of personhood and sense of emptiness and loneliness in a society marred by technological (mis)communications.

On a less complex level, Sid Vicious (lead singer of the Sex Pistols), in a memorable image from the file "The Great Rock and Roll Swindle," emptied "a revolver into the audience suddenly attacked by the spectacle they had come to consume." Punk cut through the commodity spectacle, but "its ability to escape recuperation depended on its lack of content; its lack of analysis, program, polemic" (Davies 14). Similarly, GenX narratives of the 1990s relied on blank and empty narratives—what I will discuss later as "blank fiction"—to undercut the artificiality (read spectacularity) of traditional narrative styles. Their ability to undercut critical discourse relied on a similar lack in content.

The negationist themes in songs like "Blank Generation" or "Pretty Vacant" by the Voidoids were appropriated by many Hispanists to feature the literary group's level of disenchantment, rebellion, nihilism, and defeatist attitudes. Whether in punk or GenX texts, the songs all motioned to a clean break, a new baseline of destruction and reconstruction. This end of the old and beginning of the new was often embodied in the image of the apocalypse, as found in Douglas Coupland's novel, *Generation X: Tales of an Accelerated Culture,* or in Agustín Fernández Mallo's *Nocilla Experience,* among many other texts. For the Sex Pistols, the apocalypse reflected two things: complete nihilism and a degree-zero response to a society of the spectacle, which deprived all utterances of content and transformed all forms of revolt into commodities to be consumed (Davies 13). For Paul Weller, the singer of The Jam, the apocalypse was a metaphor for an alienating and violent urban society that problematized identity construction (Davies 10). The apocalypse as a baseline—a blank—defined the paradox of Generation X: it allowed a new identity to be born out of the ashes of the old.

> *The idea of the apocalypse is playfully set up by Alex de la Iglesia in his film,* El día de la bestia *(1995), in which a Basque priest, accompanied by a heavy metal rocker and the host of a nighttime esoteric/occult television program, sets out to save the world from an antichrist who will be born on Christmas Eve.*
>
> —*Samuel Amago, in response*

The dichotomy of death and rebirth leads back to the role of the "blank" in the evolution and expression of a Generation X consciousness. Richard Hell, front man of the Voidoids, explained in an interview that his lyrics, "I belong to a _____ generation," from the song "Blank Generation," were misunderstood. What most people interpreted as a glorification of indifference and failure or unwillingness, was for Hell a space that could be filled in with anything at all: "To me 'blank' is a line where you can fill in anything. It's positive. It's the idea that you have the option of making yourself anything you want, filling in the blank. And that's something that provides a uniquely powerful sense to this generation" (Ulrich 13). Several years later, in 1989, Greil Marcus, in his infamous book, *Lipstick Traces: A Secret History of the Twentieth Century,* confirmed that punk was indeed "a voice that denied all social facts, and in that denial affirmed everything was possible" (2). The duality inherent in the blank, the positive that can fill an emptiness, is a perspective often denied or ignored when critics examine Generation X, yet it appears repeatedly in social studies on the subject. For example, Douglas Rushkoff, in the *GenX Reader* (1994), points to critics' interpretation of the GenX rant as "pointless whining." Yet, he says, its style and passion has strong connections to the productive and creative function of African American blues: "And like the blues, no matter how angry, cynical and forlorn, or hopeless the rant gets, the underlying energy is a pure joy of expression, inventiveness, and a deeply felt urge to entertain those around us" (206). In 2008, with a good dose of historical perspective, Jeff Gordinier also appropriates this dichotomy in his book *X Saves the World.* His goal is to outline the role of who Generation X'ers had become, shifting from his own defeatist perspective of an in-between generation lost to inattention to a more optimistic take that identified the role of this demographic as silent innovators.

> *It is hard to imagine a more joyful expression of emptiness and failure than Beck's "Loser," an anthem in which the GenX rant becomes a celebratory raison d'être.*
>
> —*Samuel Amago, in response*

The essence of Generation X resides precisely in the paradox of its designation. One of the most powerful and underexamined characteristics of Generation X is the space that the designation affords to multiplicity and contradiction, to both anger and expression, to destruction and creation, to cynicism and idealism. The essence of the "X" resides in its permutability. To be an "X'er" defines a state of mind centered on a mentality of change, interiorization, and search for alternative models of meaning making. This is a state of mind that allows for the inclusion of opposites in the same space (margin and mainstream, blank and filled, negative and positive) and for the emergence of different patterns; it is a state inherently determined by movement and change.

The Brat-Packers, 1970–80

The alternative modes of expression that underline the GenX repertoire of the 1990s are rooted in the 1970s and 1980s in both the United States and in

Spain, despite the fact that each country experienced different sociopolitical conditions. In the 1960–80 period, the American publishing industry had lost sight of college-age readers and was caught "between hysterical promotion of trash and obsequious worship of old-timers like Paul Bellow and John Updike" (Young 3). In the 1970s in the United States, ambitious, money-hungry artists and writers went into advertising, and boy poets went into the music industry and flung themselves at the microphones as the "heirs to the oral tradition […]" (Young 6). The experimental/best-seller divide of the books on the market did not attract a young audience of voracious readers, who instead looked toward the music press, the style and listing magazines, the pulp and horror fiction, crime, and fantasy to find material more in tune with their realities (Young 6).

In Spain, a mixture of literary and social factors most likely conditioned changes in fiction. The publishing industry, which had been partially squashed in the 1940s and 1950s due to strict censorship laws, gave way in the 1960s to an influential series of new novels (*nueva narrativa*) whose cycle began with Luis Martín Santos's *Tiempo de Silencio* (1962) and Miguel Delibes's *Cinco horas con Mario* (1966), and continued with the highly experimental and influential novels of Juan Benet and Juan Goytisolo, among others. What these texts had in common was "a search for new non-mimetic forms, in itself an implicit recognition that the stark realism of the 1950s and early 1960s was no longer adequate for a new, more complicated world in which ideologies were no longer black and white" (Longhurst 25). Adding to this world was the European importation of the Latin American Boom novels in the early 1960s, which already in that period displayed the power of literary agents, critics, and commercial publishing houses to provide readers with different transatlantic models. And it was in the 1980s that Spain saw a boom in narrative genres previously unimaginable. But similar to the U.S. case, the language of the literati did not necessarily speak to Spain's youth. The time and space for artistic innovation was, rather, found in the 1970s and 1980s Spanish *Movida*, where the young also looked toward the music world, fanzines, comic books, dance, photography, and video clips for alternative means of expression, as I will examine at length in the next chapter.

It is during the 1970s and 1980s that punk culture expanded its cultural reach from the United States and Britain to Spain and beyond. For example, Czech writer Jàchym Topol wrote lyrics for his brother's rock/punk band Dog Soldiers in the 1970s; Scottish novelist Irvine Welsh got involved in the punk scene in London in the 1970s and he co-wrote the musical script to *Trainspotting* with Vic Godard, member of the punk group Subway Sec; and American novelist Bret Easton Ellis grew up in Los Angeles in the 1980s "where he played keyboards for many New Wave groups and hung out in the LA punk scene" (America and Laurence). In China in the 1990s, the "hooligan writer," Wang Shuo, was referred to as a punk novelist based on his use of colloquial language and unorthodox and antiauthoritarian views. Many female Generation X'ers, such as Australian writer Justine Ettler or French filmmakers Virginie Despentes and Coralie Trinh Thi, were also identified as hard-core grunge and punk artists whose neorealist lens on women's lives

and bodies and violent portrayals of women's victimization and empower-
ment presented controversial takes on the female GenX consciousness.

Punk constituted a (sub)culture in movement and mutation in which individuals negotiated and created its dynamics as much as they were determined by
its larger philosophies (Sabin 5). One of the most important and wide-reaching
literary outgrowths of this phenomenon occurred in the United States through
the work of the US Brat-Pack writ-
ers in the mid-1980s. The original
group included Bret Easton Ellis
(b. 1964), Tama Janowitz (b. 1957),
and Jay McInerney (b. 1955).[5]
Their first novels, *Less Than Zero*
(1985), *Slaves of New York* (1989),
and *Bright Lights, Big City* (1984),
respectively, appealed to a young
audience who could easily relate to
their urban experiences. The Brat-
Packers were also known as "post-
punk urban writers," "downtown
writers," "neorealist writers," and
"minimalist writers," and Elizabeth
Young and Graham Caveney, in
their influential book, *Shopping in
Space: Essays on America's Blank
Generation Fiction*, labeled them
the "Blank Generation" to evoke
the novelists' relation to punk and
the flat and stunned quality of their
writing (iii).

The Brat-Packers directly and indirectly influenced a series of GenX writers
on the world stage. For example,
Australian writer Justine Ettler
appropriated Ellis's work in her
novel *The River Ophelia* (1995) to
dislodge readers by adopting an
interventionist position through
a female point of view. That said,
the Brat-Packers were, of course,
not the only writers to influence
Spanish authors, nor did their
work reach all of its members, but
they are a significant part of the
puzzle that makes up the larger
"Generation X" picture. From
an overarching perspective, they
were some of the first writers to

deal with the plights of contemporary urban life: alienation, violence, crime, sexual excess, drug addiction, commercial culture, and the mass media. They presented life in the fast lane through fast narrative styles that portrayed a sense of paralysis and disaffection. Their narrative structures lacked historical contextualization and centered on the present time by diminishing plots and character developments and emphasizing the banality of everyday life. Their linguistic styles ranged from the purely flat to the sarcastic and cynical. David Foster Wallace called their writing "ultraminimalism" to refer to a "flat, understated and undersold" style of writing directly influenced by the aesthetic norms of the mass media, especially television and advertising. Their relationship to television and MTV was considered an essential expression of their contemporary lifestyles. And much like in the case of Spain, their work was often referenced as negative and less worthy versions of the minimalist aesthetics of dirty realist writer Raymond Carver.

From the beginning, the work of the Brat-Packers became a marketing phenomenon that was hyped similar to the novels of Spanish GenX writers seven years later. Publishing houses promoted their youthful appearance and young age (Ellis was twenty-one when his first novel was published), and critics reacted to the "literary Brat-Pack" in pejorative ways, as the *Village* pictured faces of the three pasted onto cut-outs of babies in diapers. Born about ten years after their U.S. colleagues, the age of the "Spanish Brat-Pack" writers José Ángel Mañas (b. 1971), Ray Loriga (b. 1967), and Lucía Etxebarria (b. 1966) was similarly hyped for marketing purposes (Mañas published *Historias del Kronen* at the age of twenty-three). Critics came up with labels such as "joven narrativa" [young narrative], "Generación Biberón" [Baby Bottle Generation], or "Generación Sesame Street."[6] In both the United States and Spain, the authors were readily confused with the actions of their characters, whose lives were filled with violence, empty sexual encounters, abuse of drugs and alcohol, and superficial attention to material culture. Critics considered their works the underbelly of contemporary life and art, reacting to the excess of commercial and technological culture. Their generally young readers, on the other hand, felt addressed by their exposition of suburban anxiety and angst. Together, both critics and readers witnessed a narrative that was giving expression to individuals' growing awareness of

Daniel Grassian's book, *Hybrid Fictions: American Literature and Generation X*, speaks to the hybridizing effects of Generation X literature. American fiction writers, says Grassian,

> "display active hybridity between opposites and extremes: between the highbrow and the lowbrow, between the literary and the popular, and between competing ethnicities and conflicting desires. They forge a middle ground between the emotionally jarring but intellectually thin writings of minimalist writers like Raymond Carver and the brilliant, but often obfuscating, protoacademic writing of Thomas Pynchon and John Barth" (16).

—Christine Henseler

changing social conditions, the presence of commercial and popular culture, the increasing role of technology in everyday life, and the need for alternative sites of expression born from the urban spaces inhabited by the youth.

Whether we talk about the work of Ellis, Almodóvar, or Mañas, in each case the word "excess" may be used to define their artistic sensibilities and their perspective on contemporary urban experiences. Larry McCaffery used the metaphor of "a hive of emergent meanings and holistic patterns" (*After* xxvii) to identify contemporary life during that time. In his description, one can almost hear the bees swarming within a "simultaneous muddle of noises, colors, and spiritual rhythms" closely related to commercial transactions and mass culture (xxvii). He believed that "this chaotic, endlessly circulating swarm of sounds, words, images, and data was actually speaking a new kind of language—a secret language of junk which expressed the inner workings of our culture's collective unconscious" (xxvii). In Spain, this hive of meanings first expressed itself during the *Movida* and was assimilated into narrative in the early 1990s, when it was more clearly related to punk than junk.

Generation X of the 1990s

In 2004, by coincidence, Douglas Coupland re-created Larry McCaffery's hive metaphor spatially when he chewed up and spit out his novel *Generation X: Tales of An Accelerated Culture* and turned it into a three-dimensional papier-mâché beehive. A photo of the beehive appeared on his *New York Times* blog alongside the question: "Why does it feel so strange to see a book removed from our own sense of history and culture and inserted into a non-cultural slot where art or music or any other art form don't exist?" Coupland answered his own question by musing through time and tradition:

> This past month has been a pleasure. It's helped me clarify in my mind my experience with society and how books have shaped it. It's made me clearer about my call to anyone involved in teaching or within institutions to try to broaden their thinking about what books are or can be. Since 1991 I've witnessed the triumph of the superstore, the near death of the independent bookseller, the rise of Amazon, the rise of the Internet, the comings and goings of the e-book and the rise of the P.D.A. Books are not under siege, but they are evolving and mutating. The more this process disturbs you, the more necessary it might be to try and engage with these changes. Right or wrong, they are inevitable, and the choice for anybody is whether they want to be able to live fully within the future, or whether they want to become a recluse and vanish into the past. The only way to go is forward. It's all there is. (Coupland "Photoshop")

The excessive swarming of codes, images, and letters that mark the emergence of new meanings and new media in the 1980s and 1990s unsettled, as Coupland remarked, conventional aesthetic practices. The evolution and mutation that he referred to presented a series of disturbances and disturbing results that began to come to light in the early 1990s in the United States, in Spain, and in many countries around the world. Elizabeth Young believes that in North America, societal shifts and anxieties related to urban life were not culturally assimilated until the publication of *American Psycho* by Bret Easton Ellis in 1991. In Spain, I would venture to say that the assimilation process caught up with North America precisely around the same time, as expressed in one of the first GenX novels by Ray Loriga, *Lo peor de todo* (1992). As mentioned in the introduction, this was the same period when *Faserland* (1995) and *Crazy* (1993) appeared in Germany, *101 Reykjavík* (2002) in Iceland, and *Praise* (1992) in Australia.

Whether these novels were influenced or appeared in parallel with North American "X" texts in the early 1990s, critics' approach to the Spanish "X" designation has lost an important part of its foundational history—including its roots in the *Movida*—because of the media's hand in commercializing a particular image of the post–Baby Boomer US generation.[7] This representation, based on a distortion of slacker and punk culture (apathy, aimlessness, and lack of ambition), has been most often linked to three cultural events that took place in 1991: the publication of Douglas Coupland's novel *Generation X* (translated into Spanish in 1993), the screening of the movie *Slacker* by Richard Linklater, and the release of the album "Nevermind" by grunge band Nirvana. The stereotypes associated with these cultural events have been studied at large, but they deserve a moment of reevaluation in light of no less than their impact on aesthetic innovation and alternative models of storytelling.

Readers of Coupland's novel learned that the "Generation X" label derived from Japanese newspapers that called the twenty-something generation that was stuck in meaningless and futureless office jobs *shinjinrui* (or new human beings). This same generation, says one of the characters of the book, Andrew, exists in the United States, "but it doesn't have a name—an X generation—purposefully hiding itself" (Coupland, *Generation X* 56). For his part, Coupland explained that, "Generation X" derived from "the final chapter of a funny sociological book on American class structure titled *Class* by Paul Fussell" (Ulrich 16). In *Class:*

NIRVANA

In 1991 Nirvana released the album *Nevermind*. Its first song, "Smells Like Teen Spirit," became the archetype of Kurt Cobain's sound and of a generation that believed to find its fight cry in words such as, "Load up on guns / Bring your friends / It's fun to lose / And to pretend […]." The song was "heard as an ironic rallying cry for thoroughly disaffected youth—an interpretation encouraged by the nightmarish high school pep rally depicted in the song's video" (Crisafulli 38). But on April 8, 1994, at the height of Cobain's fame and income, the artist took a gun to his head—three years after he wrote "Load up on guns"—and committed suicide. In his final letter, Cobain decried the loss of his art to the demands of a society whose commercial appropriation of the band was asphyxiating the grunge artist and leading to fans high on stardom and fame. His vigil was attended by thousands who mourned the loss of a great musician.

—Christine Henseler

A Guide Through the American Status System (1983), Fussell positioned youth both within and without American mainstream culture, the "X" marking a "paradoxical borderline status (inside and outside, within and against the mainstream), with 'X' capturing the dual sense of negation and freedom and 'generation' signifying a kind of hyperbolic assertion of subcultural, rather than demographic solidarity" (Ulrich 19). What Fussell's study emphasized was the alignment of GenX's philosophy along two matrixes. The first one regarded the self-conscious awareness of its paradoxical location within both the subcultural and mainstream realms, and the second considered their political attention to everyday life (a perspective derived from the avantgarde). In addition, in his final chapter, Fussell related this "X" to a category of people who "wanted to hop off the merry-go-round of status, money, and social climbing that so often frames modern existence" (Coupland, "Eulogy" 72). Taken together, Generation X constituted a group of people of similar mind-set who deliberately left mainstream society in search of venues of identification that allowed for a dual space of inclusion and exclusion.

> ### GENERACIÓN X
>
> Douglas Coupland's novel appeared in Spain in 1993, by Ediciones B. In the introduction of the Spanish edition, Vicente Verdú describes the novel as a radiography of a group of postyuppies. These were individuals who did not protest or explode. Their pacifist positions reminded him of the hippies of the 1960s although he felt they were more complex and subtle, and better equipped with a critical eye toward contemporary society. According to Verdú, the "X" referred to a social group that defined its position as outsiders, as separate from the general functioning of society.
>
> —Christine Henseler

The three characters of the text, Andrew (the protagonist-narrator), Dag, and Claire, were born between the early 1960s and the late 1970s; had high levels of education; but viewed the world as an insecure, hopeless, and unhealthy place. They consciously decided to jump off the bandwagon and escape from a world defined by their Baby Boomer parents, where money ruled, people measured their worth through material objects, and human relationships were down-played. Instead, the characters went in search of alternative spaces of identification marked by simplicity, honesty, less emphasis on material objects, true friendship, and love.

Talk of the end of the world, of an approaching apocalypse, and a desire to literally and metaphorically be struck by lightning led to a fixation on the present and on the futurelessness of North American society. Their sarcasm, and their often superior attitudes of dismay and rejection of the state of current affairs and the world left by their elders, necessarily led to withdrawal, contemplation, and the seeking of margins—"albeit with the volume knob cranked to eleven" ("Eulogy" 72). Yet even though they escaped their families and professional lives and took on low-wage jobs, the three characters rented three bungalows in Palm Springs, California, enjoyed a pool and owned an old Saab, and they were aware of fashion and furniture. Their need for alternative physical spaces was not fully disconnected from material

SMELLS LIKE TEEN SPIRIT

Through Nirvana's song "Smells Like Teen Spirit," millions of youth expressed their generational anger through a tune inspired by a deodorant of the same name. The story of this misinterpretation is worth mentioning because it exemplifies the degree to which even the most extreme image of social angst and outcry was already intertwined with commercial culture as an everyday affair:

> "Kathleen Hanna, from the band Bikini Kill, sprayed the following sentence on a wall while graffiti painting with Cobain: 'Kurt smells like Teen Spirit.' Cobain took it as a compliment, thinking it was Hanna's way of saying that he still had the rebellious edge of an angry kid. But Hanna was actually putting some arch humor to use—'Teen Spirit' was actually the rather insipid, niche-marketed brand name of an under-arm deodorant for young women put out by the Mennen Company. It wasn't until after Cobain had written, recorded, and released the song that he realized a trendy anti-perspirant had provided the title for his tune" (Crisafulli 37).

—Christine Henseler

What a terrific anecdote! I didn't know this! I wonder if misattribution could not be explored as part of the GenX aesthetic. I seem to remember several misquotations of songs in Historias del Kronen.

—Samuel Amago, in response

comforts, but led, rather, to an infusion of alternative storytelling spaces marred by angst, sarcasm, and humor.

The dozens of stories that make up *Generation X* are extremely important in critics' appreciation of the novel's narrative innovation. Throughout the entire novel, the characters tell mini-stories to comment on social and personal mores, with the desert presenting an arid baseline upon which deconstruction and reconstruction becomes possible. The mini-stories are joined in the margins by quotes, cartoons, Pop Art images, and cynical social commentaries that combine to present a hybrid and, one could say, a more interactive or hypermedia product. Coupland's professional background in the visual arts tellingly embodies the "hive" of no longer "emerging" but rather "emerged" cross-disciplinary signifiers, as first identified in the 1970s and 1980s in both the United States and Spain.

The work that pushes the fragmentary presentation of storytelling to an extreme, and that best exemplifies the basic tenants of Fussell's book is Richard Linklater's film *Slacker*. The production trailed ninety-seven characters of mostly but not exclusively twenty-something youth through ten city blocks in Austin, Texas, with no apparent plot save the causal relationships created by their non-narratives. These individuals seemed sane, crazy, eccentric, bored, listless, floating, questioning everything and nothing. Despite their apathetic languishing, they were highly politically engaged, if not actively, surely metaphysically. While many of the adjectives I use here have contributed to the stereotyping of the "slacker," Linklater suggests that a more modern notion might see slackers as a "people who are ultimately being responsible to themselves and not wasting their time in a realm of activity that has nothing to do with who they are or what they might ultimately be striving for" (qtd. in Ulrich 18). In other words, much like Coupland's characters, these individuals contested social and political practices and searched for alternative spaces of existence.

Jeff Gordinier, author of *Generation X Saves the World* (2008), adds to Linklater's more positive spin an essential slacker trait: "the encyclopedic brain" (27). He clarifies that what the media failed to point out was that slackers were hyper-smart, as seen in both Coupland's and Linklater's work and in mainstream GenX films like *Reality Bites* (1994) or *High Fidelity* (2000). In fact, GenXers "took great pride in knowing things in a way that the Millennials, ten or fifteen years later, would not" (Gordinier 26). Quoting the filmmaker Quentin Tarantino (best known for *Pulp Fiction*) and the American musician and multi-instrumentalist Beck Hansen, Gordinier explains that "even when it looked like the slackers were wasting their time, they weren't. They were learning; they were sponging up information" (26). In the case of Tarantino and Beck, critics felt that they presented an icy existential detachment in their "dazzling virtuoso collages that had nothing to say" (Gordinier 28). This criticism, says Gordinier, was not only true, it was, "in the eyes of the Xers who bought the tickets, one of the most attractive features of their work, and the artists themselves didn't seem to disagree" (28).

Linklater's film, *Slacker*, similarly followed Tarantino's and Beck's aesthetic philosophy; the film transposed its content to its form by presenting viewers with a hybrid cinematic product where documentary and fiction conjoined. Through a reality television approach and smooth transitions between scenes, the film became "a documentary of characters acting out a fiction" (Linklater 10) in a vertical narrative structure "in which each shot, each event and character, [led] only to the next" (Linklater 10), and each new scene defined a new start. This was a space where fiction met the real representation of characters' lives and where anything was acceptable and integrated into the film. Linklater himself appeared in character in the first scene to decipher the purpose of these effects. In a dialogue with a disinterested cab driver, he questioned the existence of parallel realities and paths not taken. He came to the conclusion that humans could only embark on one path

---

> ### WHO'S A SLACKER?
>
> "I'm what, a slacker? A 'twenty-something'? I'm in the margins. I'm not building a wall but making a brick. Okay, here I am, a tired inheritor of the Me generation, floating from school to street to bookstore to movie theater with a certain uncertainty. I'm in that white space where consumer terror meets irony and pessimism, where Scooby Doo and Dr. Faustus hold equal sway over the mind, where the Butthole Surfers provide the background volume, where we choose what is not obvious over what is easy. It goes on…like TV channel-cruising, no plot, no tragic flaws, no resolution, just mastering the moment, pushing forward, full of sound and fury, full of life signifying everything on any given day…"
>
> —Richard Linklater, interior cover of *Slacker*

One of the more entertaining encounters in Slacker *is with a character who, after offering a harrowing account of a freeway shooting spree she has just witnessed, produces for sale from her jeans pocket a sample of what she insists is Madonna's pap smear. She offers this "high-dollar item" as a way to get closer to the superstar: "it's a little bit getting closer to the, you know, the rock god herself than just a poster." The sequence at once illustrates the GenX sense of humor about itself, while demonstrating some of the issues you are discussing here: the contingent notion of authenticity and the absurdity of global stardom (who is Madonna, anyway?); mediation in the 1990s (what is the most direct mode of access to Madonna?); the GenX entrepreneurial spirit (selling a tissue sample?); within the context of an absurd, random, alienated, violent, unpredictable society (guns on the freeways). To see the clip, go to: /www.youtube.com/watch?v=JoCuUgxMU_Y*

—Samuel Amago, in response

at a time because "we're kind of trapped in this one reality restriction type of thing."

In this movie, viewers follow the multiplication of paths taken and *not* taken. The individuals portrayed in the film inherently partake in a tension "between chance and design, at once tragic and laughable" (Jaffe 123). When at the end of *Slacker* the camera is thrown into a ravine, leaving its eye to record a confusing array of circular blackness/blankness, its visual space functions as a self-conscious "rejection of certain mainstream values, as well as a space within which new or 'alternative' lives might be constructed" (Ulrich 18). With a view toward this marginal space, the ending is ultimately, ironically and contradictorily, self-destructive of its own artistic production.

When positioned side by side, *Slacker* and *Generation X* set the stage for a growing vision/version of a Generation X consciousness. Topics such as marginalization, escapism, antimaterialism, antisocial behavior, the end of time, and generational discontent combine to recenter the importance of storytelling in innovative ways. Much like today's definitions of the hypertext, both renditions display short narratives connected through barely identifiable links (a character, an action, a thought) or visual material placed on the margins of the book itself. In addition, these links occur at varying points in the narratives and can terminate as quickly as they begin, often resulting in a layering of voices, ideas, and symbols only scarcely interconnected, if at all. Both pieces include self-referential components steeped in technology and commercialism. As mentioned earlier, Coupland's text is surrounded by Pop Art cartoon images à la Roy Lichtenstein, as well as short blurbs and neologisms about Generation X demographics, displaying a highly ironic and visual stance toward the sanctity of the word; *Slacker* uses the camera as an intertextual medium to comment on the construction of its own reality. In other words, as content and form, fiction and documentary interconnect, it becomes clear that we are encountering aesthetic productions that are redefining the act of being and being created.

Most often, literary critics have felt that Generation X'ers' immersion into commercial culture depoliticized their work and relegated their significance to surfaces, their narratives lacking analytical depth and artistic value. Linklater argues against such assertions, explaining that readers forgot that they were standing before a group of writers and artists who had grown up on television and advertising and whose reading strategies were much more sophisticated than that of their elders. In fact, Linklater himself went from thinking that his generation had nothing to say,

to thinking that it not only had everything to say but was saying it in a completely new way. It was a multitude of voices coexisting and combining and all adding up to something that certainly "meant" something but couldn't easily be classified. Each individual had to find it in [his or her] own way and in the only place society had left for this discovery—in the margins. (4)

> ### GENERATION X AND TELEVISION
>
> "Generation X learned to handle television like a team of lawyers handle a hostile witness—we did not raise a stupid generation here. The ground rules were established early: Generation X would take from the media what they needed and what they found entertaining, but they would never accept information from the media at face value. They would learn to be critical. They would learn to recognize hype, 'weasel words,' and exaggeration. And, like all good lawyers, they would always seek to control the communication" (114).
>
> —Karen Ritchie
> *Marketing to Generation X*

The self-conscious awareness of GenX'ers' position in the margins made the generation all the more conscious of the role of media technologies in selling out people's souls to homogenous myths and stereotypes. As the first generation to have fully grown up with television and advertising, GenX'ers were able to recognize their manipulating forces. To construct personal identities in a society determined by constructs, they either adopted a language radically opposed and outside of this intrinsic apparatus or they appropriated and manipulated commercial meaning-making machines for their own purposes. Generation X'ers did both. They joined the negationist themes centered on youth cultural rebellion and a minimalist and physical linguistic style with a fascination for commercial and popular culture. Then they added a pinch, or several tablespoons, of cynicism, sarcasm, and irony; or they removed all tone and presented unpalatable, flat speech patterns void of piquant flavor.

Left Between the Blank: Tales of Generation X

The "X" marker that has often been designated as empty, negative, and meaningless also provided artists with a space to move, change, and grow. It was a space of rejection and rebellion, but also of an awareness of positive and alternative self-constructions—punks' do-it-yourself (DIY) philosophy. Both the GenX punk philosophy of the 1970s and the sociological work of Fussell in the 1980s presented an "X" that exhibited a sense of release and freedom. Generation X'ers presented readers with meta-mediatic storytelling techniques in which the technologies that defined their realities were translated into innovative signifying practices or intertextual sites of critical meaning making. Based on this history, the "blank" afforded to the generation's "X" marker is today one of the most fruitful spaces of analysis. The term accommodates a set of spatial and temporal multiplicities that includes the GenX label's chronological evolution and its geographic idiosyncrasies in fiction and film from around the world. In addition, the "blank" allows for a better understanding of the ephemeral dimension of the "X" as a space of convergences and contradictions, of displacements and misplacements.

The critic who has analyzed best "blankness" on a literary level is James Annesley in *Blank Fictions: Consumerism, Culture, and the Contemporary American Novel*. Annesley begins his project by pointing to the emergence of a new scene in the 1990s. This scene was sprinkled with a set of extreme expressions, such as the disturbing early teen sex, alcohol, drugs, and AIDS in Larry Clark's film *Kids* (1996); depression and drug addiction in Elizabeth Wurzel's novel *Prozac Nation* (1994); or the sense of indifference in song lyrics by musician Beck (Beck Hansen) in "Loser" ("I'm a loser baby…why don't you kill me?"). This was the same scene that, as I indicate in the introduction, was also perceived on an international front in the drug addiction themes of Scotland's *Trainspotting*, the indifference and sexual habits in the Australian novel *Praise*, or the "loser" and "slacker" qualities of Iceland's *101 Reykjavik*.

Annesley refers to violence, sexual experimentation, drug use, and urban despair in American fiction of the 1990s to develop a wider perspective on the contemporary literary panorama. He contends that writers such as Donna Tartt, Susanna Moore, Douglas Coupland, and Mark Leyner, among others, were loosely held together by a common reference point, namely the New York Brat-Packers of the 1980s. These writers shared some common ground. Their novels centered on American youth in their twenties, they were urban in focus and concerned with the relationship between the individual and consumer society, and, instead of dense plots and elaborate styles or political subjects, they preferred blank and atonal perspectives (2).[8] He chooses the term "blank fiction" to describe this group, above other labels such as "fiction of insurgency," "new narrative," "downtown writing," or "punk fiction" because these authors "prefer blank, atonal perspectives and fragile, glassy visions" (2). He relates their narratives to the subjects of sex, death, and subversion that occupied the likes of William Burroughs, George Bataille, and Marquis de Sade.

More useful than Annesley's analysis of these individual texts (and GenX's possible associations) is his theoretical excising of explanations that have been used to make meaning of this emergent literary scene. The arguments strongly resemble those that have been used to understand Generation X, even though "Generation X" is one of the labels Annesley rejects as too strongly related to slacker culture to explain "blank fiction." There are several arguments the critic disregards as not encompassing of scholarship on the subject. They include an "apocalyptic culture" reacting to millennial angst, an aesthetic of the radical and the extreme that uses marginal statements and pronouncements, and a postmodern condition that reflects "the material structure of late twentieth-century American society" (4). Annesley explains that this latter interpretation on postmodernism, much like the critical work on Spanish GenX fiction, has been used as an all-encompassing explanation that does not differentiate between narrative forms:

> Fiction, from this perspective, seems passive. Lost in the abstract sign-space of contemporary American culture, it is unable to offer anything more than a blank reflection of this 'cultural logic.' Postmodern culture thus becomes a catch-all, a category that is used in so many different circumstances that it loses its explanatory power. (5)

For a more fruitful approach to the interpretation of blank fiction in the 1990s, one cannot ignore the centrality of the texts' place in late-twentieth-century American culture. That said, Annesley cautions critics not to read literature as a direct representation of social conditions. Scholarship on blank fiction, he contends, must go beyond models of reflection and interpret "the links between the material realities of 'existence' and the aesthetic structures of the literary 'sign'" (5). Quoting V. N. Volosinov, he emphasizes that the analysis of fiction in contextual terms must not be straightforward, but must focus on the processes "through which a text thematizes contemporary conditions on structural, stylistic, linguistic and metaphorical levels" (6).

> *BLANK FICTION, A WELL-MADE BEER COMMERCIAL*
>
> "Blank fiction may well be like a 'well-made beer commercial,' but it can still provide a surprising amount of 'intellectual nourishment'" (10).
>
> —James Annesley
>
> *Not just empty calories!*
>
> —*Samuel Amago, in response*

Annesley uncovers these mechanisms in how authors do not just detail or reconstruct commercial culture, but incorporate commercialized products into their writings—they do not refer to "a car," but to a "BMW." Dates do not matter, nor do situations or personalities, but rather the commercial features of the environment that provide these novels with their reference points. Most importantly, "blank fiction does not just depict its own period, it speaks in the commodified language of its own period" (7). In other words, Annesley proposes an analytical shift from product to process, one that, as I mention in the introduction, mirrors the process-based digital environment in which we live, and, as Juan Manuel Espinosa argues in one of the side boxes, feeds into the process-oriented function of hybridity itself.

In this book, I embrace Annesley's approach and take it a step further. In line with the work of D. Chaney, Steven Miles, and Paul Willis on youth culture, I agree that material culture's meaning goes beyond its monetary value to provide a code or language within which identities or lifestyles are constructed. Young people respond to this culture in a host of positive and creative ways, and contrary to popular belief, "they do not buy consumer goods passively or uncritically, but transform, appropriate and recontextualize meanings" (Miles 31). To understand the reality of youth in today's world, one must entertain the role of popular media technologies in the transformation of global network societies and the changing and participatory nature of the "consumer" and the "consumed." Therefore, to limit the literary analysis of contemporary literature to intersecting points between subjectivity and consumption, as does Candace Bosse on the Spanish front, is limiting. Instead, I propose to engage in the changing structural dynamics—relations to time, space, identity, and reality—that consumption practices of technology may facilitate.

In line with the critical reevaluation undertaken by Annesley, I end this chapter by filtering through four half-truths, or "tales" as I call them here, to refocus and reposition scholarship on the Spanish Generation X oeuvre. The tales consist of critics' references to "dirty realism" as a literary equivalent to Generation X literature in Spain, to direct and generalized correlations made between economic and social conditions and their impact on the representation of youth, to the perception that Spain's rapid transition and development led to a society traumatized by "information overload," and to the critical evaluation of GenX narratives within extreme examples of violence and horror. Scholarship on Spanish GenX narrative needs to rid itself of some of these partial, causal, extreme, and abstract readings to allow for more complex, correlational, and grounded interpretations centered on a deeper understanding of the history and meaning of "Generation X."

Tale #1: Dirty Realism

The tales of Generation X that I unravel earlier focus on the "blank" as an empty space appropriated for aesthetic means and as a site of classification: "blank fiction." To better understand the significance of this space of possibilities in the GenX context, it is essential to look at the meanings lost in translation between "dirty realism" and "realismo sucio." Although "realismo sucio" is the literal translation of "dirty realism," the two labels embody very different phenomena. My aim here is not to present a comprehensive comparative analysis, but to look at two components, language and commercial culture, to point to critics' unfitting application of the label.

Cintia Santana's enlightening essay "What We Talk About When We Talk About Dirty Realism"

> *"Dirty realism" was a term first coined by Bill Buford in the spring 1983 issue of the British literary magazine* Granta. *The volume featured short fiction by Raymond Carver, Frederick Barthelme, Richard Ford, Bobbie Anne Mason, Jayne Anne Phillips, Elizabeth Tallent, and Tobias Wolff. In the fall of 1986, Anagrama published Carver's* Catedral, *the first collection of short stories to appear in Spain by a so-called dirty realist writer. Over the next decade, Anagrama would continue to publish the work of these writers, as would Alfaguara, Seix Barral, Edhasa, and Grijalbo.*
>
> —*Cintia Santana, in response*

provides a valuable insight into the translation of American minimalism into Spanish "realismo sucio." She argues that although certain similarities may be found in both cases, Spain's "realismo sucio" was markedly different from its expression in the United States for four main reasons that have gone virtually unnoticed: there were far fewer Spanish women writers in Spain; in the United States characters belonged to lower-middle classes instead of the upper-middle class scene found in Spain; the degree of violence was much higher in Spain, and the location was generally rural in nature in the United States while more urban in Spain (36).

Santana explored how the US working-class speech characteristic of "dirty realism" was "cleansed" by removing class markers in the Spanish translations. The oral, colloquial language used in Spanish texts was often referenced as a "dirty realist" trait, despite its marked differences with the speech represented in US "dirty realist" writing. Yet the roots of Generation X's language patterns were found in Spain's *cheli*, "a slang that originated in the 1970s and 1980s and that the Real Academia Española's dictionary defined as "Jerga con elementos castizos, marginales y contraculturales" [Slang with Castilian, marginal, and countercultural elements] (Santana 43). Quoting Miranda Stewart, Santana reveals that this slang first originated in criminal subgroups in major cities in the 1970s and then spread into the cultural elite and wider youth communities in Spain; it was not tied to face-to-face manifestations, but flourished in the underground fanzines and creative arts of the *Movida Madrileña* (43).

Transcriptions of colloquial dialects were not new to Spanish literary traditions as previously found in the works of figures such as Benito Pérez Galdós, Pío Baroja, Ramón del Valle-Inclán, Carlos Arniches, and Sánchez Ferlosio (39). But, explains Santana, the type of language and characters "portrayed in the work of Mañas, Loriga, Prado, and Wolfe, [captured] not the speech of the small town or urban Spanish proletariat, but of young, urban 'pijos' whose speech simultaneously [attested] to their consumption of North American cultural products" (39). When Francisco Umbral published the *Diccionario cheli* in 1983, *cheli* had already undergone a process of co-optation and appropriation by higher economic classes and was fully integrated into speech by the 1990s. Subsequently, Umbral and Pilar Capanaga called the work of Mañas, et al. *post-cheli* given their use of neologisms that attested to the consumption of Anglo-American culture (*rocanrol, Jenriretratodeunasesino, Yinkases*). Santana convincingly argues that "as 'hick became chic' in the U.S. in the 1980s so *cheli* became increasingly co-opted and appropriated by a higher socioeconomic class in the 1990s in Spain" (44). Spain's dirty realism rendered a language that was cleansed and was "largely readable, and commodifiable" (44). Ultimately, the inclusion of the literary dialect of a truly marginal element of Spanish society would have resulted in a much "dirtier" fiction than that found in the diluted *cheli* of Spain's realismo sucio or Generation X (45).

> *The "dirty realism" label was such a commercial success that Anagrama retroactively marketed Charles Bukowski as such. Bukowski (1920–94), who belonged to a prior generation of US writers, had first been introduced to a Spanish audience in 1978.*
>
> *—Cintia Santana, in response*

Santana's argument motions to Spain's imaginary of the United States as linked to an urban setting, to youth, and to violence, despite the fact that, for example, Carver's work was neither urban nor violent (46). Soon after the appearance of Carver's fiction in Spain, the translation of the work of Bret Easton Ellis and Jay McInerney in 1987 also reinforced the use of the term "dirty realism" on the Spanish peninsula. Although these Brat-Packers were a generation younger than the "dirty realist" writers, their use of a minimalist style and their references to North American culture led to their conflation on a critical front. Subsequently, the term "realismo sucio" was applied to GenX authors with little regard to cultural distinctions and translations.

"Dirty realism" may have been a convenient way for the Spanish literary elite to emphasize GenX novels' *dirty* qualities and to reinforce the contaminating qualities of contemporary colloquial language and culture. In addition, references to North American popular culture, while certainly not exclusive of GenX texts (meaning that other authors similarly included them into their fiction and that Spanish cultural references were also frequently used), also fed into critics' larger perception of a book market that was selling out to US commercial culture. Critics claimed that GenX authors readily embraced the work of blank fiction writers such as Ellis or McInerney in part because they added a dose of "nothing" to the narrative mix in Spain (see Jason Klodt's essay "Nada de nada de nada de nada"). Articles emphasized minimal plot developments, first-person narratives, abject subject constructions, fragmented narrative styles, the thematics of disenchantment, and the negative effects of commercial commodification. But as Santana's analysis intimates, critics did not sufficiently engage with the inherent cultural and linguistic differences of the two literary groups nor with the role of commercial culture in the cleansing of Spanish slang. They did not rush to make better sense of the blank that marks the generation's X spot, a spot not to be termed "realism sucio" [dirty realism].[9]

Tale #2: Social Reality

In the 1990s in Spain Generation X texts flattened and remodeled literary practices to contend with political, economic, social, cultural, and technological changes occurring on both a national and an international stage. Lest we speak of a GenX resurgence in light of the global economic crisis of the twenty-first century, to make direct connections between real social conditions and their fictive constructs is too symmetrical of an activity to explain multileveled changes occurring in any period. As Annesley, quoting Terry Eagleton, observes, a direct reading relationship is "unable to accommodate the dialectical conflicts and complexities, the unevenness and discontinuity, which characterize literature's relation with society" (6). In the case of Generation X, social reality alone is not able to take into account the group's attention to contemporary culture's emerging global and networked dynamics.

Mark Allinson wrote an essay on the "youth problem" in Spain that defines the 1980s and 1990s as a time marred by unemployment, lack of housing, alcohol abuse, drug addiction, and AIDS. His article has been quoted frequently to justify GenX'ers' gloomy and disenchanted takes on reality. While data support the serious status of these conditions, critics have not paid enough attention to the details, the larger picture, and the consequences. For example, little consideration has been given to how certain realities affected individuals differently. Because of the entrance of more women into higher education and the workforce, unemployment in Spain has been and still is the highest among young women, but gender is rarely considered in scholarship on Generation X. For example, unemployment for men went down from 15.1 percent in 1982 to 13 percent in 1989, while for women it went up from 18.9 percent to 25.4 percent, mostly for younger women (Zaldívar 54). If unemployment is a definite marker of the disenchantment expressed by GenX'ers, why are there not more GenX women writers? Why is it that, in fact, women tend to be left out of the GenX equation altogether?

> ### GENERATION X AND SOCIAL CLASS
>
> The "nevermind" (in Spanish, *pasota*) attitude of characters in Spanish narrative of the 1990s, like Carlos and his friends in *Historias del Kronen* by José Ángel Mañas, was intricately tied to the middle-upper-class money that made their outings possible. Their virtual flights into antiestablishment behaviors express themselves through punk and rock music heard loudly through the speakers of their Volkswagens while driving at high velocities. The Volkswagen "Golf" had become European, especially German, Generation X'ers' car par excellence as described in Florian Illies's book *Generation Golf: Eine Inspektion*, 2001.
>
> —Christine Henseler

Another question to consider is how these social factors in Spain compare to the rest of Europe and the Western world. Data show that similar conditions existed in many parts of the world. While Spain's (and Italy's) case may have been more extreme, lower living standards and unemployment were also found in countries such as Japan in the 1990s. Can we find similarities in the aesthetic expression of youth in both Japan and Spain? What role should Spain's national history and cultural idiosyncrasies play in an understanding of GenX narrative? What is the consequence of unemployment in different geographic and physical spaces, such as the *okupas* (squatters) in Spain? A fascinating study by anthropologist Carles Feixa, for example, determines how the GenX phenomenon of the *okupas* in the Catalan region allowed for stronger group dynamics, new possibilities for identity construction, and alternative forms of artistic expression (performance theater) that contributed to a changing conception of citizenship in Spain ("Movimientos"). The essay emphasizes that high levels of unemployment do not necessarily lead to destructive or negative developments, but may contribute to alternative and innovative cultural constructions depending on the multifarious assimilation process that takes place in each country and in each case.

Another perspective that should not be disregarded in discussions on the social reality of youth in the 1990s is that, while examples of lower-class representations exist in Spain and internationally, such as in *Trainspotting* by Irvine Welsh or *Praise* by Andrew McGahan, Generation X is widely seen as a white, middle-upper-class phenomenon. Many GenX characters seem to have money to spare and toys at their fingertips. Carlos's home with a swimming pool in Mañas's *Historias del Kronen*; Vania's lifestyle of expensive fashion and nights out on the town, buying drugs and alcohol in Bustelo's *Veo veo*; or Ana's designer furniture and professional home design in Etxebarria's *Amor, curiosidad, prozac y dudas* portray a socioeconomic period steeped in an overindulgent capitalist and consumerist culture rather than a world defined by difficult economic conditions brought about by the peninsula's recession years.[10]

> ### SPANISH VALUES, 1991
>
> A survey conducted in 1991 gave an overview of Spaniards' secular values: Spaniards only attributed 5 percent in value to the importance of politics in their lives, and religion was attributed 25 percent. The most important value was attributed to the family, at 83 percent, and to work, 64 percent, as the fundamental happiness attributed to personal lives and social positions. Once these two elements were guaranteed, the population stated friends (44 percent) and entertainment and activities (37 percent) (42).
>
> —Carlos Alonso Zaldívar and
> Manuel Castells
> *España fin de siglo*
>
> Also in 1974, 85 percent of households had a washing machine and a fridge. Car ownership grew even more rapidly: "The SEAT factory in Barcelona, which turned out 30,000 saloon cars in 1960, produced over 360,000 by 1972. Spanish levels of car ownership rose from 500,000 (one car for every fifty-five inhabitants) in 1960, to over 3,300,000 (one for every nine) in 1974" (265).
>
> —Borja De Riquer I Permanyer
> *Social and Economic Change*

As outlined earlier, I believe Generation X's philosophical roots are buried less in a reaction against real social conditions (unemployment, AIDS) than in the metaphysical questionings of larger social patterns (a questioning that does not deny social awareness). Coupland's three Generation X characters and Richard Linklater's dozens of *slackers*, consciously downgrade jobs and lives, they prefer to intellectualize life and art, and they search for alternative sites of meaning-making, even if those sites remain empty and insignificant. In Spain, characters escape into sex, drugs, and rock and roll; they hit the road; or they lock themselves into rooms from where they point to society's abusive practices, outdated institutions, and grand narratives. Some of these characters make conscious decisions, others do not, but their general goal is to allow new meanings to emerge and converge. I do not deny that unemployment and other material social factors affected Generation X'ers, but I would go so far as to claim that social reality has become a convenient way to justify GenX fiction's expressions of disenchantment and disengagement without looking at a broader and more complex and intersecting set of factors, such as gender, class, and the metaphysical questioning of social patterns.

Tale #3: "Information Overload"

In line with the disenchanted and disillusioned perspective taken on social reality in GenX fiction, critics also misconceived of the impact of socio-economic and technological changes on urban life and culture in the 1990s. Cristina Moreiras Menor theorized that Spain was "ushered overnight into the postmodern era [and emerged] as a traumatized and defenseless society—what Mark Seltzer would call a 'wound culture'" ("Spectacle" 141). She viewed this trauma as a psychoanalytical underlying weight (referring to history) that affected the narrative and filmic production of the 1990s. The mental, albeit unconscious, consequences of a fascist past coincided, she said, quoting French philosopher Jean Baudrillard, with an excess of meaning and a society collapsing under the burden of information overload (138). The result, she claimed, was a post-1992 Olympic response to the trans-nationalization of mass cultural forms of entertainment expressed through violence and fantasies of violence (designed to conceal the absence of meaning) (*Cultura* 206).[11]

I agree with Hispanist Paul Julian Smith that to engage with the social and cultural reality of the 1990s in Spain one does not have to rely on a negative model of loss (of a Francoist past), lack, historical amnesia, nostalgia, violence, trauma, or shock, but rather on empirical data which have shown to be positive repositories for the exploration of historical memory. Smith attests that "empirical indicators of social attitudes [...] tend to support neither the 'mourning and melancholia' hypothesis of pathological grief nor the 'spectacle and simulacrum' theory of irresponsible and apolitical hedonism" (*Spanish* 72). In support of Smith's thesis, Carlos Zaldívar affirms that in 1984, 61 percent of Spaniards considered the

> *In this regard GenX literary culture mirrors, in part, the emergence of product placement in US hip-hop culture—also in ascendancy in the 1990s. See Monae A. Davis, "Hip-Hop and Product Placement: The Struggle to 'Keep It Real.'"*
>
> —*Samuel Amago, in response*

development and integration of new technologies as something positive; only 21 percent of Spaniards viewed it as a negative evolution. Data validate that positive attitudes were found particularly among young people, those of higher classes and educational levels, and in urban areas and in groups that have historically had easier access to new technologies (Zaldívar et al. 184). Data indicate that to present the image of youth as passively and traumatically taking on what Moreiras Menor calls the "burden of information overload" is misconstrued. To examine GenX literature through this lens underestimates the positive, welcoming, and naturalized position that popular and commercial culture and media technologies had on youth since the 1960s, as indicated in the introduction. In addition, these studies disregard young people's *active* engagement with media technologies, their constant exposure, participatory involvement, and conscious critical applications in life and art.

Raw numbers determine that the greatest, and perhaps only, shock perceived by Spaniards was felt among the forty-plus age group in Spain in the 1990s who quickly fell out of sync with a highly secularized, apolitical, pacifist, environmentally conscious, and media- and technology-savvy youth. To give a few examples of this generational divide, it warrants mentioning that while 84 percent of young people consider normal having sexual relations outside of marriage, the majority of individuals over the age of 40 do not agree. While 30 percent of people between the ages of fifty-one and sixty and 46 percent of people over sixty believe that living together without being married is immoral, only 4 percent of young people believe the same (Zaldívar and Castells 43). In regard to the use of computers and electronic devices in the home, the schism between the forty-and-over and less-than-forty population is especially significant. The population born before 1951 found itself at great odds with new media technologies, an important perspective to keep in mind when we talk about Generation X in Spain or elsewhere. All in all, the period presented a considerable generational shift in social and cultural values and power structures still visible in today's literary production and reception. In this context, the result is that to speak of Generation X as a negative, traumatized expression of information overload does not present a truthful representation of the contemporary mindset of democratic youth in Spain. No matter how accelerated Spain's social, economic, and political changes may have been, the tales that reflect on this accelerated culture, have always been an inherent part of the "X" consciousness itself, as Coupland's subtitle supports.

Tale #4: The Radical or Extreme

Generation X literature is often deemed "radical" or "extreme," especially as it relates to violence and sexuality. GenX novels are often associated with a branch of "trangressional" or "transgressive" fiction and film that deal with death, murder, and sadomasochism. The Italian "Gioventú Cannibale" Marquis de Sade (*Justine*, 1787), Herbert Selby Jr. (*Last Exit to Brooklyn*, 1964), William Burroughs (*Naked Lunch*, 1959), J. G. Ballard (*Crash*, 1973), and Anthony Burgess (*Clockwork Orange*, 1971) are quoted as forerunners of Spanish GenX writings of the 1990s as well as the twenty-first century. Based on these perceived connections, critics' general impression of the "Generation X" label is skewed. Although extreme violence and horror may be found in GenX narratives of men and women alike, these novels are precisely what the term suggests: an extreme expression of Generation X that does not conform to a more broad-based view of the term when other examples are included in the mix, especially in the case of Spain.

When scholars place the work of Mañas and Loriga next to the ultra-violent films of directors Alejandro Amenábar (*Tesis*, 1996) or Álex de la Iglesia (*El día de la bestia*, 1995), the result distorts GenX's perception as a whole.[12] This overlapping approach has led Moreiras Menor to conclude that in one decade, from the 1980s to the 1990s, the experience of a celebratory and spectacular reality has shifted into an experience of violence.[13] Quoting Fredric Jameson, Moreiras Menor finds that Spain has moved into "una cultura que marca la huella de la sangre, la tortura, la muerte y el terror" [a culture that marks a path of blood, torture, death and terror] (274). She claims that Spain moved from an artistic utopia to a dystopia, one in which the consequences of the process of modernization has led to experiences of the abject and to deconstruction. Her comments ask us to question the logic of making *extreme* generalizations in which several select novels and films come to represent the psycho analytic conditions of an entire nation (a nation of people who, as data indicate, are generally happy with the country's direction). In addition, can the increase in violence found in life and art all over the world be used to augment the historical condition and development of one nation?

Alain-Philippe Durand and Naomi Mandel, editors of the volume *Novels of the Contemporary Extreme* (2006), place Spanish authors Ray Loriga

In my essay on Tesis *I argue that Amenábar does not so much celebrate violence in the film, but instead elaborates an ambivalent critique of audiovisual violence that implicates the viewer and, by extension, Spanish society. The film is also a reflexive meditation on the future of Spanish filmmaking in a home market that is increasingly dominated by Hollywood.*

—Samuel Amago, in response

YOUTH LIFESTYLES IN A CHANGING WORLD

"The sociology of youth has tended to treat young people as troubled victims of economic and social restructuring without enough recourse to the active ways in which young people negotiate such circumstances in the course of their everyday lives. In this context, youth becomes little more than a term describing an undifferentiated mass of people of similar age experiencing similar things, when what it should be describing is a highly differentiated group of people of similar age subject to a whole variety of experiences depending on a diverse range of personal circumstances" (10).

"Sociologists have traditionally tended to focus on extreme cultural expressions of youth at one end of the spectrum and conceptions of 'disadvantaged' youth on the other. On this basis there has been a tendency to extract meaning from either melodramatic expressions of lifestyle or from structural conceptions of youth disadvantaged as a basis for further generalizations about the nature of youth as a whole" (3).

—Steven Miles

Another "extreme" manifestation that is worth mentioning for its more metalinguistic and mediatic approach is that of a group of writers whose narrative production parallels that of the Brat-Packers. Instead of residing in the West, they resided in the East and are also identified as "downtown writers" working in the early 1970s and 1980s (peaking between 1979 and 1982). Robert Siegle in his book *Suburban Ambush: Downtown Writing and the Fiction of Insurgency* (1989) argues that these writers are less well known than the Brat-Pack writers in part because of their much more radical and self-reflexive (and feminist) prose. The work of Kathy Acker, Constance Dejong and Lynne Tillman present a much deeper, angry, polymorphous, and astute reading of the shifts in American society. Siegle calls their work "fiction of insurgency" because they express the 1970s "guerrilla campaign against the imminent transformation of American consciousness into a shopping mall" (4). Downtown writing is insurgent, says Siegle, but its alpha and omega reside in the other half of the double genitive—in its status as fiction rather than revolution" (2–3). What this literature does is "it shakes up reified relations—roles, genders, social structures—so that at least momentary experiences of various sorts of Other might take place before the great culture machine swallows it up again" (3). He explains that, "this is an insurgency against the silence of institutions, the muteness of the ideology of form, the unspoken violence of normalization. But it does not expect of itself the pure voice of the Other—it knows its own language, the position of the speaking subject at the end of the twentieth century" (4).

—Christine Henseler

and Lucía Etxebarria also alongside an emerging movement of extreme violence in literature across the globe. The editors identify a worldwide phenomenon marked by "a hyper real, often apocalyptic world progressively invaded by popular culture, permeated with technology and dominated by destruction" (1). In this category, they include writers such as Americans Bret Easton Ellis and Don Delillo, Quebécois author Nelly Arcan, Belgian Amélie Nothomb, Israeli Orly Castel-Bloom, Chilean Alberto Fuguet, and Frenchman Frédéric Beigbeder. The editors relate the "extreme" in these novelists' works to political extremity and to a fascination with transgression as found in scenes of rape, torture, murder, mutilation, death, pornography, terror, and cannibalism. These events are often channeled through media and technology and described in everyday, colloquial, and flattened language that naturalizes the horrific events.

Certainly, GenX texts often display acts of gratuitous violence, including the gun killings in Loriga's *Caídos del cielo*, homicide in Mañas's *Historias del Kronen*, and suicide in Etxebarria's *Amor, curiosidad, prozac y dudas*, but the explicit and detailed horror that we assume with "extreme" violence cannot be found to the same degree in Spanish GenX narrative as in Bret Easton Ellis's novel *American Psycho*. Hispanists Kathryn Everly and Catherine Bourland Ross, in their studies on Loriga and Etxebarria in the *Contemporary Extreme* volume, discuss individuals' relationship to popular media culture and their sense of dissatisfaction, violence, sexuality, and drug use and abuse. Their studies, while interesting pieces in and of themselves, do not evince a sense of extremism, especially when read parallel to fiction concerning terrorism, rape, and sadomasochism. Does explicit sexuality still count as extreme? Does the portrayal of city life marked by drugs and alcohol still shock people? Does it shock us to learn about the construction of beauty and death through televisual manipulations? Isn't a certain level of gratuitous violence a naturalized part of today's cityscape (as sad as this affirmation may be)?

To talk about the "extreme" in GenX texts, under any circumstance, demands a more nuanced approach. Eloy Fernández Porta and Vicente Muñoz Álvarez, editors of the short story volume *Golpes: Ficciones de la crueldad social* (2004), define the extreme in Spain in a slightly different but related context as "social cruelty." Social cruelty delves into the extreme, the negative, the destructive, the traumatic, and the bloody to present a sociopathic vision they call "psiquiatría espectacular" [spectacular psychiatry].[14] Porta and Álvarez relate this extreme to Slavok Zizek's post-9/11 vision of society described in *Welcome to the Desert of the Real* (2001) and to Hal Foster's conception of "traumatic realism," as expressed in *The Return of the Real* (1996). "Traumatic realism" may be applied to one version of the expression of violence in narrative and art, one that may interestingly reside on the margins of what may be considered *literary* (comics; fanzines; punk music; hybrid pieces that join writing, illustration, and art). But this is not a concept that should be generalized to only Spain's social domain in the 1990s, nor to Generation X literature overall. The "extreme" of GenX texts pertains to a much more moderate rendition of *marginal* subjectivity, and it does not reside in a *traumatic* ground *zero*. Ground zero in GenX narrative is a space for escape, questioning, and innovation (often expressed through the apocalypse), and "the desert of the real" literally functions as a place for physical and emotional escape (as in Coupland's *Generation X*), a space of contradictions and interconnections (as in Mallo's *Nocilla Dream*) that allow for new beginnings and innovations. In sum, while examples of extreme violence and horror do exist in the GenX repertoire, they are not representative of Generation X as a whole.

Chapter 2

Punked Out and Smelling Like Afterpop

"It's hard to imagine a modern Europe and America not transformed by punk" (5). These words by Roger Sabin in his edited volume *Punk Rock: So What?: The Cultural Legacy of Punk*, amplify the cultural and political reach of the punk rock movement around the globe. Sabin posits that punk was not an isolated or bounded phenomenon, but that it had extensive impact on a variety of cultural and political fields in the United States, Great Britain, and beyond (2). Sabin argues that punk defined a cultural and political movement that influenced a larger shift in Zeitgeist, a turn found in everything from literature, fine art, comics, film, theater, television, comedy, journalism, body modification, and more (5). To understand the impact of this shift, especially on the cultural dynamics in Spain, one must first define punk not as a historically and culturally fixed construct but as "a process of construction" (5) ridden with contradictions and tensions. This process begins in the world of music, but it advances in a series of countercultural and commercial manifestations that the *Movida madrileña* and the work

> *This quote illustrates the great optimism about the power of music to transform individuals and societies, an integral part of the energy of the youth movements originating in the 1960s. Seen from today, this optimism seems naïve and unaware that not flowers, drugs, punk daring, or rock 'n roll would stop the wars or the effects of an uncaring international capitalism.*
>
> *—Randolph Pope, in response*
>
> *After thirty years of punk, one wonders if the movements succeeded. I believe the answer is no. As anticipated by its own slogan, "No future," the punk movement ended up being absorbed by the international music industry. What remains of punk today is more a style than a revolutionary movement. But punk gave us an iconoclastic musical genre, perhaps the most original music of the last fifty years. For generations to come, the songs of groups such as Eskorbuto, Parálisis Permanente, Kaka de Luxe, and La Polla Records, will be regarded as classical masterpieces.*
>
> *—Carmen de Urioste, in response*

> *Roger Sabin's statement is undoubtedly overblown. As youth subculture, punk was ineffectual in changing anything. It was essentially designed as a protest movement and not as a political, social, and economic game-changer. A youth subculture heavily fostered by drugs, sex, and rock 'n' roll, one wonders how punk, conceived as a mass movement, could have achieved political change. While punk's community spirit is palpable in large crowds during punk rock concerts because of the sense of common purpose, the community spirit engendered by such gatherings is transient. The energy produced by such crowds is transitory and impossible to harness into any effective and meaningful political or social movement. One needs to remember that punk is not a global phenomenon. Most youth in Africa could care less about punk.*
>
> *—Yaw Agawu-Kakraba, in response*

of José Ángel Mañas expound. In the texts by Mañas, whose novel *Historias del Kronen* I examine at length at the end of this chapter, the tension may be observed in a punk stylistic that converges with a Pop Art sensibility and narrative techniques found in television. These diverse components result in a new generational perspective on reality best brought into focus through what Eloy Fernández Porta calls an "Afterpop" critical lens.

La Movida and Generation X

Punk in Spain was not monolithic but included a range of individuals and displayed a philosophy that changed from city to city and band to band. The artifice that characterized the punk movement in the United States and Britain and helped usher in heavy metal, prog, stadium rock, and symphonic collaboration with a twist of posthippie darkness was an artifice that ran deeper in Spain and grew into the maximalism of the *Movida madrileña* of the 1980s ("Drogas"). American and British punk was initially conflated with the *Movida* or *Nueva Ola* (new wave) as a stance against Franco's political conservative *movimiento* and the beginning of a booming drug culture ("Drogas").[1] Interestingly, the conflation of the *Movida* and *Nueva Ola* terminology emphasized the relation between punk and punk spin-offs and was first used by Malcolm McLaren to talk about bands that were not exactly punk but were related to it or were part of the same musical scene.[2] That said, in 1977, the "New Wave" (taken from French New Wave filmmakers) replaced "punk" in Great Britain to talk about underground music that tended toward experimentation, lyrical complexity, or more polished productions ("Drogas"). The New Wave was also marketed in the United States to talk about the anticorporate and experimental work of the Ramones and Talking Heads.

> *The interconnectedness of all these cultural manifestations defines the times. Participants tried to create a brand for themselves, in a still Modernist and even late-Romantic effort to break from the past, at the same time that the great wave of the postmodern swallowed them up into the transient multiple offerings of an international entertainment industry.*
>
> *—Randolph Pope, in response*

The punk movement that was first born in New York City and then travelled to Great Britain was imported by some of the major figures of the Spanish *Movida* in the latter half of the 1970s. The most famous *Movida* club, *Rock-ola*, put Spain on the concert series map by signing on international bands such as Iggy Pop and Spandau Ballet. In addition, the club housed everybody from writers, musicians, photographers, comic artists, and film directors, thus presenting an underground space where alternative artistic practices and figures coalesced. This symbiosis led to a host of collaborative projects, such as the famous *La luna de Madrid* (1982–88), that corralled hundreds of writers and artists and included segments on the visual arts, photography, advertising, design, fashion, music, theater, and more serious documentary reports meant to provoke and transgress. In line with these media events, the *Movida* permitted and promoted a variety of "crossings," whether they were related to dress, culture, or nation. These intersections lead to innovative projects, such as the joining of fanzines and photography in the work of Alberto García-Alix, or rock and comics in the "nuevo cómic ibérico" [new Iberian comic].

> *In Spain, the Movida madrileña was a "new" cultural manifestation that brought the country closer to Europe and marked a departure from its francoist past. Two countercultural European movements influenced the Movida: the British "punk" movement and the French revolutionary wave of 1968. But its emergence as a festive and aesthetic movement had deep Spanish roots as a response to the desolating situation of the country at the beginning of the 1980s, when the unstable Spanish democracy was under the continuous threat of coup d'états. In the midst of this instability, the Movida represented a cultural lifeline and a word whose emptiness captured the sociopolitical confusion of all parties, as the hopes raised by the Socialist electoral victory in 1982 gave way to rapid disillusionment. The Movida reformulated the countercultural aspects inherited from the British and French movements toward the purely aesthetic and superficial. It disseminated a discourse of the fragments, centered on narcissistic individualism—with expectations of pleasure, hedonism, seduction, complacence, and frivolity—that can be regarded as a perfect match to the discourse deployed from the political power centers.*
>
> —Carmen de Urioste, in response
>
> *A notable shift you are observing here is the shift of the cultural vanguard, as imagined in Spain and Latin America, predominantly from Paris to London and New York, from French to English.*
>
> —Randolph Pope, in response

The *Movida*, explains Héctor Fouce in his overarching book *El futuro ya está aquí: música pop y cambio cultural*, was determined by a plurality of cultures, often interlacing and joining expressions, while simultaneously presenting attitudes of rejection and contradiction (51). The *Movida* gave birth to alternative modes of expression that were in part rooted in punk's underground, do-it-yourself philosophy and inherently served as one of the baselines from which Spain's Generation X was formed. Although artistic

> *While critics have the tendency to characterize this cultural movement as the "Movida madrileña," it is important to point out that other Spanish cities also contributed to the movement. Such is the case of Barcelona's Movida that was influenced heavily by its unusual political circumstances due to Franco's repression of the Catalan cultural and language identity. The same is the case with Bilbao's Movida in the Basque country. The cultural production that emerged in these cities and others around the country ultimately shared the same traits that constituted the "Movida madrileña": eclecticism and versatility, adoption of foreign artistic forms mixed with different Spanish traditional styles. In its totality, the "Movida" movement was designed to attack the institutional pillars of the system: power, repression, alienation, and authoritarianism.*
>
> *—Yaw Agawu-Kakraba, in response*

results differed, especially as they related to the *Movida's* infusion of kitsch and glam, a surprising number of similarities may be found between the two aesthetic movements. Semblances include youth's sense of hedonism and individualism, their rejection of intellectual elitism for a more street-based and colloquial realm of experience, their apolitical attitudes centered on the present time instead of the past or the future, their rebuff of high art's musical excellence for simplicity, roughness and "noise," and their dismissal of grand transcendental narratives and ideas, preferring instead spontaneity, improvisation, and the experience of everyday life. In many but not all cases, youth also applied a large dose of humor, sarcasm, and irony to their arts and everyday expressions, thus permitting, among other things, the distancing of the subject from social expectations.

The *Movida* youth associated as much with the lower-class punks and mods found in Great Britain as with the North American middle to upper class scene more closely connected to commercial culture. In fact, many *Movida* songs conveyed a love/hate relationship with consumer capitalism, as in Alaska's famous song *Bote de Colón.* This affinity was probably best embodied by the arrival of Andy Warhol in Madrid in 1983 and his design of Miguel Bosé's 1983 front album cover "Made in Spain." His visit

> ### *BOTE DE COLÓN*
>
> Quiero ser un bote de Colón
> Y salir anunciado por la televisión
> Quiero ser un bote de Colón
> Y salir anunciado por la televisión.
> Qué satisfacción
> Ser un bote de Colón.
>
> *—Alaska y Los Pegamoides*

symbolically solidified Spanish youth's relation to North American popular culture, as well as the *Movida's* often over-the-top use of bright neon color and kitsch in everything from Almodóvar's films to the magazine covers of *Madrid me mata.*

The repetitive sameness of Warhol's Marilyn Monroe or Campbell soup images echoed throughout the 1980s—arriving in Spain albeit a few years later than in the United States—and colorfully disrupted Franco-centered social boredom. In Generation X, this repetition of the same as always, despite slight disturbances in aesthetic outcome, fell in upon itself and under-lined individual apathy. The glamour of the repetitive Marilyn Monroes of yesterday were now supplanted by Warhol's orange car crash serigraph, as seen on the cover image of José Ángel Mañas's 1994 novel *Historias del Kronen*. Mañas stripped the *Movida* punk of any kitsch and glam, and presented in writing a series of "naked" close-ups less related to erotic and sexual experimentation than to a violent and obscene "pornography" of punk. And while sex, drugs, and punk rock were acknowledged as the most important components of the *Movida*, they were at that time still cast in a celebratory light, suggesting freedom from convention and aesthetic innova-tion. Less discussed, and more clearly apparent in the late 1980s and 1990s were the darker, nega-tive and dying effects of AIDS and addiction despite the fact that these dynamics were already present in *Movida* punk culture, which featured concerts at *Rock-ola*, among others, that included spitting, cutting, bleeding, or throwing. This darker lens on reality was also visible in the dis-concerting stark photographs of the likes of Alberto García-Alix, and may be found in a variety of other artistic expressions when focused in on more broadly. In essence, the *Movida*, as one of the first visible and audible youth cul-tures on the Spanish Peninsula, set the scene for what was later to become "Generation X," a move-ment stripped of glam and kitsch to portray a more realistic, yet aes-thetically diverse take on life and art. Generation X augmented the *Movida*'s pornographic expanse of punk. In the process, youth spurned elitist artistic patterns, and gave expression to diverse aes-thetic practices and social models.

> *I believe that it was Susan Sontag in* Styles of Radical Will *who quipped that pornography is the new opiate of the masses.*
>
> —*Paul Begin, in response*

> *The question arises as to how unified was this youth culture. We should not forget the continued vitality of deep-rooted other music, such as the Spanish rock found in Saura's 1981* De prisa, de prisa *(with the memorable "Me quedo contigo" of Los Chunguitos). In many of Almodóvar's movies some of the most moving tracks are boleros. Particularly memorable is Caetano Veloso singing "Cucurrucucú paloma" in* Hable con ella *of 2002. One could consider the Spanish resistance to the English invasion as one more factor to help us provide the complex cultural space where punk was deployed in Spain. Aerolíneas Federales's 1987 "Soy una punk" is a mar-velous, sweet version of the naturalization in Spain of punk.*
>
> —*Randolph Pope, in response*
>
> *An understanding of Generation X defi-nitely benefits from a wider engagement with the influence that the prior group of urban artists, musicians, and intellectuals of the Movida have had on the Generation X writers, such as Pedro Almodóvar, Rosa Montero, Alaska, and other punk and rock music groups born between 1950 and 1961–64. I think they are crucial to an understanding of Generation X, since many of the older members of Generation X lived through la Movida as precocious teenagers.*
>
> —*Gema Pérez-Sánchez, in response.*

Historias del Kronen exhibited a communication style similar to that found during the *Movida*. Mañas believed that physicality and gesture captured the everyday expression of the 1990s generation when he explained that,

> La gente joven no comunica en el sentido clásico, aunque luego comunica de una manera gestual mucho más elaborada que la generación de mis padres, que era más verbal o literaria. Esta gente se expresa más físicamente... bailan en la discoteca, en un concierto, se suben a un escenario y se tiran al público... Es otra manera de comunicar aunque muchas veces, y es el caso de los personajes que hay en mi novela, se traduce en insatisfacción. (Ribas 33)

In *Historias*, this physicality is expressed through capital letters that visually represent shouts and swear words, phonetic orthography, transcriptions of telephone conversations, and intertextual references to pop and punk songs. In addition, Anglicisms, colloquialisms, and neologisms serve to contradict academic and institutional practices of written language, allowing emotions to flow "de la vida al texto con menos impedimentos, sin el filtro del buen tono" (Gullón, "Historias" xxii).

—Christine Henseler

Although punk performances provide a sense of community, such communities are ephemeral. Participants attain only a fleeting moment of hallucination and ecstasy. To some extent, the novel underscores the absence of physicality and the inability to have meaningful conversations as Roberto recalls in the sessions with his therapist.

—Yaw Agawu-Kakraba,
in response

Punk's Dictum to "Tell It Like It Is"

When, in June 1998, novelist José Ángel Mañas declared the revival of a postpunk consciousness in his essay "El legado de los Ramones: literatura y punk," he infused Spain's literary scene with a minimalist do-it-yourself philosophy, originally at the heart of pre-*Movida* punk. Mañas, born in Madrid in 1971, quickly became the very young "father" of a generation of youth nicknamed "Kronen" by the press based on the title of his first novel *Historias del Kronen* (1994). His book became a cult novel significant for giving voice to a generation of youth whose experiences could not be represented through traditional storytelling techniques.[3]

In "El legado de los Ramones: literatura y punk," Mañas conceptualized his narrative approach through the concept of "punk."[4] He defined his punk narrative recipe in the following way: "Koge esa paradoja que los formalistas rusos llaman *skaz*, añade mala hostia, y procacidad y tendrás una oralidad punk" [take this paradox that Russian Formalists call *skaz*, add a bloody bad attitude, impudence, and there's your punk orality] (42). This recipe seemed easy enough at first, but when cooked correctly, the dish presented a complicated mix of unconventional spices and a prose that was "antitékniko, antiliterario y anárkiko" [untechnical, unliterary, and anarchic] (42). This was a narrative that provoked with brute adversity and with a maximum of stylistic incorrection, an orality that mimed colloquial language and gestures and combined them with an attitude of unrepentant anger and anguish. Mañas's undressing of the word from its artificial attires was not a slow and pleasurable striptease, a spectacle more available during the promiscuous *Movida* years, it was, rather, an ugly and harsh frontal look into pornographic close-ups of contemporary life. Nothing was left to the imagination and nothing was adorned, touched up, or edited, even when empowered by a play, rewind, or forward button.

Mañas once said that whenever he felt the dialogue in his novel becoming too artificial, he would strip that language to its bare bones, intentionally creating an in-your-face, straight-to-the-gut prose that removed any barriers between the text and the readers. For him, the biggest compliment was for someone to say that his language sounded ordinary and screamed out the noise of Madrid's nightlife, playing something like a direct recording off the streets. For Mañas, then, the basic feature of punk—"tres acordes, ningún punteo, tomar por culo que puedas cantar aunque tengas la voz muy mala" [three chords, no plucking, and not giving a shit whether you can sing even though you have a bad voice]" (Arbilla)—played on the minimalism of the Ramones, on an orality stripped down to fundamental features, to an economy of words, to brisk syntax, to a focus on surface descriptions, to little or no plot development, and to an almost anarchic stance toward society.

SKAZ = (from skazat', *"to tell")*

While the term originally referred to traditional oral narratives, the Russian Formalists used *skaz* to describe a technique in written narratives that imitates a spontaneous oral account through the use of dialect, slang, and the peculiar idiom of the narrator. The narrator in *skaz* is often conveyed as different from the author. www.macalester.edu/russian/glossary.html

---

How hard it was to sustain such an approach is revealed by the shift in tone at the end of the novel, where we return to a very conventional and traditional language. Just as El Jarama *introduced a melodramatic event at the end of a masterfully presented uneventful day, the shift in voice, point of view, and vocabulary at the end of* Historias del Kronen *betrays, in my opinion, its best accomplishments, which you have well described here.*

—Randolph Pope, in response

Glocalization: The key to understanding GenX literature, at least in Spain, is to understand how subjects use "imported" products within a given context. Mañas, for example, provides ample intertextual references to American and British popular culture, which require a second and third reading before one can fully grasp their narrative logic within the context of Historias.

—Paul Begin, in response

THE RAMONES

"With just four chords and one manic tempo, New York's Ramones blasted open the clogged arteries of mid-1970s rock, reanimating the music. Their genius was to recapture the short/simple aesthetic from which pop had strayed, adding a caustic sense of trash-culture humor and minimalist rhythm guitar sound" (532).

—Ira Robbins and Scott Isler, "Ramones"

Mañas's punk philosophy called for an emergence of youth cultural voices that did not sell out to contrived literary techniques.[5] He proclaimed the need to end the—according to him—artificial and imposing world around which "grand styles" had been valued by the literary establishment. He was referring here to novelist and essayist Juan Benet's 1965 ideas in the book *La inspiración y el estilo* [*Inspiration and Style*] in which Benet "attacked the *costumbrista* and realist traditions, including 1950s politically committed literature, arguing for the centrality of style over content in literature and the superiority of the 'poet' (the writer of fictions) over the historian (the latter merely constructed what was already there while the poet had to 'invent' reality)" (Perriam, et al. 170). Mañas believed that Benet's expressed values were still attributed special status in the literary arena of the 1990s, where other, more lyrically-inclined writers like Juana Salabert, Belén Gopegui, or Juan Manuel de Prada remained favorable sons and daughters of the literary establishment.[6]

> *The punk literature written by J. A. Mañas seeks to eradicate the grand style practiced by Juan Benet. Mañas defends the anti-style that emerges from the representation of violence and nihilism. This anti-style is characterized by anguish, orality, humor, argot, musicality, fragmentation, noise, transgressions, a ludic sense of life, and everything that antagonizes the bourgeois society. Mañas uses the anti-style as the punkers use black leather and chains.*
>
> *—Carmen de Urioste, in response*

Mañas was not alone in his criticism. Novelist and poet Roger Wolfe, born in 1962 in England but residing in Spain since his infancy, is Mañas's poetic soulmate. Categorized within "la poesía de la experiencia," "el neo-realismo" and "el realismo sucio," his work echoes that of Mañas and his GenX colleagues, especially those, such as Ray Loriga or Benjamín Prado, in whose writings one can perceive a more lyrical strain. According to critic Jordi Gracia, Wolfe's poetry applies,

un lenguaje desgarrado, la oralidad de jerga y las técnicas que se nutren de espontaneísmo, confesionalidad, [...]. Una poética de la agresión y del desplante con visos autodestructivos porque relatan la construcción de un personaje supervivente de sí mismo. La elipsis forzosa de la poesía y la construcción del poema permiten una rara forma de expresionismo lírico y abrupto—obsceno aquí, tartamudo allá, banal, soez o impúdico—con horizontes cerrados: nihilismo desafiante, autosuficiente y sin consuelo.

[a raw language, the orality of slang and the techniques that feed on spontaneity, confession.... A poetics of aggression and rudeness with self-destructive overtones because they tell of the construction of a character who survived himself. The forced ellipsis of poetry and the construction of the poem allow an unusual form of lyrical and abrupt expressionism—obscene here, stammering there, banal, raunchy or smutty—with closed horizons: defiant nihilism, self-sufficient and of no consolation]. (qtd. in López Merino 3)

Contrary to critics' perceptions of a dehumanized and commercially confused voice, Wolfe considers his own especially human, one that is not imprisoned in the "corsé retórico de la literatura" [rhetorical corset of literature] (López Merino 3), but whispers and even shouts out credible and live hardwires. He clearly positions himself against poets whose "ejercicios [son] vacíos, huecos, banales, frívolos, [y están] enamorados de sí mismos en el peor de los sentidos. Yo *hablo*; ellos *se escuchan hablar*" [exercises are empty, hollow, banal, frivolous, {and who are} in love with themselves in the worst of all senses. I *speak*; they *listen to themselves speak*] (López Merino 3). Wolfe turns the blanket of blankness and emptiness upon itself and wraps the "Stylists" within it. Like Mañas, he believes that behind the artificiality, surface, and exaltation of "Style" remains

> Wang Sho, China's Generation X'er, echoes Wolfe's and Mañas's sentiments when he says: "My writings are targeted specifically at one particular species—intellectuals. I can't put up with their sense of superiority and aristocratic sentiment. They think that common folks are all hooligans, only they themselves are the conscience of society. Isn't this aggravating?...I particularly want to attack this 'nobody else but me' mannerism" (269–70).
>
> —Jing Wang, *High Culture Fever*
>
> *By resorting to punk as a literary artistic mode, Mañas and his cohorts essentially demystify the stylistic and linguistic integrity of writers who belong to the literary establishment. Although one might contest the effectiveness of their novelistic message, it is imperative to recognize that the GenX audience is one that is fully aware of the ironic pose embedded in punk as well as the tantalizing allure of the virtual world and mass communication.*
>
> —*Yaw Agawu-Kakraba, in response*

absolutely nothing. Whether expressed in poetic or narrative form, this "nothingness" becomes the center of a true, real voice from the barracks of the young. In the process, it begins to mutate James Annesley's conception of "blank fiction."

The dissemination and assimilation of punk in the Western world pronounces a shift in Zeitgeist that uses culture not to escape reality, but rather to confront reality. Punk's emphasis on issues pertaining to city life, including alienation, violence, and commercial culture, adds to discussions concerning the problematization of new social constructs and its effect on identity in a changing world. To understand the role and importance of Mañas's punk philosophy within this changing world, it warrants looking at how punk was assimilated into a literary style, without disregarding its dictum to "tell it like it is." In the novelistic output of the 1990s, the intersection of punk, commercial culture, and technology did not eradicate the real for its representation. Punk aesthetics did not erase origins in order to expose a society of spectacle, simulation, or science fiction (although "cyberpunk" is an outgrowth of this), nor did it self-consciously entertain the role of fiction in the deconstruction of traditional narrative models.[7] In fact, according to Young and Caveney, Bret Easton Ellis himself sought "truth" and "meaning" and

Hispanists believe that GenX texts display a movement from the concrete to the abstract in which simulation and the hyperreal—concepts that define human's inability to distinguish reality from fiction—have consumed individuals' real relations to life and art. Contrary to this perspective, I consider punk's "pornographic" stylistics an *augmentation* of individual's perceptual experience, not an erasure of it. Mañas and his contemporaries do not present us with subjects who lose sight of their identities or live in a convincing illusion or simulation of the world despite, or perhaps because, many GenX characters say that their experiences appear to be *like* the movies or they reference television shows, video clips, videogames, or advertisements. When a character, such as the one in Ray Loriga's 1993 novel *Héroes*, locks himself in a six-meter large room and psychologically travels into the past and the future, intermittently referring to and quoting from pop and rock songs, he does not necessarily lose his identity *or* his reality, as Jason Klodt has suggested in "Nada de nada," but he uses music and media to enhance, expand, intensify, multiply, and reinforce his real life experiences. He does not lose himself along the way. On the contrary; he finds himself within and through a set of multimedia storytelling techniques that define a different era (as I make clear in the next chapter).

—Christine Henseler

For me, the question of identity within the context of consumer culture is inextricably linked to the notion of authenticity and its undertones of being "original." Adorno would classify Carlos's identity as false or inauthentic because it is constructed from a palette of consumptive choices, all of which are predetermined (or "predigested") by the culture industry itself. One could complain, for example, that a Spaniard wearing ripped Levis, Converse

→

judged and rejected the hyperreal (33). Punk ethos underlined the existence and importance of the real where it joined visual and verbal surface culture into what Mañas called "una pornografía técnica y emocional" [a technical and emotional pornography] ("El legado" 40). The surplus with which Mañas brings the ugliness of contemporary urban life into public light is an obscenity that in the literary scene may well be likened to the power of punk as a transcendental exposure of thought brought to the surface.

There is a clear relationship between Mañas's punk philosophy and a worldwide generational outlook that rejects artificially constructed fictions and witnesses everyday hypocrisy and abuse of power. As analyzed in the previous chapter, these repudiations are intimately tied to aesthetic innovations related to the development and acceleration of new media technologies as well as the influence of popular culture in everyday life. When one narrative pattern is rejected, another is embraced. Larry McCaffery, in the introduction to his volume *Some Other Frequency: Interviews with Innovative American Authors* (1996), underlines that writers in the 1980s and '90s retained an allegiance to realism's dictum to "tell it like it is." He said that it was the nature of the telling, as well as of the "it," that was transformed as writers increasingly recognized that fiction's inability to produce truth-functions concerning our shared postmodern condition in no way precluded its ability to render "the real" in a realistic manner (10). There was also a growing awareness on the part of our best writers that the "real"—of the self and of the world we live in—was not some discrete, isolable entity that could be represented objectively but was in actuality a network of relationships that could be rendered "realistically" only via formal methods that emphasized rather than denied the fundamentally fluid, interactive nature of this network (10). The representations of this network of methods and media technologies underline their role in the fictionalization of contemporary reality.

From Avant-Pop to Afterpop

The question at the heart of this chapter is how to coalesce punk's dictum to "tell it like it is," its augmented relationship to the representation of reality, the acceleration and heightened influence of technology, and a Generation X worldview. This convergence of distinct elements presents the key to a changing world environment whose outgrowths are materializing today. The cynicism, disillusionment, slacker-dom of the "X'er" of the 1990s displayed discontent and powerlessness. Their rebellion consisted in a retreat from mainstream society, a movement toward the margins, an escape into substances and media entertainment. These characteristics began to change as individuals learned to adopt and adapt their new environments into everyday life and art. The stereotypical Generation X mindset shifted and expressed different world visions, new leadership practices, more participatory and anti-hierarchical outlooks, and more integrative and interdisciplinary aesthetic practices.

In the 1990s, the answer to these changes, mutations, and recombinations on an artistic level may be found in what Larry McCaffery diagnosed in the United States as "Avant-Pop," a term revived in the Spanish literary panorama as "Afterpop" by Eloy Fernández Porta. In *Avant-Pop: Fiction for a Daydream Nation* (1993), a title derived from an indie-rock Sonic Youth

> *One Stars, and a slightly tight cardigan while indulging in the music of Nirvana and Smashing Pumpkins is an imposter, since this "grunge" identity is the derivative of a simulacrum that was born in a distant Seattle, Washington. On the other hand (and I believe this is the best way to understand consumptive praxis in GenX culture), one could try to understand how subjects consciously use and manipulate cultural artifacts to forge an authentic identity within the context of contemporary culture. Though "imported" and then adjusted to fit, this GenX identity is no less real than that of the religious leader whose life is based on a model that is distant by thousands of years and hundreds of miles.*
>
> *—Paul Begin, in response*
>
> *How different is modeling a life on the movies to Don Quixote living out chivalry novels, or Emma Bovary or Ana Ozores being inspired by books or the opera? That new signifying coordinates do not always provide good sense to the real world is one of the traditional plots of the novel as a genre. Perhaps there is great wisdom in the 1984 movie* Stop Making Sense.
>
> *—Randolph Pope, in response*

album from 1988, and in *After Yesterday's Crash: The Avant-Pop Anthology (1995)*, McCaffery outlines one of the most applicable models for understanding the changing social and technological effects on cultural production at the end of the twentieth century. McCaffery believed to be witnessing the emergence of a new age, one defined by what he called "hyperconsumer capitalism" (*After* xiii). He invoked Fredric Jameson's argument that the world as we know it had culturally expanded primarily because of the exponential growth of technology. This development, he said, had colonized both inner and outer emotional and physical realms in almost every country on earth (*After* xiii); it was a landscape, he clarified,

where the real is now a "desert" that is "rained on" by a ceaseless "downpour" of information and data; "flooded" by a "torrent" of disposable consumer goods, narratives, images, ads, signs, and electronically generated stimuli; and peopled by media figures whose lives and stories seem at once more vivid, more familiar, and *more real* than anything the artist might create. (*After* xiv)

How does writing, he then asked, and how must we, he questioned, "adapt within a landscape whose surface is *already comprised* of the kinds of signs and replications that had once been available from art?" (*After* xiv). Expanding to Generation X, how do writers produce a convincing sense of the exponential increase of sensory input and render in fiction the enormous changes that this increase wrought on people's view of themselves and the world around them (*After* xiv)?

McCaffery finds answers to these questions in the sort of organic amalgamation of postmodernism called *Avant-Pop*. The roots of this term are found in an album called "Avant Pop: Brass

---

In a *New York Times* article titled "30 Years of Making 'Avant Pop' Music," Mike Zwerin gives readers an idea of what Lester Bowie and his music are all about. He writes that, "Lester Bowie is a blue-collar trumpet player. A working-class musician. He gets paid for making music. Period. No frills, fanfares or tangents. He earnestly believes in this image and he hopes people see him that way." His common-man approach is enhanced by a punk-like no frills style that rejects involvement in any vocabularies not his own (such as government-sponsored grants), or doing anything that is not simply walking on stage or into a studio and making music. The article says that Bowie plays what he calls "avant-pop" music, which is a style that seems to reject the brass band's traditional approach to George Gershwin, and plays instead "Michael Jackson, Marilyn Manson and Madonna songs." He underlines that the difference lies not in "what I play. It's the way that I play it. It's not the repertoire, it's the interpretation." Zwerin explains that his "interpretations [...] feature the visual as much as the musical. There is a strong African presence. The stage is full-up with all sorts of conventional and ethnic instruments. African ceremonial designs are painted on their faces. They wear colorful robes and outlandish hats." This recombination of styles and genres add to Bowie as the guiding light behind the free jazz movement, which Zwerin defines as "improvisation without rules."

—Christine Henseler

Fantasy" (1986) by jazz trumpet player Lester Bowie. Bowie used the term to defy traditional brass band conventions and rather than play George Gershwin, he reinterprets popular music, from Michael Jackson to Madonna. McCaffery appropriated Avant-Pop to refer to the combination of "Pop Art's focus on consumer goods and mass media with the avant-garde's spirit of subversion and emphasis on radical formal innovation" (*After* xvii–xxviii).While not new in itself, and rather simplified, the subversive (and now elitist) avant-garde spirit of the early twentieth century is expanded upon through more active, collaborative, and process-oriented approaches. That said, both the Avant-Pop and Pop Art movements share a focus on popular culture and media technologies as a source of artistic inspiration, supplanting classical references (art, painting, music, literature) for consumer products, advertising jingles, and material stemming from television shows, movies, music, and other mass media. The difference between the two concepts lies in Pop Art's faithful duplication of popular cultural elements, which leave materials untransformed. Avant-Pop's goal, rather, is to create multimedia representations in print that speak to our current relationship to the multimedia manipulating potential of media technologies and their changing relation to reading and production. This activity may be marred by a deconstructive spirit—in the words of McCaffery, it may "confuse, confound, bewilder, piss off, and generally blow the fuses

But let us remember René Magritte's 1928 La trahison des images.

—Randolph Pope, in response

The historic avant-garde (HAG) artists were equally interested in collaborative, active, and process-oriented approaches (surrealist practice alone would stand as an example). For me the main difference is that the HAG was much more overtly political than the Avant-Pop, Pop Art, or any other "new" vanguardist movement has been ever since. The simplistic view is therefore: HAG– pursued political and cultural revolution in earnest; 1970s British punk– nihilistically ridiculed the established culture and politics with no hope, and, to quote the Sex Pistols "No Future"; GenX– a total ambivalence toward politics and cultural revolution. One could make the argument that GenX subjects might even prefer that others not follow their cultural practices in order to maintain a sense of having a more authentic identity in the face of mass culture.

—Paul Begin, in response

LA VANGUARDIA Y EL PUNK

"Del dada los punks recuperan el sentido lúdico, la conversión del estigma en emblema ('Dadá, dadá, es el Ya de los malditos') y la negación del futuro ('Llevo el estigma de una muerte apremiante / donde la muerte verdadera no supone terror para mí', dice Artaud, pero lo podría decir cualquier punk). Del surrealismo toman la obsesión por la ruptura de códigos, las asociaciones metafóricas, la subversión como política, el privilegio de lo visual (doy fe que las películas de Buñuel, tanto *Un chien andalou*, como *Los olvidados*, apasionen a los punks). Del futurismo comparten la pararefernalia tecnológica, la identidad urbana y el colapso de los símbolos por la proliferación de signos. De hecho, el punk anuncia nuevos lenguajes estéticos: fanzine, video, adornos, graffiti, etc.".

—Carles Feixa, *De Jóvenes, Bandas y Tribus*

of ordinary citizens exposed to it" (*After* xix)—or a reconstructive strategy whose intention it is "to create a sense of delight, amazement, and amusement" (*After* xix).

> ### AVANT-POP STRATEGIES
>
> - The improvisational, digressive structures of jazz and cartoons.
> - The slam-dance pacings, surrealism, and visceral intensity of punk and MTV.
> - Hypertext's reliance on branching narrative paths.
> - Television's flow of different worlds, its casual-but-intimate interaction between what is going on in the tube ("the programming flow") and the real world ("household flow"). [...]
> - The information-dense feel of advertising, with its flash of seductive images, microminiaturized narratives, and in-jokes designed not to convince but to seduce or gain attention.
> - The windows-within-windows structures of computer software and video games, with their dizzying sense of infinite regress.
> - Rap music's sampling techniques, with an endless recycling of "bites" feeding the hand that rearranges them into new aesthetic contexts.
> - Principles of collage and other forms of spatial, visual, aural, and temporal arrangements borrowed from video and cinema. (xxii–xxiii)
>
> —Larry McCafferey,
> "After Yesterday's Crash"

The Avant-Pop results of the 1980s and 1990s in the United States undermined or modified conventional plot structures, sequences, and endings for the visceral intensities of punk and MTV, the digressive structures of cartoons and jazz, the windows-within-windows structures of the personal computer, or the sampling techniques from rap music (*After* xxiii). McCaffery argued that the more kinetic, dynamic, and nonliterary formal manifestations of Avant-Pop narratives were first witnessed in the works of early, post-Beat figures like Ronald Sukenick and Raymond Federman, but also in rappers like Ricardo Cruz, hacker Marc Laidlaw, cyberpunk godfather William Gibson, Brat-Packers Bret Easton Ellis or David Foster Wallace, and postfeminists like Lynn Tillman (*After* xvii). While the movement began in the 1960s, it was not until the 1980s and 1990s that their work clicked with the developments of a televisual and computer-driven society, which eventually reached far into the twenty-first century.[8]

In 2007, Spanish scholar and writer Eloy Fernández Porta published his book *Afterpop: la literatura de la implosión mediática* (2007). Fernández Porta finds inspiration in McCaffery's *Avant-Pop* philosophy to talk about Spain's aesthetic and critical turn in the twenty-first century (Humanes 9). He prefers the preposition "after" to "avant" because he believes it implies a more extensive, historically posterior moment in which Avant-Pop existed but is over, and in which our deconstructive and negative positions have given way to attitudes of nostalgia, of fascination, of transcendence and discord with popular culture (Humanes 9). We live in a period, Fernández Porta argues, that can be defined as "el pop en la era de su disipación" [pop in an era of its dissolution] (Macgregor).

By this he means that although traditional conceptions of the "popular" still exist—the mass media, the object, the audience—new conditions have led to more fragmentation in the markets, to localized tastes, new audiences, new storytelling spaces, a wider reach, more interaction, and participatory readers and critics (Humanes).

In the blank space momentarily left empty by the nullification of the traditional pop object, Fernández Porta uncovers the hypocrisy and backwardness guiding traditional literary criticism in Spain. Using as examples novels by Javier Marías and Ray Loriga, Fernández Porta unveils the level of duplicity involved in the use of "popular" terminology by the literary establishment, essentially concluding that Marías is more "poppy" than Loriga when their work is analyzed in an anonymous, fair, serious, and comprehensive fashion.[9] Fernández Porta's subsequent call for an "Afterpop" aesthetic condition—one that naturally, simultaneously, and fully reads across, through, within, and between high and low cultural disciplines—serves to underline the need to break down what Mañas previously reacted against and conceived of as a series of stylistic iron bars still in place in the critical arena. The discussion boils down to certain critics' lack of ability or desire to converge literary and audiovisual cultures. Fernández Porta believes that they reduce some texts to superficial sites of popular surface culture, with little understanding that there has been "un cambio de signo del objeto pop, que desde Adorno hasta McLuhan lo habían teorizado como leve, fácil, superficial. Y cada vez más se convierte en un objeto sofisticado, que implica lecturas de segundo y de tercer grado" [a change in the sign of the pop object, which since Adorno to McLuhan

> *Creo que el momento histórico en que nos encontramos puede definirse como "el pop en la era de su disipación". Esto lo ha comprendido muy bien el crítico cultural Nick Currie —más conocido por su faceta de cantante, con el nombre artístico de Momus—, que en uno de sus artículos nos propone hacer un viaje organizado a lo que él llama "el yacimiento arqueológico de Disneylandia". En efecto, vivimos en las ruinas de la antigua cultura de masas, y ahí empezamos a definir un nuevo paradigma estético.*
>
> *Ahora bien: cuando digo "pop" no me refiero sólo a Disney, sino, más allá, a algunas supuestas modalidades de alta cultura que, de hecho, no son sino pop ataviado de frac. El establishment literario español, con su pompa, sus Premios Nacionales y su severidad, es lo más poppy que ha parido madre. Logos de editoriales como marcas registradas, nombres de autores como garantía de calidad, confianza ciega en el criterio de los mass media, desdén por los medios y editoriales independientes, búsqueda del "autor comercial de calidad" como Santo Grial del mundo literario... El autor poppy es el que publica en un suplemento dominical, con el respaldo de un gran sistema de marketing, hablando en un grado medio del lenguaje apto para todos y presentando un producto editorial que reformula de manera light la tradición literaria. En comparación con eso el escritor que publica en medios independientes es un outsider.*
>
> —Eloy Fernández Porta, "Retórica y punk en el relato contemporáneo."

Mañas's essay on "literatura y punk" anticipates by almost ten years some of the ideas that Eloy Fernández Porta criticizes the Spanish literary establishment for blindly categorizing in certain texts as "high" or "low" culture with no concern for close textual analysis. Fernández Porta believes the reading of contemporary novels has been limited to political friendships, to a lack of close textual analysis, and to preconceptions of the role and value of popular culture. He points to a book review of *Un milagro en equilibro* by Lucía Etxebarria. The critic considered it too *poppy* and vulgar on one hand and too theoretical (referring to a quote by Jacques Derrida, *La carte postale*) on the other. Which is it, Porta asks, too popular or too sophisticated? Porta believes that there is a generational divide in Spain that separates the authors born in the 1960s and 1970s, nurtured on communication and entertainment media, and those of all ages who have ingested the high cultural inheritance steeped in literary studies.

—Christine Henseler

had been theorized as light, easy, superficial. And more and more it turns into a sophisticated object, which implies readings of second and third degrees] (Humanes 9–10). He suggests that critics now talk about "low popular culture" and "high popular culture," the latter referring to pop culture's highly interactive relation to its metamedia expressions and the need for a new critical language to understand the new frameworks.

Fernández Porta's goal in his influential *Afterpop* book is to develop a high pop-cultural criticism that undermines traditional literary practices in Spain. He vacillates between suggesting the need for a new vocabulary and approach to an understanding of the role of popular culture in high literary texts and an acknowledgment of already existent models. This oscillation is indeed understandable if one considers that during the first GenX wave, narrative was already naturalizing the new, more immersive, and technologically driven mass media. In other words, Avant-Pop in the 1980s and 1990s, on an aesthetic level, was already demanding new narrative and critical approaches to make sense of a more pop- and media-driven society. Fernández Porta's choice of the preposition "after," then, highlights a disconnect between reading and writing practices in Spain. This is important since it points to an Afterpop sensibility already in place in the 1980s and '90s as first indicated by McCaffery, and it demands that we ask ourselves what a successful *Afterpop* critical approach might look like, and why it is that such a proposition is so hard to come by. Fernández Porta's book presents one example of how to conduct a *poppy* reading, how to apply popular cultural reading practices to literature. His book suggests that one should, "leer las camisetas como si fueran novelas, interpreter los relatos como anuncios, combinar la crítica libresca con la musical y el manifiesto con el dibujo animado" [read t-shirts as if they were novels, interpret stories like advertisements, combine criticism from the literary and musical worlds, and the manifesto with comics]. In essence, Fernández Porta asks critics to read, "la literatura con el pop, desde el pop, contra él y después de su fin" [literature with pop, from pop, against it, and after its ending].

Historias del Kronen by José Ángel Mañas, *Afterpop*

In this chapter I embrace Fernández Porta's reading of, with, against and after pop to spin the work of José Ángel Mañas into a new direction. The "popular," as it has been traditionally conceived, brings with it a value judgment seated in the masses, in the meaningless, and in the surface of television culture. In this analysis of *Historias del Kronen*, I take the "popular" literally by comparing it to Andy Warhol's Pop Art sensibility.[10] Warhol's cold and objective lens, repetition of sameness, representation of violence as "light," his flat artistic techniques, all contribute to present a deeply impressive series of events whose reality-effects are augmented through televisual techniques. The linguistic and emotional presentation of commercial surface culture in *Historias*—found in empty tones of repeated dialogues and events, in conversations and lives cut short—seeks to foreground the techniques of a new (yet decade-old) aesthetic: punk style in an *afterpop* critical framework.[11] This is a narrative that is based on a combination of commerciality (everyday speech and events rooted in capitalist culture); of technology (the character's televisual translation of the world); of an erasure of time, space, and affect (one body and event is like the next, emotion is dehumanized); and of a stark, almost journalistic representation of the reality of the 1990s.

Repeating by Not Repeating Precisely

The photograph on the cover of Historias del Kronen functions as a visual metaphor for a novel in

Douglas Coupland's *Generation X: Tales of An Accelerated Culture* in Canada/the United States and José Ángel Mañas's *Historias del Kronen* in Spain, combine the Pop-Art sensibility of Roy Lichtenstein and Andy Warhol with a new cultural sensibility steeped in technology. Douglas Coupland, a visual artist by profession, entertained a long-standing love relation with Pop Art. Warhol's Campbell soup cans inspired Coupland to become an artist and showed him that ordinary things could be viewed as art. When he first used Photoshop in 1998, Coupland started appropriating pop imagery from a variety of places and found that he,

> was able to learn about layering and gradation and cutting and pasting and…in the end I came to the conclusion that the 1960s Pop artists were merely dry runs for the year 2000 imaging software. For example, Andy Warhol's work was about cutting, pasting and cloning, while that of Robert Rauschenberg and Jasper Johns was about opacity, layering and filtering. (Coupland, "Photoshop")

Coupland's novel *Generation X* presents readers with a literary continuation of this Pop Art sensibility. Each chapter is presented in a box formation. The pages are justified, paragraph breaks are integrated into the text through a paragraph symbol, a box of pixilated clouds rests at its center, with subsequent pages showing Lichtenstein-like comic strips and a series of neologisms defining a new GenX sociology.

—Christine Henseler

which Carlos is as indifferent and as cold to emotions as the Warhol images suspended in gazed repetition. If we follow Andy Warhol's mantra that "the more you look at the same exact thing, the more the meaning goes away, and the better and emptier you feel" (Foster 131), then we could claim that *Historias* brings to the surface of the page the emptiness of an individual's take on life through repeated doses of sex, drugs, and violence. If, continuing with Warhol, repetition leads to emotional emptiness, then the cover of the 1994 Destino edition of the novel may best depict the outcome of this life led in the fast lane.

> *It is odd that the cover shows, mediated many times, an evocation of an event—a car crash and a resulting death—that could happen in the novel, but never does.*
>
> —*Randolph Pope, in response*

The reproduction of Warhol's orange car crash series (repeated fourteen times in the original 1963 silkscreen) shows an unidentifiable woman apparently dead beneath the hood of a car, her eyes staring defiantly at the viewers; two other subjects lie to the right, their condition indistinguishable to the naked eye.[12] The orange glaze that covers the photograph reduces the shocking effect of the accident as if providing a protective lens from its traumatic reality. The choice for the cover of the novel may have been a fortuitous accident, or the publisher, Destino, or Mañas himself, may have shown exceptional foresight into the relationship between Warhol's work and *Historias*. Whichever the case, the association makes clear that Warhol's art, "governed by the principles of interchangeability, multiple reproduction, serial repetition, manufactured glamour, and self-conscious commodification" (Shaviro 2), impresses upon the novel, the character's emotional emptiness, and the technological construction of his identity.

The cover of *Historias* triggers a repetition of Warholian-like car crashes. These are loud instances of metaphorical, and literal, deaths that crystallize the relationship between the flatness of the surface of emotions and self-representations made real through repetition. These reappearances are driven by a televisual framework of temporary subjects and conversations, of interchangeable locations and events, of an absence of character development, of a spatial and temporal framework emptied of meaning, and of superficial schematized repetitions at the control of the viewer's fingertips. In front of this televisual framework squats a dehumanized subject—Carlos—who materializes the emotional emptiness of a culture in motion.

> *Summer and vacation help in creating this erasure of past and future. As in other novels, such as García Hortelano's 1962* Tormenta de verano *or Aldecoa's 1967* Parte de una historia, *or in movies such as Antonioni's 1960* L'Avventura, *the postwar idle rich get into trouble. For most of the real nation the long summer vacation was less eventful and only increased in popularity during this period.*
>
> —*Randolph Pope, in response*

Historias del Kronen presents not only several stories *of* or *in* the bar Kronen, but a series of stories that are like the ones that take place in the bar Kronen. They are much like Warhol's silk screens in which he repeats "by not repeating precisely" (Wilson 4), and in which he magnifies repetition into "a theme of variance and invariance, and of the success and failure of identicalness" (Wilson 4). Whether at the bar "Kronen," the "Riau-Riau," or the "Barflais," social spaces seem to leave no identifying marks on the group of twenty-something youth that inhabits this novel. In the two weeks of the summer of 1992 in Madrid, Carlos and his posse drive from one bar to another and participate in an almost indistinguishable, empty sequence of drinking, taking drugs, and lusting after women. The bars, and events, become so indistinguishable that the word "Historias" in the title of the book ends up absorbing them all.[13]

> *The action of Kronen is located specifically in Madrid—the streets, clubs, and neighbourhoods all locate the narrative firmly in the Spanish capital. Even the cultural references stress the need to, in certain terms, reject that Spanishness, such as when Carlos claims that tortilla española is only for tourists or the references to the Olympic Games in Barcelona of 1992 or the Expo in Seville the same year. Thus, space and time are not irrelevant to the text but perhaps presented so by the protagonist.*
>
> *—Kathryn Everly, in response*

If one were to take a poppy approach and represent *Historias*'s narrative visually, one might liken the story to a black-and-white negative. In the text, the scenes of Madrid nightlife are never realized, they are never developed into a colorful picture with content and form in the sense that none of the places or characters (except perhaps Roberto) is detailed on a descriptive or psychological level. Carlos actually enjoys this rather superficial portrait of the city: "a mí me gusta Madrid. Aquí nadie te pregunta de dónde vienes ni se preocupa de si tienes una camiseta de Milikaka o no. Cada cual va a su rollo y punto" [I like Madrid. Here nobody asks you where you are from or care whether or not you have a Milikaka shirt. Everybody does their thing and that's that] (95). Every individual, in Carlos's version, has the ability to strip him- or herself of societal and commercial norms and do what he or she pleases. Fredric Jameson might liken Carlos's city image to Warhol's car crashes, in which "it is as though the external and coloured surface of things—debased and contaminated in advance by their assimilation to glossy advertising images—has been stripped away to reveal the deathly black-and-white substratum of the photographic image which subtends them" (557). Rather than a clean, clear, and textured space of socialization and identity formation, the text/subtext formula portrays a space of black-and-white depth that brings to light a crass documentary of contemporary life. Like in Warhol's car crash series, the journalistic photograph of the wreck, albeit flat, shines through the glossy pigmentation to paint a disquieting picture of reality.

> Carlos's vision of communication and community also likens itself to the view of sociologist Michel Maffesoli, who explains that the contemporary individual lives in a community that, "can be completely disindividualizing by creating a diffuse union that does not require one's full presence for the other (referring to the political); it establishes rather a relationship in the emptiness—what I would call a tactile relationship. Within the mass, one runs across, bumps into and brushes against others; interaction is established, crystallizations and groups form" (73).
>
> The emptiness that defines the GenX consciousness, then, is one that is being filled with signifiers that do not fall in line with modernist notions of linearity, presence, and truth, but rather within spaces, like clubs and bars, in which large numbers of individuals congregate, shift, move, and communicate in more physical than verbal ways (which the instances of screaming in bars underlines in the novel) (33).
>
> Maffesoli helps us understand that what marks the wanderings of individuals like Carlos is the act of "switching from one group to another" (76). Whether individuals switch from place to place, from subject to subject, or from channel to channel, they "can give the impression of atomization or wrongly give rise to talk of narcissim," says Maffesoli, for "neotribalism is characterized by fluidity, occasional gatherings and dispersal" (76).
>
> —Christine Henseler

A Generational Ethos: Literature and Television

Carlos projects himself into *networks* of communication before he entertains spaces of *human* communication. The use of colloquial speech patterns, semi-anonymous dialogues, one-sided telephone conversations, mini-chapters, and references to the mass media and popular culture join to represent a culture closely connected to media and communication technology. Carlos shifts from the television to the telephone to headphones and the car stereo with more ease than he does from one human being to another, technology resulting in more meaningful moments than human interaction. For example, while sodomizing Rebeca, Carlos emulates the rape scene he watches in *Clockwork Orange*. Not only does he place himself into the role of the protagonist, as many scholars have already noted, but once the act is performed, he returns to the movie and ignores the consequence of his violence on real life. In this space within a space, he uses technology to disassociate himself from the act—presence—not the after-act or the act that precedes the event. Violence is turned into nothing more than a flat and neutral surface of instantly discounted affairs whose reproductive qualities are of self-reflective proportions mediated through technology.

In *Historias* audiovisual media is, according to the protagonist, the main component needed in the construction of a generational identity and communicational understanding, references to films and rock and punk culture abounding in the novel as in other GenX texts. To present such a subject, the emotional emptiness and superficial portrayal of Carlos work together to construct an identity that cannot be devoid of its relation to the media, especially to television. In the novel, one voice may take the place of another, one female body for another (as Warhol's Marilyn Monroes), and one Carlos for another image of himself (as when he looks at himself in the mirror and finds his nose bleeding from too much drug intake). Detachment allows for a repetition of acts—driving, drinking, sex—that seemingly collapse into the concurrence of empty images, like a sound bite—a succession of different noise levels (such as shouts) and short, almost simultaneous pronouncements (such as telephone conversations)—in which meaning is reduced to a flash (Moreiras Menor, *Cultura* 208). Similarly, one of Warhol's most famous pronouncements was: "If you want to know all about Andy Warhol, just look at the surface of my paintings and films and me, and there I am. There's nothing behind it" (qtd. in Berg 56). Warhol's self-promoted construction of an identity, like Carlos's, is to be found no further than in the flat surfaces he portrays. Critics have wanted to find the *real* Warhol behind the surface of his images only to realize that the surface *is* the man behind his work and the meaning behind his art. Warhol "made use of the notion of surface both as aesthetic credo *and* as a provocative and polemical tool for establishing his own identity (even if it was an identity that insisted on having no identity)" (Gemunden 237). Similarly, the superficial, supposedly light and popular characterization of *Historias* is precisely where its value may be found.

Andy Warhol, whose persona has made many critics search for the depth behind the self-proclaimed surface of a man, could be considered the first embodiment of this turn toward a new ethos. In his book, *The Philosophy of Andy Warhol*, Warhol proclaimed the death of his own emotions by pointing his finger at technology, especially television and the tape recorder:

> When I got my first TV set, I stopped caring so much about having close relationships with other people...I started an affair with my television which has continued to the present...The acquisition of my tape recorder really finished whatever emotional life I might have had, but I was glad to see it go. Nothing was ever a problem again, because a problem just meant a good tape...You couldn't tell which problems were real and which problems were exaggerated for the tape. Better yet, the people telling you the problems couldn't decide any more if they were really having the problems or if they were just performing. (26–27)

For Warhol, television killed off his emotions. He admitted that "when things really do happen to you, it's like watching television—you don't feel anything" (Shaviro 2). His perception echoes the thoughts of Carlos, who believes that "cuando vemos algo que nos impresiona siempre tenemos la sensación de estar viendo una película" [when we see something that impresses us we have the sensation of watching a movie] (42). According to Carlos, he is an "[hijo] de la televisión, como dice Mat Dillon en Dragstorcauboi" [son of the television, as Matt Dillon says in *Drugstore Cowboy*] (42). At a birthday dinner for his father, he appropriates the television as an emotional guard against involvement in family affairs. Television

In *Historias del Kronen*, Mañas uses the aesthetic philosophy of Andy Warhol to present readers with repeated and juxtaposed linguistic and televisual subject constructions that rely on emptiness and ultimately subvert this empty emotional space. Mañas admits to doing exactly what Warhol inspires, which is to paint,

> igual una botella de Coca-Cola, una Marilyn Monroe, un suicidio o un coche estrellado. Es absolutamente indiferente a su sujeto. Yo quería trabajar un personaje así, también en la línea de *El extranjero*. Un personaje impermeable a los sentimientos, que intentara retratar lo que ve con la máxima objetividad posible. Este personaje sólo describe gestualmente lo que ve, lo que hace la gente y nunca se mete a analizar lo que significan sus actos. (Sanz Villanueva 33)

The protagonist of *Historias*, Carlos, emotionlessly lives from day to day, the discourse on his meaningless life increasingly simulates the televisual effects of repetition, pausing, and zapping. He wards away emotional depth through the obsessive pressing of the rewind button while watching violent scenes in films like *Henry, Portrait of a Serial Killer* and by repeating life's daily events (barhopping, having sex, and taking drugs). The result of this repetition is increasingly integrated into Carlos's psyche for the sake of subverting and ignoring his own lack of social and spatial significance. The more often the protagonist watches violent videos, the more violent his actions become and the better and emptier he feels.

—Christine Henseler

reflects the continuity and boredom of everyday life as scenes of war are increasingly evaluated by their level of spectacularity: "La [guerra] del golfo, con los moros, era más espectacular. Además, estaba mucho más claro quiénes eran los buenos y quiénes los malos" [The Gulf War, with the Moors, was more spectacular. What's more, it was much clearer who were the good guys and who the bad guys were] (66).

It is no coincidence that Carlos's deliberations about the news on television are framed by his father asking about his summer plans. Carlos's answer, before and after looking at the screen, is "nada," a response that leads to a paternal sermon and divulges one of Carlos's more critical comments about his own generation's need for rebellion. The silence, the *nada*, that allows this conversation to progress, is not embraced in and of itself, but filled with television and advertising images: "El silencio se alarga y miro la televisión.... Luego,... otro silencio... llena la publicidad" [The silence extends and I look at the television.... Later, ... another silence... fills the advertisement] (67). Television takes the space of feelings, but, more importantly, the medium gives Carlos a sense of control over his own life, since advertisements allow him to ignore emotionally charged family moments and videos allow him to push the pause or rewind buttons when he wants to fantasize, masturbate, or have sex to the scenes that best fit his present state of mind. Television, advertising, and music add content and context to Carlos's everyday life experiences.

In *Historias,* one televisual image follows another and a third, a fourth, and a fifth, all lacking effect or surprise. This effect presents readers with not only the boredom of the same old, same old, a mass-media take on intrigue and high critical value, but also with a sort of "zapping literature" of new technical proportions. Beatriz Sarlo demonstrates that the self as image in postmodern (video) culture loses all intensity because it does not produce "asombro ni intriga; no resulta especialmente misteriosa ni especialmente transparente. Está allí sólo un momento, ocupando su tiempo a la espera de que otra imagen la suceda" [amazement or intrigue; it does not end up being especially mysterious nor especially transparent. It is only there for a moment, occupying its time waiting for another image to follow it] (57). In the novel, this logic is presented through the role of human beings in Carlos's world mind-set. One woman follows another in Carlos's sex-capades, leaving no more identifying marks than those that connect the visual objectification of women to Carlos's image of them as "cerdas" [pigs]. Carlos uses people only to the degree that they are medium-empowering. Carlos's parents are only valuable to him insofar as they provide him with money to go barhopping, buy drugs and alcohol, and secure the services of prostitutes; he values his sister only to the degree that he shares a car with her; his friends' value lies in the drugs, alcohol, music, and videos they consume; and

Critics have interpreted the role of commercial and popular media culture in both *Historias* and Bret Easton Ellis's *Less Than Zero* as defining a detrimental world of stimuli overload. Excess appears to lead to a human's inability to digest cultural signifiers in healthy ways. But, we must remember that both novels include voices by the characters themselves and by others that place the extremity of this dehumanized vision into perspective. As Young has determined, the very existence of this level of dehumanization denotes vast outrageous affect. Within *Less Than Zero* (and *Historias* as well) "lies a furious subterranean humanism fully cogni zant of the threat opposed by all varieties of lack of affect" (Young 34). To generalize the negative effects, leads, I believe, to a dead-end road of deterministic interpretation that ignores GenX's influence on future paradigms. Michel Maffesoli adds to this point that "we have dwelled so often on the dehumanization and the disenchantment with the modern world and the solitude it induces that we are no longer capable of seeing the networks of solidarity that exist within" (72). Maffesoli believes that pointing to examples "of narcissism and the evolution of individualism [. . .] represents thinking at its most conventional. [It is] of little merit unless to illustrate the profound upheaval occurring within the ranks of intellectuals" (72–73). He explains that while in many instances social existence may be alienating, individuals naturally search for solidarity and reciprocity. In short, he theorizes that each era is defined by a particular style "which specifies the relationship we forge with others" (72). He underlines that today's "tribes," or micro-groups, arise "as a result of a feeling of belonging, as a function of a specific *ethic* and within a framework of a communications net

→

> work" (139). The individual and his or her sense of individuality, then, is more and more tied to the role of media technologies in the creation of a network of human connection.
>
> —Christine Henseler

> *When you discuss "stimuli overload" it made me think about its interest in the context of early 1990s Spain and about the relativity of the ever-evolving concept of Modernity and its literary or filmic representation. Global brands of drinks or cars, MTV and English-language music, music videos and films were modern then, but these are very dated when compared with the generations of 2000s and, even more, 2010s. Kronen was prior to iPods, iPhones, modern computer games (PlayStation, Wii , etc.), Internet film and music downloads, and online gaming. In fact, mobile phones and the Internet are not even mentioned in the novel. In recent years my students have commented on this a lot when we study the novel (and the film).*
>
> *—Santiago Fouz-Hernández, in response*

the value of female acquaintances resides in their potential for sexual escapes and satisfaction. It is no wonder, then, that those friends who distance themselves from these skewed images and emotions (as in the case of Carlos's friends after the death of Fierro) disappear from the circle of his acquaintances. Carlos can substitute—or "zap"—one group of "friends" in Madrid for another in Santander without much more than a fleeting look back.

Carlos's (in)actions ask readers to experience his world through a series of televisual "zappings" and "close-ups" that bring the visual to the surface of his raison d'etre. When Carlos's "best friend," Roberto, is given voice at the end of the novel, he puts the "blank parody" of Carlos's frame of mind into perspective. Roberto confesses to a psychiatrist the homicide of Fierro by Carlos and talks about the simulative powers by which Carlos entranced his groupies. Roberto says that Carlos, "nos veía a todos como si fuéramos personajes de una película, de su película. Pero él era como si no estuviera ahí. No le gustaba vincularse afectivamente" [he viewed us all as if we were characters in a movie, in his movie. But it was as if he were not there. He did not like to attach himself emotionally] (237). Carlos's absence from his own film denies his guilt in the action and reflects on Andy Warhol's premise that the repetition of media events (the imaginary creation of one short film after another by Carlos) contributes to the disappearance of the subject within the performance of his own storyline. While Fierro functions as a metonymic catalyst for a character crashing toward emotional death in Carlos's storyline, Roberto becomes a character in search of a new author to steer him out of the emptied image of himself. One could claim that Roberto serves as the prototype for the neotribal individual who, in Maffesoli's framework, seeks for affect and community within the same disindividualizing and tactile world inhabited by Carlos.[14]

The component that places *Historias* into a more critical and aesthetically valuable context is the pre- and postscript function of the song "The Giant" by "The The."[15] This song redirects the emotionless and flat portrait of Carlos's life within a temporal and spatial framework involving self-reflection.

This is an important piece of the puzzle since it is the insertion of music that disrupts traditional television culture for a more multi-dimensional critical interpretation of this and other GenX books, as I will highlight in the next chapters.[16]

The piece was written and performed by a "part pop, part post-punk, part poet for the disillusioned, ("The The") singer Matt Johnson in 1983. His album "Soul Mining" was said to "ripple with menace and tension; as Johnson broods and snarls his way through diatribes of self-doubt [...] and thinly-veiled attacks on the powers that be" ("The The"). The first lines of the song: "The sun is high and I'm surrounded by sand / For as far as my eyes can see / I'm strapped into a rocking chair / With a blanket on my knees" suggest a stopping of fast-paced metropolitan life as well as the existence and effect of traditional notions of time, which in Carlos's case, are constantly disrupted and ignored for a more synchronous, stacking, or zapping engagement with the present. Carlos's storyline defies traditional spatial and temporal patterns as he rejects the past—"el pasado es siempre aburrido" [the past is always boring] (83)—the

> ### THE GIANT by The The
>
> The sun is high and I'm surrounded by sand
> For as far as my eyes can see
> I'm strapped into a rockin' chair
> With a blanket over my knees
> I am a stranger to myself
> and nobody knows I'm here
> When I looked into my eyes
> It wasn't myself I'd seen
> But who I've tried to be
> I'm thinking of things I'd hoped to forget
> I'm choking to death in a sun that never sets
> I clogged up my mind with perpetual greed
> and turned all of my friends into enemies
> and now the past has returned to haunt me
> I'm scared of god and scared of hell
> and I'm caving in upon myself
> How can anyone - know me
> When I don't even know myself
>
> "La novela *Historias del Kronen*, de José Angel Mañas narraba las andanzas de un grupo de jovencitos de esta ralea, que se enrollaban, se drogaban y salían de marcha al ritmo de grupos como los Pixies o The The. En Madrid la sala Revólver—que aparece retratada en mi novela *Beatriz y los cuerpos celestes* bajo el seudónimo de "La Metralleta"—se constituyó en templo de esta selecta modernidad grungie, aunque existían otros bares, como el *Maravillas*, el *Agapo* o el *Louie Louie*, que también serían de obligada referencia. De la noche a la mañana un aluvión de grupos indies calcados a imagen y semejanza de los de la escena Seattle—Nirvana, Pearl Jam, Smashing Pumpkins...—inundó las estanterías de las tiendas de discos. Bandas ya desaparecidas o casi como Sexy Sadie, Australian Blonde, Penelope Trip...Nombres en inglés y letras en inglés" (130).
>
> —Lucía Etxebarria,
> *La Eva futura/La letra futura*

old—his parents for their sense of power and allegiance to a cause—and the weak—his grandfather and Roberto for his display of human emotion. The repetitive dimension of Carlos's life—"siempre lo mismo" [always the same] (215)—is only interrupted when his emotions are augmented through drugs and he flirts with death when by driving against traffic: "Vivir sólo se vive cuando se siente, y te juro que fue como un subidón de coca" [To live one only lives when one feels, and I swear to you that it was like a high on coke] (215). Similarly, Warhol valorized "stasis rather than acknowledging his own avoidable passage through time. Warhol was a voyeur; he wanted to believe death and old age happened to other people, but that in his case he could control or deflect it" (Yau 6). In both cases, it is the unavoidable passage of time and space that ultimately crashes into the technologically mediated space within which the two men desire to remain. In Warhol's case it was an inadequately monitored routine gallbladder operation that cut his life short; in Carlos's case, it is a song that turns the lens upon itself and makes readers rethink the flat televisual portrayal of life in the 1990s.

A Poppy Beginning

If we reduce Carlos's take on life to a set of insignificant references and events, to a deeply dehumanized subject reacting to a contemporary reality in crisis, our critical understanding of the novel will stagnate in space. But if we re-interpret the novel through a televisual framework that is ultimately infused by a dose of music, the narrative can be reactivated. For example, we can claim that Carlos's concept of life mirrors what Margaret Morse in the context of the television screen sees as "the representation of stacked planes which can be tumbled or squeezed and which, in virtual terms, advance toward and retreat from the visual field of the viewer" (115). His actions emulate spatial televisual techniques in the sense that, according to Morse, pictures are organized "by a mise-en-scene of light and darkness, and by proxemic indicators of nearness and distance within an unanchored situation" (116). Instead of perceiving life sequentially and temporally, Carlos brings events closer and emphasizes his role in their viewing or pushes them away to ignore their transcendental qualities. In the novel we can observe this technique when he interrupts conversations and debases their content, thus pushing people away, or he expresses his thoughts through continuous "blocky paragraphs" of short and quick sentences that visually take up the entire page and lack breaks. These sections contain information about movies such as *Henry, Portrait of a Serial Killer* (30), sexual encounters such as the one with Rebeca (34), a multitude of telephone conversations (43, 99, 124, 133, 188, 211), the description of a Nirvana concert (106), and one-sided conversations with friends—"escucho vagamente el monólogo de Amalia, que es como la voz en off" [I vaguely listen to Amalia's monologue, which is like the voice in off] (71–72). His telephone conversations emphasize the mutability and interchangeability of the individuals on the other end of the line since it does not really matter from whom Carlos buys his drugs or with which woman he has sexual intercourse. This nearing visual field takes over the text in chapter 14 during the continuous "monologue" of Carlos that leads to Fierro's death. In this nine-page, one-sided dialogue the voices of his friends are completely leveled through parentheses; they portray the erasure of the group's identity and Carlos's full and solitary immersion in his own video recording of himself (as the movie version of *Historias* directly displays). This lengthy "soliloquy" becomes a one-dimensional space that imprisons the "I" in the present moment with nobody to "pause" or "zap" the action.

María T. Pao believes that Carlos's strong associations with characters such as *American Psycho's* ("Americansaico's") Pat Bateman, together with his use of verbal strategies that mirror film techniques such as "slow dissolve," "smash cut," and "jump zoom" (252), transform him "into essentially a human video camera" and embody "the relationship between the act of look-ing and the act of consuming" (255). While it is undeniable that the novel furnishes a reality steeped in commercial culture and that these acts do indeed take place, the eye of a camera implies a critical distance between the viewing subject and the scene filmed that does not apply to Carlos. "Consumption" implies using up, expending, wasting, destroying, or absorbing an action. While Carlos certainly "uses up" other people for his entertainment, wastes his own life, and destroys Fierro in the process, he reduces life to an absolute presence in which time and space deny a before and an after. In other words, consumption implies a fulfillment of desire that is absent in this novel. In this case, looking becomes an act in itself, albeit an empty one, not a precur-sor to the establishment of a desire for an other. Carlos, in a sense merges the black and white negative of his existence with the orange Pop Art infusion of a commercially inspired rendition of life. The use of colloquial language and narrative techniques inspired by television and Pop Art work together to erase any perception of critical distance in Carlos, subsequently diminishing any critical distance between the novel and its readers.

The lack of critical distance that the novel inspires leads us back to Annesley's conception of the blank as a space in which both time and space has been erased and may be reconceived. As mentioned in the previous chap-ter, Annesley concerns himself with novelists such as Douglas Coupland, Bret Easton Ellis, Dennis Cooper, and Evelyn Lau whose works "offer images of extreme sex and violence—reflections of the body's commodification as consumer and consumed—in flat, neutral tones, providing a blank record of events" (Jameson 114). These blank copies, best embodied by Carlos, lack "humor" and critical distance as he moves from scene to scene always in search of disembodying experiences of sex, drugs, and rock music. Carlos

---

EL CINE DE LOS DESARRAIGADOS

Films that enter into this category in Spain include *Los golfos* (1960) by Carlos Saura, *La llamaban la Madrina* (1974) by Mariano Ozores, *Perros callejeros* (1977) by José Antonio de la Loma, *El pico* (1983) and *El pico II* (1984) by Eloy de la Iglesia (an incursion into heroin addicts), and most recently, the works that best present a youth-cultural search for identity in marginal social situations: *Historias del Kronen* (1994), *La pistola de mi hermano* (1997), *Barrio* (1998) by Gernando León de Aranoa, *El Bola* (2001) by Achero Mañas, and *Siete vírgenes* (2005) by Alberto Rodríguez.

—Christine Henseler

collapses his life's timeline into places where each day, bar, and city is like the next, where inaction reigns, and where lack of linearity and traditional plot development deny the construction of a personal and political history. His emphasis on speed and movement, in terms of his nightly *movida*, falls in line with what Christopher Stanley, in "Not Drowning But Waving: Urban Narratives of Dissent in the Wild Zone," sees as a denial of order and fixity, a way to disrupt spaces. Urban nomads, he argues, "seek not to territorialize or colonize particular spaces, but rather temporarily to reconstitute and reconfigure particular spatial forms and then move on" (52). Mañas's construction of Carlos's spatial "reconfiguration" may appear utterly empty to most of us, but it is precisely in this emptiness that a poppy generational ethos is born.

Chapter 3

Generation MTV

Bart Simpson: *Nothing you say can upset us. We're the MTV generation.*
Lisa Simpson: *We feel neither high nor lows.*
Homer Simpson: *Really? What's that like?*
Lisa Simpson: *Meh (shrugs).*

Around the same time that Robert Capa published his photographs of Generation X, John Clellon Holmes wrote an essay titled "This Is the Beat Generation" (1952) in which he quoted a conversation with Jack Kerouac from 1948. Based on this interview, Holmes conveyed that "more than weariness [...], *beat* implies the feeling of having been used, of being raw. It involves a sort of nakedness of mind, and ultimately, of soul; a feeling of being reduced to the bedrock of consciousness" (qtd in Ulrich 20). Beneath the detachment of the Beat state of mind lie "the stirrings of a quest" (Ulrich 20) that is not meant to disrupt or undermine postwar society, but rather to evade it by searching for spiritual meaning through new forms of expression. *Beat*, in the work of Kerouac, takes on a tripartite vision that includes the marginal, the spiritual, the

BEATS VS. GENERATION X

Many scholars, most prominently Adelaida Martín Caro, refer to the Beats as an essential influence on Generation X writers. While several elements coincide—in particular, the search for meaning, physical and spiritual escape or mobility, resistance to conformity, references to the ills of society, and the use of substances—it is essential to point out how Generation X moves beyond the Beats. One of the main components that differentiates GenX is its relationship to commercial and televisual culture (from one of antagonism to integration), the shift from the road story as a metaphor of self-awareness and finding to the road, as in Loriga's *La Pistola de mi hermano,* as a site of parody and commentary on social and commercial mores (in which even the road story itself is commercialized). John Ulrich motions to the testimony of a Cornell University student to point to a significant generational difference. The student "testified that 'I and many of my friends show symptoms of belonging to this Beat Generation. We all want to believe in something, or possibly be defiant nihilists. But we do neither. We are caught in between, left merely with a longing to believe in something'" (Ulrich 21).

—Christine Henseler

creative, and the artistic (the rhythm of bebop and spontaneous prose) (Ulrich 21).

The Beat's highly symbolic, personal, and self-conscious vision spoke to Generation X'ers whose own quests were quickly related to Kerouac's oeuvre, with sales of his novel *On the Road* quadrupling to 100,000 copies in 1991. But the Beats, remarks Katie Mills, had drugs and alcohol, not to mention sex without the fear of AIDS, to embolden them in their dharma. Alcohol killed Kerouac, and in the 1990s "jacking into technology [became] the transformative path for Generation X" (Mills 225). The Beats were the last generation to not grow up with television, decrying the black box as capitalism's triumph in universalization (222). In contrast, Gen X'ers grew up ingesting and identifying with television, the first of many new media technologies to transform their personal and cultural landscapes. In particular, the generation came to define itself through the rebellious and experimental videos of MTV, a channel based on music videoclips that spoke to these rebels so well in their own audiovisual language that teens used MTV and Nickelodeon to escape from the family without ever leaving the home (Mills 227).

> *En España, los componentes de la Generación X fueron los primeros en crecer completamente con la televisión en casa, de modo que muchos se autocalificaran como "hijos de la televisión" (Mañas) o "hijos de las pantallas". Este aspecto determinó, sin duda, la manera de leer y de escribir, marcando un "antes y un después" en la manera de apreciar el mundo y por tanto las producciones culturales —también las "tradicionales"— como la literatura, como demuestra la producción literaria de la Generación X. A este respecto expresó Ray Loriga, de forma crítica con el panorama literario español de finales del siglo XX, que "en este país la gente sigue escribiendo como si no existiera la televisión".*
>
> *—Eva Navarro Martínez, in response*

The influence of MTV on a generational ethos was as strong in Spain as it was in the United States, even if it arrived and was disseminated at a slightly slower rate. In novels written by Spanish GenX writers, references to "Emeteuve" abound either explicitly or implicitly. For example, in a passage in *Historias*, "Amalia calienta las pizzas en el microondas y las corta en pedazos. Comemos en el salón, cogiendo las pizzas con servilletas. La tele sigue encendida y la Emeteuve pasa un vídeo de Madonna: Laikavirgen" [Amalia warms up the pizzas in the microwave and cuts it into pieces. We eat in the dining room, taking the pizzas with napkins. The television remains on and MTV shows a video of Madonna: Like A Virgin] (*Historias* 127). In Ray Loriga's novel *Héroes* from 1993, the protagonist evokes the video recorder as a machine that allows him to recapture, repeat, and reembody emotions stemming from rock and roll songs. The young protagonist, who has locked himself in a six-meter-large room, watches Japanese anime in silence while listening to the Red Hot Chili Peppers at high volume. The emotional charge of this audiovisual convergence leads him to think of a series of disconnected material objects and elements from everyday life. The synergetic combination of speed through image and music makes him think of "todas las cosas que volaban por ahí fuera" [all the things that were flying around out there]. His thinking shifts between the inside and the outside as his narrative (or thought process) jumps from one element to another: "neveras, zapatos de cordones, autobuses, bombillas, supermercados, puentes colgantes, sellos, sopas preparadas, anuncios por palabras" [fridges, shoes with shoelaces, buses, light bulbs, supermarkets, hanging bridges, stamps, canned soups, ads paid per word] (25). Image, sound, and text clearly join to define the speed of life through an interiorized expression of material things.

This scene, which I emulated in a video remix (and can be found on my website), points to a very important phenomenon that gains contour at the end of the twentieth century: the increased mixing of media technologies by producers and consumers, or what media studies expert Henry Jenkins has termed "convergence culture" and Lawrence Lessig has called "remix culture." Returning to *Héroes*, then, one could consider Loriga a contemporary remix writer and the text could be said to anticipate the movement toward what we know today as an example of hybrid media. In other words, I suggest that the novel, as well as other GenX texts, not just be analyzed as a story set to a song,

> *Loriga's successful career as a film director and scriptwriter supports the idea of him as a contemporary remix writer. Camera angle, editing, close-up, long shot, slow motion all find a way into his narrative. Perhaps there is a close connection between his novels and his film scripts, which have been directed by such luminaries as Carlos Saura* (El séptimo día) *and Pedro Almodóvar* (Carne Trémula).
>
> *Given the fact that Loriga is indeed a film director, scriptwriter, and novelist, it remains interesting that he returns time and again to the novelistic form. There is something about the novel that creates an intimacy between reader and writer that film cannot. It is individual, intimate, and immediate, and the investment a reader makes pays off doubly.*
>
> —*Kathryn Everly, in response*

but rather as a vivid example of one of the first breakthroughs in the mixing of media on a narrative level, namely as a powerful example of "video clip literature."

Although critics have used the term "video clip literature" to define the structural stylistics of GenX texts, they have only done so on a superficial level, usually centering their comments on the negative, illogical, and emptying qualities of a particular novel.[1] My goal in this chapter is to question the stereotypes that a theoretical examination of music video clips has carried into the field of literary criticism and to survey the inner dynamics and potential signifying spaces of the videos through concrete examples. Contrary to popular belief, the medium entails a series of complex multimedia convergences that can enrich and augment critical interpretations of Generation X narrative. A translation of the medium's strategies in text allows us to appraise GenX novels, like Ray Loriga's *Héroes*, from a radically material, academically rebellious, and *poppy* angle.

<table>
<tr><td>

MTV SLOGANS ON INTERNATIONAL CHANNELS

- "MTV Every Day," "MTV Araw-Araw" (MTV Philippines)
- "Musical Tele-vis-i-on" (MTV UK—The "Music Man")
- "There's Something in the Water!" (MTV Canada)
- "Don't Give Up Your M" (MTV Australia, MTV New Zealand, and MTV Baltics)
- "MTV will make New Zealand music history" (MTV New Zealand)
- "Follow The Music, Follow MTV" (first introduced on MTV Italia in May 2001, later shown also on MTV France and MTV Portugal)
- "I Like…" (MTV Asia)
- "Because MTV Brings Out the Bitch in You" (MTV New Zealand)
- "MTV May Contain Nuts" (MTV New Zealand)

http://en.wikiquote.org/wiki/MTV_slogans

</td></tr>
</table>

The Rise of MTV

MTV was the brain child of Robert Pittman (executive vice president at Warner Amex Satellite Entertainment Company); it was launched in the United States on August 1, 1981; MTV Europe was first aired in Amsterdam on August 1, 1987, and MTV España was born in September 2000 (to be found at www.mtv.es), regulated by MTV Networks Europe out of Great Britain. In 1992 MTV Europe beamed to twenty-seven countries and claimed thirty-six million viewers ("Mtv Networks"). The birth of MTV was sparked by the desire to harvest the nascent videocassette recorder (VCR) boom in the United States and to develop new promotional tools (Gorman). In the beginning the cable station presented twenty-four-hour music video clips interrupted by on-air hosts known as VJs (some of whom became well-known celebrities). The first video shown in the United States was, tellingly, "Video Killed the Radio Star" by British New Wave group The Buggles (released in 1979); the song celebrated the golden days of radio and talked about the end of a career cut short by television (yet ironically indulging in new celebrity status on MTV). In Europe, MTV was launched with the song "Money for Nothing" by Dire Straits in which airing on MTV was ironically seen as a job much to be desired: "Now look at them yo-yos that's the way you do it / You play the guitar on MTV / That ain't workin' that's the way you do it / Money for nothing and chicks for free / Now that ain't workin that's the way you do it / Let me tell ya them guys ain't dumb."

Although the MTV legacy is steeped in an avant-garde approach to video clips and the creation of a new expressive style for young people in the 1980s, the station slowly reduced its music offerings in the 1990s and began to change with the advent of new technologies and more participatory cultures. Since 1997, MTV reduced its video rotations (moving from eight-hour-a-day music display in 2000 to only three hours in 2008) for more conventional television shows, including dance shows (*Club MTV*), animation (*Liquid Television*), and a host of influential reality shows (*The Real World* and *Road Rules*). Toward the end of the 1990s and into the twenty-first century, the station included more politically interactive programs, such as prodemocracy campaigns like *You Choose or Lose*, *Fight for Your Rights*, and the activism campaign called *Reflect. Decide. Do.* The development of MTV clearly changed over time and presented similar characteristics to those found in the shift from a GenX consciousness in the 1990s and the 2000s, including more reality shows, more participatory programs, a stronger Internet presence, and dozens of MTV music-branded channels around the world.

MTV's contribution on an aesthetic level consisted in the creation of "MTV-style editing" (the details of which I will examine later) that permeated a host of media outlets and entertainment, from *CNN News* and *USA Today* to cartoons, television series, and major motion pictures (as, for example, in the Brazilian film *City of God*). Although MTV expressed most vividly the speed of urban life in the 1980s as identified by Young and McCaffery, its editing techniques did not arise out of nowhere. Its antecedents are found in the surrealist work of Luis Buñuel (*Un chien Andalou*, 1929); the Dadaist results of René Clair (*Entr'acte*, 1924); Russian formalists such as Sergei Eisenstein (*October* 1927); and New Wave filmmakers of the 1950s and 1960s such as Jean Luc Godard (*Breathless*, 1960), John Cassavetes (*Shadows*, 1959), and more than sixty films by none other than Andy Warhol (Vernallis). MTV was generally considered an avant-garde station that attracted artists and directors interested in moving away from traditional (Hollywood) techniques and structures. In this regard, Ann Kaplan notes that, "video artists [often played] with standard high art and popular culture images in a self-conscious manner, creating a liberating sense by the very defiance of traditional boundaries" (*Rocking* 47).

MTV's mythology and rebellious nature was met with a variety of conservative reactions from its birth. Stephen Levy wrote in 1983 that "MTV's greatest achievement has been to coax rock and roll into the video arena where you can't distinguish between entertainment and the sales pitch" (qtd. in Beets). The sexually provocative and often misogynist, heterosexist, and initially diversity-devoid videos led the Parent-Teacher Association in 1987 to lobby for MTV to label certain videos with an "X" category (Gorman). Their desire for the "X" designation is especially telling, even ironic, when viewed in light of "Generation X." Gen'Xer's delight in claiming MTV's "inappropriate" content and style relied on the medium's "ability to package rock and roll music for popular consumption while retaining the appeal of the music's twin themes, sex and rebellion" (Gorman).

The rebellious aspect of rock's commercialization was not only exhibited in its sexually explicit content and fashion, use of foul language, and movement, but also in the speed of its presentation. Kay Dickinson, author of *Movie, Music. The Film Reader*, suggests that speed had been interpellating youth identity for a long time. That said, the X'ers relationship to speed was different from that found in works like Kerouac's *On the Road* or the experience of the Baby Boomers with rock and roll in the 1960s. For the "X" youth, speed was more all-encompassing, it was a way of life, and it was ingested "in b.p.m. [beats per minute], in increasingly commodified sports, speed the amphetamine which enables prolonged dancing, fast food, speed in computer games" (147). Contrary to the perception that speed leads to superficiality and empties the video clip of meaning, or the novel of human and cultural significance, speed in music video clips brings to light a simultaneous juxtaposition of visual, aural, and narrative threads that demands a much more sophisticated, complex, and quick reader. Youth's rebellion in the 1990s resided in the creation and appropriation of a language that few of their elders could follow.

MTV was from the very beginning a site of rebellion and liberation that clearly differentiated itself from the socially censoring dynamics of mainstream commercial culture. One of the best examples of MTV's power of subversion may be found in Madonna's *Pepsi* commercial from 1989 and the subsequent MTV clip of the song "Like a Prayer." In this advertisement, targeted at a mainstream, young audience, Madonna's song "Like a Prayer" was juxtaposed with images from her past (in black and white) and present (in full color). The temporal polyphony joined at the end of the ad when both the eight-year old Madonna, with a 1960s bottle of Pepsi, and the thirty-year old Madonna, with her 1980s Pepsi can, toast to each other and the older says to her childhood image: "Make a wish."

> *HAVE YOU SEEN THIS?*
>
> Madonna's *Pepsi* commercial:
>
> www.youtube.com/watch?v=LnIO4ChkPTY
>
> William S. Burroughs selling Nike shoes:
>
> www.youtube.com/watch?v=85zCwCQPDI8
>
> —Christine Henseler

When the ad first hit the airwaves, the producers' wish came true; it was a big success. When Madonna's own version of "Like a Prayer" hit the MTV airwaves, its visual content displayed an entirely different reaction and story:

> In Madonna's video she witnesses a murder, runs into a church in a brown slip, kisses a statue of a saint, makes love with a black man on a church pew, dances in front of burning crosses, sings with a church choir, and shows bleeding stigmata on both palms as though she had survived a crucifixion. Only Madonna could pull this video off—it is stormy, mysterious, tragic, violent, dark, and exciting. (Bego)

Needless to say, Pepsi pulled the ad under pressure, showing that a countercultural zeal could only sustain so much pressure. MTV, on the other hand, continued to encourage artists to combine rebellious or shocking material and cutting-edge techniques to identify with a "rebellious" young audience. It goes without saying that MTV made money and headlines with this magical combination.

By the early 1990s, MTV was not only contributing to the exposition of shocking or alternative content, but it was also mainstreaming countercultural popular culture, such as punk and grunge, and leading to a reevaluation of the relationship between commercial and subcultural dynamics. In 1991 MTV brought alternative music groups such as Nirvana, Pearl Jam, and Alice in Chains into mainstream commercial culture, and it continued to do so between 1994 and 1996 with punk rock bands like Green Day and The Offspring. While not erasing the existence of underground bands that rejected being commercialized, the station did contribute to and coincide with Generation X's own boom on the media stage. The commercial success and lasting impression of a supposedly anarchic, antihierarchical, and defiant GenX philosophy may explain why X'ers were dubbed the "MTV Generation" and were perceived as walking contradictions in speedy motion.

> *MTV YOUTH*
>
> Hispanist Santiago Fouz-Hernández, in respect to the globalizing advances and reach of technology and the media, considers MTV to be intimately linked to the identity of all Generation X'ers (91). He motioned to "[Douglas] Coupland's *Shampoo Planet,* in which MTV is mentioned as one of the 'chemicals needed to be a truly modern person'" (91).
>
> —Christine Henseler

MTV Aesthetics and Generation X Fiction

While many studies have contextualized and theorized MTV, most notably Ann Kaplan's *Rocking Around the Clock,* Andrew Goodwin and Lawrence Grossberg's *Sound and Vision: The Music Video Reader,* and Carol Vernallis's *Experiencing Music Videos,* the term "video clip literature" has become more of a buzzword than a clearly defined designation. In Hispanism, critics have used the term "video clip" in passing to pay nondeferential tribute to the supposedly superficial and overly spectacular dimensions of individual authors such as Lucía Etxebarria or Ray Loriga (Naharro Calderón, Bengoa). Other critics have taken a direct approach and analyzed separately the influence of television and rock culture on Spain's contemporary literary scene (Navarro, Steenmeijer, Dorca, Pao, Urioste, Henseler, and Pope). Only a few scholars have taken a more inclusive approach and applied the term to a new sociocultural reality and narrative style. Cristina Moreiras Menor is one of the few Hispanists who have detailed the literary logic of the video clip. Her definition emphasizes a fragmentation of narrative that gives way to,

> una presentación rápida y [...] una superposición constante de imágenes débilmente conectadas entre sí, insinuación más que tematización, imposibilidad de marcar distancia crítica con el espectador (éste se ve subsumido por la rapidez del acontecimiento visual, por la perpetua transformación de una imagen en otra) y, finalmente por su incapacidad (consciente y, me atravería a afirmar, deseada) de presentarse o convertirse en un gran relato.

> [a rapid presentation and a constant superimposition of weakly connected images; insinuation more than thematization; impossibility of creating a

critical distance with the spectator (who sees him- or herself subsumed by the speed of the visual happenings, by the perpetual transformation of one image into another) and, finally by the (conscious and, I would venture to say, desired) inability to present itself and transform itself into a grand narrative]. (*Cultura* 209)

Moreiras Menor identifies the effects of a "video clip narrative" as it relates to the presentation of events, characters, and reader responses. Although many of the attributes she mentions ring true, her definition still restricts critics' analyses to the abbreviated notion of an emptying form of communication through words like "weak," "impossibility," or "inability." By not expanding on the logic and possible meaning-making connections, video clip characteristics remain stuck in their negative qualities.

As Porta argues in *Afterpop,* the synesthetic complexity of music video clips is often denied value by those who still hold on to singular and linear narratives of high art. Critics have used phrases like the downgrading of the plot and characterized the medium's exposition as free-floating, decentered, fragmented, anti-narrative, and lacking substance. In the field of Hispanism, Carter E. Smith suggests that Mañas himself senses that "his MTV-like prose style threatens to become as banal as MTV itself" (10). He contends that the author's only claim to fame is his use of irony to create a critical edge, but the examples he supplies provide weak evidence of such an approach (which I view in the previous chapter, rather, as the workings of "blank parody"). Carter's remarks also ignore that MTV has been, as seen in the first videos to appear on its network and in hundreds of subsequent clips, a powerful metafictional and ironic medium right from the start, one that has often used videos to comment/critique its own form, content, and position in society. In addition, MTV's banality is quickly undermined when one watches videos like hip-hop artist Young Jeezy's music video "Put On," which comments on unemployment, record-high gas prices, and foreclosures in the black community through a hybrid documentary style set to an urban rap beat. To describe MTV as banal or apolitical simply underscores critics' lack of close attention to the medium.

Mark Allinson, who also finds the work of Mañas to contain little aesthetic value, echoes Carter's opinion: he believes the author's work is hedonistic, escapist, and lacking creativity (271). Allinson recognizes, albeit in negative and homogenizing terms, that a globalization of the youth cultural phenomenon has taken place when he says that,

CD-ROMS, the Internet and satellite television offer a diet of international consumption in which the standard communication mode for young people is the MTV style of spectacular, fast-moving, short-duration video clips. And the products promoted are also the same world-wide: a Doctor Marten [sic] fan in Spain, who is also into raves, piercings, fanzines, Beavis and Butthead and Tarantino, now has little to distinguish him (or her) from young people throughout the Western world. (271)

This homogenized perspective adds to the "desolate picture" presented in *Historias,* finding little value in GenX texts when compared to the work of *Movida* artists (271). Allinson takes exception to the "limited resurgence of Spanish grotesque humor among young creators, following the line that stretches from Quevedo through Goya and Valle-Inclán to 1990s films such as *Justino, retrato de un asesino de la tercera edad* [*Justino, Pensioner Assassin,* 1994]" (272), among others. What Allinson does not diagnose in this essay from the year 2000, one that admittedly lacks historical perspective, is MTV's role in the innovation of formal narrative strategies and the significance of those applications within a world in which globalization does not necessarily lead to homogeneity and lack of originality, but to those alternative and innovative third (local and global) spaces in which popular media culture plays a significant role in the creation of new hybrid storytelling techniques.

> *The Baroque, then as well as today, was an age of uncertainty, mobility and fluidity, and authors did not attempt to create homogenized pictures of the world. Just look at "Oráculo manual y Arte de la Prudencia" by Gracián. It is a treaty that simply helps, without explaining where the world comes from or how it works, to not screw up in a world without order and in which the only tool is wit. And just like today, Góngora and Quevedo can be said to hang on to form—not video, images or sound, but rhetoric, conceits and cultist twists and references—to produce their own subjectivity and positions as authors.*
>
> *And let's not forget Joaquín Sabina—Patron of Spain's Gen X generation if there ever was one—and the profound influence Góngora and Quevedo has had on his lyrics.*
>
> *—Juan Manuel Espinosa, in response*

Although many narrative techniques may be found in texts of previous epochs, "MTV aesthetics," one could claim, is born with the work of Bret Easton Ellis. Peter Freese, in his essay on *Less than Zero* subtitled "Entropy in the MTV Novel?" explains that although reactions to the book differed, critics did agree on two statements: that the novel was understood as an updated version of *The Catcher in the Rye* (1951) by J. D. Salinger, and that it could be classified as an "MTV novel" (68). When this text and McInerney's *Bright Lights, Big City* were turned into film, John Powers also declared that, indeed, "the MTV novel [had arrived]" (qtd. Freese 85). Repeated references to the protagonist, Clay, watching MTV —"I turn on my MTV" (12), "I go into my room and turn on MTV really loud" (40), or "I'm lying on my bed, watching MTV" (64)—to the novel's a short and flat narrative style, and to a prose steeped in colloquialism and speed undoubtedly placed the medium at the center of this new generation's attention and added to Annesley's conception of blank fiction.

> ### *LESS THAN ZERO AND MTV NOVELS*
>
> Readers' initial impression of formlessness and contingency in *Less Than Zero* was underscored,
>
> > by the fact that the 208 pages of the novel are divided into 108 very short chapters with an average length of less than two pages. These chapters are obviously geared to the limited attention span of both the drug-impaired narrator himself and the readers he addresses. Each chapter presents a self-sufficient slice-of-life, a short "take," as it were, defined in space and time and unfolding as a visible action, with the available "actions" limited to partying, watching television, driving around, taking drugs, having sex, eating out, and talking at cross purposes. (71)
> >
> > —Peter Freese
>
> The excess for which Generation X is known could be subscribed to the complex convergence of audio, visual, and narrative modes of signification as much as the elements that this coagulation leaves out: the names of characters, the absence of place names, a lack of activity, weak or inexistent links between the past and present, the absence of psychological development, the existence of strange or unlikable protagonists, and the frames' questionable dichotomy between heroes and villains. All of these characteristics encourage readers *not* to consider these videos/texts easy, light reads, superficial takes on life. They demand, rather, multiple readings in order to reveal the pieces of all that is revealed and concealed, all of the connections between the blanks. In other words, the novels ask you to reveal their "X" spaces, now definitely unveiling a plurality of sources.
>
> > —Christine Henseler

While most read the presence of MTV in *Less Than Zero* as just another example of the emptying qualities of commercial culture, a look at international novels such as Irvine Welsh's *Trainspotting* or Jàchym Topol's *Sister City Silver* displays a more connected set of stylistics. These texts, in addition to other GenX novels mentioned in the introduction, undermine traditional aesthetic expectations by foregrounding multiple (often anonymous) narrative voices, emphasizing the oral and visual dimensions of language, increasing fragmentation and points of view, shortening sentence structures that heighten the perception of cultural speed, and presenting colloquial speech patterns that, in the case of *Trainspotting*, almost demand an oral reading experience to understand the Scottish dialect. These GenX texts from around the world undermine one of the great tales—to continue with the "Tale" terminology I use in chapter 1—about music video clips, which is that the medium's signifiers are supposedly free-floating, and therefore insubstantial. To conteract such claims, Kevin Williams stresses that while,

> the video-logic of music videos is less narrative than musical [...] a musical logic is still logical. These "images" are thus not "free," and they are not "outside the control of normal sense and sense-making" but are, in their musical presentation, the stuff [...] given to us for sense making, and a way of making sense. There is at least an awakening of a way of "seeing"

and "speaking" the world, and at most the emergence of a new discourse or mythology. (98)

Williams defends the visual presentation of music videos reasserting that MTV's logic interconnects and interrelates music and images intertextually in what he calls "the mediascape of everyday life" (97). The process of creation is simultaneously internal and external, it consists in developing a multidimensional structure easily attributable to our contemporary YouTube era.

Moreiras Menor gives a good example of the instantaneous identification between the text and the readers as produced by video clip aesthetics. In Loriga's novel *Días Extraños* (1994), readers' vision is equated with the lens of a camera, she says, allowing for a heightened experience of the character's feelings, and therefore accentuating the affectual dimension of the text (*Cultura* 209). Williams underscores this insight by suggesting that "music makes sense of the world in part because it does not reduce the world to prose, information, or messages (although lyrics and programmatic music are free to do so), but moves the body and world as rhythmic, harmonic, lyrical communication" (99). The observations by Moreiras Menor and Williams blunt the supposedly dehumanizing effects of popular media culture for an understanding of music videos as a space where the sensorial, gestural, and physical communication, embodied in many GenX novels and in today's youth, can allow for augmented and multifaceted interconnections.

By emphasizing connections instead of isolations, contemporary critical discourse can accentuate the complex interplay of a multimedia and multidimensional systems of communication in narrative. This perspective cannot be denied in a culture that, as this book suggests, is based on convergence and remixings rather than the compartmentalization and hierarchization of cultural expressions. Given the subsequent breakdown of traditional notions of authorship, it should not surprise us to find novels firmly rooted in first-person narratives. These characters appropriate audiovisual media as expressive sites of identification and sense making, thereby allowing them to overlap, struggle for superiority, undermine each other, and play together in an almost infinite game of show and tell. What becomes painfully clear is that there is no *one* GenX text that can be representative of a "video clip literature," since each author presents a uniquely individual relationship to the machines that define their communication and entertainment habits. But, what also may be emphasized is that the multiplication of media events and their meta-media outgrowths allow for new and innovative aesthetic combinations that continue to spin and shape the direction and identification of Generation X in the twenty-first century.

Setting the Scene: Reading Music Video Clips

Literary scholars have overblown and distorted several music video clip characteristics, while they have nailed others right on the head. Generally speaking, I think it is fair to say that critics have judged music videos without closely examining the material at hand. In this section, and as a framework to a better understanding of my subsequent analysis of *Héroes* by Ray Loriga, I give a short overview of the complexity and logistics behind music video clips. I center my discussion on two essential elements: on one hand, clips' appropriation of blank space and on the other their complex representation of time. I rely on the close structural readings of Carol Vernallis in her excellent book, *Experiencing Music Video* (2004), instead of the more often referenced works of Andrew Goodwin, Ann Kaplan, Marsha Kinder, and Jody Berland, who take a more postmodern, theoretical, and, from my perspective, too abstract approach to the subject.

Vernallis examines the structural codes, processes, and techniques at play in music video clips, and she looks at the construction of narrative and antinarrative spaces, editing techniques, the role of actors, settings, props, spaces, colors, textures, time, lyrics, and musical patterns. She also supplements her incredibly thorough and valuable study with visual examples and supports her work theoretically and historically. Her book makes apparently clear that the supposed *banality* of music video clip aesthetics is a myth that has remained in circulation because of a lack of close examination of the medium.

In the first chapter of her book, "Telling and Not Telling," Vernallis presents the two interpretations largely attributed to music video clips. On one hand, critics read the videos as narrative constructs that function similar to television or film. On the other, critics, especially literary critics, view clips as an essentially antinarrative medium, "a kind of postmodern pastiche that actually gains energy from defying narrative conventions" (3). The truth is that music video clips present a large range of both narrative and antinarrative dimensions, although most of them pertain to the non-narrative genre. This is because videos follow a song's cyclical form and they *consider* a topic rather than *enact* a topic (4). In addition, music video as a rapid multimedia genre does not translate film narrative techniques very well, but presents readers with three stories—the lyrical, musical, and visual—in one space simultaneously. Complicating this tri-partite scenario is that sound, image, and narrative each possess their "own language with regard to time, space, narrativity, activity, and affect," (13) and shift in relation to one another. They do not usually merge or move parallel but might play against or with one another to emphasize a chord, a color, or a feeling; they might move into the background or the foreground; they might harmoniously dissolve in a variety of spaces and times, or contradict each other and create a disheveled feeling of textured unrest and defiance.

> ### *VIDEO CLIP EDITING*
>
> "It may be helpful to picture the succession of images in a video, and the edits that join them, more as a necklace of variously colored and sized beads than as a chain. This picture not only emphasizes the heterogeneity of shots in music video, but it also suggests the materiality of the edit itself. Indeed, sometimes the edit seems to function as a part of the image and sometimes as a gap" (28).
>
> —Carol Vernallis

Video editing can respond to modulations in the music; it can elucidate a particular element of a song, rhythm or lyrics; or it can function as a counterpoint to other elements of the clip, never allowing one feature to gain the upper hand. Although we certainly cannot hear the musical references in GenX literature, for a true experience critics might want to listen to or even watch the music videos of the songs while reading the text. Not only does this reading experience heighten the emotional and rhythmic charge of the narrative, but it also emphasizes the well-worn idea that life experience is often captured or enhanced by a song and/or an image. How does it sound and feel to get physically and emotionally charged by The Door's "Light My Fire"? What is the effect of watching anime while listening to the Red Hot Chili Peppers? In *La pistola de mi hermano*, Loriga prefaces the novel with an epigraph that says, "Leave those kids alone." The meaning of this song in relation to the text becomes no clearer than in the music video clip of Pink Floyd's disturbing *Another Brick in the Wall* album. When read in light of this clip, the entire novel is relocated within a more sociopolitical and charged framework, thus undermining right from the start readings that might point to music and television as "popular" (read "empty") sites of signification.

When we watch music videos, we are often left with dozens of questions and untied plot developments that create a sense of unsettlement and uncentering.[2] This emotion, enhanced by rapid editing techniques, is a characteristic that is often referenced to undermine the value of music video clips. In line with my overarching analysis of Generation X narrative as "blank fiction," Vernallis underlines that the reason why music videos function like puzzles is because "each of music video's media—music, image, and lyrics—are to some extent blank" (13). Music videos, initially conceived as advertisements set in motion, started as marketing devices that gained "from holding back information [and] confronting the viewer with ambiguous or unclear depictions" (4). Videos were not meant to tell stories, and if there was a story, it existed only in the dynamic relation between the song and the image as they unfolded in time (4).

A good example of this interrelationship among media and its unfolding in time is Erykah Badu's video "Love of My Life." This 4.20-minute video begins by emulating storytelling conventions and presenting script-written words on the camera screen: "Once Upon a Time on the Planet, Somewhere a Bombastic Beat was Born…Let's Call Her Hip Hop," followed by the words, "A Story by Eyrkah Badu." The narrative quality and the lyrics of the song intersect with a series of fragmented and rapidly changing scenes from the past (childhood and adolescence) and the present (adulthood), as well as changing genres and rhythms, such as break dancing, segments from a feature film, mug shots, the spoken word, male hip-hop voices and dance numbers, and slightly disturbing slow-downs of music and image. The story of "hip-hop" intersects with the fictitious love story and life of Erykah Badu, presenting a rapid, complex, and fascinating interplay between voices, rhythms, and narratives over time.

Erykah Badu's video is a good example of a piece whose complexity can lead to utter confusion, decenteredness, and rejection, or to fascinating, multileveled interpretations. The viewers' role in this process is, certainly, much more active than a linear narrative might demand (even though this video presents a temporal linearity). In fact, critics' unsettled position before videos like Badu's speaks to the goal of creating "a sense that any element can come to the fore at any time" (Vernallis 27) and of maintaining a perception of openness—what some might read as *blankness* in the context of Generation X or as *innovation* (open source and remixing) in the context of new media.

The empty spaces that define music video clip editing may or may not be filled in with sensical meaning. In fact, it is the site of difference, the presence of an unexpected image or voice or action that makes the audience pay attention to the clip. For example, Eminem's video clip "Guilty Conscience" is a fascinating representation in which the voice of a white, middle-aged crime investigator, in suit and tie, presents the crime scenes that Eminem and Dr. Dre react to in bad/good roles. In this clip, the transference of the voice of a reality television show like *America's Most Wanted* or *Cops* injects itself into the representation of the song. This unexpected framing device helps interrelate the narrative of the song with the short stories of individual cases in a hybrid docufiction format.

The "yoking" of different media allows us to see music video clips as an inherently hybrid medium. Not only does this hybridity concern the interplay of the visual, verbal, and textual, but also how these interconnections can cross the traditional boundaries and create unexpected, unusual, and powerful messages. The medium can allow for significant and self-conscious social and political content, and even political commentary and savvy—such as when during the 2008 presidential campaign, Barack Obama appropriated the gesture of "brushing off" his shoulder during a speech from hip-hop artist Jay-Z's video "Dirt Off Your Shoulders," and immediately connected with a certain audience. Other examples include the song "Megalomaniac" by Incubus, which comments on power, self-exhaltation, and destructive behavior through a surreal collage of historical and urban images in which barbed wires and flying Hitlers absurdly critique the brainwashing of a population through the media. In Coldplay's song "Don't Panic," technology allows for a representation of the band members as paper cutouts, literally showing the effects of environmental destruction through comic-like figures floating through a natural disaster.

Similar to GenX texts, time in music video clips, says Vernallis, is indefinite rather than exact, never definitive of the day or the moment. This is a point worth emphasizing because all too often, Hispanists have criticized GenX'ers' narrative expression of time as "lacking multidimensionality." Gonzalo Navajas, for example, contends that "presentness or strict placement of text in the present time is reflected in the narrative mode of these works in which temporal multidimensionality is absent" ("A Distopian" 6). I do not fully agree with this assessment since, although GenX narrative may emphasize the present, a temporal multidimensionality still takes place. As I demonstrate later, a novel such as Loriga's *Héroes* presents a complex and multidimensional temporal and spatial collage whose manifestations are simply not expressed in traditional ways. A representation of the present, as music videos pronounce, is created through synchronous yuxtapositions of the past, present, and future, and through simultaneous perceptions of time in one or more spaces. In other words, advances in media technology have allowed artists to reconceive the way they experience and express personal and political histories through time and space.

For Manuel Castells, the concept of "timeless time," or what many critics have referred to as an absence of time or ahistoricity in postmodernism, does not hold true. He believes that critics must add something new to their discussions by relying on,

> the specificity of new cultural expressions, [individuals'] ideological and technological freedom to scan the planet and the whole of history of humankind, and to integrate, and mix, in the supertext any sign from anywhere, from the rap culture of American ghettos, mimicked a few months later in the pop groups of Taipei or Tokyo, to Buddhist spiritualism transformed in electronic music. The eternal/ephemeral time of the new culture does fit with the logic of flexible capitalism and with the dynamics of the network society, but it adds its own, powerful layer, installing individual dreams and collective representations in a no-time mental landscape. (493)

"Bring Me to Life," by Evanescence

In "Bring Me to Life," by Evanescence, the idea of "waking up" is literally presented by a sleeping/sleepwalking singer who wanders the outside top edge of her building to find her "answer" (lover/ singer). Before she reaches his window, she sees the scenes that take place in each room. She is confronted by images of social conformity, boredom, and performance, while the lyrics go:

> "How can you see into my eyes
> like open doors
> leading you down into my core
> where I've become so numb without a soul my spirit sleeping
> somewhere cold
> until you find it there and lead it
> back home."

When she reaches her (rock) star/lover, when the harmony of voices joins, he is unable to save her from falling. Her fall from high altitude and into space contrasts with the interior spaces and faces of sadness and disgust, thus suggesting freedom in the fall, with a camera's span across the building tops.

—See the music video at: www.youtube. com/watch?v=3YxaaGgTQYM

Castells finds that the mixing of personal "times in the media, within the same channel of communication and at the choice of the viewer/interactor, creates a *temporal collage*, where not only genres are mixed, but their timing becomes synchronous in a flat horizon, with no beginning, no end, no sequence" (492). The merging of all times, he argues, "is the recurrent theme of our age's cultural expressions, be it in the sudden flashes of video clips or in the eternal echoes of electronic spiritualism" (494), a view that echoes the work of Larry McCaffery on one hand and, as will become clear in subsequent chapters, that of Agustín Fernández Mallo and his *Mutantes* colleagues on the other.

While the merging of times might not allow for an immediate recognition of synchronicity, and, upon first sight may appear hollow or empty, a closer look often unravels its coalescent components. For example, in Félix Romeo's *Dibujos animados* (1995), the narrative jumps from disturbing scenes and references to death and dying to moments in which characters reappear and are continuously revived, as in the Wile E. Coyote and Road Runner cartoon series or films such as *The Invasion of the Body Snatchers*. The effect is a profound reflection on the life and pain of the protagonist through a multidimensional and intersecting set of seemingly unrelated time frames: the finite frames of human life and the infinite revivals of cartoon characters. The temporal collage at play in Generation X texts, contrary to its appearance as flat and insignificant, represents, rather, a way of expressing personal histories within the coordinates of contemporary (media) culture.[3]

To strengthen this argument on temporal complexity, I return to Eminem's "Guilty Conscience" video. Just as the characters in this clip are about to entertain a criminal act, the camera freezes their motion and Eminem and Dr. Dre sing to opposing morals and values. Time stops. The clip literally allows for a change in the direction of the storyline (presented through dizzying camera angles) while the video and its song continue. This multidimensionality of temporal perceptions evokes Vernallis's observation that each medium can suggest different types of time, and each can undercut or put into question the temporality of another medium (14). Even when image, music, and sound converge seemingly harmoniously, one may shift into the background and linger in palpable ways, it may change and shift in relation to another, or it may be riddled with its own ellipsis (Vernallis 14). In other words, narrative tempo is presented in constantly changing shapes and forms of dizzying, albeit fascinating proportions.

Music videos also powerfully highlight differences in perceptions of space, as determined by

> Technological access to the world's cultural products and social and political events allows for a heightened consciousness of space and juxtaposition of spaces. The watching of films and television shows, the listening of similar types of music all over the world, understandably suggests a minimization and erasure of space. But we should not forget that individuals, no matter how global their experiences, are still embodied in time and space and their identities are determined by both physical and virtual, both global and local forces—"people, as long as they are physical beings, cannot but live and act in space, and the spaces they create reflect and shape social life in its totality" (Stadler 141). I concur with Castells who believes that "contrary to postmodern visions of finality, time and space are fundamental categories of social life and cannot disappear. Computer networks are not black holes. At one point, the negative, quantitative dynamic of compression (less space, less time) turns into a qualitative new condition (a new type of space/time)" (Stadler 146). Transformation should not, and cannot, deny embodiment, but should, instead, play at the intersecting boundaries between movement and stasis.
>
> —Christine Henseler

new media technologies. For example, and to transition into my analysis of *Héroes*, although the protagonist of the novel locks himself into a small interior space, he is able to "wake up inside" and explore a variety of constantly changing exterior spaces through references to dreams; rock and roll songs and artists; and a variety of first-, second-, and third-person narrators and interlocutors. Moreover, by shifting from one virtual place to another, he seems to acquire a better sense of personal direction. Similarly, one of music videos' greatest pleasures is the ability to extend our sense of inside/outside beyond that of concrete physical boundaries and the capacity to guide us through an unfolding of multiple times and spaces (Stadler 111). This stability and fluidity between inside and outside spaces is most beautifully expressed in a video by Oren Lavie called "Her Morning Elegance." In this clip a white bed becomes the scenic background for two figures whose movements reimagine seasons, emotions, and events. This beautiful music video demonstrates the power of technology in juxtaposing interior and exterior spaces in an ever-changing and imaginative dynamic, the result being an innovative take on life and art in motion.

What is Video Clip Literature?: *Héroes* by Ray Loriga

Desde que Bob Dylan triunfó sin saber cantar,
la posmodernidad nos enseñó que no hace falta
ser un erudito para conmover.[4]

—*Agustín Fernández Mallo*

In March 2003, the Spanish culture magazine *La Revista* of *El Mundo* published a special issue in honor of Bob Dylan called "Dylan en versión española." This homage presented seven Spanish singers, including Julián Hernández of the punk rock group *Siniestro Total* and Ray Loriga and his wife, singer-songwriter Christina Rosenvinge. They each chose one of Dylan's album covers and re-created the photo in dress and pose, adding a short and personal letter of their own. Loriga and Rosenvinge fancied Dylan's 1963 debut album, *Freewheelin'*, which showcased a photo of twenty-one-year-old Dylan with his then-girlfriend Suze Rotolo. The photograph was taken at the corner of Jones Street and West 4th Street in Greenwich Village, New York, just a few yards away from where they lived. For the Spanish couple, the image spoke to their own experience in New York City from 1999 to 2004, from which was born Loriga's 2004 novel *El hombre que inventó Manhattan*.

> *TO SEE THE LORIGA/DYLAN ALBUM COVERS, GO TO:*
>
> w w w . 3 a m m a g a z i n e . c o m /litarchives/2004/jan/interview_ray _loriga.html

In Loriga's compilation of essays, *Días aún más extraños* (2007), it becomes clear why the author was included in this project. In the piece titled "Gracias, Señor Dylan," he explains that if his son were to ask him why we were born, Loriga would answer: "para escuchar discos de Bob Dylan" [to listen to Bob Dylan records] (51):

En un mundo perfecto todos y todas, vascos y vascas, seríamos Bob Dylan y
en lugar de carnets de identidad tendríamos números de teléfono, para llamar
y para que nos llamen. Habría religiones, a pesar de Lennon, pero no iglesias y
cada uno de nosotros llevaría dentro una estampa de Dios, con los rasgos de su
propia cara. Un rosario con cuentas de nuestra vida, la cruz de nuestros brazos
y más fe en nuestros errores que en nuestras virtudes. Y un espejo por altar, y
en el escapulario, una foto de Bob Dylan.

[In a perfect world all of us, Basque women and men, would be Bob Dylan
and instead of IDs we would have telephone numbers, to call and be called.
There would be religions, despite Lennon, but no churches and each one of us
would carry within us a holy card of God, with the features of our own face.
A rosary with the beads of our lives, the cross of our arms and more faith in
our errors than in our virtues. And a mirror as an altar, and on the scapular, a
photo of Bob Dylan.] (52)

The religion, then, to which Loriga subscribes places Dylan's image on a
scapular as a symbol of faith, but also as a protecting object against physical
or spiritual dangers. Yet instead of a photo of the musician on the altar of
the literary scene, the author places himself on the cover of his second novel,
Héroes, within which can be heard the ringing tones and tunes calling out
to Dylan and friends.

Loriga's work has generally been described as simulating records,
Polaroids, photo albums, sound bites, videos or tape recorders, of words
turned into images and into song. These definitions speak to Loriga's
early beginnings in the underground magazine scene of the 1980s *Movida
madrileña*. At the age of eighteen, Loriga worked at a magazine often fre-
quented by figures such as Almodóvar and headed by photographer Alberto
García-Alix (b. 1956). In Loriga's first three novels—*Lo peor de todo* (1992),
Héroes (1993), and *Caídos del cielo* (1995)—his use of often crass, colloquial
language to describe urban life and growing up mirrors much of the work
of not only Mañas and his contemporaries, but also of García-Alix. The photographer engaged with subjects such as junkies and prisoners, tattooed, and
porn stars in black and white, frontal, and almost documentary takes on real
life (what he terms "pura vida"). In addition, the later collaborative work
with Almodóvar in *Live Flesh* led Loriga to extensive filmmaking and a visual
approach to the representation of the real influenced by one of the greatest
punksters of them all—Pedro. In other words, his love for music *and* his
work in film joined to define Loriga's GenX worldview from an early age.

Eva Navarro Martínez is one of the few critics who has recognized
the highly innovative quality of audiovisual material in *La novela de la
Generación X*. She superbly details some of the narrative techniques
derived from the formal and lyrical compositions of music in the work
of GenX writers. She says that the novels of Loriga, Mañas, Prado, and
Macstrc all present certain parallels with the work of Bob Dylan, Nirvana,
David Bowie, Lou Reed, or Jim Morrison. In *Héroes*, for example, Loriga
often plays with one idea (such as the loss of his brother's ear), repeats
it, and ends at the same place he began. The repetition of the same idea

expressed in short phrases in an entire paragraph simulates the verse of rock songs (138). Loriga also uses many periods and commas and simple phrases without connecting prepositions to emphasize the closed and independent nature of each sentence, one that disrupts narrative continuity (139). His prose converges the highly lyrical with the crass and mundane, much like in song and melody. The novel's short and disconnected chapters allow readers to either read the novel sequentially or open the book to any chapter, skipping from one "tune" to another. Navarro Martínez elucidates that the reappearance of certain images in *Héroes* and *Caídos del cielo* functions similarly to the lines of a chorus and that time and space take on a more simultaneous and intercalated dimension (139).

Ignacio Echevarría has declared that "en el campo de la joven narrativa española, Ray Loriga es, hoy por hoy, una estrella de rocanrol" [in the field of young Spanish narrative, Ray Loriga is today, a rock and roll star] ("Un artista"). This stardom is impressed on the

> *La influencia de la música rock en las novelas de la Generación X, y muy especialmente en* Héroes *de Ray Loriga, no sólo está en adoptar la estructura lírica de las canciones, sino también —y con igual importancia— en la temática, que actúa en completa simbiosis con el tono de la obra literaria misma. Su carácter intertextual demuestra que la polygenesis de estas novelas (no sólo literaria sino también musical, audiovisual, etc.) es, más que un mero recurso estético, una muestra de que una obra literaria, como cualquier otro producto cultural, no es un hecho aislado (Kristeva) sino que se crea en simbiosis con otros elementos de su tiempo. Así lo reconoce el propio Loriga cuando se pregunta qué significan las raíces en una época en la que gracias a la televisión te conectas a todo el mundo. Tal vez el postmodernismo ha acentuado este aspecto, pero la intertextualidad es tan antigua como la producción literaria y artística misma. Es importante por eso, saber apreciar estas obras en toda su complejidad antes de ver —como hizo, en general, la crítica española— la introducción de la cultura "no literaria" o la cultura popular como un handicap de las mismas. Estas novelas son un claro reflejo de la cultura global y española de su tiempo: de las convergencias culturales internacionales y de la explosión de la cultura audiovisual en España.*
>
> —Eva Navarro Martínez, in response

cover of his novel *Héroes*, which displays a photograph of the author himself. Although Loriga originally wanted a different image (for which he could not get the copyright), he thought that the reproduction of himself would make sense because this book was made "con el espíritu de un 'disco sin música'" [with the spirit of a 'record without music'] ("El hombre"). Although various critics, and Loriga himself, conceived of his novel *Héroes* as a record—"de tanto pretenderlo, este libro parece casi un disco [from wanting to be one so badly, this book seems almost like a record]" (Echevarría)—in my mind such a characterization simplifies the result of his audio *and* visual writing style. Rock in this text creates a dialogue between a variety of voices and images as rock stars take on voice, figure, and mythical roles. The novel simulates music video clip aesthetics by amplifying a quality that has always been operative in rock, namely

Cover Photograph of the novel *Héroes* by Ray Loriga.
With special thanks to Ray Loriga for permission to reproduce the cover of his novel.

its status as an art between sense and non-sense, communication and noise, form and meaning. Already rock plays aurally on a dialectic in which words hover between sound and semantics. Video music adds to this a further difference in which the sense and non-sense of words enters into a dialectic with the sense and non-sense of images: hence, the possibility of a complex dialogism or polyphony. (Polan 52)

It is precisely in the spaces between sense and non-sense, narrative and antinarrative, the seen and unseen, that *Héroes* creates a dynamic and polyphonic dimension that emulates music video clip aesthetics.

> *Marsha Kinder's article, "Music Video and the Spectator: Television, Ideology and Dream" is a solid point of reference for the discussion of rock and roll videos. According to her, one of the most eye-catching aspects of such videos is their power to evoke specific visual images in the spectator every time she or he listens to music on TV. When the spectator listens to the same song on the radio or in a different context in which visual images are absent, his or her memory conjures up music images, accompanied by the desire to see them again. In most video clips, what one sees is the chain of images that accentuate discontinuities in space and time, a structure that is similar to that of dreams.*
>
> *—Alfredo J. Sosa-Velasco, in response*

I Will Let You Be in My Dreams

Héroes is a novel about a young man of an unknown age, an unknown name, who locks himself in an unknown six-meter-large room and converses with rock stars. The words of Bob Dylan, "Te dejaré estar en mis sueños, si yo puedo estar en los tuyos" [I will let you be in my dreams if you let me be in yours] (12), mark the end of the first chapter (a short two pages long), and they provide the clue to the interrelationship between selves (that of the stars and the protagonist) and between the world of music and dream. Dylan's words link to the first paragraph of the novel that begins with a dream by a third, anonymous individual driving a truck with dynamite into Moscow's Red Square. Nonsensically, this person comes to the realization that there is nothing to do in this space. The individual, whose dream is described in the third-person singular, then remembers a photo of Iggy Pop and David Bowie in Moscow. He tries to find them, cannot, feels increasingly anxious, and wakes up. For two short sentences the voice changes to the first person, from a description to a dialogue, then to the third person and the beginning of another dream where a first person, presumably the narrator, begins to dream himself.

In the second dream, now in the first person, the narrator starts to kill people randomly, throws the gun away once the bullets are gone, and begins to run. When he reaches Moscow, now old and tired, he looks for Iggy and Bowie, encounters a man in a red leather jacket who tells him that the singers are now in Berlin. The narrative changes abruptly. The verbs shift to the second-person singular as he talks about "your" girl who showed up and ran more than "you." New paragraph. Many years later, "I" am in Berlin, with a girl, and although Bowie is already gone, "I" feel oddly happy and remember Bob Dylan's words: "I will let you be in my dreams if you let me be in yours."

To call this chapter a song would overestimate the simplicity of rock and underestimate the confusing multidimensionality of this text. Yes, images and ideas recur. Yes, sentences are short and verselike. Yes, interrupted and disconnected sentences exist. But there is more. The protagonist escapes into a different realm and a structure that is determined by a new set of laws and freedoms. Each mini-chapter works like a vignette, connected yet separate from the life of the protagonist who seems to be falling in and out of dreams and memories in a series of temporally and spatially overlapping layers. The disjointed narrative style functions to erase conventional expectations from the very first moment: it disrupts and interrelates the lyrical with the mundane, the aural with the visual, the first with the second and third persons, space and time, reality with dream, and the past with the present.

In much the same way, music videos are discontinuous: time unfolds unpredictably and without clear reference points; space is revealed slowly and incompletely; a character's personality, goals, and desires are only hinted at but never fully disclosed; actions are incomplete. Stories are suggested, but not given in full; movement is cut off by edits; lyrics do not always tell us what we need to know; and stars pull at videos' meaning in unknown ways (Vernallis 37). MTV editing plays with the spaces *in between*, helping to create a sense of discontinuity and lack (Vernallis 37, 38). Is it any wonder, then, that the *in between* generation finds MTV aesthetics so appealing?

Much like the blank that defines this generation and its fictive outgrowths, with music video clips, viewers note the "shifts of activity, affect, and time, but cannot fill in the blank" (Vernallis 13). As mentioned earlier, each of the music video's components—music, image, and lyrics—are to some extent blank. As we watch a video, we might ask ourselves:

> Are the lyrics for me or a lover, or are they the singer's personal reflection? To whom do the empty sets and characters belong? What are the music's uses, and what spaces should it fill? Music, image, and lyrics each possess their own language with regard to time, space, narrativity, activity, and affect. (Vernallis 13)

Similar questions may be asked of the first chapter of *Héroes*. Who are the characters that belong to each pronoun? What is the relationship between the "I," "he," "we," and "us"? Who is "your" girl and "my" girl? What happened in the years between dreaming about being in Moscow and going to Berlin? Between the action of running and remaining still and realizing that all was a dream? What is the meaning of the endless search for Bowie and Iggy and the embrace of Bob Dylan's words?

The answers to these lapses might be found in the first sentence of the next page in *Héroes* where the narrator admits that "como casi siempre, yo había perdido el ritmo" [as almost always, I had lost my rhythm] (13). Not only does this comment refer to his inability to remember the lyrics of a song, but to a sense of feeling disconnected from his social surroundings.

Frustrated, he says, "No puedo seguir con esto; el trabajo y la apisonadora RESPONSABILIDAD-CULPA-DIOS TE QUIERE-TU FAMILIA TE QUIERE-TÚ NO TE QUIERES PERO ESO SE PUEDE ESPERAR" [I can't continue with this; work and the steamroller RESPONSIBILITY-GUILT-GOD LOVES YOU-YOUR FAMILY LOVES YOU-YOU DON'T LOVE YOURSELF BUT THAT IS TO BE EXPECTED] (14). Placed into question through the absence and lack of rhythm—the capital letters themselves breaking the rhythm of reading—are the grand institutions of work, religion, family, and self. The text connects this person's life narrative with the words, sounds, and emotions of song. Even when the character attempts to substitute his memory lapse with the verses of a famous "canto legionario" called "El novio de la muerte" (first sung by Lola Montes in 1921), the narrator is silenced by a beer can thrown at his head by a fifteen-year-old boy. Not even the appropriation of a grand historical intertext, one that radically contrasts with the bar and drug-induced scene of despair and desire, can interpellate this man in time and (personal) history.

At the end of the second chapter, the protagonist comes to the conclusion that he needs to retire into a small room "para buscar mis propias señales" [to find my own signs/traits] (15). He decides not to leave this space until he is able to "engrosar las filas de los ángeles" [enter the ranks of angels]. To do so, he creates a relationship between the song—the protagonist's life narrative—and the images of rock stars (who he refers to as angels). In other words, to find his "señales," his discourse must include a certain emotional charge and expression that he defines as a "dolor extraño al que sólo las estrellas de rock and roll están expuestas y quería explicarlo todo de una manera confusa, aparentemente superficial, pero sincera, algo que sólo pueden apreciar los que han estado enganchados a la cadena de hierro y azúcar del rock and roll" [a strange pain to which only rock and roll stars are exposed and I wanted to explain it all in a confusing, apparently superficial way, but sincere, something that only those who have been hooked on the chain of iron and sugar of rock and roll can appreciate] (191). Rock provides the drug that trips emotion, confusion, simplicity, and enlightenment. [5]

The reading of *Héroes* is complex in its simplicity, and it demands putting its pieces together like a puzzle. It warrants beginning with the protagonist himself, who expresses feelings of disconnection, fragmentation, and loss: "A veces me he sentido desnudo y a veces me he sentido como un puzzle en las manos de un imbécil" [Sometimes I have felt naked and sometimes I have felt like a puzzle in the hands of an imbecile] (16). Another time he equates his life to "esos muñecos del cuerpo humano en los que había que ir montando todas las piezas" [those dolls of the human body in which one had to put together all the pieces] (35). Physical embodiment emulates storytelling practices in music videos where viewers do not encounter a harmonious unfolding of a story or a figure, but rather a series of relations among images, sounds, colors, and forms. Far beyond a simple surface reading of the book or the music video as an empty space of signifiers, we find that readers must actively search for interconnections. Even when image, music, and sound converge seemingly harmoniously, one may shift into the background and linger in palpable ways, it may change and shift in relation to another, or it may be riddled with its own ellipsis (Vernallis 14, 17).

A key to the unfolding of the puzzle of *Héroes* is that the protagonist equates the emotional charge of song to that of video (instead of film) because it allows him to store and revisit certain sensations. As he explains, "Cuando tuve mi primera cinta de video sentí algo muy extraño: almacenaba sensaciones que antes perdía dos o tres días después de haber visto la película" [When I had my first videotape, I felt something very strange: I stored sensations which earlier I had lost two or three days after seeing a movie] (72). Video allows the protagonist to center his emotional experience and reconstruct his identity. The ability to repeat, to store, to make reappear at will an emotion or an image resides at the center of this character's connection to technology and awareness of contemporary participatory culture.

Time and Space in Narrative

In *Héroes* several time frames converge in unanchored ways presenting the temporal collage of events referred to earlier. There is only one event that allows the readers to place the novel in a definite time in history. On page 174, the narrator talks about leaving his room for the very first time to visit his brother who had just lost an ear in an accident. He travels to Seville and encounters millions of people visiting the Expo, which took place in 1992. In the beginning of the novel, the narrator makes reference to leaving his room for the first time, "hacía casi diez años" [about ten years ago] (15). This information would place the present narrative in the future, in 2002 (the novel having been published in 1993). But we never know the present age of the protagonist, even though he makes reference to several moments of his adolesence—when he was fourteen, seventeen, and eighteen years old.

Contrary to this "futuristic" vision, the main references we enjoy are those that pertain to the world of rock and to film. Bob Dylan, Keith Richards, David Bowie, Jim Morrison, Jimi Hendrix, and Lou Reed were all born in the 1940s and became stars in the 1960s to 1980s. The Sex Pistols and Red Hot Chili Peppers, of the 1970s and 1980s are the most contemporary intertexts. And one of the only concrete references to time is when the narrator remembers learning about the death of John Belushi on March 5, 1982. Much of this information disappears in the constant shifts between childhood memories, present-day emotions, and future desires. These are narrated in a mixture of first-, second-, and third-person pronouns inserted questions, direct and indirect dialogues, and descriptions whose tempo shifts from the static and unchanging to the quickening and forward moving. Traditional notions of time really do not matter for a human being who acknowledges that,

algunas mañanas eran iguales a otras mañanas en las que yo era considerablemente más pequeño, en las que era pequeño de verdad y aunque venía rebotado de circunstancias muy distintas, la sensación era casi la misma. Como dos caídas separadas por veinte años pueden suponer el mismo daño.

[some mornings were the same as other mornings, in which I was considerably younger, in which I was really small, and although I was bounced between very different circumstances, the sensation was the same. Like two falls separated by twenty years can cause the same pain]. (17)

Two main temporal planes intersect and juxtapose with the act of storytelling in *Héroes*: the first one includes the innocence of childhood associated with the home, with beauty, and with a feeling of togetherness; the second is related to the influence of society, the city, the streets as spaces where beauty and meaning disappear: "cuando llegué a la calle lo primero que noté es que las cosas dulces y bonitas ya no estaban allí" [when I got to the street the first thing I noticed was that all things sweet and pretty were no longer there] (109). To understand these two spheres, the protagonist differentiates between "their" narrative—referring to socially imposed stories—and "my" narrative—referring to the need to tell his own stories. It becomes readily apparent that they do not coincide but present frictions and differences that often undercut each other's temporal references.

In order to embody his own texts, the narrator needs to slow down time. Speed disallows for identification when he states that, "esta ciudad puede matarte de un millón de maneras distintas antes de saber qué coño ibas a decir" [this city can kill you a million different ways before you can figure out what you were going to say] (36). Contrary to the perception of speed as an essential component of youth culture in the 1990s, this protagonist desires to take a break, to stop, and to breath. He asks,

> Por qué hay que hacer siempre algo?
> ¿Por qué tiene uno que pasarse la vida yendo y viniendo?
> ¿Por qué no puedo quedarme quieto un momento sin tener que
> decidir de qué sabor quiero mi helado?
>
> [Why does one always have to do something?
> Why does one have to spend life coming and going?
> Why can't I stay still for one moment without having to decide which
> flavor I want my ice cream?] (12)

His desire to stay still is why he ultimately locks himself into a six-meter-large room. The subject rejects speed for stasis, knowing that the slowing down of time and action may make possible the emergence of his own voice. By removing himself from one space and placing himself into another, he is able to merge the past and the present, resulting in a narrative of multiple and reversed proportions (outside = speed/inside = slowing down).

In music video, space, says Vernallis, is experienced directly as having room in which to move. Moreover, by shifting from one place to another, a person acquires a sense of direction (as can be seen in the stories within stories that quickly shift from one unidentified place to another in *Héroes*).

One of music videos' greatest pleasures is their ability to extend our sense of inside/outside beyond that of concrete physical boundaries and their capacity to guide us through an unfolding of these spaces (111). This ambiguity is well expressed by the narrator when he explains that, "el cuarto mide seis metros, así que puedo recorrerlo entero varias veces al día. Todo lo que un hombre necesita es viajar" [the room is six meters long, therefore I can traverse it completely several times a day. All a man needs is to travel] (92).

In *Héroes* the narrative quickly shifts from spaces marked by society and related to the past to spaces marked by the individual and the present, and to those determined by myth—the rock star—as represented by the future. In other words, space and time are interrelated in the reformulation of the self in story. This relationship is similar to what occurs in music videos, which "can heighten our awareness to the fact that lived time can be personal and subjective, different from the rhythms of the environment and that of other people" (Vernallis 129). In addition, the three spheres constantly shift and take turns coming to the foreground, in part depending on the production itself, in part depending on where the viewers/readers place their attention and fall in synch with their subjective experiences (Vernallis 129). The result is that the three levels of storytelling in *Héroes* contend for space; they take turns coming to the fore, they push each other out, they hide or they fly sky high.

To tell his story or to write himself back into story is the main goal of the character in *Héroes* who appropriates erasure, blankness, or emptiness *before* and *for* self-definition. Self-definition evolves from the dream from which he has been denied—"si alguien se hubiera tomado la molestia de preguntar sabría que siempre he querido ser una estrella de rock and roll" [if anybody had bothered to ask, they would know that I have always wanted to be a rock and roll star] (21). Because nobody cares, the narrator interpellates himself through a series of disembodied voices. Questions that were never asked are now spread throughout the text—¿Dónde te gustaría estar? [Where would you like to be?] (88), ¿Qué es lo más triste que recuerdas? [What is the saddest thing you can remember?] (40). Anonymous voices, rock angels, provide meaning to a personal song that had been left without a tune.

Heroes – If Only Just for One Day

The title of the book—*Héroes*—suggests a multilayered relationship between the protagonist and the main characters, as well as the rock "hero"—David Bowie—and the other rock stars sprinkled throughout the text. The entire novel is dedicated to "Ziggy," a figure created by David Bowie for a concept album in 1972 called *Ziggy Stardust and the Spiders from Mars*. The album told the story of Ziggy, a human manifestation of a gay alien rock star who presents humanity with a message of hope. A blogger, Charlotte Robinson, explains that for her, the album presented one of,

> the most splendid celebrations of teenage pleasures and priorities ever committed to tape. Its obsessions with gender-bending and outer-space aren't dated

gimmicks or cheap escapism, but representations of a road of infinite possibilities lying ahead, of worlds—sexual, sensual, literal—not yet explored, and the music captures the madness, frustration, confusion, and (let's not forget) joy and wonder of adolescence. It sounds young, it sounds curious, it sounds like it's in love.

Despite this blogger's slightly romantic take, to view the role of the real and constructed roles of Bowie/Ziggy in this light adds awareness to the characters' emotional state and search for new artistic paradigms—a road of infinite possibilities lying ahead.

The idealistic role of the hero/star/angel contrasts sharply with the crude social subtext better known in the work of Mañas. *Héroes* places flatness in relief when the character says "uno a veces persigue ángeles y otras veces, media hora después, se saca la polla y se la machaca" [at times one runs after angels and other times, half an hour later, one pulls out the penis and jacks off] (124). The affectlessness so often ascribed to GenX texts is one that is more clearly associated with the outside world; with the abuse of children and women; with institutional hypocrisy, violence, fear, abandonment, disenchantment, and isolation. Rock's rebellious, lyrical, and idealist dimensions *crash* into these discourses and create a hybrid narrative of almost perverse proportions. One could claim that the result speaks to the Warholian-like crashes found

---

"LIFE ON MARS" by David Bowie

"Life on Mars," first released in 1971 on the album *Hunky Dory*, was called by BBC Radio 2 "a cross between a Broadway musical and a Salvador Dalí painting," and Neil McCormick from the British newspaper *The Telegraph* expressed his desire "to raise your voice and sing along, yet Bowie's abstract cut-up lyrics force you to invest the song with something of yourself just to make sense of the experience."
http://en.wikipedia.org/wiki/Life_on_Mars%3F

In the music video, David Bowie displays his famous red hair and blue eye shadow. Much like in *Héroes*, the lyrics also point to a social reality marked by disenchantment and the desire for a better world:

"It's a God awful small affair
To the girl with the mousey hair
But her mummy is yelling, 'No!'
And her daddy has told her to go
But her friend is nowhere to be seen
Now she walks through her sunken
   dream
To the seats with the clearest view
And she's hooked to the silver screen
But the film is a sadd'ning bore
For she's lived it ten times or more
She could spit in the eyes of fools
As they ask her to focus on
Sailors fighting in the dance hall
Oh man!
Look at those cavemen go
It's the freakiest show
Take a look at the lawman
Beating up the wrong guy
Oh man!
Wonder if he'll ever know
He's in the best selling show
Is there life on Mars?

To watch the video, go to: www.youtube.com/watch?v=ueUOTImKp0k&feature=related

—Christine Henseler

in the previous chapter. But the black-and-white surface that subtends the image—the documentary photograph of the crash—is now not related to the affectlessness of the subject (or to television), but rather to social reality. If before television was equated to (low) popular culture, now the repetition and musical sensation projected by video provides alternative and powerfully political possibilities.

HAVE YOU SEEN THIS?

The music video, "Show Me the Feeling of Being Lonely" by the Backstreet Boys, uses changing exterior spaces to express interior emotions through a variety of voices and visions. In addition, the video makes use of a similar technique as *Héroes*, namely the use of black and white with targeted dabs of red (until the end, when all characters come together and the video turns full color).
w w w . y o u t u b e . c o m / w a t c h ? v =PaZWQHzfGXs

—Christine Henseler

On a visual plane, *Héroes* appears to be recorded in black and white. The only color that materializes in the text is red, and the red pertains to a red leather jacket and boots associated with the world of rock (and hope). The technique of sprinkling just one color throughout a story is often used in video clips where a color can serve as a thread between frames and scenes. It is also used to disrupt a primary color scheme. For example, in Lil' Kim's video "No Time" the black-and-white video includes dabs of red and yellow to motion to different spaces and group identities. In *Héroes*, the color red, first in the form of a red leather jacket, migrates from a boy the narrator sees in his dreams (12) and a jacket on himself while dancing in the beginning of the novel (20) to red leather boots at the end of the text. The boots define the sound of his own footsteps (178) along a path where "las carreteras serán muros, las baldosas colmillos, los puentes agujeros y los agujeros, agujeros [the roads will be walls, the tiled floors fangs, the bridges holes, and the holes holes] (178). The various voices, time frames, spaces, messages, sights, and sounds found in the three short paragraphs of this third-to-last chapter present a dizzying array of meanings strung into a narrative thread by the color red.

The voice that evolves from this staggering amount of information is marked by clarity and equilibrium. The narrator speaks in the first person and in the preterit tense and motions to the end of his search, when he finds Bowie seated below a bronze angel (179). Bowie's eyes are surrounded by blue eye shadow and tainted red hair. The image of Ziggy Stardust appears in full color at the moment when the character realizes he has arrived. It starts to rain, they both sit below the angel, and they do not move (179). Color stands in for sight, stasis for movement, and the image of the star and the character together in the rain leaves readers with a feeling of hope.

Much like the figure of Bowie in this novel, in music video, "the image speaks to us in two languages at once, first as literal meaning (this is the musician singing, this is the meaning of words) and, at second order, the place of myth, as form, which puts the meaning at a distance so that it can be appropriated into a new situational intentionality" (Berland 37). When taken together, the rock stars presented in the novel most obviously portray an alternative space and meaning marked by a certain rebellion, lifestyle, emotion, and dress. It becomes repeatedly clear that the emotional charge provided by the world of rock is essential for the character's social survival, as when he says: "yo nunca saldría a la calle sin sentirme como Jim Morrison o Dennis Hopper por lo menos" [I would never go out into the street without feeling like Jim Morrison or at least Dennis Hopper] (73).

But rock presents more than just an emotional intertext; it presents readers with an interplay of present and absent meanings that contribute and combine to create a series of textual rhythms. References to Bowie, Marlon Brandon, or Nico do not serve to develop deep psychological characters, but to keep "musical and verbal connotations open, especially when they are at odds" (Vernallis 143). Yes, these references are sprinkled throughout the text to develop a sense of cohesion and meaning, but they also provide an alternative space of identity formation, as seen on pages 76–77, when the narrator talks about a band whose music all teenagers kept from their parents.

> **WHO WAS NICO?**
>
> Nico is the only female character named in Ray Loriga's novel *Héroes*.
>
> Nico (aka Christa Päffge, 1938–88), was a German musician, fashion model, and actress. She recorded with the Rolling Stones, Bob Dylan, Andy Warhol, and the Velvet Underground. She was romantically involved with Lou Reed, Jim Morrison, Jackson Browne, Brian Jones, Tim Buckley, Bob Dylan, and Iggy Pop.

Figures from the world of rock are not included arbitrarily or uncritically. In fact, the protagonist makes several remarks that are self-aware of the absence of power in song and his own cynical use of rock lyrics. He admits that songs cannot tell the whole story, that listeners do not want to hear the whole story, that they have an emptying effect when listened to hundreds of times: "Las canciones que escriba a partir de ahora no van a explicarlo todo, pero quién coño quiere oírlo todo" [the songs that I will write as of now are not going to explain everything, but who the hell wants to hear everything] (36). He recognizes that songs may even empty themselves of meaning, as when the narrator explains, after talking about his parents, that there was "una canción de la Velvet Underground que decía: 'Mis padres van a ser la muerte de todos nosotros.' Claro que también había una canción de la Velvet que decía: 'Ninguna nariz es una buena noticia'" [a song by Velvet Underground that said, "My parents are gonna be the death of us all." Of course, there was also a song by Velvet that says: "No nose is good news"] (114). While the first reference clearly falls in line with the character's stream of consciousness, the next satirizes his intertextual usage of song, thus displaying a meta-awareness of its multidimensionality.

As I examine in my essay, "Héroes de Ray Loriga como literatura videoclip," the novel is formally constructed by fragments that, as a video clip, recreate visual images that can be seen at the same time as music videos extracted from the adolescent young man's memory confined to his room. On the one hand, the fragments that constitute the narrative of the novel are present as video clips since their structure is neither linear nor cyclical, but discontinuous. On the other hand, such fragments make reference to songs and singers of the history of rock and roll (David Bowie, Mick Jagger and Bob Dylan, among others) with an intertextual function as they refer to contemporary pop culture and the lyrics of such songs can be read as intertexts of the novel. Loriga's thoughts on this matter are noteworthy: "Héroes era casi un disco, era[n] las canciones que uno oye en su cabeza, y el narrador era yo: me pareció una jugada honesta" (www.elmundo.es/larevista/num95/textos/ray1.html).

The mere title of the songs refers, then, to the problem of the divided, fragmented subject, among unconscious and conscious motivations, on the one hand, and physiological processes and social limitations, on the other. Intertextuality at the formal level allows us to read Héroes as a polyphonic text, characterized by its semantic, syntactic, and phonic plurality. The different voices present in the novel are not only enunciated by a "subject in process," but also define his/her plural identity. The identity of the subject as an organic and unitary entity is questioned, because s/he is constantly in crisis. The protagonist of Héroes reconstitutes his identity as a plural identity at the fictional level and, simultaneously, affords the reader the same experience in the process of reading. In doing so, popular culture serves as a point of reference, creating a game of interrelationships, identification, and distancing between the young man as the protagonist of different video clips and the novel as a television station, such as MTV,

→

Rock in *Héroes* functions much like hook lines in music videos. Lyrics are not repeated in their entirety in the novel, but only the titles appear. Titles like *Walk on the Wild Side* or *Starting Over* serve to motion to "a generalized truth or a crystallized point of view" (Vernallis 145). Often the hook can display tension and be extended to remarkable lengths. In the novel, the hooks refer to stages of emotion and physical actions; they present a continuity of references; they can pique readers' interest in wanting to know more; they misalign temporal relationships and echo events that occurred earlier or later; they present us with open beginnings and endings, with dreams and realities, and, in the case of Bowie, with an image that strings throughout the entire text and pulls it together in a circular, yet open-ended fashion.

Wrapped up in the title of the novel is the dual notion of the social and musical hero and antihero. David Bowie's line from the song "Heroes"—"I, I will be king, you, you will be queen, if only just for one day"—beautifully mirrors the protagonist's need for interpellation, *if only just for one day*. To understand the elusive qualities of the character in *Héroes* and in a music video is to accept both realms as,

short, almost mute [forms] whose purpose is to showcase the star, highlight the lyrics, and underscore the music. This requires that the viewer's attention be directed to various parameters; constant shifts of focus precludes the construction of a unified subject. In addition, music video possesses multiple senses of time and space. A music video's star is a phantasmagoric multiple: the songwriter, the performer, and the figure on the screen embody different subjectivities. When the video is finally edited whole, the image follows the music, and there is the eerie sense that the music, rather than the subject's intent, animates the figure. Generally, the image, in order to match the speed and energy of the music, reflects a more heightened experiential state than ordinary consciousness, and the characters seem like mythical automatons. (Vernallis 16)

Héroes may appear simply like a record in which the character follows the songs of his life story, but the text's use of rock in relation to space (social/physical/mental) and time (the speed associated with the outside world and slowing down for inner self-awareness) complicates the picture. Rock places social reality at a distance to highlight its flattening effects. The music's political power resides in its rejection of complete, linear, finely wrought and closed narratives (the narra-

> *in which the availability of music videos 24 hours a day and the uninterrupted programs of such videos metaphorize the representation and internalization of the music videos. The reader becomes the spectator and his/her identity comes under crisis, as does that of the protagonist of* Héroes.
>
> *—Alfredo J. Sosa-Velasco, in response*

NARRATIVE OF THE SELF

"[Anthony] Giddens discusses the experience of self-identity in the context of the massive 'intentional and extensional' changes which are sent into being by the onset of modernity. However, he also argues that it is misleading to suggest that contextual diversity in everyday life will necessarily promote a fragmented self. An integrated self is equally seen as a possibility, depending upon the ways in which individuals use the cultural resources at their disposal. The suggestion here is that an individual uses such resources through the everyday interpretation and negotiation of lifestyles. For Giddens, the narrative of the self is the product of a balance between structural influences on everyday life, such as standardized consumption patterns, and the personal appropriation of such influences" (21).

—Steven Miles

tor even argues that the outside world does not want "historias con finales abiertos" [stories with open endings]) (105). Rock emphasizes, rather, the cyclical and episodic style of song and video to break out of the grand narratives prescribed by society.

Héroes is one of the earliest and most complex narratives to appear on the Spanish GenX scene in the 1990s. Its construction of identity takes on a more open-ended quality steeped in the mixing of media as portrayed through songs and images. Vernallis explains that the best way to grasp a video's meaning "is to learn the patterns, and to make conjectures about what happens in the gaps—time lapses, activity not shown, unexplained motivations" (15). Much like the goal of blank fiction, its sense and nonsense constantly play with what is lost and found, with what is seen and unseen between spaces. In the end, as the words of the hero of *Héroes* pronounce,

> todo es cuestión de agujeros y la vida se escapa por agujeros en los que no quieres entrar y vuelve en agujeros de los que no quieres salir.

> [everything is a question of holes and life escapes through holes into which you do not want to enter and it returns through holes from which you do not want to leave]. (152)

Chapter 4

From MTV to the *Real* World of Generation X Fiction

In February 2010, MTV changed its famous logo after twenty-nine years. The company kept the three-dimensional letter "M" and its signature "tv," but removed the "Music Television" tag line. The black "M" gained new contour as designers integrated photographs of celebrities from reality television shows like *Jersey Shore, The Buried Life*, or *My Life as Liz*.[1] The logo fed into MTV's evolution from the projection of music video clips one hundred percent of the time to the ever more participatory, interactive, and celebrity culture of the "real." The designs celebrated the star power of the average folks of these shows at the same time that the ever-changing MTV logo pointed to the temporality of their stardom. As its popularity suggests, the "real" turned into a media phenomenon that broke down boundaries between technology, culture, identity, and authenticity. Reality television shows became one of the most popular success stories in multi-platform aesthetic hybridity.

When MTV first broadcast the reality show *The Real World* in 1992, it became one of the first commercial companies to harness the power of the "real." Their success—driven by popularity and low production costs— significantly promoted the development of "people shows" on network television during the 1990s, events that involved important shifts in the definition of who constituted the audience and how performance was mediated (Tincknell and Raghuram 207). It is no exaggeration to say that reality television shows quickly became the most successful programs in the world, with audiences tuning in by the millions and spin-offs appearing by the dozens. Although show formats varied and cultural differences applied, the success of almost all these shows begged the question: what makes reality TV so popular? And why should literary critics, of all people, care?

We should care because the phenomenon that is reality television has redefined the parameters and paradigms around projects like "Generation X" fiction and film. In this chapter, I give an overview of the industrial development and rise of reality television shows in the United States and in Spain. Why have reality shows become so successful? What makes the medium so

> *Published in February 1996, Veo veo was written at the very beginning of the 1990s, when European TV had nothing even remotely similar to* Big Brother *and* The Real World *was just taking off in the United States. Its main influences, therefore, are literary and cinematographic: H. G. Wells, Huxley, Orwell, Chandler, Hitchcock, Buñuel, and De Palma, among others.*
>
> —*Gabriela Bustelo, in response*
>
> "Yo escribí la novela entre 1991 y 1992, aunque se publicó cuatro años tarde, porque un amigo editor me aconsejó meterla en un cajón y no enviarla a ningún sitio. Fue otra amiga editora, Marianne Ponsford, la que al leerla en 1995 me aconsejó mandarla inmediatamente a las diez mejores editoriales del país, cosa que hice. Pero, en todo caso, se publicó tarde. Si hubiera salido en su momento, habría sido anterior a *Historias del Kronen* de Mañas, por ejemplo."
>
> —Gabriela Bustelo, e-mail

innovative and groundbreaking? The answers to these questions pronounce new relationships among media, cultures, and audiences as well as new critical approaches to the "reality effects" of popular media technologies (and literatures). Given the vast number of reality television shows, I center my sights on the success of *Big Brother* since this show was among the first to cross media platforms. I concentrate on the structural similarities between narrative and reality television, and on the role of the shows in reconstructing the *real* world through different editing techniques. This study serves as the baseline from which to consider the performance of the real in Gabriela Bustelo's novel *Veo veo* (1996), but also in the work of other "X" and *Mutantes* authors. What can reality television tell us about the way identity and authenticity are constructed in the digital age? How must the representation of the "real" be critically reconceived to better understand the effects of media technologies on everyday life and art? To pronounce this shift toward new intercultural and interactive practices, Gabriela Bustelo herself comments and reacts to the ideas presented in this chapter and to my interpretation of her novel.

Reality-Based Television

Reality television is not a new phenomenon. It has been around since the 1950s when *Candid Camera* hit the airwaves and was presented to the public by Allen Funt as a "social experiment." The second wave occurred around the 1960s and 1980s with shows like *The Newlywed Game* (1966), *An American Family* (1973), and *Living in the Past* (1978). The third wave may be flatly positioned in the 1990s when shows like *The Real World* (1992), *Cops* (1989), *Who Wants to Be a Millionaire?* (first produced in the UK as *Cash Mountain*, 1998), *Survivor* (first produced in Sweden as *Expedition Robinson*, 1997), and *Big Brother* (first produced in the Netherlands in 1999) appeared on global television and intensified the interactive quality of the shows through web-related media (Hill 14). Much like MTV before it, reality TV represented a radical departure in the history of television programming. But unlike MTV, which evolved from the vision of one particular, alternative cable station, reality television emerged from within the corporate structure of major broadcasting systems, expanding a commercial television culture on a global level while speaking directly to youth.

Several scholars have speculated on the reason for the rise of reality television. In general, popular entertainment production increased in the early 1980s in the United States, Western Europe, and Australia as a result of deregulation; marketization of media industries; and the convergence of telecommunications, computers, and media (Hill 15). But the success of reality television is attributed to a series of economic difficulties that influenced the US broadcasting system in the 1980s. Chad Raphael, in "The Political Economic Origins of Reali-TV," details the events that affected the restructuring of US television, including the expansion of video distribution channels due to new cable channels, VCRs, the FOX network, independent stations, the fragmentation of the viewing audience, and budgets. These occurrences led to strong cost-cutting measures by the major television channels, FOX, CBS, and ABC (119–25). Although reality television had existed in the United States and Europe for decades, 1988 is cited as the year that officially gave rise to the genre as a cost-cutting, back-up strategy to control labor unrest during the twenty-two week "Writers Guild" strike. This situation would repeat itself about ten years later, although this time walkouts by writers and actors coincided with the success of game shows like *Who Wants to Be a Millionaire?* (1999) and *Survivor* (2000) (125–26). The economic and audience success of reality television was also affected by growth in tabloid journalism (such as *America's Most Wanted*, 1988) and the use of more hybrid genres, such as docu-soaps or game-docs.

The basic structure of reality television shows could easily be sold and adapted to a variety of countries around the world. Already in

---

> ### THE SUCCESS OF REALITY TELEVISION SHOWS
>
> Reality TV is not only popular for Americans, but all over the world. Annette Hill highlights an interesting statistic regarding reality TV in the UK by stating that, "in 2000, 70 percent of the population (4–65+) has gone on record in having watched reality television occasionally or on a regular basis." The United States has similar reality TV statistics. One report indicates that, "for girls ages 12–17 years old, 3 out of 4 of their favorite television shows were reality TV shows."
> www.jobmonkey.com/realitytv/reality-tv-statistics.html
>
> —Christine Henseler
>
> *Even though reality TV has been encouraged for economical reasons, modern literature has followed an approximately parallel course toward realism or "truthism." But the phenomenon is not that new. During the Golden Age of Ancient Greece—fifth century b.c., when Western culture was established—poetry gave way to prose and biography was born as a literary genre. So the relationship between fact and act, so to speak, has been going strong for ages.*
>
> *—Gabriela Bustelo, in response*

1991, shows like *Unsolved Mysteries* could be seen on television screens in Spain, Canada, France, and Japan (Raphael 130). Because the shows could be sold on a pure profit basis, producers began to create models that transcended national differences and attracted global markets, but could be sensitive to the "particularities of local markets and differentiating consumer segments" (130). Some have called this the "McDonalds" model—or "McTV"—which allowed local regions to insert their own video clip preferences into general marketing models.[2] This model gained ground in the twenty-first century as regional preferences infused almost all shows and some were created directly within national borders. For example, Australia created its own version of *Cops* and *Australia's Most Wanted*, and Spain developed a version of *Big Brother* called *Gran Hermano* whose house, unlike in other nations, included an outdoor swimming pool.

Media sociologist Divina Frau-Meigs, in "*Big Brother* and Reality TV in Europe," has found that while former studies centering on the acculturation process of reality television have been infused by power struggles and concerns of Americanization, more recent studies have focused on audience reception and localized resistance strategies centered on moral values (such as China's censorship of shows that were "ethically inspiring"). She suggests that in Europe a dual process of "acculturation"—subject to globalizing power relations—and "interculturation"—a process centered on voluntary nodes of contact—"may produce new cultural inventions" (35). These processes are not abstract constructs but spin-offs of concrete situations, such as the European Union's "Television Without Frontiers" directive, or American media industry import and export strategies.[3] Not only business models, but also the audience's perception of a media genre or program may influence the extent of its cross-cultural circulation.

> *One should keep in mind Spain's hot weather. But the house where Spanish* Gran Hermano *was filmed, though minimally furnished, was considered by its ten young tenants—students, waiters, flight attendants, models, and hairdressers—a luxurious setting. The pool was famous for the sex that took place under its blue waters. :)*
>
> —Gabriela Bustelo, in response

> Big Brother's *success is totally understandable. The idea is brilliant, halfway between a docudrama and a TV contest, with its Warholian share of ephemeral fame. When democracy meets art, the show must go on!*
>
> *Though reality TV is considered trash culture, it has an underlying morality. The whole thing can be seen as a giant confession booth or the spectacular enactment of what Spanish author Gracián recommended in the seventeenth century: "live as if you were being permanently watched."*
>
> —Gabriela Bustelo, in response
>
> *Another good example is* Who Wants to Be a Millionaire, *which not only became a popular game show in Great Britain and the United States, but also inspired Vikas Swarup's best-selling Indian novel, and the internationally produced, multiple-Oscar-winning film* Slumdog Millionaire.
>
> —Debra Castillo, in response

The program must think twice about the specific cultural similarities and stereotypes it presents and the way audiences will perceive its content in relation to their own heritage (35–37). In other words, the blind "McTV" model presents a complex process of acculturation and transculturation that, in the context of narrative, has led to interventions such as the "McOndo" manifesto in the Latin American context.[4] This complex interrelationship is essential to an understanding of Generation X narrative because it allows us to shift our focus from beyond traditionally "passive" or "victimized" notions centered on the influence of North American corporate culture to more dynamic, active exchanges and innovations.

Big Brother has been considered the original paradigm of a successful transcultural reality television show, one that has radically changed the relationship among media, culture, and audience. Many believe that the show was inspired by the Arizona Biosphere 2 project (built between 1987 and 1991); others relate its major influence to MTVs *The Real World*, small sections of which were projected in the United States and Great Britain in 1992; and there is no doubt that the show was inspired by George Orwell's novel *1984* (1949) and Peter Weir's film *The Truman Show* (1998). What we do know is that *Big Brother* was conceived by the independent branch of the Dutch company Endemol, and it was first broadcast on September 16, 1999, by the channel Veronica (part of the Holland Media Group). On their website, they describe this "non-scripted" "revenue rich multi platform interactive application" as follows:

Twelve people, who've never met before, are suddenly catapulted into the Big Brother house where they must share every minute of the next 100 days. In their fenced-off compound they're denied any contact with their loved ones, and the outside world. No phones,

---

REALITY TV IN THE MIDDLE EAST

"Airing 24 hours a day on a satellite channel, *Star Academy* features 16 contestants cloistered in a villa, who attend singing, dancing, and acting lessons, devour take-out pasta, and compete for a recording contract. Each week, viewers dial their cell phones to vote off one of two candidates. Results are announced Friday, after a live performance. This week Ahmad, a dimpled Tunisian, is up against Muhammad, a lanky Saudi Arabian.

Star Academy, produced by the Lebanese Broadcasting Corporation (LBC), is on the crest of a wave of Western reality formats to debut in the region in recent months. Arabs with satellite dishes can now watch other Arabs navigating their way through foreign cities in a version of the British *Three for the Road*, Arabs auditioning to be the next *Superstar*, Arabs swimming with snakes on *Fear Factor*, and soon Arabs jostling to be the next *Survivor*.

But reality TV's entry here has not been entirely smooth. Early this month, the Middle East Broadcasting Center canceled an Arab *Big Brother* in its second week—amid cries of immorality from Islamists in Bahrain, where the show was filmed. At the same time, some viewers complained that restrictions, such as bans on kissing, rendered the show 'very boring'."

—Samar Farah, *"Can Reality TV 'survive" in the Middle East?"*

newspapers, radios or televisions. They're all alone…except for the millions watching and judging their every move.

Cameras and microphones are placed all over the house. Everything the housemates do is recorded and broadcast on television and the internet. They can't eat, sleep or chill out without the nation clocking their every move.

Yet somehow, the residents are desperate to stay in the Big Brother house. All the pain and embarrassment is worth the prospect of landing the title of Big Brother winner. All the stress of knowing that at any moment your housemates could be trying to kick you out!

On a regular basis, the housemates must nominate two or more of their fellow participants for eviction, but the viewers ultimately decide who has to leave. The last participant to leave the house wins the programme, and the huge cash prize that comes with it.[5]

Despite this rather disavowing, angst-filled description of a microsocial experiment, individuals flocked to perform in a show that was an instant hit in the United States and throughout the world. Its visibility and popularity was such that even its "communally recorded song *Big Brother* and the tune *Leef* (Han van Eijk) [reached] number one in the pop charts" and two of the contestants received photo shoot contracts in the Dutch *Playboy* magazine.[6] The show's success led other countries, including Spain, Germany, Portugal, the United States, the United Kingdom, Belgium, Sweden, Switzerland, and Italy, to buy and project the show in the year 2000.[7] Since then, there have been dozens of spin-offs of the show worldwide created for regional audiences, including *Back to Reality* (UK), *Za Steklom* (Russia), *Cabin Fever* (Ireland), *De Gouden Kooi* (Netherlands), *El bus* (Spain), and *Uttaradhikar* (Bangladesh).[8]

At the onset of *Big Brother*, the worldwide media giant Endemol published a "bible" that consisted of a series of unchanging and transcultural rules that applied to

---

> *EXAMPLES OF THE WORLDWIDE RECEPTION OF BIG BROTHER:*
>
> - "During the first series of *Big Brother* in Holland, up to 6 million viewers tuned in to watch an intimate moment between two contestants.
> - In Germany, the first series of *Big Brother* was so successful that a second was commissioned immediately for the autumn 2000 schedule.
> - In Portugal, TV1 broadcast *Big Brother* in 2000, and its average share rose from 9 percent to 50 percent, with its highest-rated episode at 74 percent in the final week.
> - In Spain, Telecinco's ratings went from 13.7 percent share to 30 percent, peaking at 70 percent for the broadcast of the final show of the first episode of *Big Brother* in July 2000.
> - More people tuned in to watch *Big Brother* in Spain in 2000 than the Champions League semifinal soccer match between Real Madrid and Bayern Munich.
> - In Australia *Big Brother* appealed to 50 percent of nineteen- to thirty-nine-year-olds.
> - In Argentina, the ratings for the eviction show on private terrestrial channel, Telefe, averaged 20 percent of the market share. They immediately commissioned a second series. (325–26)
>
> —Annette Hill,
> *"Big Brother: The Real Audience"*

all reality shows around the world, independent of local customs and values (Frau-Meigs 38). But since the show's selection of contestants was based on authentic affectual and emotional voices, the shows implicitly expressed what Frau-Meigs called "intercultural underpinnings" that often undermined bible rules (38). Interestingly, one of these "underpinnings" that infringed on the rules occurred in Spain. In its first season, the contestants refused to name one of their own for elimination, nominating everybody and obligating the viewers to choose (Frau-Meigs 41). Spain was also an exception when it came to limiting its intercultural exchanges with other countries in Europe. Instead, producers created exchanges with *Gran Hermano* participants from Mexico and Argentina to allow for a larger audience through broader cultural relations of language, identity, and compatibility (Frau-Meigs 41).

The rise of reality television in Spain displayed other unique conditions determined by the development of commercial cable television. The deregulation practices initiated by the private television law of 1988 favored the appearance of the first commercial channels in 1990 and 1991; in 1995, a second law (Ley 37/1995) regulated cable and digital television and led to a multiplication and specialization of large businesses, such as the cable station ONO and or the satellite conglomerate Canal Satélite (Roel Vecino 815). For José Ángel Cortés this change defines a movement from what he terms "el paso de la paleotelevisión a la neotelevisión" [the step from paleotelevision to neotelevision] (qtd. in Roel Vecino 814), referring to the movement from a monopolized model of programming based on education, information, and entertainment to the coexistence of national and autonomous public programming and commercial channels that compete for similar audiences (Roel Vecino 814). Marta Roel Vecino believes that the coexistence of public and commercial stations led to a healthy competition for audiences. This competition, in turn, demanded the creation of new formats, new programs, and the synergy between different media and commercial programs. Although the quality of these shows differed, in Spain, some of the best examples of this "neotelevisión" could be found in *Gran Hermano* or another Spanish reality television show called *Operación Triunfo*, an *American Idol*–type show involving competition for the best solo singers (814).

Spanish reality television's splendor occurred at the beginning of the second wave, or the "neotelevisual" epoch, between 1992 and 1993. During this period reality TV programs proliferated on several Spanish channels (Roel Vecino 816). Right after the Netherlands and Germany, Spain was one of the first countries to air *Big Brother* (on Telecinco 2, now called *La siete* and produced by Endemol) on April 23, 2000. The show lasted for three months, until July 21, 2000, and attracted an audience of 8,286,000. The house, located twenty minutes outside of Madrid, was under twenty-four-hour surveillance, and the contestants' actions were digitally streamed for the first time through Vía Digital and Quiero T. To save storage space, the show, for the first time, was stored on disks that could easily be searched by reporters for footage (Roel Vecino 814). Spain was the first country to air ten main editions, and has had the third-largest number of contestants (208), after the UK (265) and Germany (284). Spain also tops the charts

REALITY TELEVISION AS A NATIONAL "EVENT" IN SPAIN

Charo Lacalle talks about *Big Brother* not just as a program, but as a national event "por su enorme resonancia, pues mientras se emitió modificó las parrillas y los hábitos de recepción de muchos espectadores, extendió sus tentáculos por una gran parte de la programación televisiva y se convirtió en tema de conversación dominante en aquel período" (25).

—Christine Henseler

Contestants being so average is one of BB's strokes of genius. TV is crammed with famous people. The intimacy of normality is what makes it click, because it's believable.

—Gabriela Bustelo, in response

media" success stories. In fact, in addition to the possibilities afforded by advances in digital technology, it is *Big Brother*'s effect on storytelling that has resonated among the public and the critics.[10]

EL FENÓMENO GRAN HERMANO

"De su presencia en el modelo generalista podríamos destacar la capacidad que adquiere el telespectador, tradicionalmente pasivo, en el discurrir de la trama narrativa del programa. El telespectador a través de sus votos telefónicos o de los SMS, se convierte en un semidiós capaz de expulsar a los participantes del programa.

Durante la última semana de la primera edición de *Gran Hermano* se activaron más de 2.300 líneas, a 136 pesetas el minuto, para que los espectadores pudieran elegir al ganador los días anteriores a la final. En julio de 2000 los participantes de esa primera edición se estrenaron como moderadores del portal "muchagente.com". En él chateaban y mantenían videoconferencias con sus admiradores con un coste para el internauta de 61 pesetas por minuto.

→

for using the highest number of anonymous (vs. celebrity) public house contestants of all countries.[9] The success of *Big Brother* in Spain and elsewhere was in part due to the appearance and transference of its content in a variety of media platforms, from the twenty-four-hour Internet streaming of the show—reduced to half-hour episodes that were screened each night of the week, three times a day—to discussions on other television programs, interviews in magazines, voting by telephone, and texting. *Big Brother* became a perfect example of what Henry Jenkins has examined in other contexts as "trans-

Big Brother, as well as other reality TV shows, turned the act of watching into a multiplatform phenomenon that allowed viewers to partake in "real" actions. In most shows, cameras and microphones took on protagonistic roles. They provided a sense of immediacy and liveness that resembled security camera footage and played off of the technological advances in handheld camera technology. The shows gave viewers the sense that the "actors" were speaking in real time, "producing the effect of a more direct relationship to the text" and to the audience (Tincknell and Raghuram 204). This effect was enhanced by the supposed absence of a script, the use of colloquial language, and a focus on so-called "normal" activities. The sensation that these shows produced of the "real" in "real-time" performances broke down barriers between the actions occurring on and off screen. The juxtaposition of TV-liveness and real-time streaming made apparent the manipulated mixings of two "temporalities of the real" (Kavka and West 144) and the duality underlined that "viewers' participation in 'the moment' in reality tv [was] predicated on discursive and aesthetic constructions of closeness—immediacy, coincidence and liveness" (151). Misha Kavka and Amy West emphasize that this immediacy did not mean that reality television had to be live or simulcast; the show, rather, had "to establish a floating-present framework that conjoined the worlds of viewing and being viewed" (142). It did so by creating an emotional charge—the "feeling that tv comes to us live, immediate, 'direct for me'" (139)—that gave both parties the illusion of the sharing of everyday intimacies. This illusion did not only make the question

> De la presencia de *Gran Hermano* en los canales temáticos destacamos la interactividad, si bien no se han conseguido desarrollar todas las potencialidades que ofrece la tecnología. Vía Digital crea el *Canal Gran Hermano* con una emisión ininterrumpida durante las veinticuatro horas del día, con objeto de que sus abonados puedan interferir con su mando a distancia en la vida de los habitantes de la casa, decidiendo la temperatura del agua o a qué hora despertarles. Pero, por el momento, lo único que se consiguió con la aplicación interactiva fue que los telespectadores pudieran seleccionar la cámara que mostraría lo que sucede en cuatro lugares distintos de la casa, algo que supuso un coste de 1.380 millones de pesetas" (821).
>
> —Marta Roel Vecino,
> *"Innovación tecnológica en la gestión de contenidos para televisión: análisis del fenómeno 'Gran Hermano.'"*
>
> *This is the—classical?—postmodern approach to life: a nonstop succession of sequences that can be disrupted and reorganized on a whim.*
>
> —*Gabriela Bustelo, in response*

of a central text uncertain, but in the word of Tincknell and Raghuram: "its relations to different media helped widen textual relations" (208). Contained storytelling techniques broke out of its closed containers to present a series of strategies in motion.

On the Road with Generation X

The trope that perhaps best defines the development and movement of reality television shows and its effects on Generation X is the "road." Inherently echoing and transforming the spirit of Jack Kerouac's now canonical autobiographical novel *On the Road* (1951), handheld video camera technology presented GenX'ers with a transformative road experience that surpassed that of the Beats. Not only were GenX'ers able to represent their reality through audiovisual formats, but their narratives were now edited, remixed, redesigned, and relocated. The long road upon which one traveled in a chronological fashion, was now multiplied, split, copied, and pasted into a technological realm in which *transformation* related to postproduction rather than direct experience. Kerouac's continuous, long writing of *On the Road* on a 119-foot scroll with no commas or page breaks contrasted sharply with X'ers short prose, mini-chapters of microsocial "experiments" that were remixed with aural and visual material to produce an inherently multiple and synchronous reading experience in which spaces and times overlapped, and even disappeared.

Generation X'ers relationship to the road and reality television may be said to have begun in 1994, when thirty-year-old Shayna Garr, formerly with MTV, created a reality show called *The Ride*, which aired on PBS in 1994. *The Ride* was an eight-part GenX "documentary" in which six teens, aged between 17 and 19, traveled in a van around the United States during one summer vacation and documented their experiences as "participatory observers" (Mills 232–33). Each teen was given a camera and allowed creative freedom of expression, although Garr chose the locations and kept authority over the final edition of the footage. In each of the cities they visited, the teens were paired and assigned a local guide who spiced up their narratives with frank discussions on bulimia, homosexuality, race, gangs, drugs, violence, HIV/ AIDS, and other problems that plagued youth in the 1990s (233). Each group presented contrasting opinions on these issues, topics not publicly discussed in frank terms on public television at that time (233). The result, observes Kate Mills, was worth watching; it was a candid "chronotope of identity and transformation" (233)—a perfect definition of Generation X itself—in which television emphasized "process rather than quick narrative closure, valuing each step of questioning, exploration, and creation, for the traveler's mistakes [were] not edited out of the final product" (233).

Big Brother *has had popular queer contestants in Europe, with several gay and transsexual winners in the Netherlands (2000) and in the UK (2001, 2004). In Spain,* Big Brother *has also had several sound queer subtexts. In the 2002 season Raquel Morillas, a very masculine-looking woman who openly identified herself as gay in the show, was one of the main attractions of the season, polarizing debates in the audience between fans and haters who reacted to the negative stereotype of the "evil" masculine lesbian. Once she was out of the house, her popularity escalated, as she declared her love for another contestant, Noemí Ungría, who had been only heterosexual until her* Big Brother *experience. The couple announced their love in the talk show* Crónicas Marcianas, *and then made money selling their romance—and especially Noemí's newly discovered sexual identity—in the tabloids, including a fake wedding ceremony in 2003 (gay marriage was not legal in Spain until 2005), and later selling their break-up and numerous fights. In the 2001 season, contestant Mari Arrabal, known for her affair with another male participant of the season, Alonso, surprised the audience when she broke up with Alonso to marry a woman. As with Raquel and Noemí, Mari has made her divorce from her wife a profitable venture.*

—*Jorge Pérez, in response*

This version is a clear exponent of reality TV's psychoanalytical factor. For both participants and viewers it's like going to the shrink for free and without having to move from the couch.

—*Gabriela Bustelo, in response*

Kate Mills points to a significant sea change that took place before and after *The Ride* was aired. What first appeared as the innovative vérité format of MTV's *The Real World* (1992), a show in which several young adults lived together in a house and their interpersonal relationships were recorded, was now marketed as a (psychological experiment) where truth could/would be revealed. Each episode began with this tagline: "This is the true story . . . of seven strangers . . . picked to live in a house . . . work together and have their lives taped . . . to find out what happens . . . when people stop being polite . . . and start getting real . . . *The Real World.*" While in the early days the show contended with serious issues of young adults, this longest-running reality show would later change and spawn the more superficial and spectacular reality show formats we know today. In series like *Road Rules* (1995) or *Big Brother* and *Survivor* (2000) cameras were no longer placed in the hands of the youth, their narratives left largely unedited and raw, the underlying narrative embracing serious issues. Individuals were placed in artificially constructed, often closed spaces, their narratives edited and constructed for public spectacularity and entertainment. The "true stories" of contemporary reality shows now remixed the value and content of the "real" through quick and smart editing techniques.

> *CRASHING*
>
> Perhaps it is a coincidence, perhaps not, that Ballard's novel, *Crash,* is often cited as one of GenX's and the *Mutantes* antecedents, or that Warhol's car crash serigraph fronts the cover of *Historias del Kronen.* These works connect well with Corner's four categorizations of "The Documentary as Diversion," for they show high-intensity incidents, such as the reconstructed accident or the police raid, within a popular entertainment framework (260). As is well known in shows like *Cops,* an "objective" camera lens reports on the actions while a voice-over narrator tells and dramatizes a story—a reality show version of Warhol's generally accepted objective/commercial cultural axis. The balance between "distance" and "entertainment" is slightly more tilted toward "anecdotal knowledge" and "snoopy sociability" when we consider hybrid versions of the documentary, such as "docusoaps" (documentaries edited to resemble soaps) or "gamedocs" (documentaries with game show elements).
>
> —Christine Henseler
>
> *Twain said it better than anybody: "Truth is stranger than fiction." Fiction has to stick to certain rules. Truth doesn't. In other words, truth is—paradoxically— freer than fiction.*
>
> —Gabriela Bustelo, in response

The narrative that only six years earlier, in *The Ride*, was placed in the hands of the participants, one in which the act of riding was intimately related to the act of creating, was in the Spanish context, in the reality program *El Bus* (airing in 2000 by Antena 3), displaced into a closed and static system within which participants had little control over their own stories, the journey now contained in space. *El Bus* garnered twenty-four percent of the public television audience in Spain. The show hosted between nine and seventeen young people who traveled all over Spain for one hundred days with little exterior contact. Their goal was not to be voted off the bus. The bus itself was engineered to include all the commodities, security, and technology they would need during this period. Although defined by its small enclosed space, the content of this show exploded from the hands of the participants into a variety of media sites, from webcams, Internet chat sites, and the show's official website in which one could find everything from cartoonish "Bus novels," sexual video games, humorous comics, and even explicit photos of the "Bustíbulo." *The Ride*'s narrative vision, "in the raw" (natural, not changed by art, not edited), now turned into "raw" (indecent, not refined, bawdy) bits and pieces of outtakes. These scenes were transfigured into endless versions of "real" people who became stars through everything from mini-series to mini-advertisements, mini-interviews, mini-narratives, mini-videos, and cartoons. The popularity of the shows created an inverse relationship between their popularity and the value of their "real" representations of everyday life.

Ray Loriga's publication *La pistola de mi hermano* (also known as *Caídos del cielo*, 1995) and José Machado's *A dos ruedas* (1996) present two powerful examples of what Hispanist Jorge Pérez has termed "rock and road novels." Within the context of this chapter, *A dos ruedas* could be interpreted as a symbolic narrative representation of *Road Rules*, written, as the back cover of the novel pronounces, in "superdirecta, sin frenar en las curvas" [in superdirect, without breaking in the curves]. In the novel, a young anonymous protagonist travels in a bus from one unidentified place to another and narrates his experiences in the first person, with several "voice-overs" in the third person that ask questions or explain elements about the character. The trip along this Spanish superhighway interlaces the experience of this individual with a host of cultural signifiers from video games, television shows, rock, and punk to Julio Cortázar and Salvador Dalí. The result reflects the everyday experience of a public with a wider cultural repertoire and simultaneous multimedia habits, an interactive relation with the cosmos made ever more explicit in the work of the *Mutantes* years later.

—Christine Henseler

In a move that I cannot but relate to Generation X fiction, these reality programs represented what Tincknell and Raghuram called "a return to the 'basics' of television and a simplification of its aesthetics and its subject matter in an age of increasingly technology-driven and spectacular media" (203). Producers minimized the distance between audience and actors by using cameras that recorded all aspects of life and made previously private spaces available for public view. As noted earlier, some shows, for instance, MTV's *Road Rules* (1995), placed cameras into the hands of the participants, thus folding their roles as "actors," producers," and "viewers" into one. The move affected the seamless filmic quality associated with feature films by integrating the real-world effects associated with documentary filmmaking and adding a strong dose of immediacy. The result mimicked a return to the real observed in Generation X fiction by featuring ordinary youth "just like us," talking "just like us," and acting like "we" do every day. In later programs, by using twenty-four-hour webcams that disclosed routine and boredom in (unedited) shows, an aesthetics was reborn that rejected "Style" (scripted shows) and spoke to the youth, in their own language and, seemingly, through their own eyes. The question of whether the shows represented "true" reality was, actually, beside the point. What mattered was that postproduction created a sensation of authenticity, the televisual effect of Mañas's return to the real.

Generation X: A Postdocumentary "Realist Project"

There may be no better metaphor to describe Generation X's relation to the changing reality effects of its age as the road upon which reality shows have literally traveled. Jorge Pérez named several GenX texts "rock and road novels," after the work of David Laderman on American rock 'n' road movies. Most interesting about his observations in this context is that Pérez identifies these texts as containing "porous generic margins, as cultural hybrids that juxtapose words, images, and sounds" (155). This porosity is more powerful than just a multimedia juxtaposition of senses; it points to a wider aesthetic move that redefines the narrative genre itself. The hybrid roots of reality shows speak directly to an audience whose awareness of the fact/fiction divide has led to narrative conventions and mutations consciously translating the structural effects of new media technologies.

Reality television exemplifies the changing dynamics of media technologies and audience relations in the 1990s, located in between the talk show, crime reporting, the game show format, soap opera, melodrama, tabloid journalism, and the documentary. Divina Frau-Meigs believes that reality television has had a particularly important place in the history of global media reception

Spanish author Francisco Umbral said it nicely: "Each of us is a link in the infinite culture chain, and culture is the only world where all Humanity is present, from the first hominid to the latest poet."

—Gabriela Bustelo, in response

In 2007 Spanish author Lorenzo Silva published Muerte en el reality show. *This novel was originally published in* El Semanal *in the summer of 2003 in weekly installments in which readers voted and decided on the development of the plot. The novel takes place in a television set where a reality show reminiscent of* Big Brother *is being recorded. One day one of the contestants is found dead in the hot tub, and surprisingly the ubiquitous TV cameras show no record of the event. The rest of the novel centers on the investigation of the murder and is charged with high doses of humor and sarcasm.*

—Jorge Pérez, in response

Chilean writer and professor at Duke University Ariel Dorfman wrote *Terapia* in 2001. In this fascinating novel, the nervous breakdown of a man turns into a telereality-based tale of voyeurism, desire, and control.

The novel *Sulphuric Acid* (2005), by Belgian-born Generation X writer Amélie Nothomb, takes reality television to the extreme, with the spectacle of a media-made death camp that obsesses a nation.

—Christine Henseler

precisely because it presents a hybrid generic and transcultural format. The genre evolved within an "old" medium—television—but appropriated "new" digital and Internet technologies; it also laid "claim to both the universal and the specific, [and as such it was positioned] at the crux of the new political economy of media" (37). Helped by digital technologies, the genre has been at the forefront of Internet use for active audience participation.

Reality television redefined the audience's relation to television, not only through the participatory possibilities of technology, but also through the psychological connection it developed between the screening of "everyday" people and the viewers before the screen. As the competition for national and international audiences became fierce, increased consumer choice in programs drove producers to create more innovative and appealing shows. Inmaculada Rodríguez Cunill, in "¿Cómo se crean nuevos códigos audio-visuales para captar audiencias?" points to several televisual techniques that were used to connect more deeply with audiences in Spain throughout the 1990s. In the talk show *Pepe Navarro: Esta noche cruzamos el Mississippi* (Telecinco 1995), the presenter, Pepe Navarro, often dialogued with the camera, not only creating a connection with the audience, but inferring, through camera movements up and down in agreement or side to side in negation, that the audience was responding to his comments (128). Spectator empathy was also deepened in the late-night show *Crónicas marcianas* (Telecinco 1997–2005), in which the presenter would refer to and speak directly to the camera team. The show also developed the sensation of spontaneity and improvisation that attracted more audience attention (128). In the reality show *Operación Triunfo* (TVE, 2001), the fragmented and repetitive character of the televisual discourse, such as the appearance of the characters in a variety of physical and virtual spaces, their appearance on screens beyond the official projection of the show, or their performative appropriation and integration of advertisements, made it look as though the characters could appear or live in the viewers' own living rooms (128). Many of these techniques, of course, are not new, and we have become quite accustomed to them, but in the context of commercial television in the 1990s in Spain, they joined the camera and Internet technology to create a more direct and immediate connection with the viewers. The one-on-one televisual relation between the show and the viewee was materialized in the shape of a camera (exemplified by *Gran Hermano*'s dual use of the camera/ eye logo) to create a direct link between the self inside and outside the screen, between the audience's reality and the projection of an artificially constructed reality.

The techniques used to define the relationship between the television screen and the viewers, or the television and everyday life, demand that we ask how the medium has changed our perceptions of "the real" by breaking down traditional genre boundaries. John Corner, in his influential essay, "Performing the Real: Documentary Diversions," determines that we can recognize elements of, say, game shows, or the "Jerry Springer experience" in reality television, but the documentary seems to be the most obvious genre to begin an analysis of the reality TV genre. Why? Because at the heart of reality shows is,

> the idea of observing what is a mode of "real" behavior. Such observation [says Corner] finds its grounding reference, and a large part of its interest and pleasure, in the real characteristics of real people, even if the material and temporal conditions for that behavior have been entirely constructed by television itself. (256)

As such, it must be said from the outset that the "real" in a reality show like *Big Brother* is predicated on "a fully managed artificiality in which almost everything that might be deemed to be true about what people do and say is necessarily and obviously centered on the larger contrivance of them being there in front of the camera in the first place" (256). *Big Brother* houses are removed from the outside world and are specifically designed and constructed as relatively self-sustaining and all-surveilling. The houses are designed to emphasize inner spaces—interior rooms and psychological states of mind—at the expense of social and political settings.[11]

<table>
<tr><td>

REALITY TELEVISION AND THE DOCUMENTARY

"First broadcast in the United Kingdom in 1964, the Granada Television series *Seven Up!*, broadcast interviews with a dozen ordinary seven-year olds from a broad cross section of society and inquired about their reactions to everyday life. Every seven years, a film documented the life of the same individuals during the intervening period, titled *7 Plus Seven, 21 Up*, etc. The series was structured as a series of interviews with no element of plot. However, it did have the then-new effect of turning ordinary people into celebrities."
http://en.wikipedia.org/wiki/Reality_television

"*Living in the Past* was a fly on the wall documentary programme aired by the BBC in 1978 which followed a group of 15 young volunteers recreating an Iron Age settlement, where they sustained themselves for a year, equipped only with the tools, crops and livestock that would have been available in Britain in the 2nd Century BC."
http://en.wikipedia.org/wiki/Living_in_the_Past_%28TV_series%29

Well, after all, reality TV's methods are scientific and if animals could talk, a standard wildlife video would be reality TV's first exponent and National Geographic might be considered the genre's creator.

—Gabriela Bustelo, in response

</td></tr>
</table>

Corner explains that the documentary changed in the nineties to include more "inner stories," such as "the road accident, about the crime, about the illness" (256). To allow the microsocial to come across on screen, the documentary has made increased use of personal interviews and dramatization techniques; the genre "has frequently become a highly defined narrative of localized feelings and experiences presented against what is often merely sketchy if not entirely token background social setting" (256). There has been a change in the documentary tone, in the voice that leads us through the story and develops empathy in its viewers (256). Consequently, and complicating the situation, adds Corner, is the fact that the objective, documentary look has changed. Instead of sounding and looking different from other genres, the documentary has been borrowing from nondocumentary styles, such as from drama, advertising, and pop videos, thereby complicating the viewer's recognition of its authorial status (262). Adding to this already muddled situation is the inclusion of more musical accompaniment and a degree of self-consciousness filled with a higher level of performativity and parody (more in line with docu-soaps).

The more hybrid and entertaining character of the once clearly delineated, informative, or questioning documentary genre suggests that we have entered, as Corner famously declared, a "postdocumentary" culture of television. This is an era in which the audiovisual formats of the traditional documentary continue to develop in changing economic and cultural settings (255). The postdocumentary era presents a moment in which reality television shows like *Big Brother* can also be examined differently, not as just "popular media entertainment" on one hand or as a distorted, diversionary "documentary" on the other, but as the legacy of a documentary that is still at work, "albeit partial and in revised form" (257) in popular entertainment.

To move toward a postdocumentary criticism, Corner suggests that the use of the term "documentary" as an adjective may be used more fruitfully than as a noun. We might want to ask "is this a documentary project?" rather than "is this film a documentary?" (258). The same might apply to Generation X texts. Critics tend to categorize Generation X as pertaining to the genre of "neorealism," "dirty realism," even "hyperrealism," when indeed it might be more fruitful to ask to what degree GenX novels are "realist projects." By asking the question in this manner, Generation X can break out of preestablished critical approaches and repeated postmodern theories and move more freely between genres, disciplines, and storytelling platforms. By examining GenX film and fiction as "realist projects," critics can focus more attention on the way in which these texts widen narrative relations through multiplatform and transcultural relations and representations of the world. Within the context of this book, the tools used by reality television shows and their construction of reality projects can allow us to see more clearly the connection between a punk "do it yourself" and "tell it like it is" philosophy and an *Afterpop* criticism emerging in the digital age.

The *Real* World of Big Brother in *Veo veo* by Gabriela Bustelo

Generation X writer Gabriela Bustelo wrote *Veo veo* in 1996. The novel displays notions of "the real" in a remixed version of *The Real World* by emulating techniques used in reality television shows. In *Veo veo*, Bustelo turns the life of her protagonist, twenty-six-year old Vania, into a "reality project" by making her the writer, director, and performer of her own "reality show." A screenwriter by trade, Vania inserts bits and pieces of information from a variety of sources into her life's performance in order to put her storyline into action. She begins by constructing an impulse, or reason for the beginning of the thriller, rooted in her intuitive sense that she is being followed and watched. The novel highlights the dual process of performance and postproduction, the viewing and the editing, the narrating and the narrated as the mystery of this project unfolds.[12] In both reality shows and *Veo veo*, as the title suggests, the story centers on seeing and being seen, and the narrative thread plays with in-between spaces: the personality traits the characters show and those they disguise, the information and perspective that Vania chooses to include and to leave out. What the emphasis on the in-between suggests is that picking out the "real" from the "fictitious" moments is a futile exercise. Readers and viewers must suspend their disbelief and accept reality as a "reality project."

Veo veo straddles genres, such as adventure, detective thriller, game show, soap opera, and romance. The text makes readers aware that characters take part in the effects of a "game" of *I Spy with My Little Eye* (the English translation of the title, *Veo veo*). The revelation of bits and pieces of a constructed "truth" increases the dramatic effect of the novel and moves the storyline forward. While reality television producers usually create cliffhangers to bring viewers back for the next episode, the novel provides readers with limited focalization points from which to (not) see and to (not) know. In both cases, plots revolve around love interests and sexual tension; conflict is built around attraction, alcohol, and, in the novel, drug use; characters are placed into increasingly difficult situations emotionally and physically; and they are "voted" off or, as in the novel, are literally shot off "the set."

GABRIELA BUSTELO

Gabriela Bustelo, born in 1962, lived in Paris from 1963–68, and in Washington D.C. from 1968–74, at which time she returned to Spain. While in the United States, Bustelo went to an Episcopalian school in which her professors taught her English after class. For many years she only spoke English with her parents and her sister (E-mail). Her earliest cultural references were North American, not Spanish, and they included *The Land of the Giants*, *I Love Lucy*, and *I Dream of Jeannie*, and books such as *The Twenty-One Balloons* by William Pène du Bois and *Island of the Blue Dolphins* by Scott O'Dell (E-mail). In the 1970s in the United States, Bustelo grew up on Bob Dylan, Pete Seeger, and Tom Paxton, records that her father bought and listened to at home. Her North American cultural references are abundantly present in her first novel *Veo veo*, and her degree in English philology clearly influenced the connection between her second novel *Planeta Hembra* [Female Planet] (2001) and the perceived influences of Orwell or Huxley. First written as a film script, *Planeta Hembra*, a cyberfeminist science fiction novel, was written in a colloquial tongue that included slang, Anglicism, and invented words, and was, according to Bustelo, "meant to revise all those old feminist (or feminine) attitudes which have their origin in the politics of the sixties" (Mora, "Gabriela Bustelo" 34).

When Bustelo returned to Spain at the turn of the democratic era in 1974, she admitted to feeling silenced, having to hide her "experiencia americana" from her peers (E-mail). Despite this setback, says Bustelo, "mi código moral lo aprendí en Estados Unidos, pero esos principios básicos frecuentemente chocan con los de mis compatriotas, que valoran menos, por ejemplo, la sinceridad, la capacidad autocrítica o la tolerancia religiosa. [. . .] Finalmente, diría que en parte debo la →

capacidad crítica y la ironía al hecho de haberme criado entre dos mundos tan radicalmente diferentes" (E-mail). Bustelo identifies herself as a postfeminist, which she defines as a more mature, autocritical, and ironic take on feminism. This is a vision, she says, that goes beyond divisionary gender boundaries to include men into life's cycle (E-mail). And, it is a perspective that she clearly positions opposite of Etxebarria, whose book title itself, *Nosotras que no somos como las demás*, Bustelo sees as more acutely separating the female from the male sex (E-mail).

—Christine Henseler

Setting the Scene

Similar to the shifts in Loriga's *Héroes* between the past and the present, between social reality and the reality he presents through rock music, *Veo veo* sets the scene through temporal oppositions. Readers glimpse approximately two weeks of Vania's life at the end of the 1980s, several years after the official ending of the *Movida madrileña*.[13] According to Vania, her life at this time is boring, her days suggest routine, and her behavior has become that of "una santa" [a saint] (12). The spectacle, excitement, and party life of "la época del Sol, del Rockola, de la Sala Morasol, del Pentagrama" (12) have passed. Vania no longer feels the center of her own, or anybody else's, attention.

Decidedly breaking out of her chains as "Santa Teresa de Ávila" (18), Vania calls a former, intermittent lover and heads to the fashionable restaurant "Archy's." She describes Archy's as a hybrid dig, an old factory converted into a non-plus ultra-chic restaurant and disco. She is acutely aware of the contrast of eating in a fine dining space and then going down into the cave to dance with the "lumpen lait" [lumpen light] (18). She observes that the game played in this "temple of modernity" (18) is "el juego de ver-ser visto," [the game of seeing and being seen] (19). This seductive game, so integral to the totality of the novel, is used here to criticize contemporary capitalist culture's social fabric. In a move that underlines Generation X'ers' ability to critically observe from within, Vania makes clear that her social interactions are stifled by artificial encounters, superficial conversations, empty flirtatious innuendos, and passing fashions. Her experience leads to a disquieting realization about Madrid's nightlife, observing that,

se podía estar meses, años sin salir de copas por Madrid, podían pasar cosas, se podía uno casar, tener hijos, podían morir parientes, podía haber guerras, podía hundirse el sistema comunista al otro lado de nuestro continente, podían descubrirse las supernovas, los agujeros negros, y los noctambuleros seguían ensayando una y

---

I SPY WITH MY LITTLE EYE

The exact translation of the title would be I Spy with My Little Eye, *the name of the children's game, often played in a car, where the lead chooses a visible object and says* "I spy with my little eye, something beginning with the letter A." *In Spanish the game is called* "Veo veo" *and the dialogue between the lead and the other players is:* "Veo, veo" "¿Qué ves?" "Una cosita" "¿Con qué letrita?" "Con la letrita A".

—*Gabriela Bustelo, in response*

mil veces las mismas escenas insulsas de una aniquilosada obra de teatro que nadie quería dirigir.

[one could spend months, years without going out in Madrid, things could happen, one could get married, have kids, relatives could die, there can be wars, the communist system could fall at the other end of our continent, supernovas could be discovered, black holes, and the night owls would continue to rehearse the same dull scene of a fossilized theatre play that nobody wanted to direct]. (20)

The space reminds Vania of Luis Buñuel's 1962 film "El ángel exterminador," in which guests at an upper-class dinner party find themselves trapped in a room (a precursor, perhaps, to the closed space of *Big Brother* houses). Her observations relate directly to her feeling of imprisonment in her own life, a life of meaningless routine and loneliness, a life in which she feels enclosed in her apartment with nothing to do, nothing of importance to care about.

Against this backdrop, the telephone caller (her alter ego?) who repeatedly asks for (the common female name of) "Soledad" [Loneliness] is interpretatively telling. This is a voice that connects to her home and office as a suggestive reminder of her inner state of mind. Perhaps more revealing than the jarring reality that the "diabolic" (15) use of the telephone imposes on Vania's increasingly constructed perception of life is her reaction to the question of loneliness. Loneliness is a feeling she consciously pushes away as not relating to herself, for, just like in reality television shows, "loneliness" has no place in a communal space where she is constantly being watched. Tellingly, she says that loneliness does not apply to herself, but rather, to "el resto de los mortales, porque a mí me filmaban en tecnicolor, con sonoro incorporado" [the other mortals, because I was being filmed in Technicolor, with integrated sound] (78).

As in much Generation X literature, escape from social reality and personal loneliness is infused with popular culture and media technologies to counterpoise stark reality and to reposition oneself within the celebrity mania of "star" culture. Similarly, the pull of reality shows consists in turning everyday people into stars through television. *Veo veo* makes this relationship between normalcy and stardom quite apparent, as, for instance, when Vania's love interest, Ben Ganza, states that, "lo que todo el mundo quiere hoy en día es salir en algún medio de comunicación, contar su vida a los cuatro vientos" [what everybody wants to do today is appear before the public and tell their life story] (140). Thousands of normal people go to reality show auditions to become heroes "just for one day," to quote David Bowie from the previous chapter.

As Vania's life is entangled in the awareness of an existent, exterior vision, she is able to realize her own presence. The process is summarized, in perhaps too obvious of a fashion, at the end of the novel when Vania has been interned in a psychiatric hospital and meets an engineer with a similar condition. This man admits that when he was watching television he felt that those who were on the other side of the screen were watching him, that his life, much like the movie *The Truman Show,* bellowed to others like a montage. When he

DID YOU KNOW?

"Mentor and manager Andy Warhol suggested that the album *I'll Be Your Mirror* sung by the Velvet Undergound have a built-in crack in it so the line 'I'll be your mirror' would repeat infinitely on a record player until the listener moved the needle themselves, but nothing ever came of this idea."

http://draweringss.tumblr.com/post/397418695/mentor-and-manager-andy-warhol-suggested-that-the

Curiously, at one point Vania says something very similar to the Truman Show remark: "Había pasado de estar fané y descangallada a estar más solicitada que la Chelito" (47). In English: "I'd gone from withered and wasted to being more popular than la Chelito." ("Fané y descangallada" is from an ever-famous tango by Discépolo, and La Chelito was a popular nineteenth-century Spanish singer).

—Gabriela Bustelo, in response

felt himself being watched twenty-four hours a day, "me sentía el protagonista absoluto de una vida apasionante en vez del segundón de siempre" [I felt like the absolute protagonist of a passionate life instead of the simpleton from always] (197). In this context, the epigraph from Lou Reed—"Seré tu espejo / Reflejaré lo que eres, por si no lo sabes" [I will be your mirror / I will reflect what you are, in case you do not know it]—suggests a process of realization and transformation, as the public "I/eye" of the other makes the very private actions of the "I" more real. The unidirectional mirror in Vania's bathroom, a mirror in which she can see herself and simultaneously be seen, is perhaps the best exemplification of this idea. Much like the novel, the song also plays with the dual nature of seeing and not seeing, as the lyrics say:

> When you think the night is in your mind
> and inside you're twisted and unkind
> Let me stand to show that you are blind
> Please put down your hands,
> 'Cos I see you

Although Vania's life appears as the object of another's attention, from the very beginning, the novel provides clear signs that Vania writes herself into a new storyline and selects particular characters to fit preassigned roles. In reality television programs producers select "types" of individuals to represent a select group of "normal" characters. In the novel, Vania's characters must also be readily recognizable as well-defined fictitious stereotypes in order to move the storyline forward in the most dramatic of fashions. She rejects the psychiatrist she names "Mickey Rourke" because he does not comply with her preconceived image of a Sigmund Freud—"lo que yo esperaba era una especie de vejete judío con barba, firme y paternal a la vez" [what I expected was kind of an old Jewish man with beard, firm and paternal at the same time] (11). Instead, this man reminds her of a character in a cheap serial novel, leading her to sexualize his image—"no pude evitar imaginar que me estaba llevando a su dormitorio. La escena me resultaba brumosamente familiar" [I could not help but imagine that he was taking me to his bedroom. The scene felt disconcertedly familiar] (9). After her session with the psychiatrist, Vania rents the erotically charged film *Wild Orchid* (1990) and folds the reality she prefers not to see back into her own fiction, a feeling made clear when she says, "Como mi ex psiquiatra se parecía a Mickey Rourke, ver la película era la forma de exorcizarles a los dos juntos" [Since my ex-psychiatrist looked like Mickey Rourke, watching the movie was a way of exorcising them both] (14). In this first mini-chapter (or "episode") of the novel, Vania begins her transition as the producer of her own narrative. She creates a world in which all figures and elements function to set the scene for *her* preconceived story, her reality as determined through storytelling.

> *Absolutely! Weary of boredom and isolation, the protagonist writes and stages her own movie, a psychodrama played by a cast of characters prompted by her, but all of them free to improvise and act unexpectedly.*
>
> *—Gabriela Bustelo, in response*

After the image of the psychiatrist fails to meet Vania's expectations, she adopts characters that more perfectly fit into cultural stereotypes. Through a newspaper ad, she finds her perfect detective (11) and hero (69), Peláez, who she also calls "El Cejas." This man works into her preconceived notion of a Hispanic "detective" albeit already infused with British and US popular culture.[14] He is, she says,

el perfecto detective hispánico. Chaparreta, cejijunto y con un Ducados en la boca. Su despacho consistía en una mesa llena de papeles y colillas. Sobre un estante precario colgado en una de las paredes había una ristra de novelas negras, desde Chandler y la Highsmith hasta Jeffrey Archer y Frederick Forsyth.

[The perfect Hispanic detective. Short and plump, eyebrows close together, and with a Ducados in his mouth. His office consisted in a table filled with papers and cigarette butts. Precariously hanging from one of the walls a bookshelf with a string of detective novels, from Chandler and Highsmith to Jeffrey Archer and Frederick Forsyth.] (11)

> ### HAVE YOU SEEN THIS?
>
> Charlie Brooker's Screenwipe – Reality TV Editing
>
> w w w . y o u t u b e . c o m / w a t c h ? v =BBwepkVurCI
>
> —Christine Henseler
>
> *This is related to the addictive element that TV series have: repetition. The fact that a TV series has a time slot is basic. Reality shows share this element of routine that is one of television's great assets.*
>
> *—Gabriela Bustelo, in response*

Slowly the other characters in her storyline fall into place: "El Bigotes" becomes the mystery man who follows her; "Ben Ganza" embodies the perfect seducer-lover turned psychopath, even by name (Ben + Ganza = Venganza [vengeance]); Vania (the vain one) turns herself into the female figure of seduction, a victim, yet active agent of her own destiny; and the

> ## FROM PARTICIPANTS IN REALITY SHOWS
>
> "I'd gone and had this experience but I could never describe the things I saw, the things I did and the feelings I felt to everyone. And then you think, oh wait, they're going to see it on TV…And that's the whole point about validation. It [being on *Road Rules*] validates what you did and why you were there" (265).
>
> —Mark Andrejevic, *"The Kinder, Gentler Gaze of Big Brother"*
>
> "You honestly get used to it; it's just part of your everyday life…I went through withdrawal for the two weeks after I got home…I looked forward to that for so long, having my own time and my own space, and then when I got there, it was so lonely" (107).
>
> —Mark Andrejevic, *Reality TV: The Work of Being Watched*
>
> *As mentioned, Spanish author Baltasar Gracián wrote in his* Oráculo manual y arte de la prudencia *(1647)—an avant age-old how-to book—that it's advisable to act at all times as if we were being watched. "The person that wants to be seen by everybody does not have to worry about being spied on at home," he claimed three and a half centuries ago (!).*
>
> —*Gabriela Bustelo, in response*

crowd and characters of Madrid's nightlife present the colorful backdrop and setting of the story. Each character functions in distinct ways to set the scene and to develop the plotline. Vania, as the internal narrator, makes up, mediates, remixes, or edits the information she receives. And much like in reality television, the editing process leaves the viewers to wonder what is true, what is constructed, and what difference it makes.

Seeing and Not Seeing

Vania develops a reverse relationship between knowing and not knowing, seeing and not seeing. She admits that the less she knows about a particular character, the longer her version of the narrative can progress. When she talks about her attraction for Ben, she admits that "lo bueno sería prolongar eternamente esta época. No saber nada de él. Inventarme el personaje a mi gusto durante todo el tiempo que quisiera" [it would be great to prolong this stage forever. Not know anything about him. Invent his character to my liking as long as I want] (45). Sexual attraction becomes the essential ingredient, or excuse, to develop the tension that moves the plot forward. As in reality shows, sex and knowledge are played off each other. Editors manipulate the relationship between knowing and seeing, consciously creating a game of hide and seek (especially at nightfall when cameras supposedly go dark).

There are several references in the novel that point to Vania's relationship to television and the image. In the very beginning of the text, while Vania is telling Peláez about her life, she acknowledges that her previously active sex life had changed, in part because of the realities of the AIDS epidemic. Instead of enjoying an active sex life, she discloses that, "cada vez me dedico más a ver la tele" [I increasingly dedicate myself to watching television] (11). Vania also admits to rejecting language as a means of communication, relegating reports, scripts, and translations to her life at work and to everyday routine (64). Because her *real* world is marked by boredom and long hours, she repositions it in relation to the visual, to a world in which "la rapidez y el instante concreto eran lo que contaba" [quickness and the present moment were what mattered] (64). Her appropriation of the image and the instant works, as Tincknell and Raghuram remark in regard to reality television culture, to "draw the audience in, producing the effect of a more direct relationship to the text" (204). Vania's appropriation of the image, then, underlines the experience of immediacy as a narrative device that centers the readers on the present.

Ironically, the presence of cameras focusing in on characters' actions twenty-four hours a day, in both the novel and reality shows, gives viewers the impression that they are privy to every detail, that they are allowed to "know" the entire story. The narratives consciously manipulate viewers' voyeuristic tendencies, making them believe in a panopticon-like power, while surreptitiously constructing particular versions of reality. Similarly, *Big Brother*'s story is mediated by the combination of editing and voice-over commentaries, which help produce preferred versions about participants and sexualized content, often totally closing off other possible interpretations (Tincknell and Raghuram 204, 206). As in the case of Vania, whose vacation from work allows her to increasingly disconnect from the outside world, contestants of *Big Brother* shows "explore and reflect on their relations with each other, as the weeks proceeded, in growing detail, becoming more self-preoccupied (if not always very self-reflexive) as the outer world [becomes] more distant from their immediate experience" (Tincknell and Raghuram 206).

Similarly, one could claim that the reality effect of Vania's experiences allows her to step outside of time, instead of returning to a past, and transgress "the laws of linear, infinite time [...]

TIME IN REALITY TELEVISION

To better understand the temporal qualities of reality TV, Kavka and West make a valuable distinction between "located" and "unlocated" time. Located time relates to calendar dates and clock time, while "unlocated" time contravenes historical linearity for more finite and cyclical references (142). The time given for the completion of a task in reality television, whether five seconds or a month, are viewed as units disengaged from historical time and may be counted backward or forward. Therefore, one of the most important features of time in reality TV is its finiteness and its renewability, shows begin again at "Day 1" or at "0" times for each group of contestants (142). As such, time in reality TV can float backward, forward, and around, "in a temporal vacuum" that is easily relatable to the work of Loriga, Machado, or Prado as well as Gabi Martínez or Agustín Fernández Mallo.

—Christine Henseler

GenX's concept of time tends to be postmodern, which means that it's fractioned and adjustable according to necessity. In this sense, life is envisioned and manipulated like a film/video/DVD that can be moved forward or backward, fast or slow, stopped here or there, paused at will, and so on.

—Gabriela Bustelo, in response

manifesting a kind of cyclical present which begins and ends whenever and wherever it is transmitted" (Kavka and West 151). "Historical location" as a temporal marker ceases to matter or register. In the novel, historical time is increasingly compressed into actions or revelations, and in the return or reflection of the image of Vania in the mirror, in video, on the dance floor, in Ben's eyes. Returning to my reference to Andy Warhol in previous chapters, time is compressed into sameness, over and over again but with slight, almost unrecognizable differences. In the words of Vania, who at one point is trying to drink water to get over a hangover: "me veía a mi misma como una serigrafía de Warhol, cada vez en colorín distinto, pero siempre con el mismo careto y la misma jarra de agua" [I saw myself as a Warhol serigraph, constantly changing colors, but always with the same pout and the same water jug] (77).

Veo veo defies traditional notions of linear temporality and re-creates a *presence* of spatial experience through the storytelling capabilities of visual and verbal media.[15] Vision is undoubtedly the driving sense in the novel; but while vision works as a tactic for realization, and Vania believes that "eyes never lie" (65), the novel also makes apparently clear that vision is multiple, complex, and changing. The embodied Ben, Peláez, friends and acquaintances, or mechanized cameras or eyes, necessarily cut out information and edit events into storylines that better fit Vania's needs. As such, the "liveness" effect that she tries to re-create to "feel alive," is, like reality television, "as much about belonging to an imagined community of viewers at the moment

---

Critics have viewed GenX novels' relation and immersion in the present as defying historical time, as presenting readers with a (negative) generational consciousness positioned "outside" of history. On the other hand, the appeal of reality TV has been described "in terms of its capacity for live transmission, a performance of the present linked with a decontextualizing of the past [thus fulfilling] the temporal potential of the medium itself" (136). In other words, the abundance of information projected from the television screen "requires the disappearance of the just-seen to make way for the now-seeing. As Stephen Heath has put it, 'television produces forgetfulness, not memory, flow, not history'" (qtd. in Kayka and West 137).

I would like to suggest that Generation X's historical location is not measured in a distancing and objectifying manner, but, as Kavka and West suggest in relation to reality television, in hours, minutes, seconds, and bits and pieces meant to develop a rearranged and transformed sense of authenticity and immediacy (136). The lack of cultural value often attributed to the here and now fails to take into account "the complex relation among effects of immediacy, reality and intimacy brought into alignment by programmes which use 'real' people in seemingly 'real' or 'live' time" (Kavka and West 137–38). In other words, reality TV does not play itself out in "real" time, but, "it reorders time, distilling it into socially recognizable units which are reiterable, and hence return as ever new, ever present" (138). Reality is less related to chronological time than to the construction of a multi-leveled sense of historical authenticity and liveness.

—Christine Henseler

of watching as it is about being able to enjoy the unpredictability of proto-climactic events" (Kavka and West 140). The novel develops a "liveness" effect through the unexpected happenings of a detective genre and the use of other media—video, computer, television, radio—that elevate the dramatic effect of the action.

Remixing Reality

Vania's construction of the *real* is directly related to its infusion of references from the world of film, advertising, and music. Her actions are saturated with moments that emulate characters from non-Hispanic film and music, such as Starsky and Hutch (24), Cybil Shepherd (126), Anjelica Huston (47), and Mick Jagger (171). These references, and more, do not present simple intertexts, but as mentioned in earlier chapters, they serve to remix reality into an authentic representation that connects to her audience. Vania's entire being, her reality, only exists in relation to her ability to talk and walk the language that connects her to you and me. Much like in reality television shows, Vania's sense of authenticity depends on how well she can, in her own mind, relate to her audience. Only those characters on reality shows that present themselves as natural and *not* role playing or performing are those that are not voted off the show. Given that audiences are unknown (for most of the novel Vania does not know who is watching her), and given that reality shows project around the world, the most obvious and authentic connection points reside in North American popular culture. "Authenticity," then, is not related to the *natural* and the *genuine* as much as it is connected to its *credibility*. If I can convince you that I am real, then I am a part of you.

> *INTERESTED IN PARTICIPATING IN A SPANISH REALITY SHOW?*
>
> Just go to Telecinco.es: http://mitele.telecinco.es/camara/index.shtml At this site you can record a video of yourself "Grábate," you can send it to the producers, "Envía," and you can become a reality television star—"Yo estella."
>
> —Christine Henseler
>
> *Like Japanese author Murakami says, Western culture is a huge bank available to everybody. Those of us who are lucky to speak the language can just stick our arm in the culture box and pull out whatever we need. Europe tends to be in denial of the fact that America's so-called soft power—news media, television, movies, literature, celebrity lifestyle, fashion, etc.—is the Western culture of today.*
>
> —Gabriela Bustelo, in response

If reality television pursues intimacy, or emotional closeness, through temporal and spatial immediacy, then it should come as no surprise that Vania's own version of "presence" is enhanced by dozens of musical references. In a beautiful essay on the trumping influence of music in *Veo veo*, Hispanist Nina Molinaro discusses Vania's identification with popular music as both connecting "to her own history while also projecting an anachronistic sense of self" ("Watching" 206). Vania is quite conscious of the emotional dynamics of music in the reconstruction of her life. She says that,

> si me ponía a hacer zapping con mi vida, siempre había una banda sonora. Siempre estaba la Música, la más abstracta de las artes, puesto que no es símbolo, como los demás, de nada real. Una melodía no representa nada, como la pintura, ni utiliza un lenguaje con significados, como la literatura. Para empezar, la música ni siquiera es corpórea. Es puro éter.
>
> [when I began to zap through my life, there was always a soundtrack. There was always Music, the most abstract of the arts, given that it is not a symbol of anything real. A melody does not represent things, like a painting, nor does it use a language with meanings, like literature. To begin with, music is not even corporeal. It is pure ether.] (134)

Vania admits to "zapping" or "channel surfing" through the pictures of her life, highlighting different sections through the emotional charge of music. This act of zapping is not forlorn because it suggests that Vania exerts power over her narrative and her chronology, and demonstrates agency and creativity in her life (Molinaro 207). The text points not only to the medium itself, but to the medium in action. In Vania's own words, the effect of music as a system allows her to be taken away ("dejarme llevar"); she says that music allowed "una conexión tan sublime entre un tema y otro que era como estar creando una obra propia, arte sobre arte" [a connection so sublime between one topic and another that it was like making my own creation, art on art] (134). The novel provides several other hints as to Vania's awareness of the role of media in her life's reconstruction, the metamedia dimension of the text. Media scholar Lev Manovich clarifies that "the idea of a metamedium is not built on 'a' finished product, but rather on a process and on the ability of individuals to 'read' and access material and tools created by others—'the ability to write in a medium means that you can generate materials and tools for others'" ("Alan"). The *Movida* past that Vania emotionally desires to recapture can then only be re-presented to the degree that she has access to the material (popular culture and media technology) that allows her to retell a story in the making.

Vania's performances before the naked eye or camera disclose an awareness of the process of production as well as postproduction, one in which acting and being are consciously interrelated. John Corner argues persuasively that the circumstances of reality television,

> are not so much of those of observation as those of *display*; living space is also performance space. The availability is both tightly spatial and urgently temporal, clearly. But it is also, in its scopic comprehensiveness, emotional. Outside and inside, objectification and subjectification, empathy and detachment, fondness and dislike—these are positional variables on a spectatorial grid across which rapid switching can occur. (257)

Veo veo is, through this lens, a text that emphasizes display rather than voyeurism as Vania constantly switches back and forth on what Corner calls "a spectatorial grid." Vania admits to seeing everything "en clave de cine" [through cinematic code] (150); she "rewinds" scenes (25) and hears the closing of a door as "el clic de una cámara que se apaga después de rodar la escena más fuerte de la puñetera película" [as the click of a camera that turns off after filming the toughest scene of the entire fucking movie] (150). When Vania has to provide a declaration to the police after shooting Ben, she views her act as a psychodrama, revealing her perception of real life. In a hyperaware fashion she comments that "la diferencia entre un sicodrama y el teatro de toda la vida es que en el sicodrama no hay texto escrito. Vale todo y puede ocurrir cualquier cosa, pero hay que dar la talla actuando, igual o más" [the difference between a psychodrama and the theater of everyday life is that in the psychodrama there is no written text. Everything goes and anything can happen, but one has to give a convincing performance, the same, or even better than in a film] (149). Her psychodramatic enactment reveals that her definition of the "theater of everyday life" is defined/confined by a text that pins the act to its storyline. Performance, then, presents a break from linearity (speak boredom and routine), which Vania beautifully identifies when she says:

> mi vida era una sesión continua estilo Rosa Púrpura del Cairo, en la que yo brincaba a uno y otro lado de la pantalla a mi antojo, actriz o espectadora según me convenía. Y así lograba mantener en todo momento un distanciamiento de los hechos demenciales que se sucedían día tras día.

> [my life was a continuous session in the style of *The Purple Rose of Cairo*, in which I jumped from one side of the screen to the other depending on how I felt, actress and spectator according to my needs. And this way I was able to keep a distance from the surreal events that took place day after day]. (150)

The reference to Woody Allen's 1985 film *The Purple Rose of Cairo* suggests an awareness of Vania's role and ability to walk on and off the screen, to present herself as character in film and in real life, and to switch between the real and the created in a seamless and playful manner that questions and constructs authenticity in both realms. Most interesting, perhaps, is Vania's conscious interpellation as actor or spectator as a coping mechanism that allows her to construct a particularly powerful story for and about herself. I would add to this positioning the role of production and edition that appears throughout the novel in different guises, as in the well-edited videos created of Vania's twenty-four-hour surveillance, or Ben's exposition of digital editing technology and techniques (87). Postproduction takes on an equally large role in the performance itself, a reality consciously remixed.

The marriage of technology and storytelling most obviously occurs when Vania defines herself as a "pastiche compacto" [a compact pastiche] (134):

"pongo una canción de Guy Beart y no sé bien qué me pasa, pero no estoy con todos mis átomos en Madrid,.... dejo de ser un *pastiche compacto* y me diluyo en no sé qué lugares remotos del espacio y el tiempo en París" [I play a song of Guy Beart and I don't know what happens, but I no longer have all my atoms together in Madrid...I stop being a *compact pastiche* and dissolve into remote space and time in Paris] (my emphasis 134). The use of the word "compact" describes not only her packable, dense physical embodiment of an artistic, literary trope, but in this context, it could also play with the word "compact disc," thus creating a direct relationship between herself and the "compact" storing and playing of digital data. Taken together, music in *Veo veo* underlines the (digital) construction of a story-song as defined by units, by bits and pieces and ultimately packaged as a compact pastiche.

In reality television, as in most (traditional) novels, producers or authors create stories with beginnings, middles, and ends. The "story editors" or "segment producers" of reality shows use an editing process known as "frankenbites" "to describe the art of switching around contestant sound bites recorded at different times and patched together to create what appears to be a seamless narrative." The word's etymology joins Frankenstein's monster and the sound bite to suggest a patching together of a story from many sources.

The ultimate goal of the frankenbite is to extract what the editor considers the sources' most salient features: to construct an especially dramatic, revealing, or sensational narrative. Similarly, John Corner talks about reality television's "mutually modifying interplay of relationships and identities [that] delivers the crucial open plot of the program's narrative. One might use the term 'selving' to describe the central process whereby 'true selves' are seen to emerge (and develop) from underneath and, indeed, through, the 'performed selves'

> The process related to "frankenbites" reminds me of a hypertext by Shelley Jackson titled *Patchwork Girl* and produced by Eastgate Systems. The author and title's connection to Mary Shelley's *Frankenstein* and the linking experience of reading the hypertext provides a powerful example of the changing dynamic between creation and created, the physical patching process of becoming a story in motion.
>
> —Christine Henseler

> *"Given your overall argument, I'm struck by how retro novel-reading truly is, given the 'simultaneous and multi-media habits' that you detail in our global visual culture. Bustelo's novel may be talking ABOUT this culture but the act of reading a novel—her novel perhaps even more than other GenX novels—is hopelessly nostalgic, chronological, time-heavy, memory-heavy, etc."*
>
> *—Nina Molinaro, in response*
>
> *I totally agree with Nina Molinaro. As I've been saying for decades, today's cultural formats are based on written genres, but have displaced them. Our younger generations watch movies/videos and surf the Web. My first novel was prenostalgic of literature's oncoming decline.*
>
> *—Gabriela Bustelo, in response*

projected for us, as a consequence of the applied pressures of objective circumstance and group dynamics" (261–62). One could claim that Vania's "true selves" are exposed through the patching together of frankenbites in *Veo veo*. Vania reaches out and upward and grabs on to bits and pieces of material here and there from the world of fiction, film, television, and music as she performs her storyline into action. With every mental "zap" or "click" Vania patches her own frankenbites into a seamless narrative of dramatic proportions, the final "bip bip bip" of the telephone foregrounding a feedback loop that underlines technology's role in the endless remixing of Vania's reality.[16]

Chapter 5

From Generation X to the *Mutantes*

Just as Mother Nature was seen in past centuries
as the source of both human behavior and physical reality,
so now the Universal Computer is envisioned
as the Motherboard of us all. (Hayles, *My Mother* 3)

If, as literary critics, we venture into the genetic code, as does Katherine Hayles in *How We Became Posthuman*, we learn that mutation "normally occurs when some random event (for example, a burst of radiation or a coding error) disrupts an existing pattern and something else is put in its place instead" (33). Hayles emphasizes that a "mutation" can only be understood if it is measured against a standard; it must be, like media in general, *connected* to something.[1] As such, "mutation" refers to "a *bifurcation point* at which the interplay between pattern and randomness causes the system to evolve in a new direction" (my emphasis, 33). The beginning of the twenty-first century presents a literary bifurcation point when new bits and pieces add new patterns to an established literary standard called "Generation X." The result leads to "information

PATTERN AND RANDOMNESS

"Pattern can be recognized through redundancy or repetition of elements. If there is only repetition, however, no new information is imparted; the intermixture of randomness rescues pattern from sterility. If there is only randomness, the result is gibberish rather than communication. Information is produced by a complex dance between predictability and unpredictabililty, repetition and variation. We have seen that the possibilities for mutation are enhanced and heightened by long coding chains. We can now understand mutation in more fundamental terms. Mutation is crucial because it names the bifurcation point at which the interplay between pattern and randomness causes the system to evolve in a new direction. Mutation implies both the replication of pattern—the morphological standard against which it can be measured and understood as a mutation—and the interjection of randomness—the variations that mark it as a deviation so decisive it can no longer be assimilated into the same" (78).

—Katherine Hayles, *"Virtual Bodies"*

narratives," as Hayles would call them, which mutate previous linguistic patterns or characteristics through technological means and techniques. These new narrative bytes have infused the production of writers known as the "Nocilla Generation," based on the work of Agustín Fernández Mallo; the "Afterpops," by Eloy Fernández Porta; and the term I prefer, the *Mutantes*, as first conceived by Juan Francisco Ferré, Julio Ortega, and Vicente Luis Mora.[2] By regarding the application of new media technologies as, on one hand, a *bifurcation point* and, on another, a *mutation* of a previously existing pattern, it is possible to view the work of the *Mutantes* as born out of and mutating from Generation X.

In this chapter I examine the role and relation between patterns and mutations. I begin by suggesting that literary criticism itself must break out of existing historiographic approximations and take a more flexible approach to the study of *Mutantes* fiction. The idea is to redefine the effects of the digital age on critical approaches to contemporary literature. When authors have at their fingertips an entire world of information with a myriad of possible entry and exit points, individual sensibilities and experiences break down pre-established categories and critical approaches. This demands that scholars engage with new media technologies not in a generalized fashion, but rather on a very material, user-based level. The design, function, and use of any given medium materializes as distinct stylistic forms with unique spatial, temporal, and identificatory dynamics. To continue to examine the materiality of media events, I engage here with the video game in Gabi Martínez's 2005 novel *Ático*. This book is a good example of the complexity and richness that a video game structure can

---

GERMÁN SIERRA

The video game model is useful for representing recombinations in predictable narrative structures. In some of my fictions I prefer the bio-game model for representing the unpredictability of complex systems.

Literature defies codification (one of the most pervasive contemporary mythologies—as in "genetic code," for instance). In my novels, bio-games are a way to demythify "codification."

—E-mail, *"Videojuegos"*

Germán Sierra, in his strong belief in "code," suggests, it seems to me, a positivism or structuralism based on information. The problem with this is clear when we turn the previous quote by Katherine Hayles on its head: instead of imagining absolute randomness, imagine absolute pattern. There is then an absolute and eternal order, even within the iteration that appears in the video game: iteration is a practical and information-wise efficient way of creating a video game (trace some vectors, let them follow a set of algorithms, iterate them, and you have an infinite background for the game). However, if you have that infinite background, there is no sense of playing, unless you only want to walk around in a deserted space (imagine playing "Second life" with no one else logged in): you need exceptions—a character in the middle of the background you can interact with, a door you can go through, an order of steps necessary to breach out of the background imposed on you—like in puzzle games, (Portal 2 is the paradigm of this).

—*Juan Manuel Espinosa, in response*

contribute to the art of storytelling. The novel's historical, cultural, and literary engagement creates a reality project in which the subject plays himself into game. Instead of the televisual flattening effects in the work of Mañas, the synchronic multimedia constructs of the contemporary "hero" in Loriga's novel, or the performance of authenticity in Bustelo's *Veo veo*, the importance of the video game in *Ático* lies in the looping relationship it establishes between levels, stories, images, themes and characters inside and outside of the computational space. The novel's metaphoric and metamedia application of the art of "playing" provides a rich example of how technology can intimately intertwine the material or mechanical construction of a (game) world and the writing of the contemporary subject into new story spaces.

"X" Mutations

Generation X, as a label that was historically and culturally rooted in the acceleration of technology and in the innovation of discursive practices, originally presented writers with multimedia techniques through which to make sense of their changing worlds, in their own language, through their own eyes. The result was more than just a powdering of texts centered on sex, drugs, rock and roll, and the boredom of everyday life. The products contended with new ways of telling stories that naturally ingested new communication models to make sense of a changing world. The mutation of the literary product in the twenty-first century translated the forms and functions of various media technologies into textual practices. As these models changed and assimilated across platforms, novels opened their narrative playing fields. The new points of entry opened the door to a continued augmentation of GenX characteristics, including its punk DIY approach and defiance of literary Style, its presentation of a generation defined by global nomads and transient individualists, its blending of margins and mainstreams, and its emphasis on the authenticity and the construction of reality projects through multimedia and multiplatform tools and techniques.

Although the *Mutantes* authors were born within the range of years

> *MUTANT FICTIONEERS*
>
> Mark Amerika identified the artists of Avant-Pop as the "Children of the Mass Media." For him, the elitist and academic presuppositions of postmodernism had died, overtaken by the popular media engine, which left in its wake the Avant-Pop phenomenon. According to Amerika, for artists not to lose sight of their artistic directive, they had "to enter the mainstream culture as a parasite would, sucking out all the bad blood that lies between the mainstream and the margin" ("Why"). By sucking on the contaminated bosom of mainstream culture, Avant-Pop artists turned into *Mutant Fictioneers*.
>
> Amerika explained that this mutating condition derived from an avant-garde lineage but developed more open-minded strategies. The goal was to place attention on popular forms of representation that constituted what he called the "contemporary Mediaspace" ("Why").
>
> — Christine Henseler

associated with the Generation X demographic, most would emphatically reject being labeled a "Generation X'er." In fact, at the "Hybrid Storyspaces" conference I co-organized with Debra A. Castillo at Cornell University in April–May 2010, I asked Agustín Fernández Mallo if he would consider himself a Generation X'er and he vehemently denied.[3] His reaction indicates two things: the degree to which Generation X is tied to early-to-mid-1990s stereotypes centered on nihilism; hedonism; negativity; flat colloquial language; and themes of sex, drugs, and rock and roll; and the fact that the act of denying is in itself a way to distance himself from the past and create a totally new persona. Vicente Luis Mora commented at the same conference that in fact what stands out in Mallo's work is that there are precisely *no* sex or drugs in his texts. The themes that some believe sold the public on Generation X are minimally represented in this new literary package where breaking taboos has taken an entirely new function. That said, by centering our critical sights less on the static stereotypes of Generation X in the 1990s and more on the shifting axis at its label's roots since the postwar period, the social and cultural impact of technology and its effects on cultural production can begin to emerge more clearly.[4]

To consider the *Mutantes* as a transformation of Generation X demands a critical resting moment in the bifurcation point that disrupts the pattern. Most importantly, it requires that we move out of the patterns that have defined previous approaches to scholarship on literature and generations. While Vicente Luis Mora, in *Luz Nueva* and Juan Francisco Ferré in the introduction to the *Mutantes* anthology begin such a process, their work is still too tied to chronological practices and displays of resistance and breaks to be considered a clear shift in critical mutation. Although Fernández Porta's contribution of an *Afterpop* criticism certainly addresses the reading of contemporary literature through a less hierarchical, more inclusive and cross-disciplinary lens of the "popular," Spanish scholar Jara Calles addresses more directly the *Mutantes'* relationship to new media technologies. In "Necesidades—en plural—ante una literatura de las nuevas tecnologías," she proposes avoiding terms that define this era as *post-*, *pre-* or *trans-* by centering her sights on the socio-cultural coordinates that define our global and integrated contemporary society

---

LOS MUTANTES, SEGÚN JUAN FRANCISCO FERRÉ

"*NUEVA: contaminada por todas las formas culturales, altas o bajas, neutrales o comprometidas, corruptas o vírgenes, que circulan en el hipermercado del capitalismo y la sociedad de consumo. [...]

*INNOVADORA: cargada con toda la historia del medio narrativo, en sus avatares nacionales e internacionales, entendida como tradición de la disidencia y la mutación, la renovación de las formas y también la inclusión de nuevos contenidos. [...]

*AVANZADA: radicada en una concepción de la cronología acorde con los desarrollos más radicales, menos epidérmicos o superfluous, del arte y la economía, la política y las comunicaciones, la tecnología y el consumo, la sociedad y la estética, la información la ciencia y la sexualidad, etc. [...]" (13–14)

—Juan Francisco Ferré, *Mutantes*

(1). Given the velocity and radical nature of this era, she believes that versatility and flexibility may function as a better strategy of thought to make sense of works that engage with and are open to new forms and functions (1). Her goal is to suspend, as much as possible, the historical character of cultural objects to give way to neutral, almost atemporal approximations to the work of the *Mutantes* (4).

In line with my embrace of the blank as a space that allows for new beginnings, Calles believes that an approach to the work of the *Mutantes* fiction first demands a process of emptying critical and often over-used signifiers, such as the word "avant-garde" to define everything from the work of Almudena Grandes to Ray Loriga and Kiko Amat. The idea it to detach the use, appropriation or copy of a sign from its previous, usually burdening, historiographical engagement (4). She clarifies that the limitation of such an approach might have more in common with the attitude of an author in regard to his or her personal circumstances than the absence of contact with other systems, disciplines, and referents, in other words, with an author's singular approach to fiction instead of the originality of his or her contribution (4, 5). Her approach makes sense when one thinks about the global dynamics of a world of information overload, one in which, as Calles highlights, everything ends up being defined by circumstantial meanings. Instead of inherited notions of high or low culture, we are now before a generation whose cultural products present horizontal relations. In other words, the "blank" that stereotypically defined a generation's anti-social attitudes, nihilistic and hedonistic takes on life, is no longer negative now that its signifier has been emptied of meaning. Instead, it is marked by a positive and unprejudiced filling of the vast amount of material that is accessible in today's digital day and age (Calles 5).

To make sense of the infinite possibilities found in the digitally enhanced blank space of this new critical mutation, it warrants underscoring several characteristics that define the *Mutantes* as a group of distinct individuals: their professional backgrounds, their appropriation of social media to entertain different critical spaces and narratives, and their expanding notion of the writer as a creator of new textual meanings and spaces. The *Mutantes* are educated and active on several professional fronts. Carrión has a doctorate degree in the humanities and teaches classes on contemporary literature and creative writing at the University of Pompeu-Fabra. He also writes for several literary magazines and produces and edits his own books. Vicente Luis Mora has a law degree and a PhD in Peninsular literature. He is directing the Centro del Instituto Cervantes in Marrakech, Morocco. He writes for various literary magazines and academic journals, and his blog, "Diario de Lecturas," was awarded the "Premio *Revista de Letras* al Mejor Blog Nacional de Crítica Literaria" (2010). Eloy Fernández Porta is professor of literature and the history of film. He writes novels and books on literary and cultural criticism, and has become one of the central critical figures of the *Mutantes*, one who also dabbles in spoken word, DJ, and video art performances. Javier Fernández studied Engineering and is presently working as editor and literary critic. Irene Zoe Alameda studied Philosophy and Comparative Literature and is currently making films and directing the Instituto de Cervantes in Stockholm. Agustín Fernández Mallo is a Physicist who works on cancer treatments, and Germán Sierra is a professor of Neuroscience and Biomedicine at the University of Santiago de Compostela.

The *Mutantes* varied professional backgrounds easily allow them to point out, counter, and attempt to move beyond traditional critics' often narrow and biased views and reviews of their texts.[5] They try to advance a field entrenched by an establishment holding on tightly to their literary and intellectual traditions and critical patterns. As such, it is through non-traditional means such as blogs, literary magazines, videos, or fanzines that the *Mutantes* insert their critical voices and break down barriers between authors, readers, and critics. For example, Fernández Mallo, Carrión, and Mora have embraced the use of blogs not only to promote their works and convey information, but also as a way to undermine the traditional spaces and voices of the closed circle of (male) literary critics in Spain. The subtitle of Mora's blog probably best summarizes this literary rebellion as a gesture that conveys the breaking out of traditional conventions of space and time, when he defines its goal in the following way: "En este blog se intenta una lectura crítica de literatura —entre otras cosas— alternativa a la común: buscamos una crítica para el siglo 21 en tiempo real" [This blog attempts a critical reading of literature—among other things—alternative to the norm: we are searching for a critical practice for the twenty-first century in real time]. In another attempt to break the norms of literary criticism Vicente Luis Mora also conceived of an entire edition of the literary magazine *Quimera* (issue #322) through pseudonyms and fake critical outtakes, thus subverting and parodying any sense of symbolic authority. Jorge Carrión, for his part, has been publishing several of his own works, including *Crónica de viajes* and *GR-83*, as limited editions filled with hybrid linguistic and visual models of storytelling. He has also been publishing a series of fanzines and critical outtakes under the title "el juguete rabioso." Robert Juan-Cantavella has a website called "Punk Journalism," in which he identifies his literary approach through a new punk stylistics. Together the *Mutantes* produce more story

---

PROVIDENCE *(2010) DE JUAN FRANCISCO FERRÉ*

"Juan Francisco Ferré compendia en *Providence* las manifestaciones artísticas contemporáneas —el cine, la tele, la omnívora Red, los mitos y falacias de la utopía cultural norteamericana— para machacarlas y mezclarlas en su batidora. Las figuras icónicas del pop art y el hip-hop, los blogueros apocalípticos y visionarios ocupan el mismo espacio que los referentes literarios de antaño. Lo alto y lo bajo, lo perdurable y lo efímero se confunden en una misma pasta compacta por las paletas móviles de su implacable máquina trituradora. Todo cabe en ella en virtud de una subversiva voluntad igualitaria en la que vale lo mismo Beethoven que cualquier roquero de Los Ángeles o de Jamaica."

—Juan Goytisolo,
"Literatura en el ciberespacio"

spaces to subvert, parody, and question the way the literary game has traditionally been played.

To better understand the level of their subversive attitudes toward storytelling, it warrants highlighting that the *Mutantes* writers, if they can still be called "writers," more than any generation before them, artistically dabble not only in narrative, but also in poetry, performance, media art, music, literary criticism, and so on. They are novelists and poets, writers and performers, electronic storytellers, authors, and critics. For example, Agustín Fernández Mallo, Manuel Vilas, and Mercedes Cebrián publish as much poetry as they do narrative, and Fernández Mallo has conceived of his "Proyecto Nocilla" in print as well as in video. Doménico Chiappe (Peruvian born, living in Madrid since 2001) has written narrative as well as hypertexts and music, and produced spoken-word performance videos of his work (for which he plays the electric guitar). A producer friend of Jorge Carrión's directed a four-part book trailer to promote *Los muertos* (2010), and photographs on Flickr accompany Gabi Martínez's *Los mares de Wang*; *Sudd*, the author tells me, will appear as a comic book published by Glénat in the near future. Similarly, Fernández Mallo's novel *Nocilla Experience* appeared in 2011 as a graphic novel published by Alfaguara and illustrated by Pere Joan.[6]

The *Mutantes* do-it-yourself philosophy toward cultural production and their multi-disciplinary engagement with all of the information the world has to offer enhances the existence of what Ferré calls a *new* chronological sensibility as influenced by some of the most radical advancements in the arts and economy, politics and communication, technology, consumption, society and aesthetics, science and sexuality, etc. (*Mutantes* 13–14). In the *Mutantes* volume, the contributors' literary appropriations of the comic and film (Javier Calvo), of sociological irony (Porta), of the world of the image and fashion (Ferré), of virtual reality (Javier Fernández), or of the Internet (Jorge Carrión) define a group whose global sensibility and experience and varied professional backgrounds clearly influence their very wide and inclusive approach to writing styles and subject matters. This is in part due to the

---

"Parte de mi intención artística es convertir al lector en coautor, sí. Lo experimenté en *La huella de Cosmos*, una novela colectiva y multimedia que dirigí en 2005. Hay grados de interacción, desde las cerradas, en que el lector elige cómo y qué lee, hasta las totalmente abiertas, en que la obra muta constantemente con las acciones de sus visitantes."

—Doménico Chiappe,
"¿Teme la literatura al lobo digital?"

HAVE YOU SEEN THIS?

- Doménico Chiappe introduces per video the benefits and dynamics of the Internet as a space for storytelling:
  www.conoceralautor.com/actualidad/index/NDA

- "Proyecto Nocilla, la película" by Agustín Fernández Mallo: http://blogs.alfaguara.com/fernandezmallo

- The four-part trailer of Jorge Carrión's novel *Los muertos*:
  http://www.jorgecarrion.com

MUTATIS MUTANDIS

"Acaba de aparecer el divertido libro de Javier García Rodríguez, *Mutatis Mutandis. Hacia una hermenéutica transficcional de las narrativas mutantes: de Propp al afterpop* (o "nocilla, qué merendilla"); Eclipsados, Zaragoza, 2009. Me gustaría explicarles de qué va este libro, pero no puedo, porque su género acaba de fundarse con este volumen. Hay teoría pero no es un ensayo; hay narración, pero no es una novela ni un cuento. Planteado como una monstruosidad epistemológica posmoderna, es un libro sustentado en el exceso interpretativo. Sé que en él hay una ironía cervantina hacia el grupo de los mutantes. Sé que hay varios chistes a mi costa ('Pangea no es pangea. Es pan (para la nocilla) y gea (que aún no sé lo que es, pero que no tardaré en descubrir). Es pangea para hoy y hambre para mañana' (p. 42). Sé que hay más chistes y juegos de palabras, algunos memorables: 'la hermenéutica contemporánea no es más que un depósito de gadámeres' (12). Lo único que sé es que no he podido parar de reír desde el principio hasta el final de esta extraña obra del profesor de Hermenéutica Javier García Rodríguez, cuyo personaje es un crítico de los de antes, incapaz de valorar un texto que lleve menos de 400 años escrito, y cuya obsesión es desentrañar la conspiración mutante, presentada como un grupo de seres alucinados que se proponen conquistar el mundo mediante indescifrables mensajes. Una obra inteligente y divertida, que los anti-mutantes disfrutarán por el arsenal de chistes que contiene sobre nosotros, y que los mutantes disfrutaremos aún más."

—Vicente Luis Mora, *Blog "Diario de lecturas"*

¿Y existe la crítica mutante?
La crítica literaria es, como todos los discursos institucionalizados, una práctica "normalizada", sin apenas margen de
→

fact that the *Mutantes*, like X'ers before them, are nomads and world citizens; they travel and live throughout the world; and they speak several languages as seen in travel writings such as *Los mares de Wang* (2008) and *Sudd* (2007) by Gabi Martínez, or *Australia* (2008) by Jorge Carrión. They travel physically and virtually and, in some cases, they juxtapose both realms, as in the case of Agustín Fernández Mallo's conception of *Nocilla Dream* (2007) in a hospital room in Thailand while zapping television stations.

As I mention in my "Spanish Mutant Fictioneers" essay, the *Mutantes* inherently live in an age in which old and new media are colliding and authorial and critical positions are shifting. Calles underlines that this shift cannot simply be addressed by shifting to more contemporary theoretical frameworks, like that from Ortega y Gasset to Michel Foucault to Deleuze and Guattari, or by reductively making direct connections between social reality and cultural practices, or by applying new tech terminology without more deeply engaging with its effects. The goal is to unravel the larger transformations that have defined a collective imaginary in light of the technological changes of the digital age (Calles 8). In the realm of literature, it is not enough to say that authors are appropriating more media technologies to promote and create their work, but rather, that they are partaking in a cultural mind shift in which their positions have changed in relation to the world at large—from computer science to science, art, society, psychology, advertising, news, and so on. Just like in the case of Fernández Porta's distinction between "high" and "low" popular culture, "high" *Mutante* authors are active cultural seekers and producers who in the process of creation transform the roles and expectations of authors, readers, and critics alike.

Material Mutations

Contemporary critics tend to talk about the *Mutantes* by relating the innovative quality of their work solely to digital media and action words such as *zapping*, *blogging*, *linking*, or *sampling*. In the same vein, critics generalize their use of different media, disregarding the material basis of each medium's design and application. For example, they will discuss the defining role of the Internet without considering the differing interactions of individuals depending on their use of technology (computer, cell phone, iPad, etc), use of application (Facebook, Twitter, iGoogle, MUDS, etc), and their personal habits and needs (such as the use of Facebook for family connectivity rather than book promotion; or the use of Twitter for minute-by-minute updates on everyday life, or for the use of political activism). Computer functions range from one-way word processing, Web surfing, and gaming to multiple user communications in social networking sites, blogs, multiuser games, and virtual reality spaces. Twitter, Facebook, and Second Life demand the use of

maniobra, algo previsible, poco dada a los riesgos y las aventuras. Aún más la crítica académica o universitaria (…). En este sentido, yo considero que somos responsables de actualizar las categorías teóricas y estéticas, de poner al día (en sentido estricto) las dinámicas críticas y sus discursos, para adecuarlas a las nuevas realidades artísticas, para que sean capaces de dar respuesta a los discursos que la actualidad nos propone. No sé si "Mutatis mutandis" es crítica mutante, pero sí que creo que el crítico, el especialista, debe sentirse libre para construir un discurso que pueda dialogar libremente con los discursos (artísticos, literarios, sociales, en definitiva) de los que se ocupa. No pretendo crear un género nuevo, pero sí quiero poder enfrentarme sin prejuicios formales a las formas significantes.

Perdone, estaba dando por sentado que era un libro de crítica y quizá era una novela…

Nada que perdonar. Es un libro de crítica porque, como decía Roland Barthes, es "un discurso sobre el discurso". Yo quería reflexionar sobre la última narrativa española (no toda, claro, específicamente la llamada mutante *o* afterpop *o* generación nocilla*) y, de esa reflexión, iban surgiendo ideas y perplejidades que fueron tomando forma en un modelo de escritura que utilizaba los mismos mecanismos técnicos, las mismas miradas filosóficas, los mismos asuntos que le sirven a esta narrativa. Así se fue construyendo un relato de ficción que sirve como hilo conductor a ese ejercicio crítico: los papeles de un profesor de literatura muerto en extrañas circunstancias presentados de manera fragmentaria y un tanto neurótica a partir de asuntos meramente anecdóticos. Esto me sirve para incluir una confrontación textual entre la filología tradicional y las modernas teorías de la interpretación; una mirada sobre la realidad y la ficción; anotaciones y recortes; reflexiones enfermizas; páginas falsas de internet; reseñas reales de libros imaginarios; reseñas inventadas de libros reales; y otra infinidad de recursos de* →

> *uso en principio exclusivamente literario y, por tanto, poco susceptibles de aparecer en un trabajo de crítica literaria. Este libro es, lo he dicho alguna que otra vez, la parodia de la novela de campus que ya no escribiré.*
>
> —*Javier García Rodríguez, in response (see also "El periodismo es el género más mutante")*

specifically designed applications, and each application involves a set of rules and actions, features, and creative possibilities and limitations. When translated into fiction, they all present unique characteristics that determine the representation of everything from character to plot development, from narrative voice to focalization techniques, from temporal to spatial world constructs.

The human-computer interfaces that largely underline today's economy, business, life, and art are based on structural applications that are material-based and can lead to different and new narrative abstractions. They have been put in place by a group of individuals (not machines) for specific reasons and goals. As stressed by Brenda Laurel in her book *Computers as Theatres* (1993), behind each machine and each application reside one or many human minds. The use of computers is based on a fine relationship between people's artistry and innovation in computer programming and the structures and tools that limit the design and use of a certain medium (Laurel 98). Therefore, to talk about "the influence of technology" on literature demands that we take a closer look at the structural dynamics of each medium in relation to its available uses and users. These mechanical structures partake in a constantly changing dynamic, most obvious in the move from the static page and individual-user application of Web 1.0 to the interactive, user-centered design of Web 2.0 and the more recent goals of the Semantic Web 3.0. In literature, these amplified uses of the Web translate into varying results in function, form, and content. For example, there is a clear difference between the novel *La vida en las ventanas* (2002) by Andrés Neuman (b. 1977, Argentinean-born writer residing in Spain), in which the "windows" in the title relate to static, in this case, one-way, electronic mail communications as defined by Microsoft, and *Algunas ideas buenísimas que el mundo se va a perder* (2009) by Alberto Olmos, in which the text imitates a fragmented, visually enhanced blog and micro-blogging format.

Although all media applications have changed over the last twenty to thirty years, perhaps one of the most powerful and underexamined realms in literary studies has been the computer or video game (I will use the terms interchangeably in this chapter). The history of this medium intimately intertwines advancements in computer technology with new storytelling practices, and, what interests me here, the heightened inclusion of the self (the reader/player) in game (or fiction). Developments in the video game, its genres and graphics, have advanced in tandem with technological advances since its birth in 1962 by three Massachusetts Institute of Technology (MIT) employees.[7] To give a quick historical overview, it is worth pointing out that the appearance of consoles in the 1970s turned video games into an industry, that game design of the 1980s was marked by the birth of the personal computer, and that in the 1990s, the PC "awoke fully as a hardcore gaming platform due to major advances in sound and graphics hardware" (Egenfeldt-Nielsen 78–79). In the twenty-first century, rapid technological changes allowed for the creation of more ambitious and innovative games that have been influenced by film production, the networking possibilities of the Web, and the use of physical sensors (Egenfeldt 52, 29, 88–89). While video games used to be tied to consoles and joysticks, to actions directly linked to the know-how of connecting and using different technologies, now cell phones, iPads, and Wii consoles are providing applications that are not only easy to use, but also provide a high level of physicality and access to a broader audience base. Grandparents, parents, and children can now find video games that suit their needs and notions of "fun," from *Super Mario Brothers* and *Halo 3* to *Scrabble* and *Club Penguin*.

While Spain is not a large producer of games (only twenty-seven companies produce games and tend to concentrate on low-end cell phone or casual games), the country has the fourth-highest audience of computer games in Europe ("Sólo 27"). The profile of the 27 percent gaming households in Spain indicates that 62 percent are men between 11 and 19 years of age, although in 2005 women's consumption of games rose from 33 percent to 37.4 percent. According to genres and both genders, 26 percent consumed adventure games, 21

WHO PLAYS VIDEO GAMES?

From the *Pew Internet and American Life Project* (2008):

- Only slightly more males (55 percent) than females (50 percent) are gamers.
- There are more women gamers (65 percent to 35 percent) in the twenty-five to thirty-four demographic than males.
- There are no significant differences due to household income, and the more the education, the higher the level of video game playing.
- English-speaking Hispanics are more likely to be gamers than whites or blacks, and urban and suburban dwellers are a little more likely to play than rural folks.
- Ninety-seven percent of all teens (99 percent of boys and 94 percent of girls), ages twelve to seventeen, play video games: computer, web, portable, or console games.
- Thirty-eight percent of adults report playing games on desktop or laptop computers.
- Twenty-eight percent play on game consoles like an Xbox, PlayStation or Wii.
- Eighteen percent play on a cell phone, Blackberry, or other handheld organizer.
- Thirteen percent play on portable gaming devices like a PSP, DS, or Gameboy.
- Only 24 percent of gamers play alone, 82 percent play games alone at times, and 71 percent of those individuals also play games with others; 27 percent of gamers play with people they connect with online (of which 47 percent play with people they know in their offline lives; and 65 percent play with others in the room).

—Larry Richmond, "Who Plays Video Games"?
—"Nearly All US Teens, 53% of Adults Play Video Games"

percent strategy games, 19 percent sports, 18 percent action, two percent music, and one percent puzzles and languages ("Sólo 27"). In sum, over time, in both the United States and Spain, the face of the gaming industry has changed, and so has its reach.

While video games have a relatively "long" history, computer game studies is a comparatively young field that professor and editor Espen Aarseth located in 2001, the year when he inaugurated the first *Game Studies* journal. My readings, as a literary critic looking in, left me with the sense that video game theory is searching for an identity and is locked in a game of tug of war between fields. Prominent video-game theorists approach video games from a myriad of perspectives, each claiming a portion of the playing field. For some, the video game is centered on the study of play and game, or what has been termed *ludology* by Gonzalo Frasca; Espen Aarseth examines the video game as *cybertext* or as an example of *ergodic* literature to reference texts that demand the active engagement of the players/readers; Henry Jenkins views games from a spatial perspective, namely as narrative architecture; and, as mentioned, Brenda Laurel considers the interrelationship between video game and theater, emphasizing the performative and dramatic elements at play in a game's mechanics.[8] Together these essays point to the medium's young history, complexity, interdisciplinarity, and hybridity. Video game theory clearly borrows from narrative, film, theater, performance, video, social networking, architecture, and traditional games, all powered by technology. Video games are multi-tiered audiovisual systems that bring together elements of storytelling, simulation, and game play on both a mechanical and a gaming level.

The complex interdisciplinary dynamics of the many video games that exist on the market make it difficult for literary critics to understand the role and the effect of "games" on fiction. My goal here is not to provide a comprehensive set of answers, but simply to present one of many possible perspectives based on my limited experience.[9] To analyze and play video games is a daunting task because of the sheer variety of game genres—from puzzle and adventure games to shooter and simulation games—and the formal complexity of the games—from the abstract boxes of *Tetris* to the 3-D graphics of *Halo 3*. Those of us who do not play computer games on a daily basis feel physically inept (*What button do I push?*) and mentally handicapped (*What do I do now?*). At times the

---

HISTORY OF GAMES

The history of games stretches as far back as Egypt, where in the Third Dynasty (2686–13 B.C.) the first observed game, called "Senet," was "a game of skill and chance not unlike present-day backgammon" (Egenfeldt 45). This and many other centuries-old games serve as the basis for computer games that are often, in their initial stages of development, tried out or compared to board games. Of course, video games had to wait until the advent and availability of computers for use by a general public. They were born in the 1960s and 1970s, with simple but effective games such as *Pong* and *Spacewar*.

—Christine Henseler

technology seems to get in the way of our enjoyment of the "game," and without our interaction with the game, a story cannot develop, nor can our understanding of the construction of the story in space. Whether we "enter" a game or not, what becomes quite clear is that one of the differentiating characteristics of video games is related to our physical connection and virtual insertion in game space as our actions connect to the circle or person we see and move on one or many screens.

Rules of the Game

It is not a coincidence that one of the most important edited volumes on game design and storytelling is *First Person: New Media as Story, Performance, and Game* (2004), edited by Noah Wardrip-Fruin and Pat Harrigan. The use of the first person is a distinctive element of video games since a player's perspective in game, through abstract symbols or personalized avatars, is generally based on agency, immersion, and transformation of the self, or versions thereof (Murray, "From Game" 1). Aarseth goes so far as to suggest that "games are not about the Other, they are about the Self. Games focus on self-mastery and exploration of the external world, not exploration of interpersonal relationships (except for multiplayer games)" (50). A video game can only unfold when the "I" inserts himself or herself into storyspace through a conscious choice of behaviors, choices, and actions. This awareness of the construction of the

Los videojuegos han sido concebidos de manera lúdica y experimental como réplicas de los procesos del capitalismo, con la finalidad de poner a prueba la adaptación de los seres humanos a las reglas cada vez más competitivas del sistema económico y la sociedad de control. La cibercultura de los videojuegos representa, en este sentido, el paroxismo de todos los conceptos en juego en la actual sociedad tecnocrática. Esto bastaría para explicar que los componentes liberadores de artefactos de esta categoría sean directamente proporcionales a su grado de complicidad con el estado de cosas.

¿Cómo romper, entonces, desde la narrativa con las estrategias de control y dominio desarrolladas en el videojuego a imitación de las desarrolladas en la realidad? ¿Cómo descubrir el código de la simulación, el lado construido y trucado de todo lo que damos por real, sin someterse, al jugar, a los designios de la máquina? De hecho, enredarse mentalmente en la fascinante mecánica narrativa de ciertos videojuegos de última generación produce una experiencia cognitiva similar a la lucha futura de la humanidad por el protagonismo perdido en un contexto totalmente tecnificado y computerizado.

—Juan Francisco Ferré, E-mail

self in a variety of worlds reminds us of Janet Murray's pronouncements that everyday experience is "game like"; it is a game that makes us aware of the constructed nature of all our narratives ("From Game" 3). Our psyches today, more than ever, simultaneously balance a vision of ourselves as one or whole and as multiple and ever-changing as we juggle the roles we play on a daily basis, from being students to partners, parents, or professionals. According to Murray, the stories that these roles narrate or negotiate emulate the shifting social arrangement of the global community and the shifting scientific understandings of our inner landscapes. Similarly the conscious construction of multiple roles on various platforms also identifies the development of new textual models as they augment the experience of readers of print fiction. Identity in general is presented in many *Mutantes* novels through metamorphosing manifestations of gender and being, as in *La fiesta del asno* (2005) by Juan Francisco Ferré or *Los muertos* by Jorge Carrión.

In video games, as in literature, there are formal and dramatic elements that join the mechanical structures and rules of a game with the imaginary construction and identification of possible avatars and the influence of multimedia systems. As in literature, computer games explicitly or implicitly include a series of rules (of reading and playing); they establish a premise or conflict that allows for immediate game play connectivity, and they demand a certain level of skill and *flow*—the combination of challenge and skill, according to Tracy Fullerton—that not only allows players (readers) to understand the structural dynamics of the game (novel), but, more importantly, to enjoy it. For example, in narrative we learn to read from left to right in Western culture, possibly in columns, by looking at footnotes and information in parentheses, and we may integrate visual images or lyrics into our readings. We may feel positioned as objective observers or as characters immersed in the action. Video games provide similar experiences by creating scenarios and mechanics that allow players to immerse themselves into game space or feel utterly left out when the game provides too many blanks, little fun or entertainment, lack of empathy with characters or immersive results. Depending on the experience that the author/programmer wants/is able to provide, the readers/players may feel more or less in control; they may enjoy their play/reading experience to a greater or lesser extent. They may keep on playing, or they may exit the game.

The complex convergences a game creates between the game and real life, and between the player, the programmer and viewer, motion toward developments in new technology that allow players to construct and expand on virtual/personal stories outside their official game time and space. Games such as *Halo 3* include features that let players take snapshots of their game play and arrange and share these shots in scrapbooks or personal webpages such as Bungie.net.[10] They can also take videos or photos of long or short segments of their game play and record their actions from a variety of perspectives. For example, a gamer has the option of pulling a camera back to "free roaming" mode or using it to create close shots from any perceivable angle. Within and without the game, gamers develop a virtual/real identity that is not just based on their actions within a simulated world, but on the story that they want to create in real life. The juxtaposition of technical know-how and creativity has even led to a new art form called *machinima*, which combines the "machine" and "cinema" to render action and actors. In other words, game players are creating new identities for themselves as characters, actors, directors, and editors. This extension of the self as producer and consumer of the game on a multiplicity of levels, inside and outside the game space, is best understood through the novel *Ático* by Gabi Martínez. It is here that the video game, especially as it relates to the continuously mutating construction of identity in a world of global technological flows, is presented in all its complexity and potential.

The Video Game *Ático* by Gabi Martínez

Gabi Martínez is a transitional literary figure. He belongs to both Generation X and the *Mutantes* and, at the same time, he belongs to neither. His work intersects with both worldviews while also moving beyond them. I engage with the work of Martínez in this chapter because the central and multilayered use of a video game in his 2005 novel, *Ático*, presents an excellent example of the developing effects of mutating storytelling practices also used by other *Mutantes* writers such as Juan Francisco Ferré or Germán Sierra. By closely examining how Martínez translates video gaming techniques and themes into fiction, this chapter teases out the multilayered and open quality of new media applications on transitional as well as on future novels. Through the thematic and technical reference to video game, *Ático* is able to construct a complex web of textual interrelations that play with spaces, times, cultures, and voices on multiple levels. Through game (story), the novel establishes a more active and involved relationship between the readers/players and the way we literally play our "reality projects" into being. To play our "reality projects" into being, an exception from the pattern is necessary. In Martínez's novel I demonstrate that this exception may be found in a computational pattern called *looping* through which human beings—readers, creators, Dj's—introduce meaning into a pre-set signifying system. Meaningful looping is, then, not an iteration of an infinite pattern, but rather the moment when an exception is introduced into a pattern.

Born in 1971, Gabi Martínez is best known as a travel writer through texts such as *Anticreta* (1999), *Sólo Marroquí* (1999), and *Diablo de Timanfaya* (2000) and novels like *Hora de Times Square* (2002), *Una España inesperada* (2005), and *Sudd* (2007), a book based on his adventures along the Nile. His books may generally be divided into two categories: those that are clearly related to travel and writing, and those that are more experimental, such as *Una España inesperada*, *Ático*, and a novel that he is presently working on

---

MACHINIMA

An example of machinima may be found in the science fiction comedy series *Red vs. Blue* (RvB), an example of which can be found at: www.machinima.com/film/view&id=275. Cocreated by gamers Burnie Burns, Matt Hullum, Geoff Ramsey, and others, this *machinima* piece and one hundred more series parodied first-person shooter games. It gave new attention to *machinima* in the gaming and the film community, and it has contributed to legitimizing *machinima* as an artform.

—Christine Henseler

concerning Australia (E-mail). His books are often accompanied by multi-media material, such as a video interview of him presenting *Sudd*, or a photo album that his publisher, Alfaguara, created in Flickr to accompany his novel *Los mares de Wang* (2008), a literary travelogue in China. Martínez's use of narrative structures with different rhythms and dynamics evolved from his physical, rather than virtual, awareness of the self in space. Martínez's parents owned a video store for over twenty years, and in his youth, he was able to view, for free, and during a time when accessing and viewing videos was not as easy as it is today, films from around the world (E-mail). In addition, he states that he, like so many other youth, grew up reading comic books (E-mail). Subsequently, his works flowed naturally from this early upbringing, residing comfortably in the hybrid spaces of fiction and documentary, readership and spectatorship, reality and virtuality (E-mail).

The flow of visual and verbal sites of new meaning-making in the narrative of Martínez is directly related to his interest in "play." Whether in virtual spaces, as table games, or on a soccer field, play, he says, presents the material answer to the saturation of literature's main themes: the manifestation of private and global conflicts and interior and exterior spaces (E-mail). To search for new sites of meaning-making is, for Martínez, a game in itself, as perceived in the conceptual stage of his novel *Ático*, which, he said, "Me supuso el desafío y la diversión de un juego" [Supposed the challenge and the fun of a game] (E-mail). For Martínez, the use of a video game in this novel constituted "una de las fórmulas más sofisticadas de juego, si bien su lenguaje, sus contenidos, no son sino la punta del iceberg audiovisual. *Ático* no es más que el resultado casi lógico de un escritor que tiene una historia, ve habitualmente películas, televisión, y se deja ir" [The video game is perhaps one of the most sophisticated formulas of a game, its language and content being but the tip of the iceberg of the audiovisual. *Ático* is no more than the logical result of a writer who has a story, habitually watches movies, television, and lets himself go]. (Martínez, E-mail).

For Martínez, the essence of writing is based on the central axis of challenge and fun inherent in play (the same characteristics that are applied to the video game). Martínez arrived at narrative "flow" not by playing himself, but rather by investigating the video game world and allowing words to play with his mind and computer keys. Not a serious gamer himself, Martínez played

> *Es cierto que cuando se publicó* Ático, *un grupo de gente atenta a las vanguardias señaló la obra como algo distinto, novedoso... y por eso se me incluyó en un grupo con el que nunca me identifiqué. De hecho, he llegado a discutir varias veces con integrantes de esa etiqueta, reivindicando las ventanas reales (sabrás que he escrito varios libros de viajes) frente al empuje de las ventanas virtuales.*
>
> *Si llego a la fórmula de* Ático *es por la experiencia del mundo físico que poseo. Recuerda que Agustín escribe el primer Nocilla en una habitación tailandesa... creo que es un dato a tener en cuenta.*
>
> —Gabi Martínez, E-mail, August 16, 2010

by watching his sister and by playing with a few friends. He investigated the world of the video game from the perspective and experience of a journalist. He talked to programmers, developers, designers, gamers, and specialists, initially wanting to write a lengthy chronicle in line with his previous book, *Una España inesperada* (e-mail). Instead, Martínez ended up writing a novel about a video game called "Ático," a game currently impossible to design due to today's technological limitations. But in fiction, he created "el summum de los juegos" [the non-plus ultra of all games] (e-mail) thanks to the playing possibilities of what I would call, to play with game titles, the unlimited "world of word crafts."[11]

On a global level, *Ático* is a novel inspired directly by the events of September 11, 2001.[12] Martínez located its action nine days after the terrorist attacks, the moment when Eduard Montes, the protagonist, was fired from his seven-year position at a computer firm. This event leads Eduard to lock himself in an attic in Barcelona for three months and to program a best-selling video game called "Ático." Much like a video game itself, the novel presents multiple spaces and times that intersect in short chapters. The text covers Eduard's personal experiences programming the game and living in the attic, it conveys the thirty-six hours of play time of "Ático" by Japanese gamer Kazuo Tanaka, and the text presents the recorded post-viewing of Kazuo's play by a group of young men and women, with Kazuo present. The novel contains over sixty-three chapters and four different third-person perspectives that interlace fragments of identities and sentences in each. Words, images, and characters appear and disappear, refracted in various scenes and media, providing a peek-a-boo effect of surprising results, all topped off with supposedly realistic sound bites and 3-D visuals.

"Ático," the video game (which I will put in quotation marks to distinguish it from the title of the novel), is described as a literary strategy game that contains a memory with the arguments and dialogues of 40,000 titles from the history of classic world literature, adapted and reproduced by the characters in colloquial language. To win, players need to traverse five

---

"Novelas como *Ático* son la punta de lanza de una presencia literaria nueva: la de jóvenes renovadores que, por la vía del pastiche y la exploración de realidades múltiples, logran componer un panóptico de nuestro tiempo. Temas y estilos que nos acercan a un Foster Wallace; pero también a un Paul Auster, en tanto que se ocupan de contar la realidad como si ésta, a día de hoy, se hubiera quebrado en mil pedazos cuyos fragmentos constituyeran una nueva imagen rota de la vida".

—Gabi Martínez, Facebook Page, quoting David Barba, *La Vanguardia*

HAVE YOU SEEN THIS?

Interview of Gabi Martínez presenting his novel *Sudd*:

www.alfaguara.santillana.es/index. php?s=multimedia_detalle&id=3

Flickr photoalbum of the novel *Los mares de Wang*:

www.flickr.com/photos/alfaguara/show

—Christine Henseler

different screens. The innovative, and at this point technologically impossible element of the game is that players must ask questions and demand answers; wrong answers are penalized by avatars losing their physical abilities and even ceasing to exist; right answers, or narrative stability, move the characters to new attics, or screens. Upon reaching the fifth level, if characters answer questions correctly, they can win and be freed from the simulated imprisonment of their bodies at play. The first person to reach the end will win an attic in any city in the world. Players may chose a masculine or feminine version of the game; they have thirty-six consecutive hours to play (the game cannot be paused); every individual gets seven chances to win in their lifetime; and, because of adult content, no players under the age of sixteen are permitted. Only three players have reached the final screen, and only Kazuo Tanaka figured out how to escape the final attic.

The historical influences and the dynamics of the video game "Ático" are explained through a third-person, journalistic narrative voice that appears throughout the novel in different guises. This exterior voice provides information on the life story of Eduard, the programmer, his vision for "El Juego Global" [The Global Game] (21), and his experiences in the gaming world. The voice explains that Eduard's programming background was most influenced by three games (games that Martínez says also influenced his writing of the text): The *SIMS*, a life simulation game in which players create their own avatars and build their everyday realities; *Resident Evil*, a survival horror game in which players must solve mysteries, uncover clues, and solve puzzles to escape a mansion; and *Tomb Raider*, an adventure, shooter game based on the female action figure Lara Croft, with fifteen to twenty levels in which she has to complete a mission at each stage. In addition, one of the games that most impressed Martínez was a game then under construction (whose name he does not remember) in which the player could choose eight travel mates from among 120. Each one of these eight would help the player with various faculties, and a large portion of the success of the game depended on their choice of mates (e-mail). Together, they provide a hybrid version of a game turned fiction, a fiction that appropriates genre elements from a variety of sources.

These games do not only configure the unusual genre hybridity of the novel; they also have significant impact on Eduard's approach to the programming of "Ático." The magic formula of Eduard's game searched to combine "simulación social + estrategia + gráficos impecables + una aventura bajo el signo de los retos que obligara a exprimirse el cerebro y apurar las reservas de astucia, orden y lógica" [social simulation + strategy + impeccable graphics + an adventure so challenging that it demands high levels of brain power and exhaustive reserves of astuteness, order, and logic] (21). The literary-adventure-strategy-riddle game of "Ático" is steeped in an intellectual and linguistic game of thinking and response or no response, since at times inaction rather than action is the best move.

In a metafictional or metamedia move, in the novel, previous players of "Ático" comment on several elements that make the game unique and first-class. They talk about the powerful basis of the game's technology, its "intelligence" as characters seem to communicate with the players in real time, its high-definition 3-D graphics and the portrayal of human emotion in the characters, the relationship of the game to life—"tiene algo—no sé, como la vida misma…despierta los sentidos" [it has something, I don't know, like life itself…it awakens the senses] (25), and the value of the game as "un desafío virtual al ser humano [a virtual challenge to the human being] (25). Interestingly, the combination of said qualities converge into a realistic, lifelike representation (another "reality project"), and the technology responds directly to the game's ability to immerse players not just into a simple game, but into a "life" challenge, a challenge to gamers' minds and bodies. Given this combination of ultimate game characteristics readers learn that the second version of "Ático" sold more than six million copies, expanded in various ways. With five hundred more novels in its memory bank (109) the game's engagement with and responses to players was made even more diverse and complex than before

The novel, as much as the game, challenges the mind through a complex network of voices and levels. The timing of the story just after 9/11 advances a culturally and politically complex framework. The attic in which Eduard works faces the apartment of a young Muslim woman, Faridza, and her blind uncle Ahmed Chaib. The US-Afghan war and Arab-Western relations directly affect their personal interactions in Barcelona, Spain. In turn, these events and emotions infuse the narrative space through news on the television and the Internet, and discussions by people on the streets below. In addition, the chapters combine a variety of voices. Readers confront a documentary, even encyclopedic, voice of an anonymous journalist and the factual pages concerning video game history, which play off Eduard's watching of the news and Web surfing—"dedicaba 10 horas al día a navegar el ciberespacio" [he dedicated ten hours a day to surf the Web] (13).

The novel establishes a strong relationship between spaces and cultures as enhanced by media technologies. The characters' connection to and understanding of the "Other" is mediated through the telephone, the television (news on the war), through e-mail (to emphasize gender differences), the Internet (for fact finding), and the game's global reach. Even in one of the deepest and most embodied moments of personal interaction and connection, when Eduard and Faridza dance together, yet apart, with their arms in the air, each standing on their own attic, their experience is mediated by music, Algerian *Raï* music. Because Raï music is based on the hybrid mix of Spanish, French, African, Arabic, and American musical forms, it enhances the novel's presentation of cultural convergences. In addition, while the blindness of Ahmed points to an erasure of visual exteriority for a process of looking within, it emphasizes the dichotomy between the interior and the exterior, elements at the heart of both the novel and the video game.

What makes *Ático* such a powerful novel is that it does not simply emulate a video game; rather, it presents a complex web of interrelations based on spaces, times, cultures, and voices. Voices constantly infuse the two main narrative strands: the one that follows Eduard while programming the game and the game play by Kazuo himself. Integrated into the chapters are telephone conversations between Eduard and his sister in Illinois, the somewhat mysterious but suggestive conversations Eduard has with his Arabic neighbor Ahmed, and the e-mails he receives from Faridza of semibiographical stories of famous characters, such as Fernando Pessoa, Friedrich Nietzsche, or Virginia Woolf. The novel establishes a constant relationship between the individual, between loneliness and being alone, and between the collective, connected, global experience, the multiple converging and connecting strands of life and art. For example, the topic of loneliness literally is presented in the video game through a figure named Soledad (a name whose reappearing effects we already witnessed in Bustelo's *Veo veo*), in the solitary and physically confining nature of video game play, in Eduard's self-confinement in the attic with little to no communication with the outside world, in Faridza's enforced disconnection from an anti-Islamist Western world, in the semi-biographies Faridza e-mails to Eduard, and in the ultimate impossibility of their love affair. Together the various outgrowths of the topic of "loneliness" form a large map of psychological, narrative, and virtual interconnections based largely on the love story between Eduard and Faridza, a love story that fails.

Producing and Produced by Looping

From the very beginning, Martínez's novel sets the scene for a shift in the contemporary mind-set by establishing a looping motion between the computer, the video game, and the novel. In computer science, looping refers to a reiterative process that occurs until a specific result is achieved. In electronic music, looping is defined as "a piece of sound that can be played again and again in a coherent sequence. Dance music consists of many types of loops layered on top of each other to create music" (DJ Dictionary). This dynamic falls in line with what Katherine Hayles identifies in the computational universe as working "simultaneously as means and metaphor in technical and artistic practices, producing and also produced by recursive loops that entangle with one another and with the diverse meaning of computation as technology, ontology, and cultural icon" (*My Mother* 4). Similarly, the novel uses a looping technique that seamlessly connects and repeats similar elements on different levels: that which takes place during the programming of the game, the textual knowledge domain as rooted in classical literature, Eduard's own personal experiences, Kazuo's gaming experience, and the experience of the viewers of the game. Images, ideas, and objects intersect on various levels and lead to a seemingly less linear and more hyperlinked product. But contrary to the act of hyperlinking, in *Ático* there is a sense of connection and (linear) movement toward a goal, an end result, which is the completion of the computer program or the video game, and it is this goal that gives meaning to the looping

There are many instances, beginning with the title, in which the looping mechanism of the novel presents itself. The title of the novel is connected to the attic within which Eduard lives, to the attic he re-creates in the game, and to the real attic the winner of the video game receives upon escaping the last attic on video. The representational quality of this interior space is extensive, re-presenting emotions related to spaces, to adventures, failures, loneliness, solitude, and success. Additional material appears and reappears on the various levels of the novel. In "Ático" the game, the avatar's name is the same as the player himself, Kazuo, thus leading to an immediate overlap of real and virtual personalities. The difference is that as the virtual Kazuo moves through space and event (play) time, the real Kazuo remains still in his chair and moves through limited real time (thirty-six hours), a time contrasted to the three months it takes Eduard to program the game. In addition, several narrative strands occur as the onlookers create a "supertext" that supersedes and comments on the responses and conversations of the characters in game.

In *Ático* the physical body is one of the clearest examples of looping at the center of human-computer interfaces. Katherine Hayles gives the name "intermediation" to the "complex transactions between bodies and texts as well as between different forms of media" ("Virtual" 7). She insists, quoting German media critic Friedrich Kittler, that "media effects, to have meaning and significance, must be located within an embodied human world" ("Virtual" 7). While virtual, the video game, and the novel, never ceases to remind its onlookers of the interrelationship between the body at play and the body in real life. To Kazuo's own surprise, the hunger, the cold, the heat, the desire, and the pain felt by his character extends to his real-life persona. When Kazuo gives the wrong answer to a question and loses an eye, he comments that he felt "una especie de punzada en el ojo que era casi dolor [...]. La impresión es tan fuerte que se parece al dolor. —Pero todo es

> **TIME AND MAPPING IN VIDEO GAME**
>
> Game theorist Jesper Juul explains that "the relationship between play time and event time can be described as mapping. Mapping means that the player's time and actions are projected into a game world. This is the play-element of games; you click with your mouse, but you are also the mayor of a fictive city" (134). The basic idea is that the action of the player, as distinct as his or her situation may be, is ultimately linked or related to that of the game scene on screen. This creates not only a personal identification, but a spatial and temporal one—my act determines what happens on screen now.
>
> —Christine Henseler

mental, mental. Interpretas de tal modo tu papel. [...] Es como un sueño, lo sufres en realidad. [Y] eso forma parte de su encanto" [a sort of prick in the eye that was almost pain. The impression is so strong that it seems like pain—But it is all mental, mental. You interpret your role to such a degree. [...] It is like a dream, you truly suffer it. [And] this is part of its charm]

(61–62). The enchantment of this "real" pain is fully embodied by Eduard's blind Arab neighbor who, motioning to his paralyzed body and eyes, provocatively proclaims that "Esto que aquí ves [...] es el producto de una fantasía" [This that you see here [...] is the product of a fantasy] (224). His comment reflects the journey of fantastic immersion that the video game character must experience in order to find his *real* self and not be pulverized in the process, even if in the end his real body feels the fictitious effects of the game.

There is a distinct relationship between storytelling, embodiment, and computing in this novel. Given that the video game is based on classical literature, the main themes of the game are universal, such as love and war, but the role of fiction within a fiction is inherently written into the program, leaving room for elements of Eduard's experiences and Faridza's biographies to appear in the game itself. In fact, Faridza's biographies of famous writers who committed suicide, such as Virginia Woolf or Fernando Pessoa, give Eduard the "meat" to place on the skeleton of his program. He admits to her that "hasta ahora he planteado situaciones pero no sabía qué iban a decir los actores. Necesitaba frases. Y ya las tengo: hablarán los escritores" [up until now I have presented situations but I did not know what the actors were going to say. I needed sentences. And now I have them: the writers will speak] (123). With this revelation, the novel pronounces the looping quality between the novel, *Ático*, and the game "Ático," which work together to pronounce the interactive quality of both game and narrative.

Playing at Being in a Mobile Labyrinth

The very first screen of the video game begins with sexual and emotional scenes of love and love making (complete with virtual nudity and explicit sexual positions) to pull the players into the game space and "sell" the game experience—they are even asked to partake in the action, touch the female character's breasts and comment on their beauty. These explicit sexual acts may be interpreted as a physical metaphor for the self in game and the game's relationship to storytelling. While perceived by some onlookers as a cheap pornographic gimmick, hidden behind the sex are dialogues filled with philosophical content. The male character, for example, motions to the construction of the world (his paradisical scenery) as an ontological site of survival when he says, "Cuando aceptas el mundo como es estarás muerto" [When you accept the world as it is you will be dead] (35). He perceives the world as limitless: "Por más lejos que mires existe un mundo sin límites, más allá" [No matter how far you look, there exists a world without limits, beyond] (30), suggesting that either the creative design of the world in the game is infinite or that there is a world beyond the game. His female half complements his remarks by pointing inward and talking about the power of love and love making as the source for disembodiment: "Dicen que cuando la luna se oscurece un hombre puede convertirse en mujer y la mujer en hombre. Ambos pueden traspasar los límites y pasar a ser otro" [They say that when the moon goes dark a man can turn into a woman and a woman into a man. Both can traverse limits and pass and become another] (3). This gender-bending/blending comment falls in line with her next words about storytelling when she says, "Follar sólo sale bien cuando dos historias empiezan a ser la misma historia. Implica permutarse, luchar, intercambiar relatos y contar mentiras hasta acceder a la verdad" [To screw only works out when two stories become the same story. It implies permutation, fighting, exchanging stories and telling lies until one accesses the truth] (34). If we were to replace the verb "to have sex" with "to play," readers and players could place the sexual content of this first screen within a more metafictional context. The couple's remarks would lay the groundwork for a dissolution of physical and psychological spaces in game, allowing not only for fluidity, but also for contradiction to occur as the erasure of the tropical scene on screen dissolves into the sound of alarms and oncoming gunshots of planes above.

As central as the role of physicality is the interlooping role of game, play and fantasy, as it relates to life and death. The programming and playing of the video game are the two main narrative events in the novel. They are enhanced by the (exterior) documentary voice that talks about video game history and the history of "Ático" at a future moment (after the game has succeeded on the market). Internally, the act of playing corresponds to Eduard's act of programming, and the awareness of this act translates into an awareness of the act of play in the game. This awareness appears most strongly in the second screen when Kazuo, the game character, gives Diego, the man who opens the door, the countersign—a coral—to enter the second screen. Diego throws this valued item into a chest with dozens of identical corals, making Kazuo aware of the existence and path of dozens of players before him. Consequently, Diego confronts Kazuo by asking him why he was playing this stupid game to begin with. Did he not have anything better to do with his time? This game, says Diego, was nothing but "una farsa, sí, una puñetera mentira" [a farce, yes, a damn lie] (53). To which Kazuo simply replies that he was there to play (53). After this comment, Diego bluntly reminds him of the linearity of his path, that unless he does what he tells him to do (which, in this case, is to build a mud wall), he will throw him over his veranda. The choice is game play or death of the character. His comment implies a suspension of disbelief, demanding that a player, as Kazuo recognizes, fully enter into this so-called farce of a world through self-deceit: "uno debe saber engañarse porque si no, jamás avanzaría" [one needs to know how to fool oneself because otherwise, one would never advance] (218). Without deceit, Kazuo dies. The screen turns black. It's over.

In video game, visual and verbal effects in motion contribute to a story within what could be imagined as a *mobile* labyrinth, a place within which players must make real-time choices, choices that change as the play moves forward. These actions involve players in more personal ways than in the act of reading because players risk making wrong decisions, being rejected and failing. The possibility of a perception of intimacy and success is the human power that moves the storyline forward. But despite having choices, the game experience is a profoundly linear experience—we make sense of the game world by walking, flying, fighting, or riddling our way toward a goal. In other words, during the process of accepting or rejecting certain choices, we develop a storyline that may be as abstract as a game of *Tetris* or as narrative as a game of *Myst*. In actuality, the programming of a treelike, or forking, game is difficult to program. For this reason, programs present the *appearance* of choice, an appearance that is often quite limited, but may present multiple possibilities. Interestingly, one of the most often referenced characteristics of contemporary Internet and media culture, open-ended finales or lack of meaningful endings, is a feature only available to those who fail and find their storylines broken off. In game, play should lead to a meaningful ending that leads to a feeling of achievement and the accomplishment of a goal; the success of a video game is inherently related to this psychological possibility of success.

> *Tu alusión al laberinto móvil que propone* Ático *tiene una especie de cara B en la novela* Sudd. *Si en* Ático *abordo el laberinto móvil desde la tecnología —la única forma en la que por entonces veía factible desarrollar un laberinto de esas características—*Sudd *presenta un laberinto móvil físico. Esa ciénaga me entusiasmó: era un espacio que sólo pensé posible en la imaginación, en fantasía. Y sin embargo, ahí estaba, existiendo de verdad. No sé si te hablé de que* Sudd *proponía una reversión del mito del laberinto habitado por el Minotauro, y esa revisitación era la que le daba absoluta modernidad: el del Minotauro era un laberinto perfecto, complejísimo, pero de paredes estáticas (esos valores antiguos inamovibles) mientras que el laberinto de* Sudd *contempla una geografía elástica, paredes que se mueven contigo, que te persiguen, significando a una realidad, unos valores, mucho más gaseosos y flexibles que aquellos que amparaban al Minotauro.*
>
> —*Gabi Martínez, in response*

To play, to transport oneself into a fantasy world, allows a character to live. As such, play becomes, in the biography of Fátima Mernissi (quoted by Faritza), a form of defense, one that in the game is closely related to death and war. When "play" is referenced through the voices of the Muslim characters, including Faridza, Ahmed, and Fátima, it is an act related to survival. In Ahmed's life, "fantasy" literally becomes a space of emotional survival and adrenaline. In his youth he partook in the festival of "Fantasy," or "tborida," a true-life Moroccan equestrian game that shows off horsemanship and leadership skills, and whose ultimate goal is harmony between riders and horses. Much like the emotional effect of video games themselves, Ahmed explains that "la fantasía es todo un acontecimiento. Le puedo asegurar que en su ejecución hay pólvora, velocidad, adrenalina, furia y belleza. Sobre todo eso, una cantidad excepcional de belleza" [fantasy is quite an event. I can assure you that in its execution there is gunpowder, speed, adrenaline, fury, and beauty. Above all, an exceptional quantity of beauty] (221). The result: an accident that paralyzes and blinds him. Subsequently, Ahmed suggestively remarks on the connection between reality and fantasy by motioning to his body and his eyes: "Esto que aquí ve [. . .] es el producto de una fantasía"

[This which you see here, is the product of a fantasy] (224). Ahmed literally embodies "fantasy," reminding readers that fantasy is not solely the domain of virtual space but also of real-life "play," or the game of life.

To play a successful game of life commands forgetting about the program and structure behind the "grand design," the path/screen upon which our experiences take shape. A player's experience, then, is supposed to be marked by a sense of immediacy and of immediate connection between the self on and off the screen. Video games remind us that at the heart of their creations, three important components must be found (to varying degrees): the game, the story (whether abstract or narrative), and the self. Together, they heighten players' physical and physiological relationship to game play and heighten the fantasy world within which we move. Any move away from this total immersion—as the previous fall from Fantasy indicates—leads to self-awareness. Ahmed's blindness plays with an awareness of form, content, and the self or subversion/interruption of game rules to discover the role of the self in game. The experience echoes the words of Patricia Waugh on metafiction when she comments that "play is facilitated by rules and roles, and metafiction operates by exploring fictional rules to discover the role of fictions in life. It aims to discover how we each 'play our own realities'" (35), or, Corner's concept from chapter four, perform within our own "reality projects." In (game) stories, we literally play our (constructed) realities into being and establish a direct (imaginary) relationship between ourselves and the objects or beings on the page or screen.

The novel's ability to mix fantasy and reality is worth describing

---

METAFICTION IN GAME

While commercial game designers tend to avoid moments of true game awareness, their goal being full immersion, they are increasingly including playful self-conscious references. For example, in *Super Paper Mario*, Mario can visit a casino in which he can play different video games. In *The Sims 2: FreeTime*, an event occurs in which a Sim version of Rod Humble, the head of *The Sims* franchise, gives the player's Sim family an unopened gift box. When opened, the family gets a computer with *The Sims 3* on it (http://en.wikipedia.org/wiki/Metafictional_video_games).

On a more subtle level, Alex Hayter suggests that the Wii Nintendo game *The Beatles: Rock Band* presents an interesting example of Linda Hutcheon's concept of "historiographic metafiction," as players use "instruments" to play themselves into the Beatles soundtrack and are intermittently bombarded with audio, video, text, and cut-scenes about particular moments in Beatle history. The artificial narrative of historical events are stylized and, to some degree, "rewritten," as players take part in the making of history—history is not only repacked, its temporal sequence redefined, but it is also individualized, stressing our subjective interpretation of historical events.

—Christine Henseler

In many GenX texts, media technology serves as a metafictional space →

of construction: the character in Ray Loriga's *Héroes* (1993) uses his personal and emotional relation to rock music and rock stars (not politics or history) as a supertext for reflection and growth; the protagonist in Benjamín Prados's *Alguien se acerca* (1998) uses filmic and classical literary references to write a second, murdering self into reality; in Care Santos's *Aprender a huir* (2002), the telephone serves to augment a feeling of loneliness expressed through monologues on answering machines; in José Ángel Mañas's *Historias del Kronen* (1994), Carlos's process of (not) becoming relies on his superficial relation to violent movies; in Lucía Etxebarria's *Amor, curiosidad, prozac y dudas* (1997) female identity is intimately connected to the self-deceiving power of commodity culture. In each case, the tools used to write the self into story involve individual cultural repertoires that converge with media technologies.

—Christine Henseler

in detail through the final pages of the novel. In the chapter after Ahmed tells his life story, the objective, exterior voice emulates a Web search on the topic of the Moroccan "Fantasy" festival, and it concludes that "la aspiración de la fantasía es siempre la armonía" [the aspiration of fantasy is always harmony] (225). This comment directly relates to Kazuo's own remarks that the only way one can win a game is to play in the same tempo used by the programmer. The next chapter is filled with screams and gunshot after someone kills Ahmed's falcon, the gunshots presenting, once again, the direct relationship between life and death in play and reality. Subsequently, Eduard receives an e-mail from Faridza on the Italian writer Cesare Pavese. The major topics of his biography—love, suffering, destruction, and suicide—are, according to her docufiction, and echoing the words of her uncle, "la culpa [...] de la fantasía" [the fault of fantasy] (229). It is at this moment, when love has taken over his mind, that Eduard loses perspective and reads himself into the biography of Pavese, angrily remarking: "¡Qué sabrá esa zorra lo que es la fantasía!" [What does this whore know about what fantasy is] (230).

Screen five begins immediately after Eduard's outburst, and it presents the culmination of the looping moments of the novel. The scene takes place in a children's room in a large house. It begins with a metamedia moment in which the boy shows Kazuo his computer game. The boy explains that the goal of this video game is simple: to make five comets fly high by answering five questions that refer back to Kazuo's own game play. If he answers them correctly, the real Kazuo wins the game and the character Kazuo wins the game within the game. As one of the most memory-high games to have been produced, "Ático" demands the power of players' brain memory. The first three questions that the video game within the video game asks are easy. Then comes the fourth: What is the name of the woman who Kazuo made love to in the previous screen? She had not given her name, but Kazuo guesses correctly: "Soledad." He intuits the answer, knowing well the rhythm and mind-set of Eduard when he programmed the game. The last question looms. Only six minutes are left. The question is: "Who are you?" As Kazuo thinks out loud, it becomes clear that his suspension of disbelief has reached into the confines of Eduard's life. Kazuo ponders out loud, saying that, well, "Esto es una fantasía, no es real" [This is a fantasy, it is not real.] (233). The boy remarks, that, yes, exactly, this is your fantasy. Then who are you? The following dialogue is worth re-creating given that it echoes Eduard's interactions with Ahmed:

> — Me gustan los caballos…árabes…
> Los has visto a cientos…
> —…y cuando Soledad sueña…
> —…en Marruecos…
> —…cree que yo soy él.
> —¿Quién?
> Y Kazuo responde:
> —Soy Eugenio. Eugenio de la Cruz.
> —Perdona—dice el niño—, pero los mocosos de ahora sabemos idiomas.
> —Eugéne —contesta Kazuo—Eugène Delacroix. Yo pinto fantasías.
> [I like horses…Arab horses…
> You have seen hundreds of them…
> …and when Soledad dreams…
> —in Morocco…
> —…she thinks that I am him.
> —¿Who?
> And Kazuo responds:
> —I am Eugenio. Eugenio de la Cruz.
> —Excuse me—says the boy—but we, today's pipsqueaks know languages.
> —Eugéne—answers Kazuo— Eugène Delacroix. I paint fantasies.] (233)

Kazuo's guess is informed by Eduard's biography. In the final chapter of the novel Eduard speaks to Ahmed about a tapestry that hung in his attic living room. The tapestry reproduced an image by Delacroix. When Ahmed talks about Delacroix, he talks about his life as filled with the words freedom, disillusionment, adventure, and new life. Delacroix's travels, he says, led him to new inspirations for which the only word powerful enough to describe its effects is "fantasy" (239). Ahmed considers himself a "maestro en fanta sías" [master of fantasies], a man who knows that religion and loneliness are fantasies, and that his own depressed life story can only be told to a person like Eduard, a man in search of "derrotas" [defeats] (240), a word we readers might interpret to refer to the many ways of losing in game.

Despite the real Kazuo's pronouncement that his game play was an effect of fantasy, not reality, the unfolding of the final moments of the video game respond to realities' relation to play. After answering the last question correctly, the fifth and final attic is on fire; Kazuo sees his own image reflected in the building before him and that of the boy desperately reaching for his help. The boy, in one of the only "true" moments of the game, calls out his name: "Kazuo," thereby interpellating him emotionally and physically in real time. In the final seconds, before the words "Game Over" appear on the black

I think that it's very interesting to go deeper into the video game and Martínez's relation with identity, but it is also fascinating to rethink the idea of the self as a video game. In the issue nº 322 of the Spanish literary magazine Quimera, *René Deloneon wrote an article titled "The Subject as a Videogame," in which he defended the radical experience of the subjectivity as a game and a piece of joy. These are the first paragraphs of the article: "Aunque parezca muy actual, la idea del yo como videojuego tiene bastantes años. Se remonta a un notable artículo de prensa de Claudio Magris de 1998, en el que el escritor y ensayista italiano reflexionaba en los siguientes términos: 'En un mundo y una cultura cada vez más virtuales, la unidad y la continuidad del Yo fundado sobre la conciencia y sus valores parecen no sólo amenazar ruina, sino casi olvidados en una pulverización indistinta en la que todo es intercambiable con todo, en una universal indiferencia que desmenuza sentimientos, visiones del mundo, jerarquía de afectos y el sentido mismo de la experiencia. El Yo individual, descompuesto y repuesto al mismo tiempo, de manera continua, como en un videojuego, trata de salvarse aferrándose a las cosas, a la memoria como conocimiento de sí mismo y como custodio de la realidad y de la vida: se salva en el inventario' (C. Magris, "Novecento. Lo scrittore nel videogame," Corriere della Sera, 12/01/1998). De este texto de Magris podemos sacar algunos conceptos que, como líneas de fuga, pueden servir para escapar de y acercarse al imaginario de la subjetividad en nuestro tiempo. Las líneas maestras serían:*

-El sujeto contemporáneo es un yo disuelto, que vive una experiencia vi(r)t(u)al intercambiable.

-El sujeto cobra la forma de un videojuego, en el sentido de proceso constructivo lúdico y mecánicamente repetible, algo que puede parecer muy poppy pero que estaba ya en Jacques Derrida, ni más ni menos.

→

screen, Kazuo observes the pulverization of his virtual self—"se observa las manos, se toca la cara, los muslos, el pecho. [Y] coge en brazos al niño" [he observes his own hands, he touches his face, thighs, chest. [And] he takes the boy into his arms] (235)—and he chooses to save the boy instead of win the game.

Kazuo recognized himself in his own name when the boy screams for help. To the question of his fans: "¿Por qué intentaste salvar al niño? Ibas a ganar. [...] Sólo era un juego" [Why did you try to save the boy? You were going to win [...] It was only a game]. Kazuo responds: "¿Estás seguro? [Are you sure?] (235). Echoing in his mind is the last question of the video game within the game, which was: "¿Quién eres?" [Who are you?]. This question pronounces, once again, the relationship between selves and stories in game, between the real self and the painters, programmers, and players of fantastic worlds. The game ultimately highlights the looping quality of the self in computational space, in the dramatic storytelling space of the game play, and in social reality.

Writing Oneself Into Storyspace

A good video game gives players the sense that they have control over the action and that their behaviors matter by presenting an attractive balance between a player's skill level and sense of immersion, or "fun." While players have control over a finite number of choices through finite and predetermined mechanical applications and rules, the first level of control is in the hands of the so-called simauthors. According to Gonzalo Frasca, the "simauthors," or authors of simulations, are the ones who craft laws and behave like sign generators or machines (229). They "educate" their simulations, they teach them rules and include a set of behaviors, but they can never be sure of the exact final sequence of events and results (although many of them are predetermined). As such, "simauthors" take risks, more risks than the author of a novel, because they cannot foresee the action of all players (220–29).

As the "simauthor" of "Ático," Eduard finishes programming his game and hands it off to marketers and gamers. At this point his narrative intersects with the narrative of others, the gamers, allowing mini-stories to be "writ-

> *-El inventario objetual y de consumo como base ontológica de datos (comprados) que categorizan al sujeto que la genera / consume. En los videojuegos el protagonista tiene que ir moviéndose para conseguir cosas, cuya adquisición le mejora como personaje y le permite armarse para llegar al final del juego. La adquisición consumista como medio de alcanzar el destino.*
>
> *-Los antiguos medios de comunicación (TV, cine, radio) y las nuevas tecnologías de comunicación y /o representación (internet, vídeo, cámaras digitales, móviles) configuran un sujeto electrónico que tiene también como características la movilidad, la inestabilidad estructural y el narcisismo."*
>
> *I do agree with Deloneon in everything. I'm so deeply involved with his thoughts, maybe because Deloneon was, in fact, one of my pseudonyms. The entire issue 322 of* Quimera *was written by me, under 22 different pseudonyms and characters of my own. That's another way to see the identity and the literary experience as a video game...*
>
> —*Vicente Luis Mora, in response*

ten" on top of his programmed story line (thereby the importance given to the process of looping). Although each player brings his or her own avatar and self to the screen, as we can see in Kazuo's game play, the novel never lets us forget Eduard's story, one that beautifully interweaves fiction and reality into the baseline of the electronic storyspace. Nor does the game ever provide a whole sense of self because "the boundaries of self are defined less by the skin than by the feedback loops connecting body and simulation in a techno-bio-integrated circuit" (*My Mother* 72). As such, Kazuo is compared to Eduard, Soledad is compared to Faridza, the character of Eugenio is compared to Delacroix, Delacroix is compared to Ahmed, the trash man is compared to Josep Pla, and the boy is compared to either a childhood version of Kazuo or a child of Kazuo's. The circuits completely loop around each other and themselves.

Kazuo's decision to save the boy rather than his fictional self suggests that the path into and out of the story line cannot be disconnected from an awareness of the role of the self in game. The reason why Kazuo ends up being one of only three players who reaches the final fifth stage is because he realizes that one has to know "quién eres y por qué vives antes de descubrir el camino de vuelta a casa" [who you are and why you live before finding the way back home] (205). It is only by full insertion but also full awareness of the transition of his semivisual, semitextual representation that he can write himself into or out of the narrative. This sentiment suggests that, indeed, according to Hispanist John Kronik, "a novel lies within each one of us, and everyone is shown to have a dual capacity: as narrator and as subject of fiction" (299). Those players who reach the final level of the game enter into the canon of gamers as their moves are forever recorded on videotape. The recording translates the players' actions and words into an epic narrative of authorial mastery, one that enters into ever-new narrative threads.

Beginning with McLuhan's pronouncement, "the medium is the message," many have argued that the contemporary mixing of media inherently implies a self-referential looping mechanism in which media speak of/to one another at the same time that they pull the self into virtual space. As media are remixed, the consciousness of their existence is heightened, and the hand of the "maker" becomes more pronounced. In video games this "hand" literally takes action as "it" presses a button, an arrow, or moves a joystick or other device that connects the "I" in real life with the "I," or "it," on screen. In the novel, this self-awareness may be found on three levels. The first one is philosophical and concerns the topic of game itself, as pronounced by all "characters" and "voices" of the novel. The second one concerns an awareness of the characters' construction in game and the role of "Eduard" as the "creator" (at one moment confused with Kazuo as his storytelling ability unravels). And the third metafictional level is exterior and includes the game's onlookers (the crowd watching the rerun), Ahmed and Faridza, and Eduard himself. What becomes clear from the very beginning is pronounced by Kazuo upon reviewing the first screen, namely that the spectacle he was witnessing was nothing but a big game of mirrors and that, as Eduard, quoting Nietzsche, frames at the end of the book: "todo afecta a todo" [everything affects everything] (217). *Ático* presents fictions within fictions where the characters-turned-creators attempt to turn the created object into one that is more concrete and palpable than its living prototype (297). Kazuo summarizes this idea when he says to one of the characters in the game: "Eres un esclavo que sin amo va a la deriva" [You are a slave who, without a master, is lost] (132).

Much like in real life, only a fraction of our time is built around the self alone, and our perceptions of self are largely built around our actions in relation to others. In game play, I would agree with Aarseth that our constructed selves are always interacting with an Other, may this entity be a real or virtual character or thing, or a combination thereof. The Other in game is more flexible and multiple in its embodiment, the fantasy world allowing for gender, race, and sexual bending and human-animal-machine blending of figures and objects (characteristics we find in more and more novels by the *Mutantes*). As in game, our relationship to the outside world is always mediated by our own action in the game of life. As one of the characters, Faridza, conveys in the novel through the Moroccan author Fatima Mernissi, "El juego [consiste] en contemplar el territorio familiar como si fuera extraño a uno" [The game consists in contemplating familiar territory as if it were foreign to oneself] (164). As subjects interact with the video game, their embodiment and interaction with an Other creates an inverse, blended, and mutated relationship between the familiar and the foreign, the interior and the exterior, the game and the real, a GenX game of mutation.

Chapter 6

Generation X and the *Mutantes,*
A Mash-Up

In *Collective Intelligence* (1997), Pierre Lévy argues for the creation of a new (potentially collective) knowledge space, or *cosmopedia,* the result of new computer technologies that provide, "a dynamic and interactive multi-dimensional representational space" (174). Lévy sees this space as containing as many semiotics as exist in the world itself, from "static images, video, sound, interactive simulation, interactive maps, expert systems, dynamic ideographs, virtual reality, artificial life, etc." (174–75). This is a space that allows for the dematerialization of "the artificial boundaries between disciplines, making knowledge 'a large patchwork' in which virtually any field can be folded onto another" (175). While best represented by the outgrowth of the Internet and a host of new and easy-to use software applications, this folding, or mapping dynamic, may be well observed in twenty-first-century Spanish literature where all the semiotic codes identified by Lévy can appear together on the printed page. The fiction of the *Mutantes* applies centrifugal dynamics that simultaneously include and exclude hundreds of references, large and small, real and fictitious, from the printed page and the mediated world. As argued in previous chapters, their work is the result of a world that is witnessing the mutation of codes and the blurring of genres and narrative styles. This development stresses interconnections, overlappings, and individual paths taken and not taken; it juxtaposes temporal and spatial time frames as events that erase roots and references and simultaneously create new nodes and beginnings.

The work of Agustín Fernández Mallo presents a new narrative beginning that mutates its generational roots. Born in La Coruña in 1967, Mallo is a physicist by day and a poet, novelist, essayist, and blogger by night. His book of poetry, *Carne de Píxel,* received the "Premio Ciudad de Burgos de Poesía" in 2007; his critical book, *Postpoesía: hacia un nuevo paradigma* (2009), theorizes an interdisciplinary poetic paradigm for the contemporary age; and his trilogy *Nocilla Dream* (2006), *Nocilla Experience* (2008), and *Nocilla Lab* (2009) constructs a web that is larger than its parts, a *cosmopedia* in print.[1] In addition, Mallo's latest novel, *El hacedor (de Borges) Remake* (2010), his blog "El hombre que salió de la tarta," and his video project "Proyecto Nocilla" cross media platforms and disciplines to embolden his ideas on the art and science of writing.[2]

As a scientist, a poet, a novelist, and a video producer, Mallo constructs worlds that are not only hybrid in their multidisciplinary and multimedia stylistic applications, but, most importantly, they *expand* the spatial dynamics of the written word. Mallo's fiction materializes the marginal of José Ángel Mañas's punk ethos. He develops a trash aesthetics that centers on the object by digitizing the GenX father's former *slam poetics* and turning it into a *spam poetics*.[3] In the process he enlarges the media archive related to Avant-Pop by applying new media techniques related to the act of cutting and pasting, remixing, mapping, and mashing. The mash-up—the digitized combination of two or more elements into one—becomes a media metaphor to understand the work of Mallo and to "mash" Generation X and the *Mutantes* onto one literary map, allowing both to coexist on different yet overlapping vectors. Both groups' aesthetic directions contribute to map the "blank" as one of Generation X's most recurring and encompassing tropes. Whether the "blank" refers to narrative style, human emotions, discarded objects, or the space left in between hypertextual links, what becomes clear is that Generation X's roots in the blank has led to powerful new narrative practices and possibilities. This is an opening that allows for spatial and temporal multiplicities, convergences and contradictions, displacements and misplacements. The blank allows for a positive and productive reevaluation of Generation X as the cultural impact of new media technologies has accelerated over the past twenty years.

One could argue that Mallo's artistic oeuvre digitizes Richard's Hell song lyrics of "the blank generation." Mallo embraces the blank in terms of the empty, the lost, the forgotten, the thrown-away, the error. Trash. Spam. He also turns the blank into a computational formula that flickers, to paraphrase Katherine Hayles, between ones and zeros. His work advances, recombines, and mutates Generation X while remaining tied to its underlying structure and system. To understand the influence of Mallo's fiction, especially as it feeds from and changes pre-established Generation X patterns, I divide this chapter into several sections that engage with previous ideas presented in this book. First, I argue that the work of Mallo remakes Mañas's punk philosophy in the digital age through his own brand of trash aesthetics and spam poetics. Second, I point to Mallo's narrative application of "error" as a material mutation of Generation X's "blank space." Third, I examine how Mallo expands on the notion of Avant-Pop by manipulating a larger set of digital bits and bytes that the accumulation of media assets offers contemporary writers. And fourth, I investigate how Mallo, in his novel *Nocilla dream,* applies the networking and mapping possibilities of the World Wide Web to create a unique narrative mash-up. Throughout this chapter, Mallo, Sierra, Carrión and Fernández Porta interact and expand on my main text to present what one could call an *after-poppy* mash-up of new critical proportions.

Mallo's Punk Remake and Spam Poetics

In 1994, José Angel Mañas's novel *Historias del Kronen* came to define a group of young writers as "Generación Kronen." In 2006, Mallo's *Nocilla* trilogy led to the naming of the "Generación Nocilla." Although these two writers may seem ages apart in stylistic output and attitude, Mallo's fiction may be considered to expand on his colleague's work in significant ways. Mallo advances a more mature and integrated experience of GenX individuals in a world now fully globalized and technologically connected. The work of Mallo is far from Mañas's urban "costumbrismo juvenil" as centered on sex, drugs, and popular culture. In fact, Mañas barely exists in the imaginary or literary tradition of the *Mutantes* author although one can claim that Mallo reconfigures the noise, the marginality, and the stylistic simplicity once related to punk music. Like Mañas, Mallo also presents empty takes on (sexual) relations but through a lens of human loneliness and socially marginal and disconnected characters. He opens addiction to a diverse set of drugs related to material objects, human relations (or lack thereof), and computer technology. Instead of limiting his extratextual references to popular and commercial

Mi idea de lo de punk en mi literatura no creo que sea la misma que la que se da en autores como José Ángel Mañas. Por mucho que me interesan sus novelas, creo que mi materialización, en cuanto a ese concepto, es antagónica a la suya. Mi idea del punk en mi literatura sería una especie de aparente contradicción: "el punk sin la suciedad del punk". El punk tomado como lo que serían para mí sus dos ideas principales "filosóficas", despojadas de su carnalidad urbana: la radicalidad en el sentido etimológico de la palabra "radical": "agarrar las cosas por la raiz", y en el conocido "do it yourself". De hecho, respecto a esto último, siempre que puedo, mi práctica literaria va más allá de lo textual y hago las portadas de mis libros o las fotografías e ilustraciones que estos puedan llevar (con excepción del cómic final en Nocilla Lab, *que corrió a cargo del profesional del cómic, Pere Joan), y las filmaciones de las películas, tanto de la película* Proyecto Nocilla, *como de las que he elaborado para "El hacedor (de Borges), Remake". Por otra parte, tanto los personajes, como el mundo que describo no comparten en nada la sordidez típica del punk, al contrario, son historias muy "blancas," muy haiku, por llamarlo de alguna manera. Ten en cuenta que, contra todo pronóstico en lo que se refiere a los requisitos que supuestamente debe tener un libro para "popularizarse", en mi trilogía no hay ni una escena de sexo explícito (o creo que sólo 1), ni una palabra malsonante, ni un solo conflicto (o creo que sólo 1), ni un asesinato (o creo que sólo 1, pero es simbólico, pretendidamente no creíble), ni realismo sucio, ni rock en el sentido de la exaltación de lo callejero, ni drogas, ni todo lo que se suele asociar a lo punk. Es como si fuera un "destilado" de lo punk (radicalidad + do it yourself) hacia una experiencia "blanca" (por blanca, quiero decir, no sórdida en los términos que la burguesía da a esa palabra, pero sí muy sórdida en el sentido de violentar las reglas del juego* →

narrativo, escarbar, deslocalizar, etc.). Esto, a mi modo de ver, da lugar a mi "poética", muy poco social y más bien deudora de universos artificiales o simulacros tipo Borges o Baudrillard. Fíjate que, por ejemplo, en Nocilla Experience, *donde hay muchos insertos de entrevistas a músicos de rock famosos, he metido las partes donde hablan de la sentimentalidad de la música, de las sensaciones, nunca de la parte más "maldita" o sórdida de la música, que no me interesa y sí le interesaría más a un autor típicamente punk.*

—Agustín Fernández Mallo, in response

Entiendo perfectamente que en un libro de historia crítica de la literatura española la literatura de Agustín Fernández Mallo viene después de la parte más visible de la obra de José Ángel Mañas, y que por tanto ambas son susceptibles de comparación. Pero lo cierto es que esa comparación me resulta extraña. Porque se trata de dos galaxias tan lejanas que sólo una ordenación cronológica y, sobre todo, nacional (una categoría que a mis ojos resulta anacrónica para hablar de literatura, aunque en tantas ocasiones nos veamos obligados a ella). Leí Historias del Kronen *a los diecinueve años, a mediados de los años 90, y, aunque me atrapó, el universo urbano que retrataba también me resultaba muy lejano, no era mi forma de vivir la juventud ni la ciudad. He leído la obra de Agustín Fernández Mallo en los últimos cinco años y no hay duda de que me siento mucho más cerca de ese mundo, por su uso de la metáfora tecnológica, por su investigación en nuevas formas y formatos, por su exploración del viaje y del escenario global, aunque algunas de sus características también me sean ajenas (como su visión del consumismo o de la política).*

—Jorge Carrión, in response

culture, Mallo opens his novel to any and all sources thereby refiguring contemporary reality through more multiple and complex signifiers and systems. Contrary to the work of Mañas, Mallo erases aggression and bitterness from his characters minds and instead centers his work on human disconnection through inner tranquility and acceptance. Rather than constructing and remaining in a cold and uncaring environment, Mallo uses objects that are material and objective to develop thematic connections and emotional warmth and growth between the characters.

The narratives of both Mañas and Mallo reject high literary Style in favor of a stylistics stripped of artificiality. Mañas once applied street jargon to prose in an attempt to transcribe the language of the young *en directo*. Mallo does not attempt to give voice to the young nor does he want their individual registers to saturate the narrative voices in his novel. On the contrary, objectivity in Mallo is meant to erase references albeit through similarly unfinished sentences that might include errors in syntax and grammar (Ors). Mallo does not reflect reality in prose, but he reconfigures reality through fiction to create what he calls a "docuficción." Docu-fiction, according to Mallo, mixes fiction and field material to erase the voice of the author/narrator, to present more objective focalization points, and to allow the aesthetics of objects to emerge on their own, "sin tener que adjetivarla" [without having to adjectivize it]. By removing the narrative filter of the adjective, Mallo's novels, like those of Mañas, resolutely *tell it like it is.* But while Mañas's "no filter philosophy" strips his narrative of lyrical qualities, Mallo finds poetry in the ordinary. In the same vein, the motor that Mallo uses to write his *Nocilla* trilogy is, in his own words, rather simple; it consists of narrating "sin el prejuicio de creer que estoy narrando, narrar de la manera en la que realmente vivo mi día a día" [without the prejudice of thinking that I am narrating, narrate like I live my every day] ("Adiós"). In a stylistic move that shifts from Mañas's colloquial street language to a more inner, subjective means of expression, Mallo narrates what he sees, hears, or does through his own individualized, true filter; his *punk remake* unsettles readers' expectations precisely because he sees the world through a uniquely poetic/scientific lens that places the dirt and trash, the disregarded and the marginal onto center stage.

Mallo's raw appropriation of brute and unfiltered reality directly relates material culture to science and information technology. Mallo remixes and interrelates individuals to objects that are thrown away, found, taken, used, recycled, or stolen. His vignettes on contemporary life center on the aesthetics of trash, of objects, and of spam. He takes "lo que está en los márgenes, el ruido, el residuo, como quien afirmase que ha aprendido a leer valiéndose de la mayor biblioteca del mundo: los contenedores de basura, que albergan millones de textos en

During the 1980s, differently from what was happening in music, movies, comics, photography, and so on, Spanish "punk" literary fiction remained mostly underground (although some collections of "nueva narrativa española" were published, most notably the one by "Ediciones Libertarias," which included the Burroughs-inspired fiction by Eduardo Haro Ibars).

The first novels by Mañas and Loriga introduced Spanish "punk literature" to mainstream readers, in part because the work of American GenX and dirty realism writers such as Carver, Easton Ellis, and Coupland was being translated in Spain. This resulted in a kind of "mainstream punk" literature, mainly depicting the life of young urban Spaniards of the 1980s and 1990s. This "mainstream punk," dubbed "Gen Kronen" following the title of Mañas's first novel, distanced itself from both the underground/pulp literature and the experimental/postmodern fiction practiced in the 1970s by older writers such as Juan Goytisolo, Camilo José Cela, and Julián Ríos, among others.

Underground punk literature continued to flourish in Spain during the last two decades, mostly unrelated to "mainstream punk" (good examples of this are the anthology Golpes *(2008), compiled by Eloy Fernández Porta and Vicente Muñoz Álvarez, and the recent tribute to Charles Bukowski* Resaca/Hang Over *[2008]). However, at the end of the 1990s, several authors started to reunite punk/underground fiction with experimental/postmodern fiction in a similar way to American Avant-Pop. This is explained in the article by Eloy Fernández Porta you quote, and it might be considered one of the Mutantes' original features.*

—Germán Sierra, in response

En cuanto a la evolución de lo punk en la novela en España, coincido con Germán Sierra, si bien añadiría que en los años 80, justo cuando en España eclosionó el →

> *"espíritu" punk en las manifestaciones artísticas, en literatura no fue así. Incluso ocurrió lo contrario: el desarrollo de una importante e influyente corriente, estéticamente conservadora, en narrativa y poesía. A mi modo de ver, y si bien en otro contexto y con otras herramientas y otros horizontes simbólicos, propios del siglo 21, aquella eclosión punk que no se dio en literatura en los años 80, se está dando ahora, tanto en la referencia que hace Germán Sierra a la antología* Golpes—*cercana a los presupuestos del párrafo, abajo citado, de Eloy Fernández Porta—como en el grupo que hemos venido llamando* Mutantes *según terminología y antología de Juan Francisco Ferré y Julio Ortega.*
>
> —*Agustín Fernández Mallo, in response*

"Desde finales de los años ochenta y hasta hoy mismo conviven en las nuevas prácticas del relato dos tendencias aparentemente dispares. Por una parte, una tendencia que cabría llamar *retórica*: referencial, en algunos casos hasta la sobredosis, abundante en sátira y parodia, en diálogo muy abierto tanto con la tradición literaria como con la popular. Por otra parte, la línea que quiero caracterizar como *punk*, y que persigue el ideal vanguardista de la escritura inmediata, del golpe de dados, en nombre de una ilusión de naturalidad. Es la combinación de estas dos líneas lo que convierte el relato en la forma más decididamente vanguardista de las letras contemporáneas".

> —*Eloy Fernández Porta, "Retórica y Punk en el relato contemporáneo"*

los envases vacíos" [what is in the margins, the noise, the leftovers, like someone who affirms that he or she has learned to read using the greatest library of the world: the trash containers that house millions of texts in their empty interiors] ("Apología"). This greatest of "trash libraries" encompasses all that surrounds the human being in the twenty-first century, creating a textual *cosmopedia* that Mallo defines as "lecturas transversales" [transversal readings]. These representations may derive from direct interactions with physical surroundings or from watching television or surfing the Web. Whether physical or virtual, these fragments from the *real world* are constructed through a compendium of semiotic codes to juxtapose individual experiences in time and space.

Mallo's "trash aesthetics" is intimately connected to the unwanted objects we discard in our daily lives and the electronic mail that fills our mailboxes with unsolicited information: spam. In an interview in the virtual publication *Público.es*, Mallo explained that he views the world as filled with spam because "la realidad está llena de Spam, información que es basura porque no nos sirve de nada, mero ruido. La realidad está llena de cosas que no vienen a cuento. Pero, ¿qué ocurre si consigues meterlo en una novela y convertirlo en objeto de poética?" [reality is filled with Spam, information that is trash because it does not serve any function, it is just noise. Reality is full of things that have no function. But what happens when you place them into a novel and change them into poetic objects?]. When Mallo integrates discarded elements, ideas, and materials into his prose, readers enter into a print-based moving map of references whose "true" and "fictitious" features are not meant to be separated. Contrary to the work of Mañas, Mallo's *spam* instead of punk's *slam poetics* does not aggressively engage in a noisy countercultural exhibition of anti-mainstream and materialist sentiments. Instead, Mallo infuses the object with emotion and spams his literature with the noise of unwanted material and meanings.

Mallo's *spam poetics* integrates the unwanted and inherently ingests and remixes punk's and Generation X's relationship with material objects, as best represented by his embrace and love of the artificial, the synthetic, and the plastic. Andy Warhol once pronounced that "everything's plastic, but I love plastic. I want to be plastic" (Bockris 66). Mallo has also admitted to loving plastic, feeling comfortable, happy, and confident in plastic spaces (Barker 348). His words return us to Douglas Coupland who has equally commented on his obsessive relationship with plastics, citing it as a central component of the present and future. In the video interview "Plastic Planet," Coupland talks about the role of plastic as a material that determines his age and generation. Plastic, says Coupland, is "intrinsically self-contradictory: the moment you find something good with it, [you also encounter] the complete opposite bad thing, the moment you find something evil about it, something altruistic and wonderful emerges" ("Plastic

las [Islas] Cíes"), si bien reelaboraban el imaginario punk combinándolo con otros estilos y usándolo como un registro musical cómico, y no como una forma de protesta política o lumpenproletaria. En este sentido, el grupo se parece un poco a algunas bandas de fun-core inteligente que proliferaron en Nueva York a principios de los ochenta, como Murphy's Law. Lo que hay ahí es una estetización del punk e incluso una intelectualización; creo que ese es el elemento punk, de segundo grado, que está presente en el Proyecto Nocilla.

—Eloy Fernández Porta, in response

Both in Mañas's novels and in Mallo's Nocilla *trilogy, "punk" is related to "simplicity," but in Mallo's work, this "simplicity" derives from his background in poetry and physics. In modern poetry, as in modern physics, simplicity is understood as a symbolic representation of complexity. This is very well understood by contemporary readers, who are used to navigating through different kinds of networks. Agustín Fernández Mallo's punk derives from "intentional ingenuity," the same way his electronic productions can be seen as "amateurish" or "naive." In fact, the simplicity sensation in Mallo's work is due to the fact that its complexity is not the result of sophisticated narrative techniques, but to the complexity of the world itself.*

—Germán Sierra, in response

De hecho me interesa fundamentalmente la ciencia. Me explico: la ciencia como creadora de metáforas —y eso es parte de lo que llamo Postpoesía *— y no la ciencia como explicación o argumentación de una trama novelística —que eso sería un uso argumentativo o justificativo de la ciencia, vía la tecnología.*

En ese sentido, creo que una de las intenciones —no pensada, pero no por ello no cierta— del Proyecto Nocilla, *puede haber sido querer ensayar nuevas puertas a una poética diferente en el terreno de la novela. Una noción ampliada de la poesía.*

—Agustín Fernández Mallo, in response

Planet"). For Coupland, plastic is "an extension of our humanity," yet it is not us, he declares. Similarly, Mallo has argued that for him, "el súmmum de la creación humana es el plástico [the greatest of human creation is plastic]." He has admitted that "me excita lo sintético, lo artificial, lo químico. Seamos claros: al final, ¿qué es una novela o una pieza artística? Pues el culmen del artificio" [I get excited about the synthetic, the artificial, the chemical. Let us be clear: in the end, what is a novel or a piece of art but the culmination of artifice?] (Lozano, "Adiós").

Mallo denies the artificiality previously associated with linguistic Style by fully embracing the materiality of the artifice and by directly engaging with the synthetic—his love of plastic come to life. His narrative approach is one that connects the synthetic to the minimalist in a disciplinary move in which both poetry and science provide Mallo with a way to narrate "sintéticamente [y] cristalinamente, es decir, contar algo con los menos elementos posibles, pero que haya transparencia. Si a un verso le quitas o le añades una palabra, lo destruyes. A una ecuación también. [synthetically and crystally, in other words, to narrate something with the least possible elements, but with transparency. If you remove or add a word to a verse, you destroy it. The same occurs to an equation]. By relating the verse and the equation to the artificial and the synthetic, Mallo allows both to infuse his narrative results. Textual transparency and clarity is closely related to his belief that everything, from fiction to science and nature, is a representation, is synthetic.

Blank Mutations in Error

The narrative objectivity and flat literary style so well known in the work of Mañas reappears in the work of Agustín Fernández Mallo and his *Mutantes* colleagues as linked to the isolating and material-based dimension of information technology. In the past thirty years, Generation X has moved from Bret Easton Ellis's perception of life as *Less Than Zero* to Javier Fernández's *Cero absoluto* [*Absolute Zero*] (2005) in terms of a reality that connects the human brain to computer software. Instead of perceiving the "zero" as an emotional metaphor, "zero" is now equated with the binary computational code. The raw "pornography of punk," as Mañas once called it, now exhibits itself as raw computational data, leading to narratives that can appear equally cold and deterministic, objective and flat, but that manipulate surfaces and explore emptiness through scientific and technological allegories (Juan-Cantavella). As the "Punk Journalism" of Robert Juan-Cantavella exposes, and French curator and art critic Nicolas Bourriaud underscores, contemporary art and narrative is now viewed in terms of a process of postproduction that hacks into reality instead of reflecting reality.

One of the most powerful creative expressions that has

PUNK JOURNALISM

"En el caso del Punk Journalism no sólo se importan las elegantes trampas de la narración realista sino también otras menos respetables que tienen que ver con la pura fabulación, la parodia maliciosa, la mentira sincera, la especulación camicace, el despropósito gratuito, la irresponsabilidad meditada, etc.…o lo que viene a ser lo mismo, el Punk Journalism también trafica con mentiras porque sabe que lo que está diciendo es verdad.

Hoy en día una fotografía es un archivo digital que con el photoshop puede convertirse en cualquier cosa. Es materia prima informativa para un alevoso proceso de postproducción y no constituye tanto un reflejo como un hackeo de la realidad.

Alguien podrá replicar que la postura del Punk Journalism es viciosa porque se hace con el bonus track del periodismo (en su trato privilegiado con la realidad y las cosas ciertas) y al mismo tiempo maneja trampas propias del cuento, la patraña, la serie B y en general la mentira…y habrá acertado."

Robert Juan-Cantavella (www.punkjournalism.net)

En la literatura española (no puedo evitar el uso del adjetivo de marras) actual la palabra "punk" remite, sobre todo, a la obra de Robert Juan-Cantavella. Tanto su crítica constante del modo en que la SGAE gestiona los derechos de autor o en que los políticos españoles gestionan la cultura, como sujeto civil enmascarado en el alter ego Escargot, como su tratamiento

→

de los materiales literarios, como escritor, apuntan hacia una reactualización del movimiento punk, en clave personal y neovanguardista. Autor de una tesina doctoral sobre la poesía objetual de Joan Brossa, uno de los artistas más radicales de la historia del arte español, en sus textos ha dado vueltas de tuerca a autores tan dispares como Marinetti o Tarantino. Y, a propósito de El Dorado, *una novela basada en una investigación periodística sobre la corrupción política y el ultra-fundamentalismo religioso católico en Valencia, forjó el concepto "punk journalism" para referirse a un periodismo gonzo más ficcionalizador que el de Hunter S. Thompson, en que conecta con poéticas de la distorsión como la de Valle-Inclán o la de Luis Buñuel.*

—*Jorge Carrión, in response*

*En mi opinión, lo que Cantavella lleva a sus textos, el así llamado Punk Journalism, es una de la piruetas más sólidas e interesantes de la novela actual en español. Aunque en apariencia no tenga que ver, hay muchas similitudes con parte de la obra del fotógrafo español Joan Fontcuberta, en cuanto en las obras de ambos se cuestiona de manera muy radical la veracidad de lo representado en los medios y la veracidad de lo presuntamente documental, a través de la manipulación + invención del material que se expone. Ambos trabajan por el sistema de la presencia física en el medio puntual del que se está hablando, la noticia en bruto, y su posterior manipulación para devenir en "falso documento". En otro sentido, lejano pero próximo en algunos aspectos, y con materiales más derivados de la historia y la sociología literaria, se enmarcaría la obra novelística de Manuel Vilas (*España, Aire nuestro*), en la que elabora ficción-documentalista, en su caso cercana tanto al esperpento como a una tradición buñuelística.*

—*Agustín Fernández Mallo,*
in response

emerged from this hacking process is Mallo's critical and creative application of error as inspired by its use in digital music. In "Apología del Error," written by Mallo for *El País*, the author said that in the act of copying and pasting, aberrant mutations can take place. For him, creativity consists in using these unexpected mutations, or errors, to his benefit. Errors present themselves as anomalies usually discarded, ignored, or forgotten, says Mallo, but history has shown us that they can be rematerialized into great works of art, as was the case with Las Vegas, Nicanor Parra, or the Sex Pistols ("Apología"). For Mallo, one of the most interesting generators of error is the act of appropriation, by which he means the taking of a fragment from one source and placing it into another, such as the taking of a fragment from an instruction manual of a washing machine and placing it into the *Quijote*. What happens, he says, is that with the proper insertion of new material,

el lector detecta un cortocircuito, y el orden simbólico, canónico y hasta semántico del *Quijote* salta por los aires. Por unos instantes el juicio sobre esa nueva obra queda en suspenso, en un limbo, en un extrarradio de la literatura muy propicio a la posibilidad de que surja una nueva e intensísima poética en virtud de ese error.
[the reader will detect a short circuit, and the symbolic, canonical and even semantic order of the *Quijote* is disrupted. For a few seconds any judgment accorded to this new work remains hanging

in the air, in limbo, on the outskirts of the literary, very favorable to the possibility that a new and intense poetics may appear in light of this error.]

Mallo adopts the negative, blank space previously discarded by critics as a generational error that should be forgotten and discarded from the memory of literary history, and instead turns error into a source of creative possibilities. You never know, he says at the end of "Apología del Error," "a qué escenario te conducirá ese error" [to which scene your error will lead you]. Mallo recognizes that errors can lead to new and innovative works of art, but they can also lead to violent crashes in linguistic codes that take you two feet under, as he suggests by referring to J. C. Ballard's novel *Crash*. Even when represented in the shape of a crash and filtered in orange, Andy Warhol's own car crash series conducted readers to a novel that some probably perceived as an error in Spanish literary history—*Historias del Kronen*. That said, it was precisely this "error" that gave rise to a generation marked by a floating or empty signifier with a host of creative and critical potential.

The possibly tragic results that emerge when a page is erased of its initial content, is an emptiness that in the work of Mallo allows for the emergence of new and ever more interesting sources and techniques on meaning-making. Contrary to

LA ESTÉTICA DEL ERROR

"La estética 'post-digital' se desarrolló en parte como resultado de la experiencia de trabajar sumido en ambientes rodeados de tecnología digital: fanáticos de los computadores, impresoras láser, sonorización de las interfaces de usuarios y el sonido de los discos duros. Pero más específicamente, es, por los 'errores' de la tecnología digital, que este nuevo trabajo ha emergido: errores/fallas, virus, errores de aplicaciones, incompatibilidad de sistemas, clipping2, aliasing3, distorsión, ruido de quantización, incluso el ruido de las tarjetas de sonido, son los materiales primarios que los compositores buscaron para incorporar a su música" (13).

—Kim Cascone,
"Las estéticas del error"

Esta referencia al artículo de Kim Cascone es fundamental para mí. Cuando lo leí, allá por el 2001 o 2002, confirmó muchas intuiciones que yo tenía. De hecho, en la versión original de Postpoesía, hacia un nuevo paradigma, *estaba citado ese párrafo de Cascone, y después, como suprimí una parte, lo quité ¡y me olvidé de volver a ponerlo! Creo que hablo de él en el artículo "Apología del Error". En mi siguiente poemario, "Antibiótico" —inédito— sí que está ese párrafo explícitamente.*

—*Agustín Fernández Mallo, in response*

Artist Miltos Manetas said: "Real space has lost its emptiness." Emptiness is a really important concept in physics and in poetry: Meaning or matter may emerge from "emptiness." Agustín Fernández Mallo's novels try to recover/re-present this "emptiness."

—*Germán Sierra, in response*

A un nivel meramente simbólico, el término "vacío" (emptiness), sigue funcionando (pensemos tanto en el vacío al modo de algunos pensadores clásicos helénicos,

→

como en el vacío al modo del misticismo, o el vacío a nivel del habla popular en referencia a estados de ánimo).

Pero, por otra parte, el vacío, verificable a fecha de hoy, en términos estrictamente científicos, no existe en tanto por mucho que se despoje un volumen de materia o energía siempre permanecen las llamadas "fluctuaciones cuánticas". Creo interesante el intento de representar esa paradoja, es decir, que el vacío no existe, y la mejor forma de representar eso es despojar una representación cualquiera de casi todos sus elementos, para ver que aún ahí se dan, y si cabe con más intensidad, los movimientos de material físico y afectivo.

Por otra parte, me parece interesantísima la evolución que rastrera Eloy Fernández Porta de la palabra "vacío", desde el existencialismo (parodiando, en la inversión de los apellidos: Jean Paul Camus y Albert Sartre) hasta la actualidad. Cómo el sentimiento de "vacío" constituyó en su tiempo un "sentimiento de lujo", accesible a las clases más intelectuales, a las élites en lo que a sentimentalidad se refiere, y hoy ha decaído en "sentimiento basura", accesible a Paris Hilton o a la clase trabadora. Naturalmente, la ironía planea sobre todo ese argumento (de €®O$ la superproducción de los afectos, Eloy Fernández Porta).

—Agustín Fernández Mallo, in response

"La literatura española tiene 'una desconexión con la calle realmente alarmante' ya que los autores no tienen 'ni idea de lo que pasa por la cabeza de la gente normal,' afirmó hoy el escritor español Kiko Amat durante una entrevista con Efe en Caracas.

Amat, quien acaba de presentar su tercera novela, *Rompepistas*, sobre un grupo de adolescentes en el extrarradio de Barcelona en los años 1980, reivindicó la 'literatura de fregadero, de clase obrera' frente a los 'ejercicios de estilo' tan comunes en la literatura española contemporánea.

→

the emptiness retained in the work of Mañas, an emptiness that remains disconnected on a human level, Mallo's *cosmopedia* of the discarded, the marginal, the overexposed, or the lonely does not remain lost in space. Mallo places "the empty" within a web of interconnections that are rooted in multiple and global locations and serve as agents of infinitely changing relations. The web that these connections provide do not remain flat as in the work of Mañas, but they take on relief as the novel presents networks upon networks, maps upon maps. The paths that link the points on these maps reconfigure Mañas's street culture as one upon which youth do not simply walk and talk, but as a series of roads upon which individuals travel and meet, disperse and reappear. The road movies and road culture that once defined the Beats and then influenced Generation X novels and reality television shows alike now become tropes for the computer links travelled upon through cyberspace, links that remake the road in the digital age.

The work of Agustín Fernández Mallo creatively and critically expands the notion of blank fiction. His focus on error, on trash, on spam, on cutting and pasting, on dislocating, and on linking, disrupts and reconfigures patterns. His mutations lead to new narrative results that render a different web of interrelations between ideas, disciplines, and technologies. To discuss the influence on fiction of technologies related to the Internet, it is essential to not view this medium as something totally new, but as an outgrowth of a complex matrix of factors that interconnect the past and the present, old and new media, as Jay David Bolter and Lev Manovich have already well articulated.

Avant-Pop in the Digital Age

In the work of Generation X writers of the 1980s and 1990s, Avant-Pop well served to understand the relationship between popular and commercial culture and the authors' relationship to emerging media technologies. *Afterpop*, as mentioned in previous chapters, functioned as a broadened and more direct and material relationship between these two components as applied to the field of literary criticism. In the twenty-first century, popular culture and media technologies are ever more intimately related, ingested, and naturalized, and they have merged to include a larger set of signifiers from any part the world. The work of the *Mutantes* expands on the use of distinct signifiers to present more complex systems of relations. Germán Sierra said it best when he explained that, *of course,* the influence of popular culture in our daily lives infuses authors' narratives. As an inhabitant of a global and mediated culture, *of course* authors write global and media-inspired stories. But when the strategy of the mass media is to present reality "de un modo tan banal que a nadie pudiera

El autor, de 38 años, explicó a Efe su interés 'en ser comprendido, sin ser recargado'. 'El cripticismo me parece nocivo y elitista', aseguró.

'Hay muy poca intención de hacer literatura para la gente, siempre se intenta hacer alta cultura, literatura seria, por eso luego salen esas cosas que no excitan a la gente a leer, porque son insufribles', afirmó en una populosa arepera del centro de Caracas.

—"Escritor español Kiko Amat critica 'desconexión de literatura con la calle'"

Es justamente así, no me interesa lo que pasa en la calle en el sentido que le da a la frase, "la calle," Kiko Amat en su entrevista. Puede que me interese, en ocasiones, como lector o espectador, pero no como material estético para mis novelas o poemas o ensayos. Para mí, "la calle" es otra cosa. Básicamente, un lugar para mirar a través de una ventana de cristal (ya sea la de la habitación o la del ordenador). Hay muchas calles. Esa ventana de cristal es a lo que yo llamo "realismo," ya que para mí es lo más real que hay. Y esto me interesa porque casi siempre me parece más real lo que veo en las pantallas que lo que veo en la calle.

—*Agustín Fernández Mallo, in response*

Es curioso que cuando escribí el Proyecto Nocilla, *así como* Postpoesía, *no tenía en mente Internet, de hecho no era un usuario muy asiduo de la Red, y creo que pocas veces había entrado en un blog —hablo del año 2004, casi aún no había blogs. Supongo que esa fragmentariedad estaba también "en el aire", en el entorno social. Pero también, creo que igualmente importante es lo siguiente: vengo de la poesía, y la poesía es el género fragmentario por naturaleza. Creo que eso provocó que intuitivamente yo expandiera esa característica, propia de la poesía, a un ámbito que yo aún no sabía muy bien cual era, y que resultó ser la narrativa. De hecho, si te fijas, en*

→

> Nocilla Dream *o en* Nocilla Experience, *la mayoría de insertos o apropiaciones, no vienen de la Red sino de revistas o libros en papel que tenía por casa cuando las escribí, que seguro que están también en Red, pero yo no las saqué de ahí. Eso no impide que, como dije arriba, la influencia de estética Internet estuviera ya "en el aire", pero insisto también en el carácter intrínsecamente fragmentado de la poesía. Y esto es la idea de texto como "lista" (idea que en ocasiones también ha trabajado Germán Sierra): texto como sucesión de items que se pueden leer sin orden, eso es la poesía también —ver en "Postpoesía", el capítulo de "Acceso a aleatorio a listas".*
>
> —*Agustín Fernández Mallo, in response*

> *Cabría hacer un añadido: hoy, tras todas esas ideas está la idea de Red o de Sistema Complejo. Creo que mi literatura se establece, dentro del libro, como una red horizontal, sin jerarquías, en la que la alta cultura y la baja cultura dialogan. Eso es un correlato espontáneo, no planeado, de la concepción contemporánea de la realidad como sistema complejo y en red.*
>
> *Entiendo que lo que hago es complejo, pero no complicado.*
>
> —*Agustín Fernández Mallo, in response*

interesarle" (las diversas versiones del *reality show*), ¿no es mi derecho insistir en la complejidad de la materia, ese bullir de larvas que proliferan bajo cada relato mediático y bajo cada explicación supuestamente técnica? [in a manner that is so banal that it could not be of interest to anybody (the various versions of the *reality show*), isn't it my right to insist in the complexity of the matter, this seething of larva that proliferates under every mediated tale and under every supposed technical explanation?] ("En búsqueda"). Sierra argues that the contemporary author must move beyond the surface of either the popularly or mediated banal to present a more complex system of material relations. His comment points to the clearly superficial examples of the "popular" as either trash TV or trash literature. As the work of Porta in *Afterpop* underlines, "pop" is not limited to the superficial and the low. Products of high popular culture demand more specialized and astute critical practices because, as Sierra indicates, they include and meld with other systems to create more complex literary results.

Avant-Pop once presented an almost radical insertion and translation of commercial and popular culture into new narrative practices. The results contributed to a vision of young writers as subversive, subcultural, and located on the margins of the literary. In the digital age, margins and borders have been melding and changing places, leading to more fluid and multiple positions that advance a postsubcultural era of more open and participatory relations. Today's *Mutantes* writers do not need to choose whether to be subversive or to be literary. They do not have to choose between popular culture and high literary references. They can include both and everything in between. They do not identify with words such as "avant-garde," "experimental," "rupture," or "marginal," says Sierra, because they are decidedly materialist and individualist, wanting to explore matter in all its complexity ("En búsqueda"). This interest in the "material" as a reconfiguration of Generation X's emphasis on material culture now expands its significance to emphasize the creative potential of the object, of material reality, of the material basis of computer technology, and the creation of more complex systems related to matter in science (and science fiction). Subsequently, more material-based critical practices are needed to make sense of what matters to the *Mutantes* authors in the twenty-first century.

Mallo's work is often related to the Avant-garde, but like Sierra, and in line with the critical lens adopted by Jara Calles, the author rejects the term "experimental," stating that his work is deeply rooted in reality and he simply narrates things as they appear before him. In other words, reality as perceived and expressed through the individual human mind, voice, or word is already a subjective experiment whose content and form differs depending on the medium through which it is experienced. Mallo's narrative result, then, may be viewed in terms of a spatial association of minimalist elements, a new type of "reality project" whose aesthetic result may be considered experimental in the sense that he infuses the arts with the "real" effects of any and all matter.

Mallo's novels filter bits and pieces of reality by ingesting and re-creating an infinite number of objects from everyday life, from the margins and from mainstream. Mallo brings often uncommon materials to the surface and mixes them with his own aesthetic sensibility in order

> *No me consta que Agustín tuviera presentes las ideas de McCaffery al escribir el* Proyecto Nocilla; *sí puedo decir que esas ideas, que habían tenido escasísima difusión en España, las tenían más presentes autores como Sierra, Ferré o Calvo (en sus primeros dos libros). Por si te interesa, señalo que, hasta donde yo sé, la primera referencia que aparece en prensa cultural española al término avant-pop está en un artículo que publiqué en el suplemento Libros de El Periódico de Catalunya, titulado "Revolución en el relato", y donde comentaba la obra de Coover, y en particular las traducciones de Pricksongs and Descants y Briar Rose publicadas por Anagrama en 1998.*
>
> —*Eloy Fernández Porta, in response*

> *Como suelen decir todos los escritores "experimentales", incluidos Burroughs, Coover, etc. el único "escritor experimental" que acepta con gusto ese término, que yo sepa, es Richard Kostelanetz. No obstante, en el caso del* Proyecto Nocilla, *como en el de otras obras recientes, veo una diferencia que cambia el sentido de esa afirmación. Ese libro, con todas sus referencias a la tecnología y los nuevos medios, está escrito en la época de las ciberculturas, años después de que el movimiento cyberpunk convirtiera, efectivamente, la ciencia-ficción en la literatura realista de la época contemporánea al presentar el análisis de los medios técnicos como un asunto sociopolítico específico, y no como una invención de "otros mundos". La afirmación "yo no soy un escritor experimental, sino realista", en boca de Coover, es una metáfora e incluso una provocación a los críticos literarios; en cambio, en boca de Mallo es "más literal." A esto hay que añadir que, así como la novela posmoderna norteamericana se presentó, en general, como una réplica al "estilo realista", en cambio en la literatura innovadora española del cambio de siglo ese argumento, aunque aún está presente, pasa a* →

> *ser secundario y menos enfático, porque en este momento y en este lugar no puede decirse ya que la poética realista sea el enemigo a batir, o el "error ontológico" que fundamenta la literatura dominante, o el elemento de oposición contra el cual se definen las literaturas innovadoras. Este es un factor importante, que, según tengo comprobado, suele perderse de vista en la recepción internacional de estas novelas, donde es frecuente presentarlas de manera oposicional, contraponiendo, por ejemplo, a Mallo con Delibes. En este sentido, podría decirse que la corriente literaria que comentas en este artículo constituye, en España, el primer caso de tendencia literaria rupturista que "no tiene rival" en el ámbito de la novela, aunque sí tenga rivales identificables en el terreno de la ideología, de la Política, etc.*
>
> —*Eloy Fernández Porta, in response*

to "deformar productos originales o de segunda generación, sacarlos de quicio, desviarlos y enchufarlos a otras corrientes, que no son casi nunca temporales sino espaciales" [deform original products or products of a second generation, irritate them, deviate them and plug them into other currents that are almost never temporal but spatial] ("Tiempo" 2). Mallo's spatial relation and manipulation of objects are connected to the conceptual art of French Dadaist Marcel Duchamp, who Mallo references in many of his interviews. By taking a urinal and placing it in the context of a museum space, Duchamp elevated the significance of the everyday object to that of a poetic subject able to seduce us like any work of art ("Tiempo" 2). Mallo does something similar by taking objects out of their ordinary and natural habitat and placing them into a series of decontextualized and unexpected scenarios, thus elevating their object status to poetic heights.

Mallo's poetic expansion derives directly from his theoretical definition of "poesía postpoética" or "poesía expandida" to refer to the use and inspiration of science and technology in poetry (Mallo "Hacia"). Mallo talks about this expanded version of the poetic process—its narrative results well embodied in the *Nocilla* trilogy—as an aspect of randomness and lack of control, a form of art in which the subject is not at its center. He likens this approach to "un televisor que cambiara constantemente de canal, pero sin que el espectador ejerciese sobre el mando control alguno, de manera que el resultado de todas estas imágenes es una obra creada con su propio palimpsesto" [a television set that would constantly change channels, but without the viewer exerting any power over the remote, so that the result of all of these images becomes a work created by its own palimpsest] (*Postpoesía* 118). The poetic result of a televisual palimpsest is one in which a text is (sometimes incompletely) zapped or erased but allows for the emergence of a myriad of unexpected but remembered connections to trace stories into space.

Mallo's spatial relation to the remixing of material is intimately tied to advances in computer technology. To better understand the changing dynamics of "Avant-Pop" in the digital age, I turn to Lev Manovich's discussion in "Avant-Garde as Software," in which he explains that, over time,

> the techniques invented by the 1920s Left artists became embedded in the commands and interface metaphors of computer software.... For example, the avant-garde strategy of collage reemerged as "cut and paste" command..., the dynamic windows, pull-down menus, and HTML tables all allow a computer to simultaneously work with practically unrestricted input of information despite the limited surface of the computer screen. ("Avant-Garde")

Manovich believes that the practice of manipulating existing media was not central to Avant-garde practices, but has become so after many years of an enlarging media archive. This enlarged archive, increasingly accessible and manipulable in recent times, stresses the "material factors in the shift towards postmodernist aesthetics: the accumulation of huge media assets and the arrival of new electronic and digital tools which made it very easy to access and re-work these assets" ("New Media" 23).

The arrival of this huge database, together with user-friendly programs of data mining and manipulation has served critics to talk about Mallo's work in terms of a literature characterized by a fragmented or bloglike structure and effect, one that creates a collage of contemporary life. But it is important here to place emphasis on the author's process of production without suggesting that the process directly mirrors social reality (as I argue in one of the "Tales" in chapter 1). There is a significant difference between a fragmented world and a process that makes the world appear fragmented. Mallo recognizes this difference and questions critics' belief that his work is "fragmented" because it somehow suggests a broken world. I agree with Mallo that while subjects might organize and ingest information about the world in new, more spontaneous ways, their views do not necessarily suggest a *broken* or *fragmented* world or subjectivity. Mallo's narrative process of collecting, recycling, and manipulating bits and pieces of material is intimately related to what I prefer to view in terms of a contemporary *expansion* or *augmentation* of the world. This

> *Respecto a esta idea de la que hablas de copiar, pegar para armar un mundo propio: a veces se dice que mi literatura es fragmentaria, como si fuera un collage, pero yo no estoy muy de acuerdo con eso. El término "fragmentado" alude a un mundo previo, que era unitario y que se rompió para después nosotros rearmar los trozos con otra disposición. Y no creo que eso sea así. Cuando escribo no tengo la sensación de trabajar con un mundo previo al mío, y ya roto, sino sobre un mundo nuevo que se me presenta espontáneamente así, "como si estuviera fragmentado", pero que no lo está bajo una óptica contemporánea. Creo que esta idea es importante, porque marca la diferencia entre la visión nostálgica de una modernidad "rota", y la visión contemporánea de un mundo en el que el conocimiento se organiza de otra manera.*
>
> —*Agustín Fernández Mallo, in response*

perspective makes use of media archives where films, advertisements, television shows, radio productions, books, music, and more, "have become the raw data to be processed, re-articulated, mined and re-packaged through digital software—rather than raw reality" (Manovich, "New Media" 22). Raw data has replaced raw reality, and in the process, it is not only allowing for creative possibilities in the connection between materials (an age-old phenomenon simply expanded upon in the digital age), but it is opening up new storyspaces.

Mashing *Nocilla Dream* by Agustín Fernández Mallo

In his first novel, *Nocilla Dream*, Mallo applies the networking and mapping dynamics of the World Wide Web. This Web, according to its founder Tim Berners-Lee, is made up of two components: the "Net," which comprises the computers, cables, and programs that underline all actions, and the "abstract (imaginary) space of information" that consists of documents, sounds, videos, and "hypertext links" (Berners-Lee). Similarly, *Nocilla Dream* presents the material basis of computer technology through references to the world of science, mathematics, and physics. Upon and through this net, a web of more abstract ideas mesh together in the shape of objects, characters, ideas, and cities. The novel is constructed as a "network of networks" by integrating webs within webs, maps upon maps that comment on and outside of each other. This self-reflexive dynamic may be visualized as a series of interlinked points on a vector, as Mallo literally does at the end of the novel, but the elements that constitute this novel are not static. Despite being in print, the bits move in relation to each other and in the process comment on their own construction. In other words, the image of a map does not pay enough tribute to the novel's emphasis on the *process of creation*, which may be better represented as a *mash-up* of a map upon a map upon a map of creative spaces.

Science + Fiction +

In "Tiempo topológico en *Proyecto Nocilla* y en *Pospoesía* (y breve apunte para una Exonovela)," Mallo motions to the global dynamics of the Internet as presenting artists with identificatory roots that are highly personal and dynamic.[4] Today's artists, he says, create their roots as they grow alongside and surf the Web, unproblematically assuming the sum of their rootedness as all places, near or far, classical or contemporary, "visited" in cyberspace. Mallo references French art curator and critic Nicholas Bourriaud's book *The Radicants* (2009) to motion to the nomad as a wanderer, or "radicant." In the words of Bourriaud, to be a "radicant" refers to the

setting of one's roots in motion, staging them in heterogeneous contexts and formats, denying them any value as origins, translating ideas, transcoding images, transplanting behaviors, exchanging rather than imposing. The author extends radicant thought to modes of cultural production, consumption and use. Looking at the world through the prism of art, he sketches a "world art criticism" in which works are in dialogue with the context in which they are produced.

Mallo understands Bourriaud's use of the "radicant" as a metaphor with etymological roots in the plant world. "Radicants" are ivy or trumpet creepers that take on new roots as they advance and cling to different surfaces. In the words of Mallo, "Van dejando atrás sus raíces a medida que ascienden y crean nuevas raíces con las que agarrarse a la tapia. No son raíces, sino pequeñas adhesions mutantes. Nomadismo estético" [Leaving their roots behind as they ascend and (create) new ones to hold onto the wall. They are not roots, but small, mutant adhesions. Aesthetic nomadism] ("Tiempo").[5] This aesthetic nomadism centered on *mutant adhesions* relates to surfaces, scar tissue, wounds that bind or deform to create new cells and structures. In print, it refers to a constantly changing and growing diversity of signifiers and interconnections as each idea, image, or thought wanders, grows, and changes in space.

Mallo's aesthetic nomadism does not present readers with roots that add up to something new—in other words, A + B = C. It refers to a system of connections that might be better expressed as A + B + C +...and so on. *Nocilla Dream*, although it begins with chapter 1 and ends at chapter 113 and is usually read in sequence, does not present a definable sum of its parts—

> *Siguiendo a Bourriaud —cuyo libro* Radicante *se editó en 2009, es decir, 5 años más tarde que de yo escribiera el* Proyecto Nocilla *(lo digo sólo para indicar que había algo, ciertas intuiciones, que estaban en el "ambiente", o que muchos estábamos trabajando en literatura lo que después Bourriaud llamó* Radicante *en el campo del arte, y que yo había llamado* Postpoesía *en el terreno de la narrativa+poesía),— decía, existe ese nomadismo estético no sólo en las temáticas que aborda el* Proyecto Nocilla, *sino en los géneros, y en la mezcla de materiales típicos de la ficción y del documental. Es decir no sólo un nomadismo en cuanto a estéticas sino también en cuanto a epistemología, o lo que es lo mismo, en cuanto al grado de verosimilitud de lo narrado, que es, para mí, ese "in between" que tú señalas tan acertadamente, tan propio del Rizoma deuleziano.*
>
> —*Agustín Fernández Mallo, in response*
>
> *Bourriaud's relational aesthetics are quite familiar to physicists. For instance: "Some of the deepest truths of our world may turn out to be truths about organization, rather than about what kinds of things make up the world and how those things behave as individuals" (Buchanan 19).*
>
> —*Germán Sierra, in response*

"No busco finales sino que se me presentan principios" [I don't seek endings but beginnings"], Mallo once said ("Tiempo"). Spanish author Juan Bonilla uses this same logic of infinite addition in the prologue to *Nocilla Dream* to identify the author's narrative result. Bonilla refers to the work of Giles Deleuze and Félix Guattari in *A Thousand Plateaus* to differentiate between the verb "to be" and the conjunctions "and...and...and ..." to point to a more rhyzomatic theory of writing. The strength of the word "and" or the mathematical sign "+" is one that Bonilla believes has the power to uproot the verb "to be," whether that *being* refers to the identity of the human or of the narrative genre.

In practice, the radicant-like theory on infinite addition spans 113 chapters and 217 pages in *Nocilla Dream*. Readers encounter everything from high academic to indie culture through direct and paraphrased quotes cited at the end of the novel and in the text, short italicized and lyrical sentences, sequences from television and reality TV, a square emulating a page with a poem, quotes from webpages, references to the cinematic planes of Hitchcock's *The Birds*, sections meant for publication and written in Courier font, and, among others, a chapter consisting of book reviews. In line with his philosophy on error and infinite addition, it is precisely the erasure of the *sum* of these parts that highlights the spatial possibilities and interconnections in the novel. But how do readers make sense of the multitude of fragments that move from the lyrical to the descriptive and the factual, spanning the world of literature, popular culture, science, and computation?

To make sense of the *cosmopedia* that is *Nocilla Dream*, it is best to turn to the end of the novel where readers find a map titled "Cartografía Universo Nocilla" and "Territorio [1] Nocilla Dream."

This representational system, entitled "*Cosmos*: n," was developed by professor of interaction design and usability Javier Cañada. On the site of this cosmos, Cañada explains that the "diagram is based on one assumption:

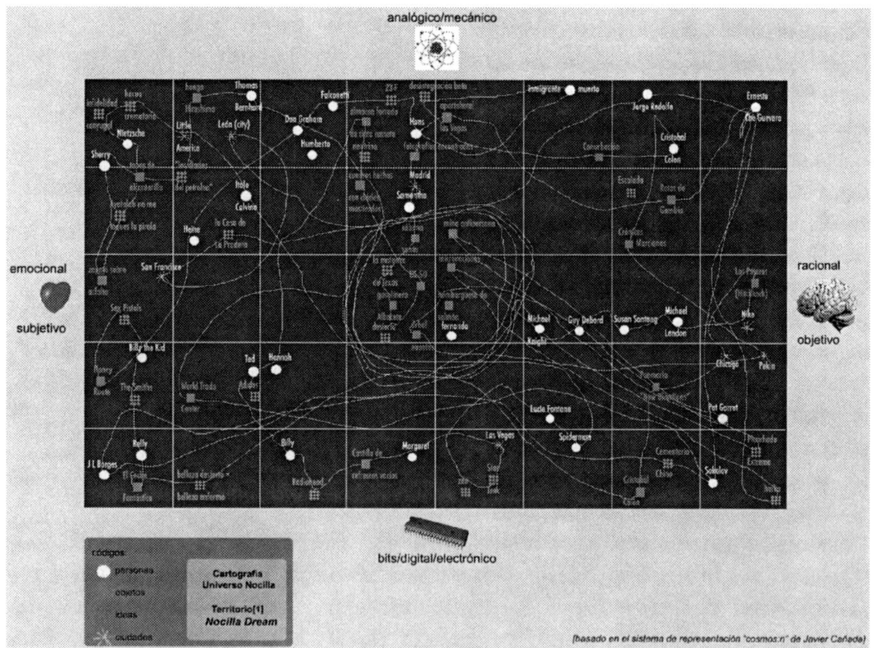

Image of Map/Cartografía by Agustín Fernández Mallo.

With special thanks to Agustín Fernández Mallo for permission to reproduce this image.

everything in the User Experience field ranges between bits and atoms, and points predominantly to the brain or the heart" (Cañada). This same assumption underlines the four vectors almost exactly reproduced in Mallo's diagram, with the difference that his web of interrelations does not represent disciplines, people, professional groups, and products, but the people, objects, ideas, and cities that appear in the novel. Cañada writes that his map was not meant to be comprehensive, but that elements may be missing and "further versions could include a different axis, categories or an increased number of points displayed. This work is open for revisions and reformulations."

While Mallo exchanges the interior categories linked in the map, he leaves the four main axes of the digital/analog/rational/emotional in place. This allows for a more fluid and inclusive paradigm to place the various elements in his book. That said, *fluidity* is not the first adjective that comes to mind when one encounters seemingly meaningless references to numbers in the space of this f(r)iction. For example, readers learn that a woman named Rosa takes care of three children in a room that is thirty square meters (34), they find out the physical dimensions of a young Mexican who suffocated to death in the back of a truck (61), they are given the exact number of inhabitants of a micronation (93), references to exact clock times (76, 89), length of knives (88), number of rats (52), and even an entire page of "constantes físicas de interés" [physical constants of interest] (102). These numbers interject the reading of "a novel" whose central property, language, is interrupted and expanded upon by a larger set of linguistic registers, including the language of programming and physics and numerical references used in everyday life.

The novel's references to mathematics, physics, and computing are inherently presented as converging, combining, and contradicting the more fluid and abstract references to the world of art and fiction. Mallo has stated that, for him, science presents axioms that are referential systems that define certain limits. He also believes that poetry departs from a relatively calculated arbitrary location in order to search for axioms it will never find ("Tiempo"). The author admits that he likes to take these two operations and mutate them, "hacerlas inversas, hacer de la ciencia una especie de poesía y de la poesía una falsa ciencia. Permutar sus funciones para crear un artefacto no muy definible, borroso" [to invert them, making a sort of poetry out of science, and a false science out of poetry, permuting their functions to create a blurry, ill-defined artifact] ("Tiempo"). To see the results of his blurry art/science/ emotional/rational axes in motion, it is best to start at the beginning of the novel where the first chapter references one of the three foundational figures of the world of computer science, Alan Turing (1912–54). This section in the novel derives from Jack Copeland and Diane Proudfoot's essay "Alan Turing's Forgotten Ideas in Computer Science." In this piece the authors make reference to Turing's work on "computing machinery and intelligence" to point out that although computers can process mounds of information in seconds, they cannot recognize faces or read handwritten material. In other words, says the paragraph in *Nocilla Dream*, computer science is inspired by the human brain, whose web of cerebral neurons can perform more operations than the machine can.

"IONES" DE GERMÁN SIERRA

"'Iones', uno de los relatos del último libro de Germán Sierra, *Alto voltaje* (Mondadori, 2004), es un buen ejemplo de esta mirada entre técnica y antropológica. Se trata de una preciosa historia de amor que sucede durante un viaje organizado en autobús. El narrador alterna la primera persona con la segunda y con la primera del plural, de tal modo que narra el encuentro entre los dos amantes desde la perspectiva de cada uno de ellos y de la multitud, sustantivizada para la ocasión como una forma de lo otro, lo desconocido con que se encuentran los dos amantes al llegar a una ciudad costera de Galicia tras seis horas de viaje desde Madrid. La multitud es aquí pensada como una masa celular, como un fluido dentro del cual ellos se atraen como iones, movidos por el efecto de una fuerza que es física, y no psicológica ('Nos dejamos llevar por un campanario barroco de influencia compostelana. Estamos cansados y sucios y sudados y hace mucho calor y nos hemos dejado llevar por la excitación de la multitud sin tener en cuenta nuestro deseo previo'). De ahí que el relato sea muy frío, en consonancia con esta especie de determinismo físico; pero también cálido e incluso tierno, pues a fin de cuentas narra la historia de un encuentro amoroso, furtivo, fugaz y al amparo de una noche estrellada, como manda la tradición. Da la impresión de que el narrador entra en la historia por cualquier sitio, y que de una perspectiva cualquiera pasa a otra igualmente azarosa, y la historia es como una secuencia que encadena estos distintos planos. El resultado es una especie de perspectiva macro de la acción, casi un plano aéreo que constantemente parece caer en picado para enfocar una y otra vez, y muy de cerca, algún pequeño acontecimiento".

—Robert Juan-Cantavella, "La ficción-ciencia de Germán Sierra"

From the outset, this reference establishes a relational dynamic between humans and machines, but it leaves it to the brain to establish superior connections. One could expand this thought to conjecture that although the novel applies numerical coordinates to present new ideas, these mutations, when connected to the human mind, always present deeper and more complex meanings. On page 30, Mallo quotes from F. G. Healt (which refers to "Heath," the author of "Origins of the Binary Code"), to talk about the binary system of zeros and ones that underlines digital computers. This is the same system, says the passage, that expands to many dual operations in nature: on/off, true/false, open/closed, and so on. The passage then relates these binary circuits to the material texture of clothes whereby the binary becomes a metaphor for "la puntada, que podrá ser como un hilo horizontal sobre otro vertical, o al revés" [the stitch, which can be like a horizontal thread above a vertical one, and back] (30). In stitching and in circuitry, what determines the binary is its electric conductivity: it conducts or it does not conduct (30). This reference to the possibility of a binary code as a conductor advances that binary codes, whether in computation or in human relations, can lead to a series of meaningful connections and webs. Ultimately, it is the number of active transmitters (links or ideas) that can create or disrupt a web of textures, or a web of texts.

A Network of Networks

Conductors, transmitters, or links convey movement or mutation as the characters in the book are presented through different types of webs, essentially displaying networks within networks. These webs are described explicitly as roots, channels, veins, roads, and so on, or they are constructed implicitly as readers begin to (actively) connect themes, names, images, and events from the different minichapters. The two most visible and reappearing concepts include that of the desert and the tree. They are described in ways that are both abstract and rooted in the material world. The image of the desert on the one hand stresses nothingness, emptiness, sameness, and death; on the other it accentuates the existence of life and human connections. The tree denotes material location while also proposing outgrowths and points of bifurcation.

Located in the desert of Nevada, connected by one road and two whorehouses on each end, a tree was planted in the middle of nowhere, yet held enough shoes to string together stories for an entire novel. The shoes found hanging from the lonely branches of this tree appeared on Agustín Fernández Mallo's screen (or perhaps it was a paper version?) in an article in the *New York Times*. When one compares the article to the words on pages 16 and 17 of *Nocilla Dream*, it seems as if the words "US50," "tree," "shoes," "Carson City," "LA," "whorehouse," "loneliness," and

NEW YORK TIMES

By CHARLIE LeDUFF

Published: May 18, 2004
MIDDLE GATE, Nev. — The Loneliest Road in America is indeed lonesome. As lonesome as a solitary shoe.

The road, officially known as U.S. 50, cuts through the heart of the Nevada high desert, stretching 260 miles from Carson City in the west to Ely in the east. There is a whorehouse at each end and not much company in between.

There was a solitary man standing in the middle of the desolation today with his thumb out. He was an oddly angular fellow and psychologically not wholly convinced of anything more than his own existence. He said that his name was Dwight and that he had spent a winter of misery in Frisco and was in search of someplace else. He had bits of sage in his shirt as he had slept in the bush the previous evening, the rides being far between on the Loneliest Road.

" 'There's nothing out here,"' Dwight offered in a slurred, nasal tone. " 'I don't mind. I'm just more comfortable in the absence of people is all it is."

—www.nytimes.com/2004/05/18/us/middle-gate-journal-on-loneliest-road-a-unique-tree-thrives.html

Para mí aquí hay dos planos. El primero es lo que comentas: el árbol es algo con raíces manifiestas, el lugar origen del que todo parte, pero también están los zapatos, que serían la dimensión nómada de la imagen, la red horizontal —no jerarquizada— de la imagen, o el nomadismo estético. En esa unión (árbol o raíz + zapatos o red), está una buena metáfora de lo que quería decir con el libro.

—Agustín Fernández Mallo, in response

La influencia de las ciencias en la obra de Germán Sierra es patente en muchos aspectos, tanto en referencias puntuales como en el modo de argumentar determinados pasajes, o elaborar conceptos. Por ejemplo en Intente usar otras palabras, *realiza una serie de insertos que son pura teoría sociotecnológica, en el sentido no sólo del tema tratado sino del vocabulario, las construcciones, los giros lingüísticos, típicamente de científico profesional cuando realiza divulgación. No hay impostación. Eso le da un tono al texto totalmente creíble, al margen de que el contenido lo sea o no, lo que aporta una exacta verosimilitud al relato. Por otra parte, la ciencia en la narrativa de Sierra también está presente en algo que la gente que se dedica a las ciencias suele compartir, y que lo aleja de los típicos relatos, o bien utópicos, o bien distópicos, me refiero al hecho de que el futuro es todo lo que vivimos en cada momento presente, ahora; el futuro nunca es lo que propone la ciencia ficción. Por ejemplo, este fragmento de la citada novela (es una conversación):*

"Lo mejor del futuro que viene es que gente como usted y como yo no tendremos cabida en él y, como no podrán deshacerse de nosotros, deberán construir ficciones a nuestra medida —reflexionó Forner. Eso es lo que permitirá la tecnología. (...) ¿No está usted deseando vivir en ese mundo?"

"Ya vivo en ese mundo —admitió Carlos para sí-, y ya me gusta".

A mi modo de ver este tipo de características, que crean no sólo un estilo sino una verosimilitud interna del relato, es lo que diferencia a los autores que aventuran presentes-futuros literariamente verosímiles, de los que simplemente hacen futurología ingenua u obsoleta.

Si se me permite extenderme, acerca de las ciencias en la práctica novelística de algunos de los autores que este libro analiza, algo parecido ocurría en la novela Ático, *de Gabi Martínez, en el sentido de que el protagonista vive en tiempo real, a través de la tecnología, toda su miseria cotidiana.*

→

"nothing" may have led to dozens of Google searches and even more links in the creative mind of the author.

The real existence of this tree immediately sets up a relationship between the content of the book and the spaces outside the bounded pages of the novel. This very first example of Mallo's docu-fiction makes readers aware of their active role in the consumption of this novel. They can either suspend all disbelief and read the book as a fictional reconfiguration of reality, or they can sit next to a computer and expand on the novel's references to real-world information, helped by a few Uniform Resource Locator (URL) addresses along the way. It is in these acts of linking that readers begin to connect the bits and pieces of material from inside and outside the book. Readers find that it is in the spaces *in between* the real and the fictitious that new stories are spun.

The image of the tree makes clear that despite the novel's reference to nodes and connections, a beginning does exist. The tree is not an image of open-ended unrootedness or uncontrolled aesthetic nomadism; it is a trope that serves to highlight a web of interconnections in which dualities and multiplicities still exist. A large tree is well rooted in the ground, it is located in a particular geographic area, and it is immobile. Similarly, an idea is born somewhere, in someone, and must begin in some way. Roots and ideas branch out and grow, they move, they change,

También es interesante cómo en Providence, *Juan Francisco Ferré pone sobre la ficción el asunto del género (sexual), en el sentido de cómo la novela puede interpretarse en clave cambios de géneros (correlato del sexual) proporcionados por la tecnología, o más específicamente, por la mezcla de tecnologías, que van de las tecnologías arcaicas del mito clásico, a las tecnologías contemporáneas en sentido estricto, asociadas a las máquinas, o las tecnologías simbólicas de las máquinas. La novela de Jorge Carrión,* Los muertos, *realiza varias piruetas puramente tecnológicas, en cuanto a proponer novedosas realidades a través de teleseries, pero además establece algo estrictamente mítico-tecnológico: resucitar a los muertos televisivos. En otro orden, en ese libro existen dos insertos de falsos informes, elaborados con la terminología propia de informe científico, en este caso de análisis de la televisión. Como si* Videodrome *fuera, en vez de la ficción, que todos conocemos, una tesis doctoral acerca de la televisión contemporánea. El caso de la tecnología como vehículo de ficción, se ejemplariza, a mi modo de ver, en* Aire Nuestro *de Manuel* Vilas: *propone cada capítulo como un canal de televisión, en los que va mezclando rigurosa documentación con el esperpento.*

"No somos una televisión inorgánica. Somos pantalla viva. Somos carne revolucionaria. Somos visión de todo cuanto ha sido, es, y será. Dios es Aene TV. Tenemos proyectos: queremos televisar el Big Bang; queremos entrevistar a Jesucristo, televisar su enigmática frase final: 'Padre, perdónalos porque nunca han salido por la televisión'; queremos televisar un discurso de Lenin en directo. Queremos a Lenin en un plató de televisión. Queremos mejorar su imagen. Porque Lenin es un monstruo televisivo todavía sin explotar. Imaginad qué sería de los presidentes de los Estados Unidos si no existiera la televisión. Lenin se merece un regreso televisivo. Cristo también. Nadie creyó en la resurrección de Cristo por el simple hecho de que no fue televisada. Estamos en ello, estamos en ello".

—*Agustín Fernández Mallo, in response.*

and they mutate that which comes before. Precisely because the tree in the novel is located in the most remote of places, in the middle of the Nevada desert between Carson City and Ely, it becomes an image for unlikely connections. These connections may span grand universal topics such as life and death, or they may tout meager dualities as found in quick snapshots. For example, one anonymous narrator compares the *strength* of the poplar on his property to the growing *weakness* in his marital relationship. Another character refers to the perpendicular motion of the hundreds of shoes and varying lengths of shoestrings as "un baile *caótico* en el cual, pese a todo, se intuyen ciertas *reglas*" [a chaotic dance in which, despite everything, one intuits certain rules] (my emphasis 23). In a scene in Mozambique, the image of *human* shoes is substituted with that of a multitude of dead *animal* bones (52). The tree becomes a vessel used to present a series of opposite relational qualities

The shoe tree in Nevada reappears in a variety of guises and places in the novel and, in line with Mallo's "apología del error," it is placed into scenes that seem at odds with its original location and meaning. One of the most curious recyclings of this image is in a scene that refers to Siniestro Total, the punk-rock band that inspired the title of *Nocilla Dream* through the song "Nocilla qué merendilla." In the novel, the Siniestro Total's song "Ayatola no me toques la pirola" inspired the work of an artist from Santa

Barbara, California, residing in Madrid by the name of Margaret. After hearing their song, she wanted to design the cover of their first LP, which was never published. When she passed away, over 120 sketches were forgotten in her attic, one of which represented a stamped image of a Renault 12 upon a flowering tree. In reality, several members of the band had a serious accident in a Renault 12, which one member described as "siniestro total." Therein lies the origin of the band's name, visually enhanced by a tree whose living and blooming branches were webbed within and throughout a metal death trap.

While the entirety of the tree emphasizes a sense of place, location, and origin, its metaphoric qualities branch out in a network of stories. Similarly, a map shows a series of points or dots without divulging which dot first started the chain of thought reactions. Although the *New York Times* article may be viewed as one of the novel's referential origins, the text provides a variety of stories to make sense of the origins of the shoe tree. Were two lovers the ones who first threw up their pair of shoes? Was it a feud between two cities? The answer is insignificant. What matters is that the tree serves as a source of continued mutation, inspiration, and creation. The tree image carries on its branches the stories behind hundreds of pairs of shoes of all brands, colors, shapes, and sizes. Their human origins are literally left hanging at the same time that they become symbols for the exchanging, the throwing away, the taking of the old to create something new.

Remixing Smallest Narrative Units

The work of Mallo most clearly differentiates itself from that of Generation Xers in the 1990s in terms of its underlying process of creation. What had most often been referred to as media hybridity gradually has become the result of *sampling* and *remixing*, which refers to any reworking of already existent material whether combining the same or different media. The process of sampling and remixing is not exactly new. Generation X, according to Kate Mills, used "contiguity and recontextualization—by sampling image or sound bites from the past, then remixing them into a new irreverent pastiche, united by the tape-looped beat of a drum machine" (230). In the 1970s, when multitrack mixers allowed artists to separate individual instruments, they were able to add, remove, or manipulate their tempo, pitch, playing time, or equalization. As such, the process of reduction, of reducing music to three chords in punk, may be equated to reducing and filtering music to its smallest, minimalist tones and tunes, then putting those bits and pieces back together in new ways. Much like punk, remixing is an art form infused by a do-it-yourself (DIY) philosophy that directly challenges the corporate industry; it began in clubs and garages where individuals set up systems consisting of electronic technologies and computers and went to task. Although precedents of remixing can be found earlier, it was the introduction of multitrack mixers in the 1970s that made remixing a standard practice. With each element of a song—vocals, drums, and so on—available for separate manipulation, it became possible to remix the song—to change the volume of some tracks or substitute new tracks for the old ones.

As mentioned earlier, more accessible software applications have directly affected artists' ability to access and manipulate material. Nowadays musicians, authors, and digital artists have at their fingertips an almost infinite number of "smallest narrative units" (SNUs) that they incorporate into their work through easy-to-use software applications. The recombinations of these SNUs in print allow us to discern them as "database narratives." For Marsha Kinder, the

term refers to narratives whose structure exposes the dual processes of selection and combination that lie at the heart of all stories and are crucial to language: the selection of particular narrative elements (characters, images, sounds, events, and settings) from a series of categories or databases, and the combination of these chosen elements to generate specific tales. Although a database narrative may have no clear-cut beginning, no narrative closure, no three-act structure, and no coherent chain of causality, it still presents a narrative field full of story elements that are capable of arousing a user's curiosity and desire. This desire can be mobilized as a search engine to retrieve whatever is needed to spin a particular tale or to provide a rich array of sensory and intellectual pleasures. These works frequently have a subversive edge. For, in calling attention to the database infrastructure of all narratives, they reveal a fuller range of alternatives. In this way, they expose the arbitrariness of so-called master narratives, which are frequently designed to appear natural or inevitable. ("About")

> ### REMIXES
>
> "It is a truism that we live in a "remix culture." Today, many cultural and lifestyle arenas—music, fashion, design, art, web applications, user-created media, food—are governed by remixes, fusions, collages, or mash-ups. If postmodernism defined 1980s, remix definitely dominates 2000s, and it will probably continue to rule the next decade as well. Following are just a few examples of the current diversity in remix practices. In his 2005 winter collection, John Galliano (a fashion designer for the house of Dior) mixed vagabond look, Yemenite traditions, Eastern European motifs, and other sources, which he collects during his extensive travels around the world. Over the last few years, DJ Spooky has been working on *Rebirth of a Nation*, a feature-length remix of D. W. Griffith's 1915 film *The Birth of a Nation*. In April 2006, the Annenberg Center at the University of Southern California ran a two-day conference on "Networked Publics," which devoted separate sessions to various types of remix cultures on the Web: political remix videos, anime music videos, machinima, alternative news, infrastructure hacks, and the like. (In addition to these, the Web houses a growing number of software mash-ups defined by Wikipedia as "a website or application that combines content from more than one source into an integrated experience.")
>
> —Lev Manovich,
> "What Comes After Remix?"

Kinder's definition of "database narratives" perfectly identifies the work of Mallo as exposing and expanding upon age-old storytelling techniques through enlarged and multimedia sources of material (not exclusively linked to the Internet). His work applies techniques that, although not totally new either (think of the cut-up methods of William Burroughs), do allow for a reduction of information into smaller and smaller bits. The result of this expansion and reduction presents innovative new literary results that similarly demand new critical practices.

Mallo's appropriation of "smallest narrative units" allows him to combine disjointed or uncommon pieces of information in a manner that is seamless and functional, but inherently original and created by the author himself. The process leads him to construct tales in which it matters little whether

> a un verso neoclásico le siga la fotografía de un macarrón o una, en apariencia, incomprensible ecuación matemática si esa solución *metafóricamente funciona*. Este talante, naturalmente, produce zonas híbridas, cartografías en ocasiones literalmente monstruosas (recordemos que monstruoso únicamente significa: *aquello que no está en su propia naturaleza*), y es ésa la zona de frontera...que precisamente nos interesa.

> [a neoclassical verse follows the photograph of a macaroni or an, in appearance, incomprehensible mathematical equation if this solution *works metaphorically*. This event, naturally, produces hybrid zones, cartographies on occasion literally monstrous (let us remember that monstrous only means: *that which is not in its own nature*), and it is this zone of frontiers...that interests us.] (*Postpoesía* 36)

As a map that is "not in its own nature," Mallo's cartography of *Nocilla* brings together elements that do not logically seem to belong together. For example, Deeck, a Danish Web surfer, developed two aesthetic approaches to create artworks out of chewed bubble gum, presenting his artistic results on his own webpage with detailed descriptions of his techniques (27). Che Guevara, also known as Ernesto, survived his simulated death in Bolivia. Now at age seventy-eight he is residing in Las Vegas, he dedicates himself to gambling and a life of luxury, and he wears Ray-Ban glasses and Playboy t-shirts. He allows himself to be photographed by a prostitute the moment before he gets hit and killed by a motorcycle (167). The hotel chain *Houses of America* created a "Museum of Found Objects" supposedly located in Chicago and Los Angeles but is also available on the Internet. In this museum people can exchange stolen hotel objects with pieces found at the hotels themselves, no questions asked (225–26). The novel lets objects and humans play off and into each other, leading to some of the most unique and absurd takes on contemporary life and art.

Mallo develops "lecturas transversales" in the same way that a sampling DJ in a Public Broadcasting System (PBS) special titled *Copyright Criminals* considered all previous artists part of his new band. In *Nocilla Dream* a DJ is literally portrayed by a young man who taped any and all sounds off the suburbs of Chicago. Once taped, he remixed and sampled those sounds with other recordings of his own and others (40), and soon became a famous avant-garde musician. Mallo has compared his own craft to that of a DJ sampling music and material from different sources and presenting new narrative results. His fiction pulls material from one source and places it into another.

> Así hago la monstruosidad [...] de crear un Frankenstein a base de trozos, citas y metáforas subterráneas. Todo eso tiene un hilo, porque si no sería una mera yuxtaposición. Es como el buen Dj que siempre pincha con hilo. Lo que me fascina es cómo puedes convertir y reconstruir la realidad. ("Llámalo nocilla")

> [This is how I dare the monstrosity [...] of creating a Frankenstein through pieces, quotes and subterraneous metaphors. All of this contains a thread because otherwise it would result in a simple juxtaposition. It is like a good DJ who always plays with a thread. What I find fascinating is how you can transform and reconstruct reality.]

Mallo does not simply choose random elements to juxtapose, but he develops threads or links without which any piece of art would fall into chaos. The author is inspired by things that propose narrative threads. He might develop them or he might leave them hanging in the air and move on to other threads. Together, that which takes center stage and that which is left behind all add up to a final text ("Tiempo"). From San Francisco to Peking, Las Vegas to León, the characters that appear throughout his novel do not follow traditional development and movement but are remixed with figures from the world of popular culture, history, literature, and philosophy. The text mixes unknown characters like Sherry, Peter, or Heine, with Spider-Man, the Sex Pistols, and Radiohead, Che Guevara, Billy the Kid, Guy Debord, Susan Sontag, even Nietzsche, allowing all to be part of his "new band."

The art of remixing is at the heart of the narrative process as both a formal technique and a central topic. In chapter 85 a narrator discusses the artificial basis of reality as an essential component of capitalism in the twenty-first century. But because this reality (or artifice) is too excessively standardized, says the character, individuals are customizing the already constructed, as in the case of "los chinos [que] hace tiempo que copian todo lo Occidental pero introduciéndole ciertas transformaciones; lo *customizan*" [the Chinese (who) copy everything that is Western introducing certain transformations, they *customize* them] (159). This Chinese process of "customization" includes the creation of a new comic hero with a mixture of Chinese, Indian, and American features; a Pekinese road movie; and, among other examples, a character named Lee-Kung who spends her time cutting out photographs from North American magazines, scanning and saving them on her Mac, and later modifying them with Chinese motifs through the art of digital copying and pasting (55–56). Remixing characterizes the rise of a global participatory culture of individuals who can customize anything and everything to their own expressive creations.

Nocilla Dream seamlessly threads together dozens of invented stories, presenting a customized meta-remix of infinite proportions. In this novel mathematics meets poetry, commercial culture meets geography, the organic melds with the inorganic, life with death, and real and fictitious characters occupy the same space. The meta-remix that is *Nocilla Dream* undermines hierarchies for more circular and hybrid results, it involves the readers in the linking properties of the stories, and it dissolves the past and the future into an ever-existing present. As such, the novel presents a different set of narrative vectors that are, as Mallo has indicated, topologically related. In other words, they serve to configure a surface and the relations between a diverse set of features to not point to the *telling* of a story, says Mallo, but to the *construction* of a story ("Tiempo").

A Narrative Mash-Up

Nocilla Dream is a product of the process of creating a story through the techniques of sampling and remixing. The concept of the map as a topological space that can visualize the points and links in the novel does not place enough emphasis on the process of creation. For this reason, I prefer the term *mash-up* to characterize the novel. On Wikipedia, a mash-up is defined as "digital media content containing any or all of text, graphics, audio, video and animation drawn from pre-existing sources, to create a new derivative work" (Wikipedia Contributors). The mash-up emphasizes the novel's integration of sources from different media into a single new interface, which in this case is the book. Thanks to new software released by Google, mash-ups have become increasingly popular because they allow individuals to organize information topologically. As such, maps have become a good source for the spatial representation of different stories, whether these define real estate sales, epidemics, or personal tales.

In the case of *Nocilla Dream*, the mash-up stresses the map or Web-like dynamics of the novel while building on the "Cartografía Nocilla Dream."

> ### *MASH-UPS: GOOGLE MAPS*
>
> "This summer, Google released software tools that make this sort of mash-up simple to create, even for casual Web users. Thousands of people began to make useful, often elegant, annotated maps. It turns out that the best way to organize much of the information online is geographically. After Holovaty's crime statistics, real-estate listings and classified ads were among the first forms of information combined with maps. Then came sporting events, movies, and gas stations with low prices. Now the social possibilities are being mined, with sites like mapchatter.com, which lets you search for chat partners by locale, and frappr.com, where you can map the physical locations of your online pals and share photos with them. The latest twist is 'memory maps,' in which you annotate a satellite photo of your hometown with your personal history. (A good example is the blogger Matthew Haughey's evocative project, 'My Childhood, Seen by Google Maps')."
>
> www.nytimes.com/2005/12/11/magazine/11ideas1–13.html?_r=1

In other words, while the map can display the location of ideas/images/people/cities on the four axes, their interactivity, say, on a subjective/bit vector might remain flat. Take, for example, the role of the micronations in the novel. These very small countries might be seen as specific small points located on a geographic map. But in *Nocilla Dream,* these points include an entire stratosphere of information and material that also moves vertically or synchronically as it connects different kinds of material inside and outside of the novel. For example, the micronation talked about in chapter 58, for which the readers receive its Web URL, was supposedly created by two artists. Their manifesto of sorts declared the occupation and joining of a physical territory, which they consider to be fluid, a mental territory, which joins the hybrid zones of "el estado frontera entre la vigilia y el sueño" [a border state between wake and dream] (110), and a digital territory, which leads to the largest global entrance of the micronation. The narrator believes that the physical territory of the micronation may be best represented as a curve that traverses each of these territories in the shape of a fractal, "a geometric pattern that is repeated at every scale." As the narrator says in the text, to represent this micronation, "la línea plana del mapa coge relieve, toma cuerpo, borbotea [the flat line of the map takes on relief, body, it begins to bubble] (11). The micronation takes on relief as it juxtaposes its

The topological view is essential to the construction of the Nocilla Trilogy. For instance, in Gilles Deleuze, Difference and Repetition, *"An idea is an n-dimensional, continuous, defined multiplicity…by definition, we mean the elements reciprocally determined by these relations, elements which cannot change unless the multiplicity change" (182).*

—Germán Sierra, in response

More on the topographic aesthetics that are evident in the Nocilla Trilogy: Manuel Delanda, in Intensive Science and Virtual Philosophy *says, "Multiplicities give form to processes, not to the final product, so that the end results of processes realizing the same multiplicity may be highly disimilar from each other, like the spherical soap bubble and the cubic salt crystal which not only do not resemble one another, but bear no similarity to the topological point guiding their production" (22).*

—Germán Sierra, in response

La visión topológica me interesa en tanto la topología habla de la deformación de cuerpos (superficies, volúmenes, hipervolúmenes), que aún deformados siguen manteniendo una serie de características que los definen. La topología es una rama de la matemática que no mide, no se interesa por lo que miden las cosas o cuantificarlas, sino por sus formas. Y eso es lo que, precisamente, es el acto de traducir: deformar un texto para acoplarlo a otra lengua, pero manteniendo en la medida de lo posible el sentido del texto. Y ese "en la medida de lo posible" es lo que me interesa, ya que al traducir siempre se pierde algo de información para ganar otro tipo de información, y esa deformación de materiales es la que acometemos cuando arrancamos un trozo de una obra, nos la apropiamos, y la insertamos en otro contexto. Hemos creado una metáfora en tanto diálogo y unión entre elementos que son disímiles, que están deformados o

→

> *"traducidos". Esto, en el fondo es la idea de "caminata" a la que antes aludí (Robert Smithson): tránsito por diferentes espacios que el ojo va deformando y reinterpretando según leyes propias.*
>
> —*Agustín Fernández Mallo,*
> *in response*

three territories without defying its location on the map.

For two meta-mashing examples, I turn to the most obvious references in regard to the effects of their mapping, forking, or webbing dynamics in print, namely Italo Calvino and Jorge Luis Borges. These references serve to link stories to one another, and they pronounce an overlapping quality in which the map serves to construct stories, albeit different ones, about the art of map-making. Chapter 13 makes implicit reference to Calvino's book from 1972, *Invisible Cities*. The novel consists of brief prose descriptions and dialogues shared between a character named Marco Polo and an emperor, Kublai Khan. What stands out in this book is that the fifty-five short descriptions of cities and interspersed short dialogues in italics reconstruct the spatial dynamics of but one space through a wide range of topics similar to that of Mallo's own *cosmopedia*. As the introduction to the novel proposes, these conversations are meant to discern the reason for the ruin of the empire through "the tracery of a pattern so subtle it could escape the termites' gnawing" (6). The pattern of this novel in *Nocilla Dream* is described as a web of water channels that spread throughout a city. The narrator relates this particular web to the system of veins and arteries that may be found throughout the human being's blood circulation system. This is a system that, unlike the city, functions on circularity and return, thereby consolidating the self and saving its identity from infinite dispersion (37). This trope displays the self as frozen in time, as "una hipótesis inamovible que al nacer se nos asigna y que hasta el final sin éxito intentamos demostrar" [an unmoving hypothesis that is assigned to us and we try to prove until the end] (38).

> *Dynamic consciousness is another concept that is represented through the Nocilla Trilogy: people are what they do. "Consciousness is not something that happens inside us. It is something we do or make. Better: it is something we achieve. Consciousness is more like dancing than it is like digestion" (Noë xii).*
>
> —*Germán Sierra, in response*

The narrator mashes a concrete system of water channels to the limits of the more open-ended construction of humans' identity, both of which ultimately comment on writing itself.

If the introductory essay to the *New Media Reader*, "New Media from Borges to HTML," is any indication, Borges has become an icon for foreseeing in fiction what computer scientists were developing through the machine. In "La biblioteca de Babel" Borges foresaw the infinite addition of textual references; in "En exactitud en ciencia," he gave space to the art of mapping; and in "The Garden of Forking Paths," he foresaw in print what later appeared in hypertext, literally translated into electronic space by Stuart

Moulthrop in 1987.[6] In *Nocilla Dream*, Borges's connection to equations, geometrics, and mathematics is referenced directly in chapter 69, where writer and scientist Ernesto Sábato is quoted saying that Borges "plantea cuentos como teoremas" [creates short stories like theorems] and that the detective in "La muerte y la brújula" is presented as "un títere simbólico que obedece ciegamente —o lúcidamente, es lo mismo— a una ley matemática" [a symbolic puppet that blindly obeys—or lucidly obeys, which is the same—a mathematical law] (132–33). Borges's mathematical and mapping projections in "Del rigor en la ciencia" take on a central role in chapter 20 in which a quote from this text is directly reproduced in the novel. This well-known scene discusses the map of the empire, whose size was as big as the spatial coordinates of the landscape itself, but whose art was forgotten and found useless by subsequent generations, leaving the pieces of the map to decompose in the deserts of the West, now inhabited by animals and beggars instead of displaying the remnants of a lost discipline (48).

In the context of this novel, the episode questions traditional disciplinary notions of the map and mapping, suggesting that it is in the bits and pieces of its desert trash where a new aesthetics may be found. To support this idea, chapter 25 refers to "Catástrofes de 1ª y 2ª Especie" [Catastrophes of the 1st and 2nd

Una nota acerca de la influencia de Borges en las literaturas innovadoras contemporáneas. Hace poco, estando en Buenos Aires, comprobé, en varias conversaciones y actos con escritores argentinos, que sigue estando presente el tema de la inevitable (y terrible) influencia borgiana, a la que aparentemente nadie puede escapar. Incluso la obra de Fogwill, que a primera vista tiene poco que ver, es descrita con frecuencia como un intento de escapar a Borges por omisión. Esto me dio que pensar varias cosas. 1) Esa influencia se vive como una "condición inevitable" y aun como una "condena" en un sector de las letras argentinas; en cambio, en otros medios literarios se vive como una liberación. En literatura norteamericana autores como Barth o Coover encontraron en las Ficciones una nueva dirección literaria, y eso partiendo de una lectura "de primera instancia" de Borges, en la cual dibujaron, con una línea simple y diáfana, una "conexión hispánica" que iba desde el Quijote hasta el Pierre Menard, y en la que había valores positivos como la metaficción, la fabulación, el ludismo o el antirrealismo pero ningún "valor negativo" del tipo de "la angustia de la influencia". 2) Puede decirse que en literatura española ese mismo temor ha recorrido las letras posmodernas (Vila-Matas se refirió a él en alguna ocasión) hasta el punto de moderar su componente metanarrativo, si bien en los últimos tiempos ha sido sustituido por una visión distinta. Ahora el Borges favorito no es el germanista y erudito de la cábala de Ficciones sino más bien el autor lúdico, juguetón y "ligero" de la última época, y en particular de algunos textos que, como "El libro de arena", pueden ser leídos como una autoparodia, o como la fase manierista del autor, o incluso, en el caso de "Atlas", como una imitación escrita por un discípulo: un pastiche de tigres, laberintos y citas de poesía china, Borges todo a cien (pennystore). 3) En este sentido, el escritor actual ya no dice "Borges es el Único, →

su biblioteca es la más grande", sino más bien "todos somos un poco como Borges, con nuestra internet-como-Biblioteca de Babel, nuestras atribuciones equívocas, nuestra erudición dudosa". El paso de una visión a la otra lo dio, posiblemente, la obra de Rodrigo Fresán. 4) Más allá del caso de Agustín, cabría considerar, en términos de literatura comparada, el siguiente factor: solucionar los problemas internos de la tradición argentina en otras literaturas (sea por medio de una simplificación, de una misreading, de cortar el nudo gordiano) es una práctica sin la cual no se entienden buena parte de las innovaciones literarias de los últimos tiempos.

—Eloy Fernández Porta, in response

El principal inspirador de esa sincronía de múltiples tiempos, o de esa arqueología simultánea, es el artista norteamericano Robert Smithson, quien a su vez está inspirado en el libro The Shape of Time *de George Kubler, o en trabajos de Levi-Strauss. Podemos hablar de un Tiempo Topológico, un tiempo que no alude a cronologías sino a las relaciones espaciales entre cosas, por muy alejadas que en el tiempo estén las cosas. Es un tiempo "estructural", hecho de capas. En mi obra, el "land-art" —ejemplificado por Robert Smithson— y el arte conceptual —ejemplificado, por ejemplo, por Baldessari — tiene una influencia fundamental. El arte conceptual, porque muchas de mis tramas de personajes, o reflexiones del narrador, son una especie de obra conceptual narrada, con atención al giro que hace esa práctica en lo que se refiere a la visión de lo cotidiano como si fueras un marciano recién aterrizado en la Tierra, es decir, llevando lo cotidiano a un absurdo para darle otro sentido. Por otra parte, el Land-Art se ve reflejado sobre todo en la práctica específica de la "caminata" a través de un paisaje —también presente, aunque con connotaciones sociopolíticas, en el Situacionismo de* →

Kind]. These catastrophes state that when objects are moved out of their equilibrium due to a foreign agent—in this case the passing of time—they create a domino effect of unforeseen events. Because deserts are levelled spaces with similar properties everywhere, they are, says the text, the least catastrophic places on earth (57). The exact same wording is copied and pasted verbatim in chapter 48, except that at the end of each discourse an action disrupts the even conditions of the desert, leading to a domino effect of events. In the first case a husband throws his wife's shoes on a tree, thus leading to the throwing of hundreds more shoes (and more ministories about the husband and wife). In the second case a gas station worker in Albacete rolls up little balls of newspaper and throws them into the desert, thus presenting a contemporary remix in which the mapping of everyday events (in a newspaper) converts the scenery of an open space in Spain. The energy of the wind moves about the bits of information without them leading to any particular reader (94). The insignificance of the result might suggest the loss of the disciplinary art of map-making or narrating, but it might also propose the construction of a new art: the creation of a moving map through the seemingly empty bits and pieces of material that make up the world, that make up *Nocilla Dream*.

The cause-and-effect energy of these catastrophes suggests

that the "user experience" of the cartography of *Nocilla Dream* continues to remix and re-mash elements beyond the pages of the book. Beyond the dream, readers experience and expand on the novel's structure and significance in the next instalment of the trilogy, tellingly titled *Nocilla Experience*. Beyond this first mash-up, readers encounter one of Mallo's perhaps most personal remakes, *El hacedor (de Borges), Remake*. Jorge Luis Borges's forethought and connection to twenty-first-century software applications and the scientific/poetic hybridity of his work makes Mallo's reference to *El hacedor* (1960) one of *Nocilla Dream*'s most significant intertexts. In the epilogue to the original book, Borges mentions that "[d]e cuantos libros he dado a la imprenta, ninguno, creo, es tan personal como esta colecticia y desordenada silva de varia lección, precisamente porque abunda en reflejos e interpolaciones" [of all the books I have sent to print, none of them, I believe, have been as personal as this collected and disorganized grouping of various texts, precisely because it is abundant in reflections and insertions] (155). Given the diversity of Borges's own *cosmopedia*, the remake may propose to be Mallo's, a contemporary maker's, most powerful mash-up yet.

> *Guy Debord. La caminata como tránsito de un espacio a otro que, en principio, no tienen relación alguna, pero que el ojo lo relaciona "topológicamente". Tanto es así que en mi libro,* El hacedor (de Borges), Remake, *hay un cuento, "Mutaciones", en el que, en la primera parte, rehago la mítica caminata que en 1967 hizo Robert Smithson, publicada como documento-obra en Artforum, "Un recorrido por los monumentos de Passaic", pero la hago a través de Google Earth, combinando el texto de Smithson con uno de elaboración propia. Desde cierto punto de vista, creo que ese cuento, "Mutaciones", es lo más ambicioso de cuanto he escrito.*
>
> —*Agustín Fernández Mallo, in response*

En mi libro *El hacedor (de Borges), Remake* –que ya en sí mismo puede considerarse un "mash-up"-, hay un poema que se llama Los Borges –el original de Borges se llama así, y en él Borges habla de su familia y sus antepasados– pero yo, tomando la idea del título hago este poema en el

Remake:

LOS BORGES
Los Smiths
Los Clash
Los Ramones

> *En* El hacedor (de Borges), Remake *he hecho un video en el que superpongo el sonido de una canción de cada uno de esos grupos, las fundo en una sola pista, y, claro, sale una melodía abstracta, un poema sonoro al que he titulado, lógicamente, "Los Borges".*
>
> *Creo que esto es un buen ejemplo de mash-up.*
>
> *La imagen del video es difícil de explicar aquí, pero resumiendo: es una van de juguete, una furgoneta, que gira sobre un disco de vinilo (LP) sin parar, y la furgoneta lleva una cartel que pone: "Los Borges, Mystery Tour".*
>
> *Puede verse, en*
>
> www.youtube.com/watch?v =jSmSBlS_hgs
>
> —*Agustín Fernández Mallo, in response*

Los Beach Boys
Los Sex Pistols
Los Nikis
Los Zoquillos
Los Strokes
Los Doors
Los Violent Femmes
Los Residents
Los B-52s

Agustín Fernández Mallo, en directo

Conclusion

Generation X Remixed:
A Conversation

The process of writing this book was ridden with resistance. The linearity of the word kept on clashing against the excess and synchronicity of Generation X texts. To make sense of this nonsense, my pen wanted to present a book of short, fragmented blurbs of thought that connected ideas as loosely as the GenX and *Mutantes* novels I was analyzing. I felt the need to look into publishing this book through hypertext software such as *Storyspaces* by Eastgate Systems. I searched for an environment in which the process of writing and analyzing could be emphasized through mapping and linking actions, something like a mobile Borgesian labyrinth. I entertained the idea of publishing my work on a participatory and open-source space like *Commentpress*, software that allows readers to turn documents into conversations by commenting, annotating, or debating in the margins or layers of the text. I thought about creating a Vook for the iPad, a hybrid electronic piece in which you could read my words then start a short video for additional information, listen to an interview with Agustín Fernández Mallo or play one of the video games I analyse in chapter five. If you were to find an academic publisher willing to support such a project, then a multimedia version of *Spanish Fiction in the Digital Age: Generation X Remixed* will literally be at your fingertips in the near future.

Each medium I came across added innovative and exciting possibilities for new scholarship. They were *hybrid* and allowed for a variety of visual and verbal material to coalesce in one space; they were *collaborative*, joining many voices from a variety of disciplines and backgrounds; and they were *creative*, presenting more democratic and inclusive techniques and approaches. My goal in this book has been to emulate these features in print, rendering side boxes that include academic material, electronic links to videos, e-mail exchanges, and responses from authors and critics alike. The conversations that develop in each chapter present, to play with a term coined by Mallo, a "crítica expandida," an expanded critical practice that can evolve and grow differently in each chapter as individuals bring their own set of expertise to the table. These

"Al principio fue la acción," traduce Fausto en la primera parte de la obra de Goethe cuando se enfrentaba al evangelio. Quizás ya intuía el escritor alemán que la acción como impulso motriz sería el rasgo epocal del futuro siglo XXI. Movimiento, velocidad, cambio…, aunque no se sepa muy bien hacia dónde nos movemos, respecto de qué queremos cambiar y por qué hay que hacerlo tan rápidamente. Sin embargo, resulta diáfano que el tiempo de la modernidad es un tiempo de discontinuidades y rupturas. Algunas de ellas profundas y de consecuencias considerables para nuestra cultura. Empieza Christine Henseler la conclusión de su Generation X Remixed *con la afirmación de que el proceso de escritura de este libro ha sido un proceso de resistencia. Y contrariamente a lo que se podría pensar, no se trata de una captatio en relación a la dificultad de escritura, a la complejidad de la temática, a la duración del proceso en sí; sino que se refiere a una cuestión estructural. Henseler está pensando las ficciones que pueblan nuestra sociedad hipermoderna y al hacerlo se encuentra con una problemática de base, una cuestión funcional: ¿cómo organizar la reflexión en el formato libro si los textos que estudia están profundamente impregnados, contaminados, irradiados de la cultura de la red?*

—*Laura Borrás, in response*

critical practices come to fruition in the final chapter in which Agustín Fernández Mallo's and Germán Sierra's backgrounds in the sciences allow us to engage in dynamic interdisciplinary conversations. By integrating their voices into the chapter and allowing the side boxes to take on an increasing amount of space, I give credence to the value of voices not like myself, to the need to listen, hear, and learn. Their responses advance interrelated artistic/critical threads that dance synchronically with my own, sometimes taking the lead, other times swaying harmoniously to the music. In a final melodic move, I remove the lines around Mallo's words at the end of the chapter to allow for a harmonious, poetic example in critical expansion and hybridity.[1]

This conclusion presents its own hybrid dynamic. It has traditionally been a space meant to pull the main ideas of a book together, but I also use it here to speak to you on a more personal level. Since there are two narrative threads that coalesce in this project—the identity of Generation X and the effects of media technologies on new narrative practices—I begin by admitting that *I am a Generation X'er*. I came after, I come between, and I will readily be forgotten in time. But before that happens, I want to set the record straight. We are the generation of change, and as the generation of change, we are in the unique position of being able to critically and creatively reevaluate the role and function of new media technologies. We have grown up and witnessed a host of technological changes, from the video recorder and the remote control to the iPhone and iPad. We are very aware of the social and intellectual effects of emerging media on our professional and personal lives. We question, we watch, we are cynical and sarcastic, and we often think in silence and avoid the limelight. As I summarize in a short essay posted on my website, "Short-*Changed*: In Defense of Generation X,"

> We are now in our 40's and 50's, we are slackers turned executives, we are
> punks turned yuppies, and we are still running high on *teen spirit*. We are
> often well-established in our professions, we have the schooling, thinking and
> writing skills needed to translate theory into practice, and we follow and ana-
> lyze new technologies, for no other reason than to keep our businesses afloat
> or to supervise and monitor our children's activities. To the surprise of many,
> our X'er worldview, whether we know it or not, has expanded on Tim Berners-
> Lee's philosophy of a free and open World Wide Web. We believe in open
> conversations, in access for all, in less hierarchical structures, and in more
> innovation and freedom of thought. Yet, we X'ers are often short-changed in
> this war of word crafts, short-changed in a world of ever-changing technolo-
> gies. But "change" is shorthand for "Generation X," and as such we feel right
> at home in these multiple, fluid, and hybrid spaces of social rebellion.

At the beginning of this book project, I did not feel *right at home* in the
multiplicities, fluidities, and hybridities that were staring me in the face.
I did not know that deep down inside I was Generation X. I did not even
know who Generation X was beyond the basic stereotypes that seemed to
have nothing to do with me. What I did know was that I was a literary critic,
not a media scholar. I did not watch MTV, nor did I play many video games.
I read books and watched films. I worked on Spanish not North American
literature. With time, one thing became very clear as I began this project:
it was time for me to move with the times and cross various lines, to finally
punk out on my own teen spirit.

Back to Ground Zero

When I started this project, I battled and was baffled by the images constructed by mainstream media about the identity of Generation X. I read
Coupland's novel, watched Linklater's film, and became readily aware that
the image of the slacker had become a cheap excuse for superficial critical
readings. Media and scholarly generated stereotypes appeared over and over
again ultimately presenting a distorted repetition of Andy Warhol's philosophy of sameness. The critical underpinnings of "the same" left untapped
and unexplored the complex roots and rich outgrowths of the "X" equation.
With this realization I knew I had to start over. I had to start from ground
zero and untangle the copies from their origins, the frozen and unchanging image of Generation X from its diverse and multiple outgrowths, and
the media hype from the generation's historical roots, political experiences,
social dynamics, and cultural expressions. I had to make sense of a youth
who, like myself, had matured since the 1990s. And in the process of figuring out how "they" had changed, I began to play video games, watch music
video clips, make remixes, and mash Google maps. In the process of figuring
out who Generation X was, I taught my traditional close reading skills how
to dance to the tunes of new technologies.

On my travels to ground zero, I encountered an image that reappeared
in many Generation X and *Mutantes* texts: the desert. Much like the more
deterministic event of the apocalypse, X'ers flocked to the aesthetic poten-

tials of the desert as a space for new beginnings and total reconnection. The desert was their metaphor for escape, for nonbelonging, for marginalization, and for new beginnings. According to McCaffery, the desert was also a metaphor for the real, a new reality rained upon by a "downpour," as he called it, of information from all walks of life (*After* xiv). In Coupland's novel, Andy, Dag, and Clair escape mainstream society by moving to the desert of Palm Springs, by searching for a new reality within which they could redefine themselves. In the second chapter of the novel the meaning of both Generation X and the desert becomes quite clear when Andy explained that,

> we live small lives on the periphery: we are marginalized and there's a great deal in which we choose not to participate. We wanted silence and we have that silence now. We arrived here speckled in sores and zits, our colons so tied in knots that we never thought we'd have a bowel movement again. Our systems had stopped working, jammed with the odor of copy machines. Wite-Out, the smell of bond paper, and the endless stress of pointless jobs done grudgingly to little applause. We had compulsions that made us confuse shopping with creativity, to take downers and assume that merely renting a video on a Saturday night was enough. But now that we live here in the desert, things are much better, *much* better. (11)

Their move to the desert presents a space of escape, of silence, of mental and physical health, and of perspective on everyday life. The passage speaks to previous discussions on the excess of emergent meanings in our contemporary culture and the need for pure spaces of thought and action—a space for an inner, instead of an outer, loud, punk nirvana that cleans out colons and leads to fresh facial complexions.

The above quotation reminded me of the words of Italian philosopher Rosi Braidotti who uses the image of the desert to represent "areas of silence, in between the official cacophonies, in a flirt with radical nonbelonging and outsidedness" (16). Yet, what most forget, and what is well represented in Braidotti's book title, *Nomadic Subjects*, is that the desert is a space of *transition*. X'ers are, as one of my students so well summarized, "transient individualists"[2] a description appropriate for the ending of Coupland's book when all three characters drive to San Felipe, Mexico, to buy a small hotel and start a new life. As Andy puts it, his move over the Southern border signifies a return: "Back to real life. Time to get snappy. Time to get a life" (171). Although his sarcastic take on life does not end here, nor his admittance that this transition will be hard, he has a life-changing experience on January 1, 2000, that suggests a more hopeful and meaningful start at the dawn of the twenty-first century. At the turn of the century, GenX'ers identity changes, evolves, and mutates, more hope than disillusionment in their eyes, as much cynicism and sarcasm on the tips of their tongues.

In Bret Easton Ellis's novel *Less Than Zero*, the desert is coincidentally also represented through Palm Springs, except this time the city is used to move back in time. Sections in italics interrupt the main storyline of the novel. In these passages, inner thoughts by the protagonist, Clay, allow him to linger in his old home in the desert. It is in these passages that readers get a sense of emotional depth, hurt, and hunger that starkly contrasts with the flat, unemotional, and cold narrative of the rest of the book (a technique also adopted in the final passage of *Historias del Kronen*). The desert also presents a comparative ground for the commercial and superficial culture of Hollywood life, there where all significance has already been corrupted and co-opted, or, rather, overdosed and oversexed. At the end of the first of these sections Clay admits to making these trips to Palm Springs because "I wanted to remember the way things were" (44). In fact, it is from a pay phone from this "Palm Desert" that he ultimately decides to return to New Hampshire, to the East, and leave his girlfriend and superficial life in LA behind (201). The desert here again presents an opening of thought and emotion; an escape from the empty mainstream; a lingering between the past, present, and the future; and a space where transition and change can be entertained.

In Agustín Fernández Mallo's novel *Nocilla Dream*, the other bookend to this project, the desert is imagined as a space of isomorphic sameness and rhyzomatic beginnings that connects individuals from around the world through micronarratives. Shoes on trees in the desert of Nevada function as visual metaphors for the coming together of hundreds of stories in an earthly paradigm that mirrors the dynamics of the Internet. The web-like form of Mallo's text falls well in line with Braidotti's metaphorical interpretation of the desert as embodying a "gigantic map of signs for those who know how to read them, for those who can sing their way through the wilderness" (17). The metaphorical act of singing one's way though the desert, this wilderness that is contemporary society, emphasizes GenX'ers' relationship of an either physical or mental escape to the margins and their relationship to new narrative models as steeped in music and song. As such, song may allow for clarity in the "wilderness" or excess of contemporary signifiers as individuals re-create and take their personal lyrics everywhere they go.

In the process of starting from ground zero and examining the meaning of ground zero, I ultimately noticed that the desert seems to have dulled the melodies of many female Generation Xers, leaving them more high than dry in the world of literary criticism. To read the gigantic map of signs that make up the GenX story must also entail the desert wanderings of the female nomad around the globe. They include the likes of Amèlie Nothomb from Belgium, Justine Ettler from Australia, Wei Hui and Mian Mian from China, Courtney Love and Wynona Ryder in the United States, film directors Virginie Despentes and Coralie Trinh Thi from France, the visual art of Sarah Lucas in Great Britain, and, as I have examined elsewhere, the literature of Lucía Etxebarria in Spain. The map of these and many other female X'ers redraws and repositions the borders that have encased critical scholarship on Generation X. The visions and voices of these GenX "bad girls" have reached across continents where they have shocked, delighted, ignored, angered, and pissed off. Their range of expression has crossed

> *Hablar de la creación literaria postgeneración X (no hay que olvidar que acaba de salir la Generación A) requiere un ejercicio previo de expansión de la noción de lo literario para percatarse de la búsqueda personal subyacente en los distintos autores por ella convocados. Nociones como "recreación", "reescritura", "palimpsesto", "intertextualidad", "irradiación," "pannarrativa", "versión", "fractalidad textual" o "texto ergódico" deben ser objeto de minuciosa reflexión para acceder a un territorio textual múltiple y complejo en que los escritores son experimentadores de lo posible. De ahí que su referencia primera en cuanto a la forma que debería de haber tomado esta reflexión sea para* Storyspaces, *el sistema desarrollado por Eastgate Systems en los noventa para desarrollar un tipo concreto de escritura hipertextual que dio resultados tan notables como* Patchwork Girl *de Shelley Jackson. La experiencia de lectura que requiere un hipertexto que en el fondo y en la forma se presenta como una reescritura de la ficción y del pensamiento y que fue vivida con desazón por lectores como Christine, que afirma que leía saliendo a la búsqueda de un hilo narrativo; se impone, paradójicamente como la forma "deseable" en su discurrir teórico. Un discurso fragmentado, anotado, comentado, irradiado, proyectado que necesita recurrir al texto, a la imagen, al sonido, a la convergencia de medios que permite Internet, que es un medio de medios.*
>
> —Laura Borrás, *in response*

artistic genres and fanned across styles and topics, from horrific violence and pornography to romantic love and utterly light humor and sarcasm; from classical high art and literature to texts saturated with popular culture; from flat and raw narrative style and content to word plays filled with utter lyricism. Female GenX writers and artists vacillate between the spaces and signs afforded by their location from below, the side, or the in-between. Their work emphasizes process over product, and they embrace hybridity as a continuously moving space of expressive multiplicities, contradictions, reconstructions, and questionings. Most importantly, and unsurprisingly, close attention to body politics encases young women's differing relation to gender politics, redefining and undermining Generation X's male canonicity in significant ways and disrupting literary practices and expectations along the way.[3]

The lack of critical attention paid to Generation X on the level of gender, race, class, or global reach motions to the need to hit the reboot button and restart conversations. A return to a critical ground zero, or a metaphorical desert plane, allows for more fluid theoretical approaches in tune with a digital age. The central idea of the blank, as first proposed by James Annesley, presents a promising theoretical thread through which to resume and renew studies on Generation X in particular. The blank is also one of the main tropes that strings throughout this book and reappears in various chapters and in different guises. In this project the blank is embodied in stories that were left out, in a punk's song of a generation, in the words left hanging between images, in flat narratives and seemingly fragmented identities, in the absence of a *poppy* criticsm, in blank screens that tell gamers "it's over," in potential errors, in spam to be avoided, in the spaces between genres, and most importantly, in the mysterious and mobile "X" of a generation. What becomes clear is that if we leave those spaces unattended, if we leave those blanks empty, we may squander the promise of the *in-between*.

From Analog to Digital Literary Criticism

In the process of teasing out the multiple meanings inherent in the "blank," in this book I emphasize the role of media technologies in the cultural production of books. As the acceleration of culture catches up with individuals around the globe in the twenty-first century, we find that technology undoubtedly is taking an ever-increasing role in the construction of new meanings. Speed, fragmentation, jumps in time and space, and the convergence of different genres, cultures, and media allow for more multiple and malleable identities to take shape. By underscoring the material effect of media on fiction, I argue that GenX writers were rearticulating their acts

> *La creación más radicalmente contemporánea se presenta como una producción de directo, de procesos, de interrelaciones, de diálogos que viajan a través de formas y géneros, y se adentran en territorios híbridos, porosos, donde el sampling y el mash-up son estrategias narrativas capitales y donde la lógica epifánica del fogonazo, del impacto se convierte en nueva estrategia cognitiva.*
>
> *Lógicas de lo pannarrativo, lógicas de lecturas ergódicas, fragmentarias, epifánicas que requieren de sus críticos nuevas estrategias expresivas, nuevas gramáticas de la creación que reclaman otros lenguajes desde la reflexión como los que se ha planteado Christine en su libro híbrido.*
>
> —*Laura Borrás, in response*

of consumption as a process of production. This shift demands a critical readjustment that one could metaphorically refer to as moving from analog to digital reading. While analog devices such as turntables read bumps and grooves from a record as a continuous signal, a digital device, such as a CD player, only reads a series of ones and zeros. The purity and unprocessed nature of analog devices, often seen as more exact, has had to give way to the manipulative potential of small bits and pieces of digital data. As "digital literary critics," then, we cannot respond to the critical potential of the remix culture we live in without engaging with it directly. We must remix ourselves in the process of remixing and reengaging our critical skills.

Remixing points to the influence of media technologies in the creative process, the changing role of authorship—one that increasingly explores concepts of originality, intertextuality, collaboration, and authority—and the more participatory and collaborative role of readers in uncovering narrative threads. When taken together, the act of reading, or what I would call *critical remix reading*, becomes dynamic and fluid at the same time that it allows for productive resistance, subversion, or parodying of critical and creative results. The remixing of Generation X is the interpretive result of a process of cultural and media hybridization that centers not only on the connections between old and new content but also on old and new techniques. There is no doubt that this process presents a complex set of dynamics often difficult to untangle; it suggests the coming together of an almost infinite amount of information from varying sources in unprecedented ways; ways that cross platforms, genres, and nations; ways that can lead to dynamic and fluid critical results with unlimited impulse and impact.

Notes

Introduction

1. These critics tended to compare position "A"—Spain, traditional, authentic, literary, and valuable—to position "B"—North America, popular culture, artifice, and superficiality. This angle ignored the global and nomadic spirit of the X generation; it also denied the multivocal, fluid, and polyphonic flows within which GenX authors had grown up.
2. See Adelaida Caro Martín's *América te lo he dado todo y ahora no soy nada*.
3. See Carter Smith's "Social Criticism or Banal Imitation: A Critique of the Neorealist Novel Apropos the Works of José Ángel Mañas," Moreiras Menor's book *Cultura herida: literatura y cine en la España democrática*, Klodt's "'Nada de nada de nada de nada': Ray Loriga and the Paradox of Spain's Generation X," and Gonzalo Navajas in "A Distopian Culture: The Minimalist Paradigm in the Generation X."
4. In the introduction to our volume, *Generation X Rocks: Contemporary Peninsular Fiction, Film, and Rock Culture*, Randolph Pope and I talk about the need to view Generation X texts not as safe commodities, but as intellectual live wires. GenX novels allow critics to explore rock in text and in film as significant cultural events that place new demands on literary and cultural criticism (xvi).
5. *Dasein* is a German word coined by Martin Heidegger that literally means being there/here. It is a term that points to one's existence in time and in presence.
6. Since so many scholars begin their essays by enumerating the negative criticism on Spanish Generation X narrative, I have decided not to repeat them here.

    See Moreiras Menor's book *Cultura herida: literatura y cine en la España democrática* and Robert Spires's essay "Depolarization and The New Spanish Fiction at the Millennium."
7. The homogenizing effects of the Generation X canon are well presented by Nina Molinaro, who includes factors such as gender, race, ethnicity, and regionalism. She argues that although scholars uniformly include women authors among the members of the generation, rarely do they follow up inclusion with any sustained analysis; likewise, considerations of gender infrequently make their way into the existing critical analyses of the novels written by these new narrators.

    Significantly, other indices of difference such as race and ethnicity, sexuality, disability, and even linguistic and cultural regionalism have largely gone unremarked, perhaps once again confirming that generational frameworks succeed predominantly through the strategy of homogenization. ("Facing" 7) These latter markers conform to a generational category in the larger sense since GenX is marked by white, middle-class individuals from Madrid or Barcelona. That said, not much scholarship has been conducted on regional or class differences, or on Generation X on a global scale.

8. See Santana's "What We Talk about When We Talk about Dirty Realism in Spain."

9. I will engage with what I call the "tales" of GenX criticism at more length in chapter 1.

10. See Paul Begin's "The Pistols Strike Again! On the Function of Punk in the Peninsular 'Generation X': The Fiction of Ray Loriga and Benjamín Prado," Adelaida Caro Martín's *América te lo he dado todo y ahora no soy nada*, and Eva Navarro Martínez's *La nueva novela española en la última década del Siglo XX*.

11. Among two comparative and transatlantic book-length studies are those by Adelaida Caro Martín and Daniel Graziade.

12. See "La generación Nocilla y el afterpop piden paso" by Nuria Azancot.

   The connection I am establishing between Generation X and the Mutantes has been suggested by a few other critics, including Jesse Barker (in his dissertation) and Eloy Fernández Porta.

13. For a comprehensive analysis of the social and economic developments in Spain in the post-Franco period, see the detailed work of Zaldívar and Castells.

14. All translations in this book are mine, unless otherwise indicated.

15. These percentages change depending on whether researchers begin to consider the generation in the United States in 1961 or in 1964. If the generation is taken to span from 1961 to 1981, Generation X'ers actually outnumber Baby Boomers (Kleber and Associates). It is important to note that those individuals born in the early 1960s can swing into either of the generational models, a factor that marketers are well aware of.

   According to the Instituto de la Juventud, the percentage of the total population of youth between 15 and 29 years of age is the following: 1960: 23.4 percent; 1970: 22 percent; 1981: 23.2 percent; 1991: 24.9 percent; 2001: 22.4 percent; 2005: 21 percent (Injuve)

   (www.injuve.migualdad.es/injuve/contenidos.type.action?type=1445831 392&menuId=1445831392).

16. Baby Boomers were born between 1946 and 1961–64 and the Millennials between 1977 and 1998, although critics disagree on specific dates for any of the generations.

17. See Strauss and Howe 317.

18. See "Suspiro de España" by Jorge Pérez for examples on GenX'ers' disenchantment with politics, general apathy, and a crisis in values in the narrative presented by Mañas.

19. As a reaction to the perceived "desarrollismo," the term "desencanto" was also used in the late 1980s and 1990s to describe disappointment with the liberal democratic system in Spain. Graham and Labanyi explain that this feeling was in part conceived of expectations of mythical proportions (that democracy could solve all national problems), an enormous investment of energy rooted in an anti-Franco struggle with minimal social

and economic reform gained in the transition, and a coinciding recession (312–313).

20. Graham and Labanyi note that despite surprising cultural changes that already began before the death of Franco, a top-down approach to culture continued well into the 1980s. One of its outgrowths was the co-optation of youth culture during the Spanish *Movida*, including the work of Pedro Almodóvar, which contributed to the making of the official image of Spain (312).

21. It bears mentioning that the Spanish autonomous regions also played a significant role in the past three decades in the voluntary perception of a united Spain, although each region underlined its territorial differences and needed to find solutions to varied administrative challenges. In addition, the professionalization of the military closed a significant chapter in its historical role in the peninsula (Zaldívar 255–56).

22. I realize I am presenting a simplified version of world affairs and flows. For a complete study see Castells.

23. In fact, I would argue that we are already seeing a backlash in global commercial practices, leading to more support and innovation on small and local scales.

24. The term "third space" has been theoretically articulated in the Latin American context by Alberto Moreiras in *Tercer espacio. Literatura y duelo en América Latina.*

25. The title of *City Sister Silver* was originally *Sestra*, published in 1994. It was translated in 2000.

26. See my forthcoming edited volume *Generation X Goes Global* for an extensive analysis of the outgrowths of this global phenomenon. I would like to give thanks to Jeremy Seekings and Jan Schenk for their insight on Generation X in South Africa.

27. For a more detailed look into the worldwide female GenX phenomenon, see my forthcoming article "Girls Who Interrupt: Going Global with the *Bad Girls* of Generation X."

28. Gonzalo Navajas begins his essay by proposing a series of methodological approaches. The third one is of particular interest to this project because he defines the new approach as a paradigmatic, correlational method. According to this method, the text should be located in a framework that is transtemporal and multidirectional. For example, he suggests that to study fiction of the last twenty years one must connect it to texts written by the likes of Milan Kundera, José Agustín, and Arturo Pérez Reverte; the visual art of Magritte and Andy Warhol; and the cinema of Almodóvar, Bigas Luna, David Lynch, and Woody Allen. Navajas calls for an end to the isolating supremacy of the written word, believing a new intercommunicative phase has been inaugurated (149).

29. I am conscious of the schizophrenic nature of this reading experience, from the disorientation, instability, and possible blanks left along the way, to the positive critical spaces that may unfold between the boxes.

30. My intellectual endeavor in this book builds upon and relies on the work of scholars such as Espen Aarseth, David Jay Bolter, Janet Murray, Katherine Hayles, and Marie-Laure Ryan. They directly contend with the intersecting qualities and differences between literary criticism and media studies.

31. For a valuable analysis of Spanish women writers of the 1990s not centered on GenX writers alone, see Carmen de Urioste's article "Narrative of Spanish Women Writers of the Nineteen Nineties: An Overview."

32. Nina Molinaro confirms that gender is an important identity marker that has not received enough critical attention: "Although scholars uniformly include women authors among the members of the generation, rarely do they follow up inclusion with any sustained analysis; likewise, considerations of gender infrequently make their way into the existing critical analyses of the novels written by these new narrators ("Alterity" 7).

1   Tales of Generation X

1. See Paul Begin's "The Pistols Strike Again! On the Function of Punk in Peninsular 'Generation X' Fiction of Ray Loriga and Benjamin Prado."

2. Over half of the young people interviewed for this project were from Western societies (Ulrich 5).

3. For insight into these GenX'er lives in 2005, see "Whatever Happened to the Original Generation X?" *The Observer.* Sunday, Jan. 23, 2005.
   <http://www.guardian.co.uk/uk/2005/jan/23/britishidentity.anushka-asthana>

4. The last song on this album was "Ready, Steady, Go!," referring to a British television rock music show first broadcast in 1963 that revolutionized the airwaves. In this song, Idol proclaimed his love for rock and roll and complemented his tune with other more extreme pieces like "One Hundred Punks" or "Revenge."

5. Others affiliated with this group are Susan Minot, Donna Tartt, Peter Farrelly, and David Leavitt.

6. For more information about the marketing of Mañas, Loriga, and Etxebarria, see my article "Pop, Punk, and Rock and Roll."

7. One of the few critics to determine the relationship between the Spanish *Movida* and Generation X is Paul Begin.

8. Daniel Grassian considers Annesley's characterization of blank fiction as preferring "blank, atonal perspectives, and fragile glassy visions" (3), a "gross generalization that carries a derogatory connotation of insubstantiability" (18). He argues that young American fiction writings of the 1990s are, rather, intellectually and culturally rich. (18). I think Grassian oversimplifies Annesley's arguments. Annesley argues for greater cultural content and significance *within* the commercial blankness that defines certain examples of contemporary American fiction. It is essential to recognize the levels of blankness and depth of content and form inherent in a variety of Generation X texts.

9. I would like to thank Cintia Santana for reviewing and providing input on this section.

10. The role of consumption is well analyzed in *Becoming and Consumption: The Contemporary Spanish Novel* by Candice L. Bosse.
    Much like the wealthy, white yuppies portrayed by Bret Easton Ellis, Tama Janowitz, and Jay McInerney, Spanish GenX characters were located within a society of excess, be it mind-altering substances, sexual, physical, musical, or electronic excesses (as in the case of Benjamín Prado's *Nunca le des la mano a un pistolero zurdo* or Ray Loriga's *Lo peor de todo*).

11. By basing her study on a profound continuity between the past and the present, Moreiras Menor places GenX fiction within "las ruinas de [. . .] unos fantasmas que siguen vivos y sin enterrar: esos espectros del pasado cuya presencia de alguna manera imposibilitan tanto la total clausura con la anterioridad democrática como la libertad de mirar hacia un futuro esperanzador" [the ruins of some phantasms that remain alive and without burial: those specters of the past whose presence somehow make impossible the total separation from a former democracy or the freedom to look into a hopeful future] (*Cultura* 17). In addition, she views GenX characters' constant movement and search for instantaneous experiences as a reduction of meaning to sound bites that, she says, ultimately lead to empty fictions (208).

12. When Moreiras Menor talks about the role of violence in the work of young writers of the 1990s, she folds within that category the novels of GenX writers like Mañas and Loriga and texts and films by artists not related to this group, and of a different age group altogether, such as Muñoz Molina (b. 1956) or Vázquez Montalbán (b. 1939).

13. Teresa Vilarós supports Moreiras's thesis by claiming that Generation X novels can "be conceptualized as a marked, scarred corpus. They were spectacular 'lites,' massively successful in the new market of mass consumption. Yet an encrypted discourse comes into play in them. Emerging as new post-modern urban narratives, they offer themselves as a tensed, and often violent, spectacle implicated in the negation of difference" ("The Novel" 257).

14. Examples might include the novel *Tirón* (2000) by Luis Ondarra or Gutiérrez Solís's *La novela de un novelista malaleche* (1999).

2   Punked Out and Smelling Like Afterpop

1. Mark Allinson views the *Movida* activity of the 1980s through a prism of nostalgia and veneration marked by the creativity, irony, parody, and postmodernism of the work of Pedro Almodóvar and Fernando Colomo, who presented Spain with new signifiers to deal with the contemporary city.

2. http://en.wikipedia.org/wiki/New_Wave_music
    As Hispanist Yaw Agawu-Kakraba proposes, "Contrary to the general belief that the *movida* ended in the late 1980's—[. . .] a mutated form of the movement's ethos is still prevalent and fundamental in Spain" (24).

3. It is worth mentioning that although Mañas was dubbed the "father" of this generation, his novel was not the first Generation X text; it was *Lo peor de todo* by Ray Loriga, published in 1992.

4. For another study on Mañas's punk essay, see Carmen de Urioste's "Cultura punk: la 'Tetralogía Kronen' de José Ángel Mañas o el arte de hacer ruido."

5. See Yaw Agawu-Kakraba's essay "José Ángel Mañas's Literature of Insurgency" for an excellent look at the aesthetic debates surrounding the appearance of Generation X writers.

6. Paul Julian Smith suggests that a similar reinforcement of traditional values between high and low cultural production occurs in the film industry where critics believe that Spanish directors like Medem are needed to "directly engage with notions of Spanishness" (4).

7. As theorized by Raymond Federman in *Surfiction: Fiction Now and Tomorrow*, or as expressed by Robert Siegle in *Suburban Ambush: Downtown Writing and the Fiction of Insurgency*.

8. Of course, the works of Jorge Luis Borges and Italo Calvino, among others, anticipate this process of jacking into the television or computer screen.

9. I would like to thank Agustín Fernández Mallo for this insight and Carlos Manuel Gámez Pérez for forwarding to me the interesting interview with Eloy Fernández Porta.

10. A version of this section of the chapter appeared in the journal *MLN*.

11. Robert Spires believes that *Historias* "does not qualify as a major work of art since it lacks the linguistic and structural finesse that combine to create for the reader a personal and transcending experience" ("José" 234). I believe the novel combines a linguistic and structural value to be reckoned with in the Spanish literary canon, one that, as Spires proposes, deals "with a whole new concept of what constitutes a work of art" ("José" 234). This value is based on an entirely different set of analytical standards, which translate the visual and aural effects of commercial art and the technological effects of the mass media—in this case, television—into a new literary style.

12. The image of Andy Warhol's orange car crash is reversed in subsequent editions of the book.

13. Carmen de Urioste examines the function of the bar in the four novels that comprise Mañas's "tetralogía Kronen," including *Historias del Kronen*, *Mensaka* (1995), *Ciudad rayada* (1998), and *Sonko95* (1999). She finds that there is an evolution in the subject's relation to space. While in his first three novels characters take on an external position in relation to the bar, in *Sonko95*, the bar appears as protagonist ("Cultura" 8).

14. Carlos is the exception, not the norm of Spain's youth, as Randolph Pope asserts in "Between Rock and the Rocking Chair" (121).

15. See Yaw Agawu-Kakraba's essay "José Ángel Mañas's Literature of Insurgency" for an interpretation of the role of the song within a larger youth cultural context.

16. See Matthew Marr who believes that the song "The Giant" presents "a kind of surrogate conscience for the remorseless and puerile Carlos" (11).

3 Generation MTV

1. My former student at Cornell University, Alfredo J. Sosa-Velasco, is the only Hispanist who has published an essay on "video clip literature" as it relates to *Héroes* by Ray Loriga and notions of "the subject in process" by Julia Kristeva.

2. Ann Kaplan theorized in *Rocking Around the Clock* that "MTV's construction of a decentered spectator indicates recognition of the alienated world teenagers confront" (47). As the analysis in my book hopefully makes clear, I do not agree with this negative assessment of the world at the end of the century. Although one could claim that Generation X is inherently a youth culture based on alienation, I do not believe a direct association can be made between the techniques used in music video clips and society at large, especially if one believes, as I do, that "decentering" can lead to a positive appropriation of different realms of meaning making.

3. See my essay in *Generation X Rocks* for another take on Loriga's *Héroes* in relation to music video clips.

4. www.publico.es/culturas/59286/llamalo/nocilla

5. Eva Navarro Martínez also makes reference to the influence of the video in the work of Mañas and Loriga in her essay "Una realidad a la carta: la televisión en algunas novelas de la última década del siglo XX."

4   From MTV to the *Real* World of Generation X Fiction

1. I would like to thank my student, Lauren Brown, for making me aware of this information.

    I would also like to thank Nina Molinaro, Debra Castillo, and Gabriela Bustelo for their suggestions for improvement of this chapter.

2. See Silvio Waisbord.

3. "The concept of 'Television without Frontiers' (TWF) is based on the free movement of European television programmes within the internal market and on the introduction of broadcasting quotas (the requirement that television channels reserve over half of their broadcasting time for European works). The 'Television without Frontiers' directive is the cornerstone of audiovisual policy in the European Community. It aims to safeguard certain important public interest objectives, such as cultural diversity, protection of minors (measures against programmes of a violent or pornographic nature) and the right of reply. Detailed rules on the content and frequency of television advertising have also been introduced." http://europa.eu/scadplus/glossary/television_without_frontiers_en.htm

4. The term "transculturation" is applied in the Latin American context because of the resonance of Fernando Ortiz's 1940's term for Cuban society. I would like to thank Juan Manuel Espinosa for this insight.

5. http://www.endemol.com/programme/big-brother

6. http://en.wikipedia.org/wiki/Big_Brother_1999_(Netherlands)

7. According to Endemol's website, *Big Brother* is now being viewed in forty-two different countries around the world. http://www.endemol.com/programme/big-brother

8. http://en.wikipedia.org/wiki/Big_Brother_(TV_series)#Near-copies_of_Big_Brother

9. http://worldofbigbrother.com/BB/Stats/Stats-General.shtml

10. For a case study of Spain's *telebasura* [trash TV] and reality television program *Crónicas marcianas* [Martian Chronicles] see Paul Julian Smith's book *Television in Spain: From Franco to Almodóvar.*

11. Some critics have linked this move toward reality television's private, interior spaces to a "feminine" or "feminization" of the genre, which no doubt has led to some of the negative critiques that sweepingly disregard reality television shows as insignificant and superficial.

12. Hispanist Candice Bosse, in *Becoming and Consumption: The Contemporary Spanish Novel*, analyzes *Veo veo* through the work of Italian philosopher Rosi Braidotti. She emphasizes Vania's practices of consumption in light of the myriad ways in which she undermines and challenges the male gaze and fixed, stable notions of gender identity. Instead, I propose a shift in paradigm, in this case toward the format and function of reality television shows. The shows' focus on authenticity, immediacy, and meta-mediacy suggests that alternative ways of construction are taking place. When we

decentralize the text by acknowledging its presence and fluid reinterpreta-
tions in a variety of media, and we break down the "text" into bits and
pieces that are appropriated from a variety of aural and visual sources, I
believe we can move "beyond gender" and better embody Bustelo's own
postfeminist position.

13. The time span of the action of the book is not clear, but one can surmise
that approximately two weeks go by thanks to a passage on page 106 that
speaks to the moment when Vania entered the office of Peláez, and Peláez
first stayed overnight at her place, from Saturday the sixth to Tuesday the
sixteenth. A reference to four years after the *Movida* appears on page 12.
In an e-mail exchange, Gabriela Bustelo verifies these clues by explaining
that,

> la novela transcurre a finales de los ochenta —principios de los
> noventa, cuando la Movida estaba empezando a acabarse. La info de
> contracubierta es correcta, pero la acción no transcurre a mediados
> de los ochenta (que todavía era plena Movida) sino a finales. Ten en
> cuenta que una de las películas emblemáticas de la Movida, 'Mujeres
> al borde de un ataque de nervios' de Almodóvar, se estrenó en 1988,
> por ejemplo, y 'Escuela de calor' de Radio Futura, un disco punt-
> ero de la época, salió en 1989. La protagonista lleva saliendo por
> la noche desde que es adolescente (antes, durante y después de la
> Movida).

> [the novel takes place at the end of the 1980s—beginning of the
> 1990s—when the *Movida* was starting to end. The information on
> the back cover is correct, but the action does not take place in the mid-
> 1980s (which was still in the middle of the *Movida*) but at the end.
> A fact to be considered is that one of the *Movida's* most emblematic
> movies was "Mujeres al borde de un ataque de nervios" by Almodóvar,
> shown in 1989. The protagonist has been going out at night since she
> was a teenager (before, during, and after the *Movida*)].

14. I would like to thank Debra Castillo for this observation.
15. Although taking a different critical perspective, Candice Bosse also determines that in *Veo veo* the backlash against authority and linearity is acknowledged through the absence of a singular tightly woven plot; one that is
mediated by a variety of discourses such as pop-psychology, detective literature, and popular media and culture. Furthermore, the defiance embodied
in this transgression is influenced by three factors: the temporal, the spatial,
and the affectual. (119)
16. I would like to thank Nina Molinaro for her thoughts regarding the connection between the final words of the novel and its relationship to the "feedback loop" as a commentary on technology or reality television.

5   From Generation X to the *Mutantes*

1. Vicente Luis Mora, in "Últimas tendencias del cuento actual: del decálogo
del perfecto cuentista al listado de Google," believes that part of today's
literature is based on "randominización," a certain level of informational
chaos based on Web searches.
2. I am stressing the term "mutante" over others because it speaks directly to
narrative function and form, independent of any particular group members.

"Nocilla" restricts the group to the work of Mallo's "Nocilla trilogy," and "After-Pop" confines it to the theoretical work of Eloy Fernández Porta.

3. See my personal webpage for more information on the "Hybrid Storyspaces" conference and working paper series.

4. One of the material dynamics that underlines this connection, but should not be confused as the category, is the often close personal and professional association between typical X'ers and *Mutantes*. They appear together in many publications and in conferences, including the *I Encuentro de Nuevos Narradores*, hosted by Germán Sierra in 2004, which included the likes of Lucía Etxebarria, Luisa Castro, and Josán Hatero next to Porta, Mallo, etc. In my own "Hybrid Storyspaces" conference the close connections and friendships between Latin American writers and Spanish authors also became readily apparent, as was the case with McOndo writer Edmundo Paz Soldán and Vicente Luis Mora. The conference program of Sierra's event may be found at http://homepage.mac.com/germansierra/fgtb.html

5. Important to note here is that despite the *Mutantes'* incursions into multimedia platforms and their varied disciplinary backgrounds, many of them are professors of Spanish literature and film. They are highly knowledgeable of Spanish and international literary history and often include literary references into their texts. As Ray Loriga pronounced in the 1990s, just because he does not apply traditional literary models to his texts does not mean that he has not been formed by works from Spanish literary history. He just chooses not to use them.

6. Carrión's book trailer may be found at: http://www.jorgecarrion.com/
   "Proyecto Nocilla, la película" by Agustín Fernández Mallo may be found at: http://blogs.alfaguara.com/fernandezmallo/

7. In 1961, Steven Russell, Wayne Wittanan, and J. M. Graetz were enlisted to create a series of demonstration programs of a large mainframe computer. They developed several interactive programs, ranging from Bouncing Ball, Mouse in the Maze, HAX, and Tic Tac Toe, but they did not attract the attention of the public because of their small role in the games. It was not until they developed a more interactive game, *Spacewar*, based on the science fiction novels of chemist Edward Smith called *Skylark*, that they attracted attention. The game was simple but effective: players were engaged in galactic warfare and they had to fire torpedoes at each other; they could turn and increase or decrease their thrust (Egenfeldt-Nielsen 50–51).

8. See Espen Aarseth's "Genre Trouble: Narrativism and the Art of Simulation," Gonzalo Frasca's "Simulation vs. Narrative: Introduction to Ludology", and Henry Jenkins's "Game Design as Narrative Architecture."

9. My own entrance into video game theory, as a literary critic, has been hands-on. As a non-gamer, I realized that in order to understand the material dynamics of video games I had to begin to play a variety of different games on various consoles. I also attended two "Games for Change" conferences in New York City (in 2008 and 2009), and I co-created and taught a course titled "Digital Games for Social Change" with a colleague in the Department of Ccomputer Science at Union College.

10. I would like to thank my student Robert Moore for this information.

11. I play here with the title of the multiplayer online game *World of Warcraft*.

12. I have written about this novel in *Romance Quarterly* in honor of John Kronik.

6   Generation X and the *Mutantes*, A Mash-Up

1. Other books of poetry include *Yo siempre regreso a los pezones y al punto 7 del Tractatus* (2001), *Creta, lateral travelling* (2009), and *Joan Fontaine Odisea (mi deconstrucción)* (2005).
2. I would like to thank Agustín Fernández Mallo for reading this chapter and adding suggestions and remarks.
3. See my piece "Ode to Trash: The Spam Poetics of Agustín Fernández Mallo" for a more detailed analysis on the subject.
4. A version of this essay also appeared in *Cuadernos Hispanoamericanos*, 721/722, July-August (2010) under the title "Acerca de lo que pienso."
5. All translations presented of Mallo's essay "Tiempo topológico" derive from Emily Eaton's translation of the text for the Hybrid Storyspaces volume compiled by Christine Henseler and Debra Castillo.
6. For an excellent review of reviews that focus on Borges and technology, see Andrew Brown's "Retasking Borges: Technology and the Desire for a Borgesian Present."

Conclusion   Generation X Remixed: A Conversation

1. To allow this conversation to spill out of the pages of this book, I have set up a page on my website
2. I would like to thank my student Laura Brown from Union College for this excellent description of Generation X'ers.
3. Given my focus on media technologies in this book, research into women Generation X'ers resides outside the scope of this project, but may be found in forthcoming articles. In addition, as my remarks in the introduction underscore, the reach of Generation X is of global proportions, which I examine at length in my forthcoming edited volume *Generation X Goes Global.*

Works Cited

Aarseth, Espen. "Computer Game Studies, Year One." *Game Studies* 1.1 (2001). Web. Nov. 22, 2009. <http://gamestudies.org/0101/editorial.html>

———. "Genre Trouble: Narrativism and the Art of Simulation."*First Person: New Media as Story, Performance, and Game.* Ed. Noah Wardrip-Fruin and Pat Harrigan. Cambridge: MIT Press, 2006. 45–56. Print.

Agawu-Kakraba, Yaw. "José Ángel Mañas's Literature of Insurgency: *Historias del Kronen.*" *Revista Hispánica Moderna* 55.1 (2002): 188–203. Print

———. *Postmodernity in Spanish Fiction and Culture.* Chicago: University of Chicago Press, 2010. Print.

"Agustín Fernández Mallo." *El Cultural: Letras.* April 1, 2007. Web. December 23, 2010. <http://www.candaya.com/nocilladream.htm>

Allinson, Mark. "The Construction of Youth in Spain in the 1980s and 1990s." *Contemporary Spanish Cultural Studies.* Eds. Barry Jordan and Rikki Morgan-Tamosunas. Oxford: Oxford University Press, 2000. 265–73. Print.

Amago, Samuel. "Can Anyone Rock Like We Do?" *Generation X Rocks: Contemporary Peninsular Fiction, Film, and Rock Culture.* Eds. Christine Henseler and Randolph Pope. Nashville: Vanderbilt University Press, 2007. 59–77. Print.

———. "Horror and Ambivalence in *Tesis*: Alejandro Amenábar's Reflections on the Postmodern Condition." *Revista de Estudios Hispánicos* 38 (2004): 143–58.

Amerika, Mark. "Avant-Pop Manifesto: Thread Baring Itself in Ten Quick Posts." N. date. Web. July 20, 2009. <www.altx.com/manifestions/avant-pop.manifesto.html>

———. "In Memoriam to Post-Modernism." N. date. Web. June 10, 2008. <www.altx.com/memoriam/pomo.html>

———. "Why Avant-Pop Is Still Cool." July 7, 2008. Web. Dec. 9, 2009. <http://professorvj.blogspot.com/2008/07/why-avant-pop-is-still-cool-historical.html>

America, Mark, and Alexander Laurence. "Interview with Bret Easton Ellis." *The Write Stuff.* N. d. Web. Nov. 8, 2008. <www.altx.com/int2/bret.easton.ellis.html>

Andrejevic, Mark. *Reality TV: The Work of Being Watched.* New York: Rowman and Littlefield Publishers, Inc., 2004. Print.

———. "The Kinder, Gentler Gaze of Big Brother: Reality TV in the Era of Digital Capitalism." *New Media and Society* 4 (2002): 251–70.

Andrés, Jesús. "Providence o la lógica cultural del capitalismo avanzado." *Salonkritik* Dec. 29, 2009. Web. July, 23, 2010. <http://salonkritik.net/09–10/2009/12/providence_o_la_logica_cultura.php>

Andrews, Margaret, and Anny Brooksbank Jones. "Registering Spanish Feminisms." *Contemporary Spanish Cultural Studies.* Eds. Barry Jordan and Rikki Morgan-Tamosunas. London: Arnold, 2000. 233–40. Print.

Annesley, James. *Blank Fictions: Consumerism, Culture and the Contemporary American Novel*. London, Pluto Press, 1998. Print.

Añover, Verónica. "Feminismo y literatura en la España del nuevo milenio: Encuentro con Lucía Etxebarria." *Letras Peninsulares* 17.1 (Spring 2004): 181–92. Print.

Arbilla, Iñaki. "Caminando por el lado de la literatura salvaje." *El Planeta* June (1998): n.p. Print.

Aufderheide, Pat. "Music Videos: The Look of the Sound." *Journal of Communication* 36–1 (1986 Winter): 57–78. Print.

Azancot, Nuria. "La generación Nocilla y el afterpop piden paso." *El Cultural*. July 19, 2007. Web. June 10, 2009. <www.elcultural.es/version_papel /LETRAS/21006/La_generacion_Nocilla_y_el_afterpop_piden_paso>

Ballesteros, Isolina. "Juventudes problemáticas en el cine de los ochenta y noventa: comportamientos generacionales y globales en la era de la indiferencia." *Cine (Ins) Urgente: Textos fílmicos y contextos culturales de la España postfranquista*. Madrid: Fundamentos, 2001. 233–70. Print.

Bakhtin, Mikhail. *The Dialogic Imagination: Four Essays by M. M. Bakhtin*. Austin: University of Texas Press Slavic Series, 1982.

Banks, Jack. *Monopoly Television: MTV's Quest to Control the Music*. Boulder, CO: Westview Press, 1996. Print.

Barker, Jesse. *No Place Like Home: Virtual Space, Local Places and Nocilla Fictions*. Diss. The University of British Columbia, 2011. Print.

Barthes, Roland. *Image, Music, Text*. New York: Hill and Wang, 1978. Print.

Baudrillard, Jean. "Ballard's *Crash*." *Science-Fiction Studies*. 18 (1991): 313–30. Print.

———. *Simulacra and Simulation*. Ann Arbor, Mich.: University of Michigan Press, 1981. Print.

Beets, Greg. "Blow Up Your Video: We Wanted Our MTV, We Damn Sure Got It." *The Austin Chronicle*. Aug. 2, 2001. Web. Aug. 22, 2010. <http://www.austinchronicle.com/music/2001–08-03/82541/>

Begin, Paul. "The Pistols Strike Again! On the Function of Punk in the Peninsular 'Generation X' Fiction of Ray Loriga and Benjamín Prado." *Generation X Rocks: Contemporary Peninsular Fiction, Film, and Rock Culture*. Eds. Christine Henseler and Randolph Pope. Nashville: Vanderbilt University Press, 2007. 15–33. Print.

Bego, Mark. "The Madonna/Pepsi Controversy." "The Eighties Club: The Politics and Pop Culture of the 1980s." N.d. Web. August 22, 2010. <http://eightiesclub.tripod.com/id135.htm>

Bellver, Catherine. "Division, Duplication, and Doubling in the Novels of Ana María Moix." *Nuevos y novísimos: Algunas perspectivas críticas sobre la narrativa española desde la década de los 60*. Eds. Ricardo Landeira and Luis T. González-del-Valle. *Society of Spanish and Spanish-American Studies*. 1987. 29–41. Print.

Bender, Mark. "Suzhou Tanci Storytelling in China: Contexts of Performance." *Oral Tradition* 13.2 (1998): 330–76. Print.

Bengoa, María. "Las descaradas chicas Etxebarria." *El Correo Español* 21 Apr. (1999): 56. Print.

Bennet, Andy. "Subcultures or Neo-tribes? Rethinking the Relationship Between Youth, Style and Musical Taste. *Sociology* 33.3 August (1999): 599–617. Print.

Berg, Gretchen. "Nothing to Lose: An Interview with Andy Warhol." *Andy Warhol: Film Factory*. Ed. Michael O'Pray. London: BFI, 1989. 54–61. Print.

Berger, John. *Ways of Seeing.* London: Penguin, 1972. Print.

Bergin. Paul. "Andy Warhol: The Artist as Machine." *Art Journal* 26–4 (1967): 359–63. Print.

Berland, Jody. "Sound, Image and Social Space: Music Video and Media Reconstruction." *Sound and Vision: The Music Video Reader.* Eds. Simon Frith et al. London: Routledge, 1993. 25–43. Print.

Berners-Lee. Tim. "Frequently Asked Questions." N. date. Web. Dec. 22, 2010. <www.w3.org/People/Berners-Lee/FAQ.html>

Bethke, Bruce. "Cyberpunk: A Short Story by Bruce Bethke." N. pag. Web. Nov. 8, 2008. <www.infinityplus.co.uk/stories/cpunk.htm>

Bockris, Victor and Gerard Malanga. *Up-Tight: The Velvet Underground Story.* London: Omnibus Press, 2002. Print.

Book Review: *Prozac Nation.* (Movie Tie-In). *Penguin.com* (USA). N. d. Web. March 20, 2009. <http://us.penguingroup.com/nf/Book/BookDisplay/0,,0 _9781573229623,00.html?sym=REV>

Booth, William. "Reality Is Only an Illusion, Writers Say." *L.A. Washington Post.* Aug. 10 2004. Web. June 16, 2009. <www.doubletongued.org/index.php /dictionary/frankenbite>

Borges, Jorge Luis. *El hacedor.* Barcelona: Alianza Editorial, 1960. Print.

"Borrón y traje nuevo: Ray Loriga bucea en la pérdida de la memoria en su nueva novela." *La Razón* 27 Feb. (1999): 17. Print.

Bosse, Candice L. *Becoming and Consumption: The Contemporary Spanish Novel.* Lanham, MD: Lexington Books, 2007. Print.

———. "El sujeto femenino y las culturas de consumo: una entrevista con Gabriela Bustelo." *Letras Hispanas* 2.1 (2005): N.p. Web. Pdf.

Bourland Ross, Catherine. "Sex, Drugs and Violence in Lucía Etxebarria's *Amor, curiosidad, prozac y dudas.*" *Novels of the Contemporary Extreme.* Eds. Alain-Philippe Durand and Naomi Mandel. New York: Continuum, 2008. 153–62. Print.

Bourriaud, Nicolas. *The Radicant.* New York, Sternberg Press, 2009. Print.

Braidotti, Rosi. *Nomadic Subjects: Embodiment and Sexual Difference in Contemporary Feminist Theory.* New York: Columbia University Press, 1994. Print.

Broderick, Mick. Hibakusha Cinema: *Editor's Introduction.* N.d. Web. June 18, 2008. <wwwmcc.murdoch.edu.au/~mickbrod/postmodm/m/text/hibakeds.html>

Brown, Andrew. "Retasking Borges: Technology and the Desire for a Borgesian Present." *Variaciones Borges* 28 (2009): 232–39. Print.

Buchanan, Mark. *Nexus: Small Worlds and the Groundbreaking Science of Networks.* New York: Norton, 2002. Print.

Bustelo, Gabriela. *Planeta Hembra.* Madrid: RBA Literaria, 2001.

———. *Veo veo.* Barcelona: Anagrama, 1996.

———. Message to Christine Henseler. 15 Jan., 2010. E-mail.

Cairns, Craig. *The Modern Scottish Novel: Narrative and the National Imagination.* Edinburgh: Edinburgh University Press, 1999. Print.

Calles, Jara. "Necesidades—en plural—ante una Literatura de las Nuevas Tecnologías." *Redacciones.* Various Authors. Valladolid: Caslon, 2011. 47–71. Print.

Cañada, Javier. "The User Experience Cosmos (V. 1.1): A Personal Representation of our Space." Blog. *Terremoto.net.* Jan. 15, 2004. Web. June 21, 2011. <www .terremoto.net/uxcosmos/UX_cosmos_javier_canada.pdf>

Carnutt, Kirk. "Generation X's Identity Politics, Consumer Culture, and the Making of a Generation." *GenXegesis: Essays on Alternative Youth (Sub)culture.* Madison, WI: Popular Press, 2003. 162–83. Print.

Caro Martín, Adelaida. *América te lo he dado todo y ahora no soy nada*. Berlin: LIT Verlag, 2007. Print.

Carrión, Jorge. *La Brújula*. Córdoba: Berenice 2006. Print.

Cascone, Kim. "Las estéticas del error: las tendencias 'post-digitales' en la música contemporánea por computadora." *Computer Music Journal* 24.4 (2000): 12–18. Print.

Castells, Manuel. *The Rise of the Network Society*. New York: Blackwell Publisher, 1996. Print.

Chaney, D. *The Cultural Turn: Scene Setting Essays on Contemporary Cultural History*. London: Routledge, 1994.

Chiappe, Doménico. "Teme la literatura al lobo digital." *Literatúrame: Actualidad didáctica y literaria*. Jan 11, 2010. Web. Nov. 21, 2010. <http://literaturame. net/2010/01/11/¿teme-la-literatura-al-lobo-digital/>

Clissold, Bradley D. "Candid Camera and the Origins of Reality TV." *Understanding Reality Television*. Eds. Su Holmes and Deborah Jermyn London: Routledge, 2004. 33–52. Print.

Colmeiro, José F. "En busca de la Generación X: ¿héroes por un día o una nueva generación perdida?" *España Contemporánea* 14.1 (2001): 7–26. Print.

Colón Rodríguez, Raúl Ernesto. "La generación X en el poder." Jan. 19, 2009. Web. June 3, 2011. <http://www.kaosenlared.net/noticia/la-generacion-x-en -el-poder>

Corner, John. "Performing the Real: Documentary Diversions." *Television New Media* 3 (2002): 255–69.

Corroto, Paula. "La Generación X se hace mayor." *Público.es* July 28, 2008. Web. July 18, 2009. <www.publico.es/culturas/138082/generacion/x/mayor>

Cortés, José Angel. *La estrategia de la seducción. La programación en la neotele-visión*. Pamplona: Eunsa, 1999. Print.

Couldry, Nick. *Media Rituals: A Critical Approach*. New York: Routledge, 2003. Print.

Coupland, Douglas. *Generación X*. Barcelona: Ediciones B, 1993.

———. *Generation X: Tales of an Accelerated Culture*. New York: St. Martin's Press, 1991. Print.

———. "Eulogy: Generation X'd." *Details* June (1995): 72. Print.

———. "Photoshop = Pop Art." *Time Capsules: Douglas Coupland. The New York Times*. Aug. 13, 2006. Web. Sept 26, 2008. <http://coupland.blogsnytimes. com/2006/08/13/photoshop-pop-art>

———. "Plastic Planet—Douglas Coupland Interview." *You Tube*. N.d. Web. June 20, 2011. <www.youtube.com/watch?v=k_ki_93LEZk>

Cover, Rob. "Audience Inter/Active: Interactive Media, Narrative Control and Reconceiving Audience History." *New Media and Society* 8.1 (2006): 139–58. Print.

Crawford, Chris. *Chris Crawford on Game Design*. New York: New Riders Games, 2003. Print.

Crisafulli, Chuck. *Nirvana: The Stories Behind Every Song*. New York: Da Capo Press, 2003. Print.

Dalmau, Miguel. "Voces de una conciencia rockera." *El Mundo* Nov. 26 (1993): n.p. Print.

"David Bowie Heroes." N.d. Web. July 29, 2004. <www.up-to-date.com/bowie /heroes>

Davies, Jude. "The Future of 'No Future': Punk Rock and Postmodern Theory." *The Journal of Popular Culture*. 29.4 (2004): 3–25. Print.

Davis, Monae A. "Hip-Hop and Product Placement: The Struggle to 'Keep It Real.'" N. d. Web. June 3, 2011. <http://dialogues.rutgers.edu/vol_05/essays/documents/davis.pdf>

Deleuze, Giles and Félix Guattari: *A Thousand Plateaus: Capitalism and Schizophrenia*. St. Paul: University of Minnesota Press, 1987. Print.

De Riquer I Permanyer, Borja. "Social and Economic Change in a Climate of Political Immobilism." *Spanish Cultural Studies*. Ed. Helen Graham and Jo Labanyi. Oxford: Oxford UP, 1995. 259–70. Print.

Delvaux, Martine. "The Exit of a Generation: The 'Whatever' Philosophy." *The Midwest Quarterly* (1999): 171–86. Print.

Dickinson, Kay. *Movie Music, The Film Reader*. New York: Routledge, 2003. Print.

DJ Dictionary. N. d. Web. December 24, 2009. <www.famousdjs.com/dj_dictionary.htm>

Dorca, Toni. "Joven narrativa en la España de los noventa: la generación X." *Revista de Estudios Hispánicos* 31 (1997): 309–24. Print.

"Drogas, sexo, y un dictador nuerto: 1978 on Vinyl in Spain." June 4, 2008. Web. March 25, 2009. <www.shit-fi.com/Articles/Spain1978/Spain1978.htm>

Druckrey, Timothy. "Introduction." *Electronic Culture: Technology and Visual Representation*. Ed. Timothy Druckrey. New York: Aperture, 1996. 12–25. Print.

Durand, Alain-Philippe and Naomi Mandel, eds. *Novels of the Contemporary Extreme*. New York: Continuum, 2006. Print.

During, Simon, ed. "Dick Hebdige: From Culture to Hegemony." *The Cultural Studies Reader*. London: Routledge, 1993. 357–67. Print.

Echevarría, Ignacio. "El fugitivo de una generación." *Babelia*, Jan. 31, (2004): 2–3. Print.

———. "Un artista del 'rocanrollo': el cuaderno de canciones de Ray Loriga." *Babelia* Nov. 27 (1993): 11. Print.

Egenfeldt-Nielsen, Simon, Jonas Heide Smith, et al. *Understanding Video Games: The Essential Introduction*. New York: Routledge, 2008. Print.

"El hombre que inventó Manhattan." *Clubcultura* N. d. Web. March 28, 2009. <www.clubcultura.com/clubliteratura/rayloriga>

"El problema de las drogas en España." N. d. Web. Aug. 1, 2008. <www.romance-languages.pomona.edu/coffey/newspain/2004Projects/Pat_Andrew_Bobback/Drogas.htm>

Ellis, Bret Easton. *American Psycho*. New York: Vintage Books, 1991. Print.

———. *Less Than Zero*. London: Simon and Shuster, 1985. Print.

Ernst, Thomas. *Popliteratur*. Hamburg: Rotbuch Verlag, 2001. Print.

"Escritor español Kiko Amat critica 'desconexión de literatura con la calle." *Soitu. es*. May 7, 2009. Web. June 20, 2010. <http://www.soitu.es/soitu/2009/05/07/info/1241651353_613631.html>

Estafanía, Joaquín. "La marcha larga." *El País Domingo*. May 3, 1998. Web. July 30, 2008. <http://www.vespito.net/historia/franco/estft.html>

Estrada, Isabel. "Victimismo y violencia en la ficción de la Generación X: *Matando dinosaurios con tirachinas* de Pedro Maestre." *Ciberletras* 6 (Jan. 2002). N. d. Web. Jan. 3, 2008. <www.lehman.cuny.edu/ciberletras/v06/estrada.html>

Ettler, Justine. *The River Ophelia: An Uncompromising Love Story*. Picador, 1995. Print.

Everly, Kathryn. "Beauty and Death as Simulacra in Ray Loriga's *Caídos del cielo* and *El hombre que inventó Manhatten*." *Novels of the Contemporary Extreme*.

Eds. Alain-Philippe Durand and Naomi Mandel. New York: Continuum, 2008. 143–52. Print.

———. *History, Violence and the Hyperreal: Representing Culture in the Contemporary Spanish Novel*. Purdue, Purdue University Press, 2010. Print.

Etxebarria, Lucía. *Amor, curiosidad, prozac y dudas*. Barcelona: Plaza y Janés, 1997. Print.

———. *Beatriz y los cuerpos celestes*. Barcelona: Destino, 1998. Print.

———. *La Eva futura/ La letra futura*. Barcelona: Destino, 2000. Print.

Farah, Samar. "Can Reality TV 'Survive' in the Middle East?" *The Christian Science Monitor*. 26 March 2004. Web. May 10 2011. <www.csmonitor.com/2004/0326/p13s02-altv.html>

Faulkner, Sally. *Literary Adaptations in Spanish Cinema*. Tamesis Books, 2004.

Federman, Raymond. *Surfiction: Fiction Now and Tomorrow*. N. place: Swallow Press, 1975.

Feixa, Carles, María del Carmen Costa, and Joan Pallarés. "Movimientos juveniles en Cataluña: de los okupas a los ravers." 1999. Web. Nov. 10, 2010. <http://www.oocities.org/terrats/jovenes/feixa.htm>

———. *De jóvenes, bandas y tribus: Antropología de la juventud*. Barcelona: Ariel, 1998. Print.

Fernández, Javier. *Cero Absoluto*. Córdoba: Berenice, 2005.

Fernández Mallo, Agustín. "Apología del error." *El País*. Feb. 2, 2008. Web. Dec. 10, 2010. <http://www.elpais.com/articulo/semana/Apologia/error/elpepucul bab/20080202elpbabese_1/Tes>

———. *El hacedor (de Borges), Remake*. Madrid: Alfaguara, 2011. Print.

———. "Hacia un nuevo paradigma: Poesía Postpoética." N.d. Web. Jan. 11, 2011. <www.circulolateral.com/pdf/mallo_1.pdf>

———. *Nocilla Dream*. Barcelona: Candaya, 2007. Print.

———. *Nocilla Experience*. Madrid: Alfaguara, 2008. Print.

———. *Nocilla Lab*. Madrid: Alfaguara, 2009. Print.

———. *Postpoesía: Hacia un nuevo paradigma*. Barcelona: Anagrama, 2009. Print.

———. "Tiempo topológico en *Proyecto Nocilla* y en *Pospoesía* (y breve apunte para una Exonovela)." *Hybrid Storyspaces* Conference. Cornell University. April 30–May 1, 2010. Reading.

———. "Agustín Fernández Mallo dice adiós al planeta Nocilla." Interview with Antonio Lozano. *Qué leer*. 14. 147 (2009): 64–68. Print, Web. June 20, 2011. <www.alfaguara.santillana.es/blogs/upload/ficheros/queleer.pdf>

———. "Llámalo Nocilla." Interview with Peio H. Riaño. *Público.es*. March, 12, 2008. Web. June, 20, 2011. <www.publico.es/culturas/59286/llamalo/nocilla>

———. "El intrascendente Agustín Fernández Mallo." *Lector iracundo*. Blog. Dec. 28, 2009. Web. June 20, 2011. <http://lectoriracundo.blogspot.com/2009/12/el-intrascendente-agustin-fernandez.html>

Fernández Porta, Eloy. *Afterpop: la literatura de la implosión mediática*. Córdoba: Berenice, 2007. Print.

———. *€®O$ la superproducción de los afectos*. Barcelona: Anagrama, 2010.

———. "Retórica y punk en el relato contemporáneo." *Tbr* 26. Sept-Oct 2001. Web. Jan. 8, 2010. <http://www.barcelonareview.com/26/s_efp.htm>

Fernández Porta, Eloy and Vicente Muñoz Álvarez. *Golpes: Ficciones de la crueldad social*. Barcelona: DVD Ediciones, 2004. Print.

Ferré, Juan Francisco. Message to Christine Henseler. January 7, 2010. E-mail.

Ferré, Juan Francisco and Julio Ortega. *Mutantes: Narrativa española de última generación*. Córdoba: Berenice, 2007. Print.

———. *Providence*. Barcelona: Anagrama, 2011. Print.

Fetveit, Arild. "Reality TV in the Digital Era: A Paradox in Visual Culture?" *Media, Culture and Society* 21.6 (1999): 787–804. Print.

Fichter, Darlene. "What Is a Mash-up?" N. d. Web. Dec. 20, 2010. <www.infotoday. com/books/books/Engard/Engard-Sample-Chapter.pdf>

Foster, Hal. *The Return of the Real*. Cambridge, Mass.: MIT Press, 1996. Print.

Foster Wallace, David. "E Unibus Pluram: Television and U.S. Fiction." *Review of Contemporary Fiction* 13.2 (Summer 1993): 168. Print.

"Fotos de una huida." *Ideal* 6 May (1995): n.p. Print.

Fouce, Héctor. *El futuro ya está aquí: música pop y cambio cultural*. Madrid: Veleció Editores, 2006. Print.

Fouz-Hernández, Santiago. "Generación X? Spanish Urban Youth Culture at the End of the Century in Mañas's/Armendáriz's *Historias del Kronen*." *Romance Studies* 18.1 (2000): 83–98. Print.

Franco, Jean. "Border Patrol." *Travesía* 3 (1993): 134–42. Print.

Frasca, Gonzalo. "Simulation vs. Narrative: Introduction to Ludology." *The Video Game Theory Reader*. Eds. Mark J. P. Wolf and Bernard Perron. New York: Routledge, 2003. 221–36. Print.

Frau-Meigs, Divina. "Big Brother and Reality TV in Europe: Towards a Theory of Situated Acculturation by the Media." *European Journal of Communication* 21.1 (2006): 33–56. Print.

Freese, Peter. "Bret Easton Ellis, Less Than Zero: Entropy in the 'MTV Novel'?" *Modes of Narratives: Approaches to American, Canadian and British Fiction*. Eds. Reingard M. Nischik and Barbara Korte. Würzburg: Königshausen and Neumann, 1990. 68–87. Print.

Frenk, Sue, Chris Perriam and Mike Thompson. "The Literary Avant-garde: A Contradictory Modernity." *Spanish Cultural Studies*. Eds. Helen Graham and Jo Labanyi. Oxford: Oxford University Press, 1995. 63–81. Print.

Friedman, Ted. "Apple's 1984: The Introduction of the Macintosh in the Cultural History of Personal Computers." N. d. Web. Jan. 30, 2008. <www.duke. edu/~tlove/mac.htm>

Fukushina, Yoshiko. "Japanese Literature, or 'J-Literature,' in the 1990s." *World Literature Today* April-June (2003). Web. July 7, 2009. <www.humanities.uci. edu/eastasian/japanese/Courses/Jp101ABC/Jp101C/J-Literature.pdf>

Fukuyama, Francis. "The End of History." *The National Interest*. Summer 1989. Web. Aug. 3, 2008. <www.wesjones.com/eoh.htm>

Fuss, Diana. "Fashion and the Homospectatorial Look." *Critical Inquiry* 18.4 (Summer, 1992): 713–37. Print.

Fussell, Paul. *Class: A Guide Through the American Status System*. New York: Summit Books, 1983. Print.

Galán Lorés, Carlos. "El estado de la cuestión." *Insula* 525 (1990): 10. Print.

Gallero Díaz, José Luis. *Sólo se vive una vez*. Madrid: Ardora Ediciones, 1991. Print.

García Rodríguez, Javier. *Mutatis Mutandis*. Zaragoza: Eclipsados, 2010.

———. "El periodismo es el género más mutante." *Lne.es*. April 11, 2010 Web. June 6. 2011. <http://www.lne.es/cultura/2010/04/11/periodismo-genero -mutante/897625.html>

Gavela, Yvonne. "Vértigo, violencia e imagen española de los noventa: novela y cine." Diss. Penn State Univ. (2004). Print.

Gemunden, Gerd. "The Depth of the Surface, or, What Rolf Dieter Brinkmann Learned from Andy Warhol." *The German Quarterly* 68–3 (Summer 1995): 235–50. Print.

"Generación Nocilla: La No Generacioncilla." *¿Qué es la generación Nocilla?* July 24, 2007. Web. Jan 10, 2009. Blog. <http://generacionnocilla.blogspot.com/2007/07/qu-es-la-generacin-nocilla.html>

Giles, J. "Generalization X." *Newsweek* (June 1993): 62–70. Print.

Goldman, Robert and Stephen Papson. "Advertising in the Age of Accelerated Meaning." *The Consumer Society Reader.* Eds. Juliet Schor and Douglas Holt. New York: The New York Press, 2000. 81–98. Print.

Goodwin, Andrew. "Fatal Distractions: MTV Meets Postmodern Theory." *Sounds and Vision: The Music Video Reader.* Eds. Simon Frith, Andrew Goodwin, and Lawrence Grossberg. New York: Routledge, 1993. 45–66. Print.

Gordinier, Jeff. *X Saves the World: How Generation X Got the Shaft But Can Still Keep Everything From Sucking.* New York: Penguin, 2008. Print.

Gorman, Paul. "MTV: Sex and Rebellion?" *Intermedia* 20.3 (1992): 26. Print.

Gottdiener, Mark, ed. *New Forms of Consumption: Consumers, Culture and Commodification.* New York: Rowman and Littlefield, 2000. Print.

Goytisolo, Juan. "Literatura en el ciberespacio." *El País Babelia.* Jan. 2, 2010. Web. Nov. 23, 2010. <www.elpais.com/articulo/portada/Literatura/ciberespacio/elpepuculbab/20100102elpbabpor_8/Tes>

———. "Providence, de Juan Francisco Ferré, es una novela ideal para quienes conciben la lectura como una incursión en lo desconocido." *Babelia* Feb. 2 (2010): N.d. Print.

Goytisolo, Luis. *Mzungo.* Madrid: Mondadori, 1996. Print.

Graham, Helen, and Jo Labanyi. *Spanish Cultural Studies: An Introduction.* Oxford: Oxford University Press, 1995. Print.

Graham, Helen and Antonio Sánchez. "The Politics of 1992." *Spanish Cultural Studies: An Introduction.* Eds. Helen Graham and Jo Labanyi. Oxford: Oxford University Press, 1995. 396–406. Print.

Grasa, Ismael. *De madrid al cielo.* Madrid: Anagama.1994. Print.

Grassian, Daniel. *Hybrid Fictions: American Literature and Generation X.* Mcfarland, N.C.: Mcfarland and Co Inc. Publishing, 2003. Print.

Graziade, Daniel. *McOndo, Crack und Avant-Pop: Neuste Entwicklungen Der Spanishsprachigen und Englishsprachigen Literatur der Americas.* Saarbrücken: VDM Verlag, 2008. Print.

Gross, Daniel. "The It-Sucks-To-Be-Me Generation." *Slate.* Jan. 9, 2006. Web. Jan. 16, 2009. <www.slate.com/id/2134007>

Grossberg, Lawrence. "Putting the Pop Back into Postmodernism." *Universal Abandon? The Politics of Postmodernism.* Ed. Andrew Ross. Minneapolis: University of Minnesota Press, 1998. 167–90. Print.

———. "The Media Economy of Rock Culture: Cinema, Post-Modernity and Authenticity." *Sounds and Vision: The Music Video Reader.* Eds. Simon Frith, Andrew Goodwin, and Lawrence Grossberg. New York: Routledge, 1993. 185–209. Print.

Guberman, Ross Mitchell, ed. *Julia Kristeva Interviews.* New York: Columbia University Press, 1996. Print.

Gullón, Germán. "Cómo se lee una novela de la última generación (apartado X)." *Insula* 58–90 (1996): 31–33. Print.

———. "El miedo al presente como materia novelable." *Insula* 634 (Oct. 1999): 15. Print.

———. "*Historias del Kronen*. Comentario. La novela neorealista de José Ángel Mañas en el panorama novelístico español." *Historias del Kronen*. Barcelona: Destino, 1994. V–XXXII. Print.

———. "La novela multimediática: *Ciudad rayada*, de José Ángel Mañas." *Ínsula* 625–26 (1999): 33–34.

———. "La novela neorealista de José Ángel Mañas en el panorama novelístico español." *Historias del Kronen*. Barcelona: Destino, 1994. V–XXXII. Print.

———. "La novela neorealista (o de la generación X)." N. d. Web. Aug. 26, 2007. <www.cervantesvirtual.com/portal/nec/ptercernivel.jsp?conten=historia&pagina=historia2jsp&tit3=La+novela+neorrealista+(o+de+la+generaci%26oacute%3Bn+X)>

Gutiérrez Resa, Antonio. *Sociología de valores en la novela contemporánea (La generación X)*. Madrid: SM, 2004. Print.

"Ha estado con nosotros Gabi Martínez." *El mundo.es*. Dec. 3 2004. Web. July 22, 2009. <www.elmundo.es/encuentros/invitados/2004/12/1353>

Hachtmann, Frauke. "Generation X and Generation Golf: What Advertisers Need to Know When Targeting German and American Thirtysomethings." N. d. Web. June 18, 2008. <www.unomaha.edu/esc/2005Proceedings/generationx-andgolf.pdf>

Hamblett, Charles, and Jane Deverson. *"Generation X."* Greenwich, Conn.: Gold Medal Books, 1964. Print.

Haraway, Donna. "The Actors Are Cyborgs, Nature Is Coyote, and the Geography Is Elsewhere: Postscript to 'Cyborgs at Large.'" *Technoculture*. Eds. Constance Penley and Andrew Ross. Minneapolis, University of Minnesota Press, 1991. Print.

Harris, Andrea L. "Generation XX: The Identity Politics of Generation X." *GenXegesis: Essays on Alternative Youth (Sub)culture*. Eds. John Ulrich and Andrea L. Harris. New York: Popular Press, 2003. 268–97. Print.

Hassam Ihab. *The Postmodern Turn: Essays in Postmodern Theory and Culture*. Columbus: Ohio State University, 1987. Print.

Hayles, Katherine N. *How We Became Posthuman: Virtual Bodies in Cybernetics, Literature, and Informatics*. Chicago: University of Chicago Press, 1999.

———. "Print Is Flat, Code Is Deep: The Importance of Media-Specific Analysis. *Poetics Today* 25.1 (Spring 2004): 67–90. Print.

———. *My Mother Was a Computer: Digital Subjects and Literary Texts*. Chicago: University of Chicago Press, 2005. Print.

———. *Writing Machines*. Cambridge, Mass: MIT Press, 2002. Print.

———. "Virtual Bodies and Flickering Signifiers." *October* 66 (Autumn 1993): 69–91. Print.

Haynsworth, Leslie. "'Alternative' Music and the Oppositional Potential of Generation X Culture." *GenXegesis: Essays on Alternative Youth (Sub)culture*. Eds. John Ulrich and Andrea L. Harris. New York: Popular Press, 2003. 41–59. Print.

Hayter, Alex. "The Beatles: Rock Band as Historiographic Metafiction." *Society Eye*. Sept. 12, 2009. Web. Jan. 29, 2010. Blog. <http://societyeye.com/?p=557>

Hebdige, Dick. *Subculture: The Meaning of Style*. London and New York: Routledge, 1987. Print.

Helgason, Hallgrímur. *101 Reykjavík: A Novel*. Trans. Brian FitzGibbbon. New York: Scribner, 2003. Print.

Henseler, Christine. "On Going Nowhere Too Fast: *Historias del Kronen* by José Ángel Mañas and the Surface Culture of Andy Warhol." *Modern Language Notes* 123.2 (2008): 356–73. Print.

———. "Ode to Trash: The Spam Poetics of Agustín Fernández Mallo." *Cuaderno Internacional de Estudios Humanísticos y Literatura*. Forthcoming.

———. "'Playing with the Game That Art Is': John Kronik's Mastery at Play in *Ático* by Gabi Martínez." *Romance Quarterly* 55.1 (2008): 29–34. Print.

———. "Pop, Punk, and Rock and Roll Writers: José Ángel Mañas, Ray Loriga, and Lucía Etxebarria Redefine the Literary Canon." *Hispania* 87 (2004): 693–703. Print.

———. "Rocking Around Ray Loriga's *Héroes*: Video Clip Literature and the Televisual Subject." *Generation X Rocks: Contemporary Peninsular Fiction, Film, and Rock Culture*. Vanderbilt University Press (2007): 184–202. Print.

———. "*Spanish Mutant Fictioneers*: Of Mutants, Mutated Fiction and Media Mutations." *Ciberletras* 24 (Dec. 2010). Web. <www.lehman.cuny.edu/ciberletras/v24/henseler.html>

———. "Videoclip Aesthetics: Gender and Popular Culture in *Amor, curiosidad, prozac y dudas* by Lucía Etxebarria." *Letras Femeninas*. XXX. No. 2. Dec. (2004): 126–42. Print.

———. "What Is All the Fuss About?: The Lucía Etxebarria Phenomenon." *Confluencia* 21.2 (2006): 94–110. Print.

Henseler, Christine, and Randolph Pope. *Generation X Rocks: Contemporary Peninsular Fiction, Film, and Rock Culture*. Nashville: Vanderbilt University Press, 2007. Print.

Hill, Annette. "Big Brother: The Real Audience." *Television and New Media* 3.3 (2002): 323–40. Print.

Holmes, John Clello. "This Is the Beat Generation." *The New York Times Magazine* November (1952): N.p. Print.

Hornblower, Margot. "Great Xpectations of So-Called Slackers." *Time Magazine*. June 9 (1997). Web. Aug. 10, 2008. <www.time.com/time/magazine/article/0,9171,986481,00.html>

Humanes Bespín, Iván. "Eloy Fernández Porta." N.d. Web. March 7, 2010. <http://www.literaturas.com/v010/sec0707/entrevistas/entrevistas-02.html>

Ibrahim, Yasmin. "Transformation as a Narrative and a Process: Locating Myth and Mimesis in Reality TV." *Nebula* 4.4 (Dec. 2007): 41–58. Print.

Illies, Florian. *Generation Golf: Eine Inspektion*. Frankfurt, Germany: Fisher Verlag, 2001. Print.

"In Memoriam to Postmodernism." *Avant-Pop: Literature and the Internet*. N. d. Web. July 8, 2008. <http://home.freeuk.com/tom.royal/litnetfinal/smellslikeap.htm>

"India's New Worldly Women." *Business Week*. Aug. 22, 2005. Web. Feb 25, 2010. <www.businessweek.com/magazine/content/05_34/b3948530.htm>

"Insects." Blog by Douglas Coupland. *The New York Times*. August 31, 2006. Web. Sept. 26, 2008. <http://coupland.blogs.nytimes.com>

Injuve: Instituto de la Juventud. "Juventud en cifras. Población Jóven." N. d. Web. July 10, 2009. <www.injuve.migualdad.es/injuve/contenidos.type.action?type=1445831392&menuId=1445831392>

Izquierdo, José María. "Narradores españoles novísimos de los años noventa." *Revista de Estudios Hispánicos* 35.2 (2001): 293–308. Print.

Jaffe, Ira. *Hollywood Hybrids: Mixing Genres in Contemporary Film*. New York: Rowman and Littlefield, 2008. Print.

Jameson, Fredric. "Postmodernism and Consumer Society." *The Anti-Aesthetic: Essays on Postmodern Culture*. Ed. Hal Foster. New York: Bay, Press, 1983. 111–25. Print.

Janowitz, Tama. *Slaves of New York*. New York: Washington Square Press, 1986. Print.

Jenkins, Henry. "The Work of Theory in the Age of Digital Transformation." N.d. Web. June 12, 2009. <http://web.mit.edu/cms/People/henry3/pub/digitaltheory.htm>

———. "Game Design as Narrative Architecture." *First Person: New Media as Story, Performance, and Game*. Eds. Noah Wardrip-Fruin and Pat Harrigan. Cambridge: MIT Press, 2006. Print.

Joselit, David. "Notes on Surface: Toward a Genealogy of Flatness." *Art History* 23–1 (March 2000): 19–34. Print.

Juan-Cantavella, Robert. "La ficción-ciencia de Germán Sierra." *Lateral* 117 Sept. 2004. Web. Dec. 26, 2010. <www.circulolateral.com/revista/revista/foco/117gsierra.htm>

Juul, Jesper. "Introduction to Game Time." Ed. Noah Wardrip-Fruin and Pat Harrigan. *First Person: New Media as Story, Performance, and Game*. Cambridge, MA, MIT Press, 2004. 131–32. Print.

Kamenetz, Anya. *Generation Debt*. New York: Riverhead Books, 2007. Print.

Kapchan, Deborah. *Gender on the Market: Moroccan Women and the Revoicing of Tradition*. Philadelphia: University of Philadelphia Press, 1996. Print.

Kapchan, Deborah, and Pauline Turner Strong. "Theorizing the Hybrid." *Journal of American Folklore* 112 (Summer, 1999): 239–53. Print.

Kaplan, Ann E. "Feminism(s)/Postmodernism(s): MTV and Alternate Women's Videos and Performance Art." *Videos and Performance Art* 6 (1993): 55–76. Print.

———. *Rocking Around the Clock: Music Television, Postmodernism, and Consumer Culture*. New York: Methuen, 1987. Print.

Kay, Ferres. "Justine Ettler: The River Ophelia." *Hecate* 21.2 (1995): 72. Print.

Kavka, Misha and Amy West. "Temporalities of the Real." *Understanding Reality Television*. Eds. Su Holmes and Deborah Jermyn London: Routledge, 2004. 136–53. Print.

Kilborn, Richard. "How Real Can You Get?: Recent Developments in 'Reality Television.'" *European Journal of Communication* 9.4 (1994). 421 39. Print.

Kinder, Marsha. "About the Labyrinth Project." N. d. Web. Jan. 3, 2010. <http://college.usc.edu/labyrinth/about/about1.html>

———. "Music Video and the Spectator: Television, Ideology and Dream." *Film Quarterly* 38:1 (1984): 2–15. Print.

———. *Rocking Around the Clock: Music Television, Postmodernism, and Consumer Culture*. New York: Methuen, 1987. Print.

Kleber and Associates. "Lingering Myths About Generation X." February 1, 2005. Web. June 16, 2009. <www.housingzone.com/article/CA503868.html>

Klodt, Jason E. "'Nada de nada de nada de nada': Ray Loriga and the Paradox of Spain's Generation X." *Tropos* 27 (2001): 42–54. Print.

———."Strangers in a Strange House: Spanish Youth, Urban Dystopia, and Care Santos's *Okupada*." *Letras Hispanas* 4.2. (2007): 58–72. Print.

Kracht, Christina. *Faserland*. Köln: Kiepenheuer und Witsch, 1995. Print.

Kristeva, Julia. "From One Identity to An Other." Ed. Leon S. Roudiez. *Desire in Language: A Semiotic Approach to Literature and Art.* New York: Columbia University Press, 1987. 124–47.

Kroker, Arthur, and David Cook. "Television and the Triumph of Culture." *Storming the Reality Studio.* Ed. Larry McCaffery. Durham, Duke University Press, 1991. 229–38. Print.

Kronik, John. "Galdosian Reflections: Feijóo and the Fabrication of Fortunata." *Modern Language Notes* 97.2 (March 1982): 272–310. Print.

Labanyi, Jo. "Postmodernism and the Problem of Cultural Identity." *Spanish Cultural Studies. An Introduction.* Eds. Helen Graham and Jo Labanyi. New York: Oxford University Press, 1995. 396–405. Print.

"La generación de los mil Euros." *El País* 31 July, 2008. Print.

"La generación X en el poder." *Kaosenlared.net.* Jan. 19, 2009. Web. July 6, 2009. <www.kaosenlared.net/noticia/la-generacion-x-en-el-poder>

"La música de los 90." N. d. Web. July 14, 2009. <http://elparaninfo.galeon.com/la%20musica%20en%20los%2090.htm>

Lacalle, Charo. *El espectador televisivo. Los programas de entretenimiento.* Barcelona: Gedisea, 2001. Print.

Lainsbury, G. P. "Generation X and the End of History." *GenXegesis: Essays on Alternative Youth (Sub)culture.* Eds. John M. Ulrich and Andrea L. Harris. Madison, WI: Popular Press, 2003. 184–99. Print.

Landon Brook. "The Literature of Information." N. d. Web. December 3, 2009. <www.altx.com/memoriam/pomo.html>

Landow, George. *Hypertext 3.0. Critical Theory and New Media in an Era of Globalization.* Maryland: The Johns Hopkins University Press, 2006. Print.

———. *Hyper/Text/Theory.* Maryland: The Johns Hopkins University Press, 1994. Print.

Laurel, Brenda. *Computers as Theatre.* Readings, MA.: Addison-Wesley Professional, 1993. Print.

Laurence, Alexander, and Jill St. Jacques. "Interview with Larry McCaffery." *The Write Stuff: Interviews.* August 1994. Web. Nov. 23, 2008. <www.altx.com/int2/larry.mccaffery.html>

Lebert, Benjamin. *Crazy: A Novel.* New York: Alfred Knopf, 2000. Print.

Lefebvre, Henry. *The Production of Space.* New Jersey: Wiley-Blackwell, 1992. Print.

Lessig, Lawrence. *Remix: Making Art and Commerce Thrive in the Hybrid Economy.* New York: Penguin Press, 2008. Print.

Lévy, Pierre. *Collective Intelligence: Mankind's Emerging World in Cyberspace.* Trans. Robert Bonono. New York: Plenum Trade, 1997. Print.

Linklater, Richard. *Slacker.* New York: St. Martin's Griffin, 1992. Print.

Longhurst, Alex. "Culture and Development: The Impact of 1960s 'desarrollismo.'" *Contemporary Spanish Cultural Studies.* Eds. Barry Jordan and Rikki Morgan-Tamosunas. Oxford: Oxford University Press, 2000. 17–28. Print.

López Merino, Juan Miguel. "Sobre la presencia de Roger Wolfe en la poesía española (1990–2000) y revisión del marbete 'realismo sucio.'" *Espéculo: Revista de estudios literarios.* 2005. Web. Jan. 23, 2008. <www.ucm.es/info/especulo/numero31/rogwolfe.html>

Loriga, Ray. *El hombre que inventó Manhattan.* Barcelona: El Aleph, 2004. Print.

———. *Héroes.* Barcelona: Plaza y Janés, 1993. Print.

————. *La pistola de mi hermano*. Barcelona: Plaza y Janés, 1995. Print.

————. *Lo peor de todo*. Barcelona: Plaza and Janés Editores, 1999. Print

————. *Nunca le des la mano a un pistolero zurdo*. Madrid: Alfaguara, 1996. Print.

————. *Tokio ya no nos quiere*. Barcelona: Plaza y Janés, 1999. Print.

Lozano, Antonio. "Agustín Fernández Mallo. Dice adios al planeta Nocilla." *Qué Leer* 147 (2009): 64–68. Print.

Machado, José. *A dos ruedas*. Madrid: Espasa, 1996. Print.

Macgregor, Joseph B. "Entrevista a Eloy Fernández Porta." *Anika Entre Libros*. N. d. Web. April 15, 2011. <http://libros2.ciberanika.com/desktopdefault.aspx?pagina=~/paginas/entrevistas/entre181.ascx

Madoff, S.H. *Pop Art: A Critical History*. Berkeley, CA: University of California Press, 1997. Print.

Maestre, Pedro. "Los nietos de Cela y Delibes." *Generación*. N. d. Web. June 20, 2007. <www.generacionxxi.com/nietos.htm>

————. *Matando dinosaurios con tirachinas*. Barcelona: Destino 1996.

Maffesoli, Michel. *The Time of the Tribes: The Decline of Individualism in Mass Society*. London: Sage, 1996. Print.

Manovich, Lev. "Alan Kay's Universal Media Machine." Sept. 28, 2008. Web. Dec. 22, 2010. <www.manovich.net/DOCS/kay_article.doc>

————. "Database as Symbolic Form." *Convergence* (1999): 80–99. Print.

————. "New Media from Borges to HTML." *The New Media Reader*. Eds. Noah Wardrip-Fruin and Nick Montfort. Cambridge, Mass: MIT Press, 2003. 13–25. Print.

————. *The Language of New Media*. Cambridge: MIT Press, 2002. Print.

————. "Understanding Hybrid Media." Sept. 28, 2008. Web. Dec. 22, 2010. <http://manovich.net/DOCS>

————. "Understanding Meta-Media." *Critical Digital Studies*. Ed. Marilouise Kroker. Toronto: University of Toronto Press, 2008. 106–12. Print.

————. "What Comes After Remix?" *Remix Theory*. Winter 2007. Web. March 10, 2010. <http://remixtheory.net/?p=169>

Mañas, José Ángel. "Apuntes sobre la forma novelesca V-Final." N. d. Web. Oct. 18, 2008. <www.literaturas.com/v010/sec0607/educomania/educomania.htm>

————. "El legado de los Ramones: literatura y punk." *Ajoblanco* 108 (1998): 38–43. Print.

————. *Historias del Kronen*. Barcelona: Destino, 1995. Print.

————. *Sonko95: Autoretrato con negro de fondo*. Barcelona: Destino, 1999.

Marchese, John. "The Short Shelf Life of Generation X." *The New York Times*. Jan. 23, 2009. Print.

Marcus, Greil. *Lipstick Traces. A Secret History of the Twentieth Century*. Cambridge: Harvard University Press, 1990. Print.

Margolis, Mac. "Is Magic Realism Dead?" *Newsweek*. May 6, 2002. Web. May 29, 2009. <www.letras.s5.com/af0812047.htm>

Marr, Matthew. "An Ambivalent Attraction: Post-Punk Kinship and the Politics of Bonding in *Historias del Kronen* and *Less Than Zero*." *Arizona Journal of Hispanic Cultural Studies*. 10 (2006): 9–22. Print.

Martín, Sabas. *Páginas amarillas*. Madrid: Lengua de Trapo, 1997. Print.

Martín-Cabrera, Luis. "Apocalypse Now: The End of Spanish Literature? Reading *Payasos en la Lavadora* as Critical Parody." *Generation X Rocks: Contemporary*

Peninsular Fiction, Film, and Rock Culture. Eds. Christine Henseler and Randolph Pope. Nashville, TN: Vanderbilt University Press, 2007. 78–96. Print.

Martín-Estudillo, Luis. "Afterword: The Moment X in Spanish Narrative (and Beyond)." *Generation X Rocks: Contemporary Peninsular Fiction, Film, and Rock Culture.* Eds. Christine Henseler and Randolph Pope. Nashville, TN: Vanderbilt University Press, 2007. 135–46. Print.

Martínez, Gabi. *Ático.* Barcelona: Destino, 2004. Print.

———. Message to Christine Henseler. December 14, 2009. E-mail.

———. Message to Christine Henseler. August 16, 2010. E-mail.

Martínez de Codes, Rosa María. "Reflexiones en torno al criterio generacional, como teoría analítica y método histórico." N. d. Web. March 12, 2009. <http://revistas.ucm.es/ghi/02116111/articulos/QUCE8282120051A.PDF>

Masoliver Ródenas, Antonio. "Critica al crítico." *Letras Libres.* February 2002. Web. March 12, 2009. <www.letraslibres.com/index.php?art=7271&rev=2>

Mathijs, Ernest, and Janet Jones, eds. *Big Brother International: Formats, Critics and Publics.* London: Wallflower Press, 2004. Print.

McCaffery, Larry, ed. *After Yesterday's Crash: The Avant-Pop Anthology.* New York: Penguin, 1995. Print.

———. *Avant-Pop: Fiction for a Daydream Nation.* Normal, IL.: Black Ice Books, 1993. Print.

———. *Some Other Frequency: Interviews with Innovative American Authors.* Philadelphia: University of Pennsylvania Press, 1996. Print.

———. *Storming the Reality Studio.* Durham, Duke University Press, 1991. Print.

McCarthy, Anna. " 'Stanley Milgram, Allen Funt, and Me': Postwar Social Science and the 'First Wave' of Reality TV." *Reality TV: Remaking Television Culture.* Eds. Susan Murray and Laurie Ouellette. New York: New York University Press, 2009. 23–43. Print.

McGahan, Andrew. *1988.* New York: St. Martin's Griffin, 1998. Print.

———. *Praise: A Novel.* New York: St. Martin's Griffin, 1992. Print.

McHale, Brian. *Constructing Postmodernism.* New York: Routledge, 1993. Print.

McInerney, Jay. *Bright Lights, Big City.* New York: Vintage Contemporaries, 1984. Print.

McInerney, Jay and Caveney Graham. "Psychodrama: Qu'est-ce que c'est?" *Shopping in Space: Essays on America's Blank Generation Fiction.* Eds. Elizabeth Young and Graham Caveney. New York: Grove Press, 1992. 43–75. Print.

McLuhan, Eric, and Frank Zingrone, eds. *Essential McLuhan.* New York: BasicBooks, 1995. Print.

McLuhan, Marshall and Quentin Fiore. *The Medium Is the Massage.* New York: Random House, 1967. Print.

Miles, Steven. *Youth Lifestyles in a Changing World.* Buckingham: Open University Press, 2000. Print.

———. "Young People in a Globalizing World." *World Youth Report 2003.* 291–309. <www.un.org/esa/socdev/unyin/documents/ch11.pdf>

Mills, Katie. " 'Await Lightning': How Generation X Remaps the Road Story." *GenXegesis: Essays on Alternative Youth Culture.* Eds. John Ulrich and Andrea L. Harris. Madison: University of Wisconsin Press, 2003. 221–48. Print.

Molinaro, Nina. "Facing towards Alterity and Spains' 'Other' New Novelists." *Anales de la literatura española contemporánea* 30 1.2 (2005): 301–24. Print.

———. "The 'Real" Story of Drugs, Dasein and José Ángel Mañas's *Historias del Kronen. Revista Canadiense de Estudios Hispánicos* 27 (2) (2003): 291–306. Web.

Dec. 16, 2009. <http://goliath.ecnext.com/coms2/gi_0199–3848693/Facing-towards-alterity-and-Spain.html>

———. "Watching, Wanting, and the GenX Soundtrack of Gabriela Bustelo's *Veo veo*." *Generation X Rocks: Contemporary Peninsular Fiction, Film, and Rock Culture*. Eds. Christine Henseler and Randolph Pope. Nashville: Vanderbilt University Press, 2007. 203–16. Print.

Monmany, Mercedes. "Rock and roll en la plaza Roja." *Diario 16* 20 Nov. 1993: 1. Print.

Montalbán, Caimán. *Bar*. Madrid: El Europeo y La Tripulación, 1995. Print.

Mora, Miguel. "Gabriela Bustelo inventa un mundo futuro gobernado por mujeres." *El País*. July 16, 2001. Web. Jan, 15, 2009. <www.elpais.com/articulo/cultura/Gabriela/Bustelo/inventa/mundo/futuro/gobernado/mujeres/elpepicul/20010716elpepicul_4/Tes?print=1>

Mora, Vicente Luis. *La luz nueva: Singularidad en la narrativa española actual*. Córdoba: Berenice, 2007. Print.

———. *Pangea: Internet, blogs y comunicación en un mundo nuevo*. Sevilla, Fundación José Manuel Lara, 2006. Print.

———. "¿Posmodernidad? Narrativa de la imagen, Next-Generation y razón catódica en la narrativa contemporánea." *Figures of Belatedness: Postmodernist Fiction in English*. Eds. Javier Gascueña Gahete and Paula Martín Salván. Córdoba, Universidad de Córdoba, 2006. Print.

Moreno Tavera, Miguel Ángel. "El Ángel Exterminador. El sueño pofético del *Gran Hermano* Buñuelesco." *Docta Ignorancia Digital* 1.1 (2010). Web. March 9, 2010. <www.doctaignoranciadigital.com/exterm_angel.pdf>

Moreiras, Alberto. *Tercer espacio. Literatura y duelo en América Latina*. Santiago, Chile: Universidad Arcis, 1999. Print.

Moreiras Menor, Cristina. *Cultura herida: literatura y cine en la España democrática*. Madrid: Ediciones Libertarias, 2002. Print.

———. "Spectacle, Trauma and Violence in Contemporary Spain." *Contemporary Cultural Studies*. Eds. Barry Jordan and Rikki Morgan-Tamosunas. New York: Oxford University Press, 2000. 134–42. Print.

Moreno Mínguez, Almudena. "The Late Emancipation of Spanish Youth: Keys for Understanding." *Electronic Journal of Sociology* 7.1 (2003). Web. August 1, 2008. <www.sociology.org/content/vol7.1/minguez.html>

Morse, Margaret. *Virtualities: Television, Media, and Cyberculture*. Bloomington: Indiana University Press, 1998. Print.

"Mtv Networks Europe." N.d. Web. Dec. 20. 2009. <http.//wn.com/MTV_Networks_Europe>

Múgica, Daniel. *Corazón negro*. Barcelona: Plaza y Janés, 1998. Print.

Muggleton, David, and Rupert Weinzierl. *The Post-Subcultures Reader*. Oxford: Berg, 2003. 3–26. Print.

Muller, Vivienne. "Waiting for Gordon—Grunge Realism and Andrew McGahan's *Praise*." *Images of the Urban: Conference Proceedings*. (1997): 152–56. Print.

Murray, Janet. "From Game-Story to Cyberdrama." *First Person: New Media as Story, Performance, and Game*. Eds. Noah Wardrip-Fruin and Pat Harrigan. Cambridge, Mass, MIT Press, 2004. 2–11. Print.

Murray, Janet. *Hamlet on the Holodeck: The Future of Narrative in Cyberspace*. Cambridge, Mass, MIT Press, 1998. Print.

Naharro Calderón, José María. "El juvenismo espectacular." *España Contemporánea: Revista de Literatura y cultura* 1 (1999): 7–20. Print.

Naqvi, Rabab. "Generation with Aspirations?" *The Hindu.* Feb. 2, 2005. Web. Feb. 25, 2010. <www.hindu.com/mag/2005/02/06/stories/2005020600630800.htm>

Navajas, Gonzalo. "A Distopian Culture: The Minimalist Paradigm in the Generation X." *Generation X Rocks: Contemporary Peninsular Fiction, Film, and Rock Culture.* Eds. Christine Henseler and Randolph Pope. Nashville: Vanderbilt University Press, 2007. 13–14. Print.

———. "Generación y canon o ley y orden en literatura." *Siglo XX/20th Century* 12.1–2 (1994): 157–70. Print.

———. *La narrativa española en la era global: imagen, comunicación, ficción.* Barcelona: EUB, 2002. Print.

———. "Posmodernismo: '¿Cómo leer una novela hoy?" *El hispanismo en los Estados Unidos: discursos críticos/práctices textuales.* Madrid: Visor 1999: 149–67. Print.

Navarro Martínez, Eva. "Una realidad a la carta: la televisión en algunas novelas de la última década del siglo XX." Feb. 2, 2006. Web. April 10, 2009. <www.usm.es/info/especaulo/numero25/alacarta/html>

———. "La novela de Benjamín Prado: Cómo construirse un mundo y una realidad propios." *Letras Peninsulares* (Winter 2001–2002): 404–26. Print.

———. *La novela de la Generación X.* Granada: Universidad de Granada, 2008. Print.

"Nearly All US Teens, 53% of Adults Play Video Games." *The Marketing Data Box.* Dec. 9 2008. Web. Jan 25, 2009. <http://www.marketingcharts.com/interactive/nearly-all-us-teens-53-of-adults-play-video-games-7114/>

Nethersole, Reingard. "Models of Globalization." *PMLA* 116.3 (2001): 638–49. Print.

Neuman, Andrés. *La vida en las ventanas.* Madrid: Espasa-Calpe, 2002. Print.

Newall Rademacher, Virginia. "The Art of Seduction: Truth or Fanfiction in the World of Lucía Etxebarria's Online 'Friends' and the Blogosphere." *Hybrid Storyspaces: Redefining the Critical Enterprise in Twenty-First Century Hispanic Literature.* Ed. Christine Henseler and Debra A. Castillo. *Hispanic Issues Online.*

"New Media Review: From the European Travel Commission." *European Travel Commission.* N. d. Web. March 4, 2008. <www.etcnewmedia.com/review/default.asp?SectionID=11&CountryID=48>

"News from Spain." March 06, 2005. Web. March 4, 2008. <www.euroresidentes.com/Blogs/2005/03/domestic-use-of-new-technology-in.htm>

Noë, Alva. *Out of Our Heads: Why You Are Not Your Brain, And Other Lessons From the Biology of Consciousness.* New York: Hill and Wang, 2009. Print.

Oake Jonathon. "Reality Bites and Generation X as Spectator." *The Velvet Light Trap* 53 (2004): 83–97. Print.

O'Hara, Craig. *The Philosophy of Punk: More Than Noise!* London: AK Press, 1999. Print.

O'Hehir, Andrew. "The Art World's Pepsi Generation." *Salon.com.* August 7, 2008. Web. Jan. 10, 2009. <www.salon.com/ent/movies/btm/feature/2008/08/07/beautiful_losers/index.html>

Olalquiaga, Celeste. "Prologue from Megalopolis." *Media and Cultural Studies: Key Works.* Eds. Meenakshi Gigi Durham and Douglas M. Kellner. Malden, MA: Blackwell, 2001. 588–97. Print.

Olmos, Alberto, ed. *Algunas ideas buenísimas que el mundo se va a perder.* Barcelona: Caballo de Troya, 2009. Print.

Ors, J. "Sueños poéticos de la estética 'blog.'" N. d. Web. December 23, 2010. <www.candaya.com/nocillalarazon.pdf>

Ortega Julio. "Propiedad Anónima." *El País*. March 18, 2004. Web. Dec. 30 2010. <http://homepage.mac.com/germansierra/proustfiction.pdf>

Ortega y Gasset. *En torno a Galileo: esquema de las crisis*. Madrid: Espasa-Calpe, 1965. Print.

Owen, Rob. *GenX TV: The Brady Bunch to Melrose Place*. Syracuse: Syracuse University Press, 1997. Print.

Packer, Randall and Ken Jordan, eds. *Multimedia: From Wagner to Virtual Reality*. New York: W. W. Norton and Company, 2001. Print.

Pao T. María. "Sex, Drugs, and Rock and Roll: *Historias del Kronen* as Blank Fiction." *Anales de la Literatura Contemporánea* 27.2 (2002): 245–60. Print.

Pelevin, Victor. *Homo Zapiens*. Trans. Andrew Bromfield. New York: Penguin Books, 2000. Print.

Pérez, Jorge. "Reckless Driving: Speed, Mobility, and Transgression in the Spanish 'Rock and Road' Novel." *Generation X Rocks: Contemporary Peninsular Fiction, Film, and Rock Culture*. Eds. Christine Henseler and Randolph Pope. Nashville, TN: Vanderbilt University Press, 2007. 153–69. Print.

———. "Suspiros de España: El inconsciente político nacional en la narrativa de José Ángel Mañas. *España Contemporánea* 18.1 (Spring 2005): 33–51. Print.

Pérez-Sánchez, Gema. *Queer Transitions in Contemporary Spanish Culture: From Franco to la Movida*. New York: State University of New York Press, 2007. Print.

Perriam, Chris, et al. *A New History of Spanish Writing 1939 to the 1990s*. Oxford: Oxford University Press, 2000. Print.

Phelan, Peggy. "The Same: Reflections on Andy Warhol and Ronald Reagan." *Umbr(a)* (2005): 65–70. Print.

Polan, Dana "SZ/MTV." *Journal of Communication Inquiry* 10–1 (1986) 48–54. Print.

Pope, Randolph. "Between Rock and the Rocking Chair: The Epilogue's Resistance in *Historias del Kronen*." *Generation X Rocks: Contemporary Peninsular Fiction, Film, and Rock Culture*. Eds. Christine Henseler and Randolph Pope. Nashville, TN: Vanderbilt University Press, 2007. 115–25. Print.

———. "The International Self: The Spanish Case of the *Kronen* Generation." *España Contemporánea* 18.2 (2005): 7–16. Print.

"Postmodernism or the Cultural Logic of Late Capitalism." *Media and Cultural Studies: Key Works*. Eds. Meenakshi Gigi Durham and Douglas M. Kellner. Malden, MA.: Blackwell Publishers, 2001: 550–87. Print.

Prado, Benjamín. *Alguien se acerca*. Madrid: Alfaguara, 1998. Print.

———. *Dónde crees que vas y quién te crees que eres*. Madrid: Anaya, 1996. Print.

———. *No sólo el fuego*. Madrid: Alfaguara, 1999. Print.

———. *Nunca le des la mano a un pistolero zurdo*. Barcelona: Plaza y Janés, 1996. Print.

———. *Raro*. Barcelona: Plaza y Janés, 1996. Print.

Prensky, Mark. "Digital Natives, Digital Immigrants." *On The Horizon* 9.5 Oct. 2001. Web. May 7, 2008. <www.marcprensky.com/writing/Prensky%20%20Digital%20Natives,%20Digital%20Immigrants%20-%20Part1.pdf>

Raphael, Chad. "The Political Economic Origins of Reali-TV." *Reality TV: Remaking Television Culture*. Eds. Susan Murray and Laurie Ouellette. New York University Press, 2004: 119–37. Print.

"Ray Loriga: El hombre que inventó Manhattan." *Clubcultura.com*. N. d. Web. Jan. 23, 2008. <www.clubcultura.com/clubliteratura/rayloriga>

Redhead, Steve. *The End of the Century Party: Youth and Pop Towards 2000*. Manchester: Manchester University Press, 1990. Print.

Redhead, Steve, Derek Wynne, and Justin O'Connor, eds. *The Clubcultures Reader: Readings in Cultural Studies*. Oxford: Blackwell, 1997. Print.

Redondo Goicoechea, Alicia. "Los modelos de mujer de Lucía Etxebarria." *Mujeres novelistas: jóvenes narradoras de los noventa*. Ed. Alicia Redondo Goicoechea, Alicia. Madrid: Narcea, 2003. 109–22. Print.

Reynolds, Simon. *Generation Ecstasy: Into the World of Techno and Rave*. New York: Routledge, 1999. Print.

Ribas, José. "Es un huracán de valentía que ha conseguido un texto frío y desgarrador: José Ángel Mañas." *Ajoblanco* March (1994): 31–36. Print.

Richardson, Nathan. "The Art of Being Forgettable: Ray Loriga's *Lo peor de todo*, the Generation X, and the New Cultural Field. *The Arizona Journal of Hispanic Cultural Studies* 9 (2005): 207–17. Print.

Richmond, Larry. "Who Plays Video Games?" *LDS Media Talk*. Dec. 18 2008. Web. Jan. 25, 2009. <http://ldsmediatalk.com/2008/12/18/who-plays-video-games/>

Ritchie, Karen. *Marketing to Generation X*. New York: Lexington, 1995.

Robinson, Charlotte. "David Bowie: The Rise and Fall of Ziggy Stardust and the Spiders from Mars." *PopMatters* Jan. 29, 2003. Web. Feb. 24 2009. <www.popmatters.com/pm/review/bowiedavid-riseandfall>

Robbins, Ira, and Scott Isler. "Ramones." *Trouser Press Record Guide* (4th ed.), Collier, 1991. Print.

Rodríguez Cunill, Inmaculada. "¿Cómo se crean nuevos códigos audio-visuales para captar audiencias?" *Comunicar: Revista científica iberoamericana de comunicación y educación* 21 (2003): 127–32. Print.

Roel Vecino, Marta. "Innovación tecnológica en la gestión de contenidos para televisión: análisis del fenómeno 'Gran Hermano.'" *II Congrés Internacional Comunicació I Realitat* (2005): 813–24. Web. March 3, 2010. <http://cicr .blanquerna.url.edu/2005/Abstracts/PDFsComunicacions/vol2/08/ROEL _Marta.pdf>

Romeo, Félix. *Dibujos animados*. Zaragoza: Mira Editores, 1995. Print.

Roscoe, Jane. "*Big Brother* Australia: Performing the "Real' Twenty-Four–Seven." *The Television Studies Reader*. Eds. Robert C. Allen and Annette Hill. New York: Routledge: 2004. 312–21. Print.

Rose, Aaron, et al. *Beautiful Losers*. New York: D. A. P./Iconoclast, 2005.

Rubey, Dan. "Voguing at the Carnival: Desire and Pleasure on MTV." *South Atlantic Quarterly* 90 (1991): 871–906. Print.

Rushkoff, Douglas. *The GenX Reader*. New York: Ballantine Books, 1994.

Ryan, Marie-Laure. "Cyberspace, Virtuality, and the Text." *Cyberspace Textuality: Computer Technology and Literary Theory*. Ed. Marie-Laure Ryan. Bloomington, Indiana University Press, 1999. 78–106. Print.

Sabin, Roger. *Punk Rock: So What?: The Cultural Legacy of Punk*. London and New York: Routledge, 1999. Print.

Sáenz Corchuelo, Oscar. "Nocilladream.afm." N. d. Web. August 12, 2010. <www.ediciona.com/portafolio/document/6/7/8/3/nocilla_dream_-_oscar _saenz_corchuelo_3876.pdf>

Sánchez, Antonio. "Postmodernism and the Contemporary Spanish Avant-garde." "The Construction in Spain in the 1980s and 1990s." *Contemporary Spanish Cultural Studies.* Eds. Barry Jordan and Rikki Morgan-Tamosunas. Oxford: Oxford University Press, 2000. 101–10. Print.

Santana, Cintia. "What We Talk About When We Talk About Dirty Realism in Spain." *Generation X Rocks: Contemporary Peninsular Fiction, Film, and Rock Culture.* Eds. Christine Henseler and Randolph Pope. Nashville: Vanderbilt University Press, 2007. 33–58. Print.

Santos, Care. *Aprender a huir.* Barcelona: Seix Barral, 2002. Print.

Sanz Villanueva, Santos. "Cambio del rumbo en el Nadal." *Diario 16* February 19, 1994: n.p. Print.

Sarlo, Beatriz. *Escenas de la vida posmoderna: intelectuales, arte y videocultura en la Argentina.* Buenos Aires: Ariel, 1994. Print.

"Says the OECD." May 10, 2007. Web. Aug. 1, 2008. <www.oecd.org/document /63/0,3343,en_2649_34487_38543551_1_1_1_1,00.html >

Scarlett, Elizabeth. *Generation X Rocks: Contemporary Peninsular Fiction, Film, and Rock Culture.* Eds. Christine Henseler and Randolph Pope. Nashville, TN: Vanderbilt University Press, 2007, 97–111. Print.

Schnapp, Jeffrey T. "Crash (Speed as Engine of Individuation)." *Modernism/ Modernity* 6.1 (1999): 1–49. Print.

Seisdedos, Iker. "A Tide of Experience for the Generation of 'Non-Writers." *El País.* March 14, 2008. Web. February 3, 2009. <www.alfaguara.santillana.es/blogs /upload/ficheros/elhombre_herald_tribune.pdf>

Shaviro, Steven. "The Life, After Death, of Postmodern Emotions." *Criticism* 46.1 (2004): 125–41. Web. March 10, 2010. <http://muse.jhu.edu/journals /criticism/v046/46.1shaviro.html>

Shevory, Thomas C. "Bleached Resistance: The Politics of Grunge." *Popular Music and Society* 19.2 (1995): 23–48. Print.

Siegle, Robert. *Suburban Ambush: Downtown Writing and the Fiction of Insurgency.* Johns Hopkins University Press, 1989. Print.

Sierra, Germán. "Videojuegos" Message to Christine Henseler. January 11, 2010. E-mail.

———. "Iones. *Alto voltaje.* Barcelona: Mondadori, 2004. Print

———. "En búsqueda de las formas narrativas de la cultura contemporánea." *Letras Libres.* March 2003. Web. Jan. 11, 2011. <www.letraslibres.com/index .php?num=18&sec=3&art=8669>

Silverstone, Roger and Eric Hirsch, eds. *Consuming Technologies: Media and Information in Domestic Spaces.* London: Routledge: 1992. Print.

Skelton, Tracey, and Gill Valentine, eds. *Cool Places: Geographies of Youth Cultures.* New York: Routledge, 1998. Print.

Slusser, George. "Literary MTV." *Mississippi Review.com.* June 16, 2008. Web. August 24, 2009. <www.mississippireview.com/1996/slusser.html>

Smith, Carter E. "Social Criticism or Banal Imitation: A Critique of the Neorealist Novel Apropos the Works of José Ángel Mañas." *Ciberletras.* Dec. 9, 2008. Web. March 9, 2009. <www.lehman.cuny.edu/ciberletras/v12/smith.htm>

Smith, Paul Julian. *Contemporary Spanish Culture: TV, Fashion, Art and Film.* Cambridge, Polity Press, 2003. Print.

———. *Spanish Visual Culture: Cinema, Television, Internet.* Manchester: Manchester University Press, 2006. Print.

———. *Television in Spain: From Franco to Almodóvar*. Woodbridge: Tamesis, 2006. Print

"Sólo 27 compañías desarrollan videojuegos en España, sobre todo para teléfonos móviles." August 10, 2001. Web. November 21, 2009. <www.elmundo.es/navegante/2007/10/08/tecnologia/1191843370.html>

Sosa-Velasco, Alfredo. "*Héroes* de Ray Loriga como literatura videoclip: la construcción del sujeto en proceso." *Explicación de Textos Literarios* 33.1 (2004–2005): 17–32. Print.

"Spain: Internet Usage Stats and Telecom Reports." March 4, 2008. Web. June 22, 2009. <www.internetworldstats.com/eu.es.htm>

Spires, Robert. "Depolarization and the New Spanish Fiction at the Millennium." *Anales de la Literatura Española Contemporánea* 30.2 (2005): 485–512. Print.

———"Information, Communication, and Spanish Fiction of the 1990s." *Romance Quarterly* 51.2 (Spring 2004): 141–59. Print.

———."José Ángel Mañas' *Historias del Kronen* and the New Spanish Democracy." *Mediterranean Studies*. 14 (2005): 225–34. Print.

Stadler, Felix. *Manuel Castells: The Theory of the Network Society*. Malden, MA: Polity Press, 2006. Print.

Stanley, Christopher. "Not Drowning But Waving: Urban Narratives of Dissent In the Wild Zone." *The Club Cultures Reader*. London: Blackwell, 36–54. Print.

Steenmeijer, Maarten. "Other Lives: Rock, Memory and Oblivion in Post-Franco Fiction." *Popular Music* 24.2 (2005): 245–56. Print.

Stone, Allucquère Rosanne. "Preface." *Electronic Culture: Technology and Visual Representation*. Ed. Timothy Druckrey. New York: Aperture, 1996. 6–11. Print.

Strauss, William, and Neil Howe. *Generations: The History of America's Future 1584–2069*. New York: William Morrow and Company, Inc. 1991. Print.

"Study Compares U.S. European Teen Drug Use." 2/21/2001. Web. Aug. 1, 2008. <www.usatoday.com/news/health/2001-02-21-teens-drugs-europe.htm>

Subirats, Eduardo. *La cultural como espectáculo*. Madrid: Fondo de Cultura Económica, 1998. Print.

Sukenick, Ronald. *In For: Digressions on the Art of Fiction*. Carbondale: Southern Illinois Press, 1985. Print.

Syson, Ion. "Smells Like Market Spirit." *Overland* 142 (1996): 21–26. Print.

Tapscott, Don, and Anthony Williams. *Wikinomics: How Mass Collaboration Changes Everything*. New York: Penguin, 2006. Print.

The Pew Internet and American Life Project. "Teens, Video Games and Civics." Sept. 16, 2008. Web. Sept. 20, 2009. <www.pewinternet.org/Reports/2008/Teens-Video-Games-and-Civics/04- 11-Who-Is-Playing-Games/3-Almost-all-girls-and-boys-play-video-games.aspx?r=1>

"The The: Soul Mining." *Leonard's Lair*. Jan. 27, 2005. Web. March 5, 2009. <www.leonardslair.co.uk/soulmining.htm>

Thornton, Sarah. *Club Cultures: Music, Media and Subcultural Capital*. London, Polity, 1994. Print.

Tincknell, Estella, and Parvati Raghuram. "Big Brother: Reconfiguring the 'Active' Audience of Cultural Studies?" *European Journal of Cultural Studies* 5.2 (May 2002): 199–215. Print.

Topol. Jáchym. *City Sister Silver*. North Haven, CT: Catbird Press, 1994. Print.

Torrecilla, Jesús. *El tiempo y los márgenes. Europa como utopía y como amenaza en la literatura española*. Chapel Hill: North Carolina Studies in the Romance Languages and Literatures, 1996. Print.

Touraine, Alain. *A New Paradigm for Understanding Today's World.* Trans. Gregory Elliott. Malden, MA: Polity Press, 2005. Print.

Triana Toribio, Núria, "A Punk called Pedro: La Movida in the Films of Pedro Almodovar." *Contemporary Spanish Cultural Studies.* Eds. Barry Jordan and Rikki Morgan-Tamosunas. Oxford: Oxford University Press, 2000. 274–83. Print.

Tsuchiya, Akiko. "Gender, Sexuality, and the Literary Market in Spain at the End of the Millennium." *Women's Narrative and Film in Twentieth-Century Spain: A World of Difference(s).* Eds. Ofelia Ferrán and Kathleen Glenn. New York: Routledge, 2002. 238–55. Print.

———. "The 'New' Female Subject and the Commodification of Gender in the Works of Lucía Etxebarria." *Romance Studies* 20 (2002): 77–87. Print.

Txetxu, Aguado. "Tokio sí nos quiso: memoria y olvido en Ray Loriga." *Letras Hispanas* 14.1. N. d. Web. Nov. 4, 2008. <http://letrashispanas.univ.edu/Vol4iss1/Aguado.htm>

Ugarte, Michael. *Africans in Europe: The Culture of Exile and Emigration from Equatorial Guinean to Spain.* Champaign, Il. University of Illinois Press, 2010. Print.

Ulrich, John MacAllister. *GenXegesis: Essays on Alternative Youth (Sub)culture.* New York: Popular Press, 2003. 3–40. Print.

Urioste, Carmen de. "Cultura punk: la "Tetralogía Kronen" de José Ángel Mañas o el arte de hacer ruido." *Ciberletras* 11. May 5, 2007. Web. August 1, 2008. <www.leahman.cuny.edu/ciberletras/v11/urioste.html>

———. "La narrativa española de los noventa: existe una 'generación X'?" *Letras Peninsulares* 3 (1997–1998): 455–76. Print.

———. "Narrative of Spanish Women Writers of the Nineteen Nineties: An Overview." *Tulsa Studies in Women's Literature* 20.1 (2001): 279–95. Print.

———. *Novela y sociedad en la España contemporánea (1994–2009).* Madrid: Editorial Fundamentos, 2009. Print.

Vecino, Marta Roel. "Innovación tecnológica en la gestión de contenidos para televisión: análisis del fenómeno 'Gran Hermano.'" *Digitalització I Nois Continguts* 8 (N. year): 813–24. N. d. Web. June 30, 2009. <http://cicr.blanquerna.url.edu/2005/Abstracts/PDFsComunicacions/vol2/08/ROEL_Marta.pdf>

Verdú, Vicente, "¿Vivir o leer novelas?". *El País.com.* June 14, 2011. Web. August 23, 2011. <http://www.elpais.com/articulo/sociedad/Vivir/leer/novelas/elpepiopi/20010705elpepisoc_10/Tes>

Vernallis, Carol. *Experiencing Music Videos: Aesthetic and Cultural Context.* New York: Columbia University Press, 2004. Print.

Vidal-Beneyto, José. "Literatura y globalización." *Actas del congreso "Literatura y sociedad: un debate en los inicios del siglo XXI."* Jerez de la Frontera: Fundación Caballero Bonald, 2004. 154–67. Print.

Vidal-Quadras, Alex. *Amarás a tu tribu: un libro inoportuno y necesario en recuerdo de España.* Barcelona: Planeta, 1998. Print.

Vilarós, Teresa. *El mono del desencanto español. Una crítica cultural de la transición española, 1983–1992.* S.A. Mexico: Editores Siglo XXI de España, 1998. Print.

———. "The Novel Beyond Modernity." *The Cambridge Companion to the Spanish Novel From 1600 to the Present.* Eds. Harriet Turner and Adelaida López de Martínez. Cambridge: Cambridge University Press, 2003: 251–63. Print.

Vilas-Mata, Enrique. "Compañeros de viaje." *El País* 7 Jan. 1998: 28. Print.

Villanueva, Darío. *Teorías del realismo literario.* Madrid: Instituto de España, Espasa-Calpe, 1992. Print.

Waisbord, Silvio. "McTV: Understanding the Global Popularity of Television Formats." *Television New Media* 5.4 (2004): 359–83. Print.

Wallace, David Foster. "Fictional Futures and the Conspicuously Young." March 18, 2009. <http://neugierig.org/content/dfw/ffacy.pdf>

Wang, Jing. "Bourgeois Bohemians in China? Neo-Tribes and the Urban Imaginary." *China Quarterly*, 183 (2005): 1–31. Print.

———. *High Culture Fever: Politics, Aesthetics, and Ideology in Deng's China.* Berkeley: University of California Press, 1996. Print.

Wardrip-Fruin, Noah and Pat Harrigan. *First Person: New Media as Story, Performance, and Game.* Cambridge, MA, MIT Press, 2004. Print.

Warhol, Andy. *The Philosophy of Andy Warhol: (From A to B and Back Again).* New York: Harvest/HBJ, 1975. Print.

Waterman, Peter. "The Brave New World of Manuel Castells." *Diálogo Solidaridad Global.* N. d. Web. Jan. 25, 2009. <www.eduglobalcitizen.net/index.php?option=com_docman&task=cat_view&gid=21 &Itemid=79&mosmsg=Est%E1+a+tentar+aceder+a+partir+de+um+dom%EDnio+n%E3o+ autorizado.+%28www.google.com%29>

Waugh, Patricia. *Metafiction: The Theory and Practice of Self-Conscious Fiction.* New York: Methuen 1984. Print.

Weinzierl, Rupert, and David Muggleton. "What Is 'Post-Sub-cultural Studies' Anyway?" *The Post-Subcultures Reader.* Eds. David Muggleton and Rupert Weinzierl. Oxford: Berg, 2003. 3–26. Print.

Welsh, Irvine. *Trainspotting.* New York: W. W. Norton and Company, 1993. Print.

"Whatever Happened to the Original Generation X?" *The Observer.* Jan. 23, 2005. Web. June 20, 2009. <http://www.guardian.co.uk/uk/2005/jan/23/britishidentity.anushkaasthana>

Wikipedia contributors. "Mashup (digital)." *Wikipedia, The Free Encyclopedia.* Wikipedia, The Free Encyclopedia, 26 Mar. 2011. Web. 21 Jun. 2011. <http://en.wikipedia.org/wiki/Mashup_(digital)>

Wiley, Stephen. "Transnation: Globalization and the Reorganization of Chilean Television in the Early 1990s." *Journal of Broadcasting and Electronic Media.* Sept. 1, 2006. Web. November 24, 2008. <www.highbeam.com/doc/1G1-157946569.html>

Williams, Kevin. *Why I [Still] Want My MTV: Music Video and Aesthetic Communication.* Cresskill, New Jersey: Hampton Press, 2003. Print.

Willis, Paul. *Profane Culture.* London: Routledge, 1978. Print.

Wilson, William. "Prince of Boredom: The Repetitions and Passivities of Andy Warhol." April 28, 2005. Web. Dec. 13, 2008. <www.warholstars.org/andywarhol/articles/william/wilson.html>

Wolfe, Roger. *Dios es un perro que nos mira.* Madrid: Espasa-Calpe, 1993. Print.

———. *Hay una guerra.* Madrid: Huerga y Fierro, 1996. Print.

Wurzel, Elizabeth. *Prozac Nation.* New York: Riverhead Books, 1994. Print.

Yau, John. *In the Realm of Appearances: The Art of Andy Warhol.* Hopewell, NJ: The Eco Press, 1993. Print.

Young, Elizabeth. "Children of the Revolution: Fiction Takes to the Streets." Eds. Elizabeth Young and Graham Caveney. *Shopping in Space: Essays on America's Blank Generation Fiction.* New York: Grove Press, 1992. 1–21. Print.

Young, Elizabeth and Graham Caveney. *Shopping in Space: Essays on America's Blank Generation Fiction.* New York: Grove Press, 1992. Print.

Zaldívar, Carlos. *Variaciones sobre un mundo en cambio*. Madrid: Alianza Editorial, 1996. Print.

Zaldívar, Carlos Alonso, and Manuel Castells. *España fin de siglo*. Madrid: Alianza Editorial, 1992. Print.

Zizek, Slavok. *Welcome to the Desert of the Real: Five Essays on September 11 and Related Dates*. New York: Verso: 2002. Print.

Zucker, Alex. Trans. *City Sister Silver*. Jáchym Topol. North Haven: Catbird Press, 2000. Print.

Index